Third Edition

SOCIAL WORK AND SOCIAL WELFARE

An Invitation

Marla Berg-Weger

Routledge

QUICK GUIDES:

For a helpful way to review for comprehension, see the Quick Guides located throughout chapters in the text and included in the detailed table of contents:

#1 Essential Competencies for Professional Social Workers (Council on Social Work Education) 15

#2 Working Statement on the Purpose, Principles, and Objectives of the Social Work Profession 48

#3 Current U.S. Social Welfare Programs 75

#4 Standards and Indicators of Culturally Competent Social Work Practice 116

#5 Ethical Principles Based on Core Social Work Values 156

#6 Ethical Principles Screen 167

#7 Principles of Client Strength 191

#8 Standards for Social Work Practice with Groups 293

#9 Guidelines for Approaching Policy Makers 330

QUICK GUIDE #1 Essential Competencies for Professional Social Workers (Council on Social Work Education)

✓ Identify as a professional social worker and conduct oneself accordingly.
✓ Apply social work ethical principles to guide professional practice.
✓ Apply critical thinking to inform and communicate professional judgments.
✓ Engage diversity and difference in practice.
✓ Advance human rights and social and economic justice.
✓ Engage in research-informed practice and practice-informed research.
✓ Apply knowledge of human behavior and the social environment.
✓ Engage in policy practice to advance social and economic well-being and to deliver effective social work services.
✓ Respond to contexts that shape practice.
✓ Engage, assess, intervene, and evaluate with individuals, families, groups, organizations, and communities.

Source: Council on Social Work Education, 2008. Available at: http://www.cswe.org/Accreditation/2008EPASDescription. aspx.

Routledge
Taylor & Francis Group

www.routledgesw.com

An authentic breakthrough in social work education . . .

New Directions in Social Work is an innovative, integrated series of texts, website, and interactive case studies for generalist courses in the social work curriculum at both undergraduate and graduate levels. Instructors will find every-thing they need to build a comprehensive course that allows students to meet course outcomes, with these unique features:

- All texts, interactive cases, and test materials are **linked to the 2008 CSWE Policy and Accreditation Standards (EPAS)**.

- **One web portal with easy access** for instructors and students from any computer—no codes, no CDs, no restrictions. Go to www.routledgesw.com and discover.

- **The series is flexible and can be easily adapted for use in online distance-learning courses as well as hybrid and bricks-and-mortar courses.**

- Each text and the website can be used **individually** or as an **entire series** to meet the needs of any social work program.

TITLES IN THE SERIES

Social Work and Social Welfare: An Invitation, Third Edition by Marla Berg-Weger

Human Behavior in the Social Environment, Third Edition by Anissa Taun Rogers

Research for Effective Social Work Practice, Third Edition by Judy L. Krysik and Jerry Finn

Social Policy for Effective Practice: A Strengths Approach, Third Edition by Rosemary K. Chapin

Contemporary Social Work Practice, Third Edition by Martha P. Dewees

Social Work and Social Welfare

An Invitation

Third Edition
by Marla Berg-Weger, Saint Louis University

In this book and companion custom website you will find:

- An emphasis on a **strengths-based perspective** and attention to diversity, social environment, theory and theoretical frameworks, levels of social work practice, and an array of fields of practice.

- The histories of social welfare and the social work profession presented as the **intertwined phenomena that they are.**

- A profile of the **contemporary landscape of the society in which social workers practice.**

- Social work practice within the framework of **planned change, encompassing: engagement, assessment, intervention, and evaluation and termination.**

- The opportunity to **hear from social work practitioners working in eight diverse and challenging practice settings.**

- Five unique, in-depth, interactive, easy-to-access cases, which students can easily reach from *any* computer, provide a **"learning by doing" format unavailable with any other text(s).** Your students will have an advantage unlike any other they will experience in their social work training.

- A wealth of **instructor-only resources** also available at www.routledgesw.com/intro provide: **full-text readings** that link to the concepts presented in each of the chapters; a complete bank of objective and essay-type **test items, all linked to current CSWE EPAS standards;** **PowerPoint presentations** to help students master key concepts; annotated **links to a treasure trove of social work assets on the Internet**; and a forum inviting all instructors using texts in the series to communicate with each other, and share ideas to improve teaching and learning.

Social Work and Social Welfare

An Invitation

Third Edition

Marla Berg-Weger
Saint Louis University

Routledge
Taylor & Francis Group

NEW YORK AND LONDON

Third edition published 2013
by Routledge
711 Third Avenue, New York, NY 10017

Simultaneously published in the UK
by Routledge
2 Park Square, Milton Park, Abingdon, Oxon OX14 4RN

Routledge is an imprint of the Taylor & Francis Group, an informa business

First edition published 2005 by McGraw-Hill
Second edition published 2010 by Routledge

Library of Congress Cataloging in Publication Data
Berg-Weger, Marla, 1956-
  Social work and social welfare: an invitation / by Marla Berg-Weger.—3rd ed.
    p. cm.—(New directions in social work)
  1. Social service—United States.   2. Poor—Services for—United States.   I. Title.
  HV91.B384 2012
  361.30973—dc23

ISBN: 978–0–415–52080–5 (hbk)
ISBN: 978–0–415–50160–6 (pbk)
ISBN: 978–0–203–11931–0 (ebk)

Typeset in Stone Serif
by Swales & Willis Ltd, Exeter, Devon

BRIEF CONTENTS

Preface   xvii

About the Author   xxv

CHAPTER 1   *A Glimpse into the World of Social Work   1*

CHAPTER 2   *History of Social Work and Social Welfare   21*

CHAPTER 3   *U.S. Poverty and the Implications for Social Work   54*

CHAPTER 4   *The Social Work Environment   84*

CHAPTER 5   *Diversity in Social Work Practice   114*

CHAPTER 6   *Values and Ethics in Social Work Practice   146*

CHAPTER 7   *Social Work Perspectives and Methods   175*

CHAPTER 8   *Fields of Social Work Practice   201*

CHAPTER 9   *Social Work Practice With Individuals and Families   266*

CHAPTER 10   *Social Work Practice With Groups   290*

CHAPTER 11   *Social Work Practice With Organizations, Communities, and Policy Practice   315*

CHAPTER 12   *The Social Work Profession   344*

References   R–1

Credits   C–1

Glossary/Index   I–1

DETAILED CONTENTS

Preface   xvii

About the Author   xxv

CHAPTER 1   *A Glimpse into the World of Social Work   1*

A Definition of Social Work   3

The Work of Social Work   4

What Social Workers Do   6

Who Is Served by Social Workers   8

Where Social Workers Work   10

Paths to Becoming a Social Worker   13

Social Work Education   14

QUICK GUIDE #1 ESSENTIAL COMPETENCIES FOR PROFESSIONAL SOCIAL WORKERS
(COUNCIL ON SOCIAL WORK EDUCATION)   15

Field Experiences   16

Conclusion   17

Main Points   18

Exercises   19

CHAPTER 2   *History of Social Work and Social Welfare   21*

Development of Social Services   22

Elizabethan Poor Laws of 1601   23

Social Services in the 17th and 18th Centuries   24

The 19th Century, a Defining Era in the United States   25

Settlement House Movement   29

Charity Organization Society   31

Social Services in the 20th Century   33

Developments During the Depression and the New Deal   35
Developments During World War II and the 1950s   37
Developments During the 1960s and 1970s   39
Developments During the 1980s and 1990s   41

Social Services in the 21st Century and Beyond   42

Professional Education in Social Work: A Historical Perspective   44

Educating Social Workers   44

Expanding Professional Boundaries   47

QUICK GUIDE #2 WORKING STATEMENT ON THE PURPOSE, PRINCIPLES, AND OBJECTIVES OF THE SOCIAL WORK PROFESSION   48

Where We Have Come From and Where We Are Going   50

Conclusion   51

Main Points   51

Exercises   52

CHAPTER 3   *U.S. Poverty and the Implications for Social Work   54*

Dimensions of Poverty   56

What Is Poverty?   56

Who Are the Poor?   58

At-Risk Groups   58
The Working Poor   60
Lifetime Chances of Temporarily Living in Poverty   61

What Causes Poverty?   62

Individual Differences   62
Social Structure   63

Challenges and Barriers to Moving Out of Poverty   64

Approaches to Poverty in the United States: Social Welfare   65

Definitions and Connotations of "Social Welfare"   66

Social Welfare in the 17th–19th Centuries   67

Social Welfare in the 20th Century   67

New Deal Welfare Reforms   69

Social Welfare from World War II Through the 1970s   69
Social Welfare in the 1980s and 1990s   71
Social Welfare in the 21st Century   73

QUICK GUIDE #3 CURRENT U.S. SOCIAL WELFARE PROGRAMS   75

Social Work and the Changing Approaches to Poverty   76

Conclusion   79

Main Points   81

Exercises   82

CHAPTER 4   *The Social Work Environment*   **84**

Changing Population Profiles   84

Changes in Race and Ethnicity   85

The Aging Population   87

Trends in Sex Ratios   89

Increasing Income Inequality   90

Trends in Religious Affiliation   93

Oppression and Discrimination   95

Cycle of Oppression   96

Social Work and Oppression   97

Challenges and Opportunities Facing Social Workers   98

Political Environment   98

Challenges in the Political Environment   99
Opportunities in the Political Environment   101

Economic Environment   103

Challenges in the Economic Environment   103
Opportunities in the Economic Environment   105

Social Impacts of the Environment   107

Challenges in the Social Environment   107
Opportunities in the Social Environment   109

Conclusion   111

Main Points   112

Exercises   112

CHAPTER 5   *Diversity in Social Work Practice*   *114*

Diversity as a Component of Social Work Education   115

QUICK GUIDE #4 STANDARDS AND INDICATORS OF CULTURALLY COMPETENT SOCIAL
WORK PRACTICE   116

Self-Awareness: An Exploration   118

Theory That Helps Us Understand Diversity   121

Ecological Perspective   *121*

Strengths-Based Perspective   *122*

The "Isms"   123

Racism   *124*

Ageism   *127*

Sexism   *128*

Classism   *129*

Ableism   *130*

Heterosexism   *132*

Religious Discrimination   *134*

Intersectionality   *135*

The Culturally Competent Social Worker   135

Cultural Awareness   *137*

Language and Communication Skills   *139*

Conclusion   141

Main Points   142

Exercises   142

CHAPTER 6   *Values and Ethics in Social Work Practice*   *146*

Social Work's Commitment to Values and Ethics   147

Values in Social Work   148

Value Conflicts   *149*

Job-Related Value Conflicts   151

Value Conflicts Related to Religion or Spirituality and Belief   151

Value Conflicts Over Limited Resources   152

The Social Worker's Values   152

Ethics in Social Work   153

   NASW Code of Ethics   154

      Organization of the *Code of Ethics*   155

QUICK GUIDE #5 ETHICAL PRINCIPLES BASED ON CORE SOCIAL WORK VALUES   156

      Application of the *Code of Ethics*   158

   Ethical Dilemmas   158

      Confidentiality   160

      Client Self-Determination   162

      Boundaries   163

      Self-Disclosure   164

      Allocation of Resources   164

Values and Ethics in Practice   165

QUICK GUIDE #6 ETHICAL PRINCIPLES SCREEN   167

Case: Cathleen's Right to Privacy and Confidentiality   167

Conclusion   170

Main Points   170

Exercises   171

CHAPTER 7   *Social Work Perspectives and Methods   175*

History of Generalist Social Work Practice   176

Levels of Generalist Social Work Practice   177

Generalist Social Work Skills and Roles   178

Theory in Generalist Social Work Practice   181

   Systems-Based Perspectives   182

      Person-in-Environment and Ecological Perspectives   182

      Systems and Ecosystems Theory   183

      Systems Theory Concepts   185

      Systems Theory in Generalist Practice   186

   Strengths-Based and Empowerment Perspectives   188

      Strengths-Based and Empowerment Concepts   190

QUICK GUIDE #7 PRINCIPLES OF CLIENT STRENGTH   191

   Strengths-Based and Empowerment Perspectives in Generalist Practice   192

Solution-Focused Model   193

    Solution-Focused Concepts   194

    Solution-Focused Model in Generalist Practice   194

Integration of Social Work Theory   196

Conclusion   197

Main Points   197

Exercises   198

CHAPTER 8   *Fields of Social Work Practice   201*

Social Work Practice With Children and Families   203

    Policy-Practice Considerations With Children and Families   203

    Angela Bratcher, BSW, MSW, LCSW, Registered Play Therapist, Great Circle   205

Gerontological Social Work Practice   208

    Policy-Practice Considerations With Older Adults   208

    Carroll Rodriguez, BSW, Alzheimer's Association Chapter   209

Social Work Practice With People With Disabilities   212

    Policy-Practice Considerations in Working With People Who Have Disabilities   213

    Mark A. Keeley, MSW, LCSW, St. Louis Arc   214

Social Work Practice With Military Family Members   217

    Policy-Practice Considerations in Military Social Work   218

    James Allen, Ph.D., MSW, U.S. Army (Retired)   221

Social Work Practice With Immigrants and Refugees   223

    Policy-Practice Considerations With Immigrants and Refugees   223

    Suzanne LeLaurin, MSW, LCSW, International Institute   225

Social Work Practice With Substance Abuse and Addiction   227

    Policy-Practice Considerations in Substance Abuse and Addiction   228

    Jon Hudson, BSW, Chestnut Health Systems, Inc.   230

Social Work Practice in Criminal Justice   232

    Policy-Practice Considerations in Criminal Justice   232

    Herbert Bernsen, MSW, St. Louis County Department of Justice Services   233

Social Work Practice in Health Settings   236

Policy-Practice Considerations in Health Settings 236

Jane Sprankel, MSW, LCSW, Health Care Social Work Across Multiple Settings 238

Lisa Parnell, MSW, LCSW, St. Luke's Hospital 241

Social Work Practice in Mental Health Settings 243

Policy-Practice Considerations in Mental Health Settings 244

Barbara Flory, MSW, LCSW 246

Social Work Practice in the Public Health Setting 249

Policy-Practice Considerations for Social Work in the Public Health Setting 250

Chae Li Yong, MSW, MPH 251

Social Work Practice in School Settings 255

Policy-Practice Considerations in School Social Work 255

R. Jan Wilson, MSW, Ph.D., LCSW, School of Social Work 257

Social Work Practice in Rural Settings 258

Policy-Practice Considerations in Rural Settings 259

Ellen Burkemper, Ph.D., MSW, LCSW, LMFT, RN, School of Social Work 260

Conclusion 261

Main Points 264

Exercises 265

CHAPTER 9   ***Social Work Practice With Individuals and Families 266***

Historical Perspective on Social Work Practice With Individuals and Families 267

The Planned Change Process in Social Work Practice With Individuals and Families 267

Skills for Social Work Practice With Individuals and Families 270

Engagement of Individuals and Families 270

Assessment of Individuals and Families 273

Interview Practice Behaviors 274
Family Assessments 278

Intervention With Individuals and Families   278

Evaluation and Termination of Intervention With Individuals and Families   283

Evaluation   283

Termination   285

Conclusion   287

Main Points   287

Exercises   288

CHAPTER 10   *Social Work Practice With Groups   290*

Historical Perspective on Social Work Practice With Groups   291

QUICK GUIDE #8 STANDARDS FOR SOCIAL WORK PRACTICE WITH GROUPS   293

Models of Change in Social Work Practice With Groups   294

Social Goals Groups   294

Remedial Groups   296

Reciprocal Groups   298

Task Groups   299

Skills for Social Work Practice With Groups   301

Engagement of Groups   302

Assessment of Groups   304

Intervention With Groups   306

Evaluation and Termination of Groups   309

Conclusion   311

Main Points   311

Exercises   312

CHAPTER 11   *Social Work Practice With Organizations, Communities, and Policy Practice   315*

A Word on Policy Practice   318

Historical Perspective on Social Work Practice With Organizations and Communities   318

Models of Change in Social Work Practice With Organizations and Communities   319

    Geographic-Community Organizing   322

    Functional-Community Organizing   323

    Community Development   324

    Program Development   326

    Social Planning   327

    Coalition Building   329

    Political and Social Action   329

QUICK GUIDE #9 GUIDELINES FOR APPROACHING POLICY MAKERS   330

    Movements for Progressive Change   331

Skills for Social Work Practice With Organizations and Communities   332

    Engagement of Organizations and Communities   334

    Assessment of Organizations and Communities   336

    Intervention With Organizations and Communities   337

    Evaluation and Termination of Organization and Community Interventions   339

Conclusion   340

Main Points   341

Exercises   341

CHAPTER 12   *The Social Work Profession   344*

Professional Outlook for Social Workers   344

    Employment Trends and Opportunities   345

        Areas of Practice   346
        Salaries   347

    Societal Perceptions of the Social Work Profession   349

Professional Socialization   350

    Social Work Education: Pursuing a Degree   350

        Bachelor of Social Work   351
        Master of Social Work   354

    Current Issues Influencing Social Work Training for the Future   354

        Health Care Social Work Practice   356

Gerontological Social Work Practice   356
Child Welfare Services   357
Technology and Social Work   358
Disaster Response and Crisis Intervention   359
International Social Work and Multilingualism   360

Your Career in Social Work   361

Conclusion   363

Main Points   364

Exercises   364

References   R–1

Credits   C–1

Glossary/Index   I–1

PREFACE

MAJOR CHANGES TO THE THIRD EDITION

Like the previous editions of *Social Work and Social Welfare: An Invitation*, this edition introduces students to the knowledge, skills, and values that are essential for working with individuals, families, groups, organizations, communities, and public policy in a variety of practice settings. The third edition provides an up-to-date profile of the world in which today's social workers practice—with updated demographic, statistical, legislative, policy, and research information; sensitive discussions of contemporary ethical issues; and new first-person narratives from social workers in a variety of fields. The call to become engaged in some of society's most challenging issues is clearer than in previous editions.

For the new editions of all five books in the *New Directions in Social Work* series, each addressing a foundational course in the social work curriculum, the publisher has created a brand-new, uniquely distinctive teaching strategy that revolves around the print book but offers much more than the traditional text experience. Quick Guides within the text offer students guidance for their field experiences. The series website, www.routledgesw.com, leads to custom websites coordinated with each book in the series and offers a variety of features to support instructors as you integrate the many facets of an education in social work.

At www.routledgesw.com/intro, the site for this particular book, you will find a wealth of resources to help you create a dynamic, experiential introduction to social work for your students:

- Companion readings linked to key concepts in each chapter, along with questions to encourage further thought and discussion.

- Five interactive fictional cases (two of them brand new with publication of the third edition) with accompanying exercises that bring to life the concepts covered in the book, readings, and classroom discussions.

- A bank of exam questions (both objective and open-ended).

- PowerPoint presentations, which can serve as a starting point for class discussions.

- Sample syllabi demonstrating how the text and website, when used together through the course, satisfy the 2008 Council on Social Work Educational Policy and Accreditation Standards (EPAS).

- Quick Guides from the books offered online for students to copy and take into the field for guidance.

- Annotated links to a treasure trove of articles and other readings, videos, and internet sites.

- An online forum inviting all instructors using the books in the series to share ideas to improve teaching and learning.

ORGANIZATION OF THE BOOK

Social Work and Social Welfare: An Invitation introduces students to the profession they are considering for their life's work. From a strengths-based perspective, students will be provided with a comprehensive overview of the major areas relevant for social work practice, including diversity, social environment, theory and theoretical frameworks, levels of social work practice, and an array of fields of practice. Presented as the intertwined phenomena that they are, the histories of social welfare and the social work profession are presented to help the student gain insight into the context of the social work profession. *Social Work and Social Welfare* offers a profile of the contemporary landscape of the world and the society in which social workers practice within the concept of planned change, encompassing engagement, assessment, intervention, and evaluation and termination. Students have the opportunity to read first-hand accounts of social work practice in an array of diverse and challenging practice settings and gain insights into the future of the social work profession.

The following paragraphs briefly introduce each of the chapters included in this book, with emphasis on the updated content.

Chapter 1

A Glimpse into the World of Social Work begins by grounding the students in a definition of social work, the ways that social workers help people, the people with whom social workers work, and the places where social workers practice. Current demographic and employment data for the social work profession is presented. In this first chapter, students are introduced to a fictitious social worker named Emily. Throughout each chapter of the book, Emily's experiences as a social work student and later a practitioner provide insights into the rewards and challenges of a career in social work that are addressed in that chapter.

Chapter 2

History of Social Work and Social Welfare enables student readers to understand and appreciate the historical backdrop of the social welfare system and the profession of social work that has produced the systems and profession that exist today. The dynamics of history as it impacts social work and social welfare is emphasized in this chapter. Profiles are provided that highlight the careers of eight individuals whose contributions have advanced the social work profession. The section on 21st-century social work has been updated to reflect the economic and social strains of the past few years.

Chapter 3

U.S. Poverty and the Implications for Social Work provides students with both a historical and a contemporary look at poverty and the programs aimed at alleviating poverty within our society. As economic philosophy and status are ever-changing, this chapter provides an up-to-date exploration of the current status of those persons living in poverty, the effectiveness of the legislation and programs that are intended to improve the quality of their lives, and the importance of social workers having indepth understanding of the policies that impact the lives of those being served.

Chapter 4

The Social Work Environment is, in fact, the global environment in which modern-day social workers live and practice. This chapter focuses on helping students understand the social forces and realities of changes that influence our society. The dynamics of oppression and discrimination have a new emphasis. Within the context of the political, economic, and social environments that impact life for the clients systems served by social workers, current information is provided on issues such as race, ethnicity, age, gender, income (social class), sexual orientation, and religion. Current realities of life in the United States are discussed, including the economic recession, unemployment, health care challenges, and the new face of poverty.

Chapter 5

Diversity in Social Work Practice introduces the students to key areas of social work practice that will impact virtually every dimension of their lives as social workers. With an emphasis on self-awareness, students are challenged to consider the evolution of their own views on persons who may be different from themselves, whether on the basis of race, ethnicity, culture, age, sex and gender, sexual orientation, socioeconomic class, physical ability, religion, or lifestyle. Framed within theoretical perspectives for understanding diversity, students are offered an over-view of the skills required to be a culturally competent social work practitioner. The intersectionality of race, class, and gender lends insight into the area of diversity. Cultural competence is emphasized.

Chapter 6

While challenging for the beginning social work student, **Values and Ethics in Social Work Practice** are introduced in this chapter as the foundation that guides social work practice. Using value and ethical dilemmas that challenge social workers, students have multiple opportunities throughout the chapter to consider the origins of their own value and ethical beliefs and to apply them to situations in which they will likely find themselves as they develop as practitioners. The commitment of the social work profession to advocating for ethical practices is emphasized.

Chapter 7

Social Work Perspectives and Methods conceptualizes generalist social work prac-tice within the levels of practice with individuals and families, groups, and organi-zations, communities, and public policy. Students are introduced to a range of theoretical frameworks that guide social workers as they practice, including systems theory, the strengths-based perspective, and a model for solution-focused interven-tions. The chapter ends with a discussion of the integration of social work theory in practice settings.

Chapter 8

Fields of Social Work Practice provides students with up-to-date perspectives on social work practice in the second decade of the 21st century. Thirteen social workers share their experiences in 12 different practice settings, including health and mental health, criminal justice, school, public health, and rural settings; and practice with children and families, immigrants and refugees, military families, older adults, persons with addictions, and persons with disabilities. It is a lengthy chapter, but through the "voices" of actual social workers, it gives students real-life insight into social work practice. This chapter also serves as an introduction to the following three chapters, in which levels of social work practice are explored, and may provide material for review and discussion throughout the next three chapters.

Chapter 9

Social Work Practice With Individuals and Families is the first of the levels of prac-tice to be presented. Students are exposed to the concepts of planned change. They will learn about the phases of the social work intervention, including engagement, assessment, intervention, and evaluation and termination. Linked to the EPAS, these areas of practice help students gain insights into the knowledge and skills required for competency-based social work practice. Students will become familiar with effective social work practice behaviors they will need as they practice at all levels.

Chapter 10

Social Work Practice With Groups continues the students' exposure to the facets of generalist social work practice. Students are presented with four models of group-level practice. Building on the foundation of social work practice with individuals and families, group-level practice emphasizes the concepts of engagement, assessment, intervention, and evaluation as they are applied at the group level of social work practice.

Chapter 11

Social Work Practice With Organizations, Communities, and Public Policy uses the insights gained about practice at the individual, family, and group levels to expand students' awareness of social work practice areas. In the third edition, policy practice is presented to students as a career opportunity as well as a critical part of any area of practice.

Chapter 12

The Social Work Profession brings to a close this introduction to the social work profession. Trends in social work employment opportunities are included along with up-to-date information on salaries. A key part of the discussion is how various current issues—health care, population aging, developments in child welfare, rapidly advancing technology, disasters and crises, and globalization—are likely to affect social work in the near future. Students are provided with various resources to help direct their interests as they continue their careers.

INTERACTIVE CASES

The website www.routledgesw.com/cases presents five unique, indepth, interactive, fictional cases with dynamic characters and real-life situations. Two of them—the RAINN and Hudson cases—are entirely new to this edition of the series. Your students can easily access the cases from any computer. The cases provide a "learning by doing" format unavailable with any other book, and the experience will be unlike any other your students will experience in their social work training.

Each of the interactive cases uses text, graphics, and video to help students learn about engagement, assessment, intervention, and evaluation and termination at multiple levels of social work practice. The "My Notebook" feature allows students to take and save notes, type in written responses to tasks, and share their work with classmates and instructors by e-mail. Through these interactive cases, you can integrate the readings and classroom discussions:

The Sanchez Family: Systems, Strengths, and Stressors

The 10 individuals in this extended Latino family have numerous strengths but are faced with a variety of challenges. Students will have the opportunity to experience the phases of the social work intervention, grapple with ethical dilemmas, and identify strategies for addressing issues of diversity.

Riverton: A Community Conundrum

Riverton is a small Midwest city in which the social worker lives and works. The social worker identifies an issue that presents her community with a challenge. Students and instructors can work together to develop strategies for engaging, assessing, and intervening with the citizens of the social worker's neighborhood.

Carla Washburn: Loss, Aging, and Social Support

Students will get to know Carla Washburn, an older African American woman who finds herself living alone after the loss of her grandson and in considerable pain from a recent accident. In this case, less complex than the Sanchez family case, students can apply their growing knowledge of gerontology and exercise the skills of culturally competent practice at the individual, family, and group levels.

RAINN

Based on the first online hotline for delivering sexual assault services, this interactive case includes a variety of exercises to enable students to gain knowledge and skills related to the provision of services to persons in crisis. With a focus on social work practice at all levels, exercises provide insight into program services and evaluation, interactions with volunteers and clients, and research.

Hudson City: An Urban Community Affected by Disaster

A natural disaster in the form of Hurricane Diane has hit Hudson City, a large metropolitan area on the northeastern coast of the United States. This interactive case will provide students with insights into the complexities of experiencing a disaster, including the phases of the human response to disaster and the social work role in responding to natural disasters.

IN SUM

I have written this book with the hope that it will provide you and your students not only with an enticing introduction to our profession but also with deep insight into the knowledge, skills, and values that are required for a competent and effective social work practitioner. The multiple options for supporting your teaching of this content are intended to help you address the diverse range of student learning styles and needs. The design of this book and the instructor support materials optimize the experiential approach to the introductory course in social work. I hope this book and the support materials will be of help to you and your students as they embark on their journey toward social work practice.

ACKNOWLEDGMENTS

I would like to extend my appreciation to the many social workers who helped this book to become a reality. To Alice Lieberman and the other authors of this book series, Rosemary Chapin, Anissa Rogers, Judy Krysik, Jerry Finn, Julie Birkenmaier, and Marty Dewees, I thank you for your continued vision, support, and feedback through this enriching and invigorating process. To my colleagues at Saint Louis University, Julie Birkenmaier, Jane Sprankel, Pam Huggins, Ellen Burkemper, Sue Tebb, Sabrina Tyuse, Sandra Naeger, and Kristi Sobbe Richter, I appreciate your willingness to provide resources, review chapters, and serve as a sounding board for my ideas. To the practitioners who contributed their "voices from the field," I am grateful for your willingness to share the stories of your professional journeys. Thank you to Michelle Siroko and Luxiaofei Li for your help with this edition. Thanks to Michael Cronin for his contributions to the test bank and website and for sharing his experiences. Thanks to the reviewers who provided feedback on the second edition: Steve Dawson, Joy Ernst, Keri Bower, Jessica Ritter, Richard Black, Linda Wells-Glover, Paula Matthews, Yvette Murphy-Erby, Ski Hunter, Aracelis Francis, Beverly Aurand, Erica Sirrine, and John Conahan. Thank you to the focus group participants at social work conferences throughout the year: Michael Cronin, Sue Tebb, Aracelis Francis, Sabrina Tyuse, Peggy Pittman-Munke, Shannon Collier-Tenison, Mary Clay Thomas, and Mitch Kahn. To the staff of Routledge, Taylor & Francis, thank you for believing in the potential of this book series.

ABOUT THE AUTHOR

Marla Berg-Weger is a professor in the School of Social Work at Saint Louis University, Missouri, where she also serves as the Executive Director, Geriatric Education Center. Dr. Berg-Weger has been a social worker for over three decades and holds social work degrees at the bachelor's, master's, and doctoral levels. Her social work practice experience includes public social welfare services, domestic violence services, mental health, and health care social work. Her research and writing focus on social work practice and gerontological social work, particularly in the areas of older adult mobility and family caregiving. With Julie Birkenmaier, she co-authored the textbook *The Practicum Companion for Social Work: Integrating Class and Field Work*. With Birkenmaier and Marty Dewees, she co-authored another book in this series, *Contemporary Social Work Practice*. She is the past president of the Association of Gerontology in Social Work and currently serves as the Secretary. She also serves as the Chair of the *Journal of Gerontological Social Work* Editorial Board Executive Committee. She is a Fellow in the Gerontological Society of America, a Co-Convenor of the Society's Transportation Interest Group, and a member of the Publications Committee.

CHAPTER 1

A Glimpse into the World of Social Work

Ask social workers what drew them to the profession, and you will hear one common message: They liked the idea that they would be helping to better people's lives. In fact, the primary reasons that people become social workers are to: (1) help others; (2) advocate for those who are disadvantaged; and (3) provide mental health services (Whitaker, 2008, p. 4). Although many might have considered one of the other helping professions, such as psychology, sociology, teaching, or medicine, they chose social work. As you will learn throughout this book, social work is unique among other helping professions because of its broad scope of concern, its strong core values, and its commitment to social and economic justice.

Social work has goals and methods in common with other helping professions, and social workers have adopted useful knowledge from many of these professions. From psychology, social workers learn to understand the impact of emotional and psychological factors on the individual. From sociology, they gain insight into populations of people. From the medical professions, they learn of the relationships between biological functioning and health/illness and the impact of these factors on psychosocial well-being. The health professions also emphasize the value of the interdisciplinary team approach, which is an essential area of practice for social workers in virtually every setting.

Social work and other helping professions certainly overlap; however, social work is also distinctive in a number of ways (Exhibit 1.1). The social work profession emphasizes a holistic, or interpersonal, perspective as opposed to the individual (intrapersonal) perspective of other helping professions. The National Association of Social Workers (NASW), the professional organization for the social work profession, issued a policy statement supporting "the promotion of social work as a distinctly different profession from other human service disciplines (such as counseling, clinical psychology, nursing, marriage and family therapy, and so forth) as it focuses on the intra- and inter-personal aspects of clients' lives" (National Association of Social Workers (NASW), 2012–2014b, p. 80). A hallmark of providing social work services to people is to consider their social environment: their family, home, work, state of health, community, and the interactions that they have with all those areas of their life. Perhaps the most important distinction between social work and other

EXHIBIT 1.1	SIMILARITIES WITH SOCIAL WORK	DIFFERENCES FROM SOCIAL WORK	
What Makes Social Work Unique	**PSYCHOLOGY** • Both are practice professions • At graduate level, both provide training in psychotherapy • Practitioners in both are trained to work in same settings with same types of clients	• Psychology focuses on internal issues as source of problem • Psychology focuses on individual as target of intervention • Psychologists administer and interpret psychological tests • In some states, psychologists can prescribe medications • Clinical practice often requires a Ph.D. for psychologists	• Social work focuses on person within the environment (PIE) • Social work interventions encompass individual and those in his or her environment • Social workers are typically not trained in this area of practice • Social workers cannot prescribe medications • Clinical practice often requires an MSW for social workers, and social workers with a BSW degree are licensed for practice in many states
	SOCIOLOGY • Both are interested in people's patterns of behavior	• Sociology is a social science that considers the population as a whole, often in the context of communities	• Social work is a practice profession
	HEALTH PROFESSIONS (nursing and medicine, in particular) • Both are practice professions • Both recognize the influence of health on well-being • Both are carried out in community or hospital settings with the same types of patients • Both require generalist and specialist expertise	• Health professions often focus primarily on physical health issues • Health professionals do not typically focus on community resources other than medical resources • Physicians and some nurses can prescribe medications	• Social work assessments routinely include biological, psychological, social, and spiritual perspectives and factors • Social workers have expert knowledge of community resources • Social workers cannot prescribe medications

SIMILARITIES WITH SOCIAL WORK	DIFFERENCES FROM SOCIAL WORK		EXHIBIT 1.1

continued

MARRIAGE AND FAMILY COUNSELING

- Both are practice professions
- At graduate level, both train students in psychotherapy
- Both have licensing and certification requirements
- Both allow clinical practice with a master's degree
- Neither allows practitioners to prescribe medications

- Counselors focus primarily on the individual as the source of the problem for assessment and intervention
- Counselors are not typically trained in community practice skills such as advocacy and organizing

- Social workers intervene with both clients and client systems and may practice at the level of individuals, families, groups, organizations, communities, or public policy
- Social work training emphasizes competence at the community level as well as the individual and family level

Sources: Ginsberg, 2001; Peck, 1999.

MSW, Master of Social Work; BSW, Bachelor of Social Work.

helping professions is the emphasis on social action through advocacy for those oppressed or discriminated against by society. Although social workers often help people by providing services in an agency setting, the profession also advocates publicly addressing social conditions such as homelessness, hunger, teen pregnancy, poverty, and discrimination.

This chapter will illustrate the meaning of social work. In the remaining chapters, a more detailed picture will emerge of what social work is and what you need to learn to be an effective social worker.

A DEFINITION OF SOCIAL WORK

Developing an accurate and comprehensive definition of social work requires an expansive view of the profession and the positions that social workers hold. As you might already know, social workers are employed in helping institutions such as schools, hospitals, mental health facilities, older adult service programs, and children's residential settings. You might not know, however, that social workers also work in banks, large corporations, theater groups, community gardens, military and veteran programs, police stations, and international settings. Social work professionals work with people in all segments of society, from those who are disenfranchised or devalued by society and living in poverty to those in the middle and upper socioeconomic segments of society. They work with the young and the old, with people in good health and poor health, with people from diverse cultures and backgrounds, including those who may be immigrants or refugees, and with people who have survived a disaster or traumatic experience.

Let us see how the profession itself defines social work. The profession's definition of social work has evolved over time. A 1973 definition developed by the NASW described social work as the "professional activity of helping individuals, groups, or communities to restore their capacity for social functioning and creating societal conditions favorable to that goal" (p. 4). This definition includes four basic goals for the profession: (1) linking people to resources; (2) providing direct services to individuals, families, and groups; (3) helping communities or groups provide or improve social and health services; and (4) participating in relevant legislative processes (pp. 4–5).

As the profession has continued to grow and change, so has its self-definition. First included in the profession's 1996 *Code of Ethics*, the definition remains relevant today:

> The primary mission of the social work profession is to enhance human well-being and help meet the basic human needs of all people, with particular attention to the needs and empowerment of people who are vulnerable, oppressed, and living in poverty. A historical and defining feature of social work is the profession's focus on individual well-being in a social context and the well-being of society. Fundamental to social work is attention to the environmental forces that create, contribute to, and address problems in living. (NASW, 2008)

Both definitions imply that the goal of social work is to empower people to optimize their abilities and quality of life, whether through working directly with people or through taking action to change society. The openness and flexibility of these definitions enable social workers to respond to those needs that exist within their communities. The populations, health crises, social conditions, and ethical dilemmas with which social workers are engaged may vary, but the work transcends time and individual circumstance because of its all-encompassing nature. This diversity and the activist bias attract many people to the social work profession.

THE WORK OF SOCIAL WORK

Consider the experiences of a midcareer social worker named Emily. Like many of her professional counterparts, Emily has worked in a number of different social work positions and settings. Early in her career, she worked in the public welfare system in several different areas, ranging from child protective services, to services for older adults and persons with visual impairments, to outreach work in a domestic violence program. Later, Emily obtained a graduate degree and, over the years, held social work positions in a mental health center, home health agency, hospital, and primary care medical outpatient clinic.

One of the things that Emily has found especially rewarding about her profession is the variety of experiences she has had because she has degrees in social work. When she worked in the program that serves persons who have experienced domestic violence, for instance, she responded to calls from emergency rooms where women had gone after being battered by their partners. Emily met the woman at the hospital and assessed her current situation, abuse history, safety needs, and resources. She then arranged housing either at the shelter or at a safe house for the woman and her children. Emily worked with the woman during her stay to explore options and make long-term plans. Sometimes, this effort involved helping the woman leave her partner for a new life, but other times it meant watching her return to the relationship. In these cases, Emily always worked out a safety plan with the woman in the event the violence occurred again. Emily used a number of social work skills in this position: crisis intervention, interviewing, assessment, information sharing and referral, brokering, intervention planning, evaluation, and documentation.

At the mental health center, Emily conducted intake assessments for persons requesting therapy services. She met with those persons for an hour-long assessment of their presenting concern, social situation, and mental health status. After completing this assessment, she compiled a report and recommended a treatment plan. In this job, Emily used skills such as assessment, diagnosis, preparation of documentation, and crisis intervention.

As a social worker in an acute care inpatient hospital setting, Emily provided services to patients and their families upon the request of the medical staff. She often assisted the patient and her or his family in making discharge plans. This process could include arranging for financial assistance, home health or hospice services, residential care, medications, medical equipment, and possible relocation. Emily was also there to support families when a patient died. When she was on call for the social work department, she covered the emergency room, which could involve just about any situation. Her crisis intervention skills clearly were a major asset here.

Because social work training provides a core set of knowledge and skills that can be applied in a variety of settings with a diverse population, Emily has been able to work in a number of challenging but rewarding positions: investigating adult and child abuse and neglect, working with women who have experienced domestic violence and their children, conducting assessments for therapy in a mental health center, arranging discharge plans for hospitalized patients, and providing therapy for persons experiencing conditions such as depression, a new medical diagnosis, or family and marital problems. You can see that Emily has enjoyed a broad and diverse career that was made possible by her social work degrees. She thrives on the opportunity to work with different types of people who are experiencing different life situations. In addition, she welcomes the opportunity to move into a new position if she chooses. Most of all, Emily enjoys being able to help people through difficult life experiences.

What Social Workers Do

While over 800,000 self-identify as social workers, over 650,000 of those employed as social workers in 2010 were professionally educated as social workers (Hopps, Lowe, Stuart, Weismiller, & Whitaker, 2008; U.S. Department of Labor, Bureau of Labor Statistics (BLS), 2012b). Over half (54%) of social workers are employed in health and social service settings, while approximately one-third (31%) work in publicly funded agencies (BLS, 2012b). To learn more about the availability of social workers within each of the states in the United States, visit HIPAASpace at http://www.hipaaspace.com/Medical.Statistics/Healthcare.Professionals.Availability/Social%20Worker/201204.

The majority of social workers work directly with individuals, couples, families, and small groups (Whitaker & Arrington, 2008). In fact, most social workers who responded to an NASW workforce (NASW, 2007) survey reported that they provide services in the areas of mental health (35%), physical health (14%), family/children's services (11%), schools (6%), adolescent programs (5%), or addiction treatment (4%)— all of which are types of **direct practice**. Social workers in the United States provide more mental health and therapy services than any other discipline does, including psychology or counseling (for more information, visit: www.socialworkers.org/pressroom). In fact, social workers provide more than 60% of mental health services. In this field of practice, social workers provide crisis intervention and counseling services to individuals, families, and groups experiencing difficulty in coping with a life crisis or transition, such as a relationship problem, death or injury, divorce, or illness.

While the majority of social workers spend much of their time providing direct services to individuals and families, a survey of licensed social workers reports that most social workers spend at least a portion of their time in one or more additional activities beyond their direct practice responsibilities (Center for Health Workforce Studies (CHWS) & Center for Workforce Studies (CWS), 2006). Supervision and teaching of social work students are the most frequently mentioned secondary areas of work. A significant number of social work professionals are also engaged, in whole or in part, in supervisory, administrative, and fund-raising activities for the agencies and organizations in which they work. Finally, social workers are often the initiators of new social programs because they have been in the field and are able to see where the needs exist. This experience also helps social workers to understand and influence social policies. Social workers can share real-life stories with legislators to help them understand the effects of their votes on constituents. In fact, hundreds of social workers serve their communities and states as elected officials, including two in the U.S. Senate and seven in the House of Representatives (NASW, 2011b).

Social workers' skills enable them to work in a broad range of areas and specializations (Barker, 2003; NASW, 2009):

- Conducting needs assessments, providing information and referrals, and accessing resources in social casework/**case management** (e.g., helping people improve personal and social functioning by referring to education, training, employment, and personal growth services).

- Serving as a case manager and counseling around specific health-related issues in medical social work.

- Determining the social, emotional, and economic concerns of persons for whom they provide services. For instance, social workers work with students and their families on emotional, social, and economic concerns to enable them to focus on the student's education in school social work.

- Counseling individuals, families, and groups in settings such as hospitals, schools, mental health facilities, and private practices in **clinical social work** through assessing, diagnosing, and treating mental health and emotional conditions.

- Supervising programs and people in **administration and management**.

- Working to influence the development, implementation, and evaluation of policies aimed at creating social justice for those impacted by the policies in policy practice. Social workers are trained to research, plan, and develop social policies and programs.

- Working with groups and communities to identify conditions and develop strategies to address them in **community organization**. For example, coordinating and working with governmental, private, civic, religious, business, and trade organizations can serve to combat social problems through community awareness and response programs.

- Analyzing conditions, programs, and policies and conducting and studying research in an effort to improve the social service system in **social policy research**. Research can be utilized to improve resources, social programs, and health services and encourage communities and organizations to be responsive to identified needs.

Social workers' skills afford them the opportunity to work with any population in any situation or setting. With all populations and settings, social workers deliver services through the use of a planned change intervention that encompasses the phases of: (1) engagement; (2) assessment; (3) intervention; and (4) evaluation and termination (**Council on Social Work Education** (CSWE), 2008). While each of these areas will be explored in greater depth throughout this book, they serve as a guide for the competency-based practice approaches that encompass the knowledge, skills, and values inherent in and unique to the social work profession. As specified in the *Educational Policy and Accreditation Standards* of the CSWE (2008, pp. 6–7),

Professional practice involves the dynamic and interactive processes of engagement, assessment, intervention, and evaluation at multiple levels. Social workers have the knowledge and skills to practice with individuals, families, groups, organizations, and communities. Practice knowledge includes identifying, analyzing, and implementing evidence-based interventions designed to achieve client goals; using research and technological advances; evaluating program outcomes and practice effectiveness; developing, analyzing, advocating, and providing leadership for policies and services; and promoting social and economic justice.

Who Is Served by Social Workers

If you are interested in being a social worker, it is important to understand that many of the people with whom you will work are struggling to function within their setting. Exhibit 1.2 provides some insight into the range of people who might find themselves in need of a social worker's services. Fortunately, most people have strengths on which to draw, and activating those strengths is the social worker's specialty.

EXHIBIT 1.2

Who Needs a Social Worker?

YOU'LL NEED A SOCIAL WORKER . . .

When you come into the world too soon

When you can't find anyone to play with

When you are left home alone

When you hate the new baby

When you don't think your teacher likes you

When you are bullied

When you don't want your mommy and daddy to divorce

When you miss your big brother

When you don't like how the neighbor touches you

When you get into fights at school

When you don't make the team

When your best friend moves away

When you get poor grades

When you always fight with your siblings

When your friends pressure you to get high

When you can't adjust to the move

When you can't talk to your parents

When you want to quit school

When your friends don't like you anymore

When you didn't want this baby

When you feel like running away

When your friend swallows an overdose

When you are the only one that thinks you're fat

When you can't find someone who speaks your language

When you can't forget the assault

When you can't decide on a career

When your family pressures you to marry

When your boss is hitting on you

When you can't stick to a budget

When you want to adopt

When you wonder if you are drinking too much

When you can't find good day care

When you think you are neglecting your kids

When you are hated because of who you are

When you lose your baby

When your community has gang problems

EXHIBIT 1.2

continued

When your kids want to live with your ex

When your partner is unfaithful

When you want to meet your birthparent

When your disabled child needs friends

When your step-kids hate you

When your mother won't speak to you

When you can't face moving again

When your spouse wants a divorce

When you want to be a foster parent

When your city officials don't respond

When your best friend has panic attacks

When you find drugs in your son's room

When your job is eliminated

When your mother-in-law wants to move in

When your neighborhood needs a community center

When you find there is no joy in your life

When your car accident destroys your career

When you sponsor a refugee family

When your legislature passes a bad law

When your brother won't help care for dad

When your partner has a mid-life crisis

When you are stressed by menopause

When your mom gets Alzheimer's

When you are caring for parents and children

When you want to change careers

When you lose your home in a fire

When you are angry all the time

When your nest really empties

When your partner insists you retire

When you can't afford respite care

When you can't find a job and you're 60

When your kids demand that you move in with them

When your daughter suddenly dies

When you are scared about living alone

When you can't drive any more

When your children ignore your medical decisions

When your retirement check won't pay the bills

When you learn you have a terminal illness

When you need a nursing home

Life's Challenges—Social Workers Are There For You!

Source: © 2001, Darlene Lynch & Robert Vernon. For free distribution information visit: http://hsmedia.biz.

From the beginnings of the profession, social workers have worked one-on-one primarily with persons facing discrimination because of ethnic background, race, gender, ability, or age, or with those experiencing life crises, or physical or mental health issues. Often working with people when they are struggling with life's most significant challenges, social workers work with clients to address issues of: "poverty, discrimination, abuse, addiction, physical illness, divorce, loss, unemployment, educational problems, disability, and mental illness. They help prevent crises and counsel individuals, families, and communities to cope more effectively with the stresses of everyday life" (socialworkers.org). However, the scope of practice and service boundaries for social workers has expanded throughout history to keep up with societal needs. Today, for example, social workers assist people who have lost their jobs, health benefits, or homes and military veterans with posttraumatic stress disorder and their families coping with adjusting to civilian life.

As an adult service worker in the public welfare agency, Emily started off one typical day by visiting Mrs. H., a woman who was 70 years old and widowed with no family. Mrs. H. lived alone in a small house that Emily could see was not well maintained or clean. Mrs. H. was referred to Emily's agency by her minister because he was concerned about her. Mrs. H. was visually impaired due to glaucoma, and had severe arthritis and diabetes. She had been trying to cover up for her increasing debilitation by isolating herself and not participating in her usual social activities. These may seem like insurmountable problems, and the only reasonable response might seem to be, at first contact, to put Mrs. H. in a nursing home.

However, Mrs. H. desperately wanted to continue living independently. Moreover, she was financially independent, and she had a small circle of caring people, such as her minister and neighbors, who provided social support. Through Emily's social assessment, which included family, financial, mobility, and health information, she concluded that Mrs. H. was a candidate for a number of social services: homemaker/ chore (help with housekeeping tasks), home health services (nursing assistance to monitor her diabetes), services for persons with visual impairments (a rehabilitation teacher to help her adjust to her visual impairment), transportation services, and telephone reassurance services (a daily telephone check-in service). With the help of these services, Emily's ongoing case management, and a willingness to build on her strengths, Mrs. H. remained independent and functional until her death 10 years later.

Where Social Workers Work

Emily's social work degrees and experience have enabled her to change positions within the social work field. Her social work training prepared her to work with varied groups of people in direct practice—children, families, older adults, and persons with disabilities or persistent illness. Her knowledge and skills have also enabled her to facilitate groups and to work at administrative and educational levels. Emily values the learning she has gained in each of these settings.

Nevertheless, she has developed her preferences. Emily's social work experience began with a community service assignment in her introductory social work course. She found an opportunity at a nursing home, helping older adults. With her under-graduate degree in social work, Emily found a job in the public social service sector. However, Emily developed an extensive knowledge of the public welfare system that was an asset in being accepted into graduate school and in being hired to work in a shelter program for women who have been abused and their children. Her experiences in public welfare and domestic violence were viewed favorably when she applied for a position at the mental health center.

Although each setting offered a different experience and enabled her to develop her knowledge and skill as a social worker, Emily also found that her personality was better suited for some settings than others. For example, she learned that she enjoys working in an agency in which she has a large group of co-workers with whom she can interact on a daily basis.

Like Emily, most social workers gain experience in a variety of settings:

- Organizations that primarily provide social services.

- Host settings, or secondary organizations such as schools, correctional facilities, or health care facilities.

- Voluntary nonprofit agencies.

- Governmental or public agencies.

Although some social workers are in private practice as counselors, most work in an organization.

As for specialty, Exhibit 1.3 describes the settings in which most practicing social workers are employed (BLS, 2012b). Social workers work most frequently in such settings as family and child service agencies, including child welfare agencies, health and mental health agencies, and elementary and secondary schools. A visit

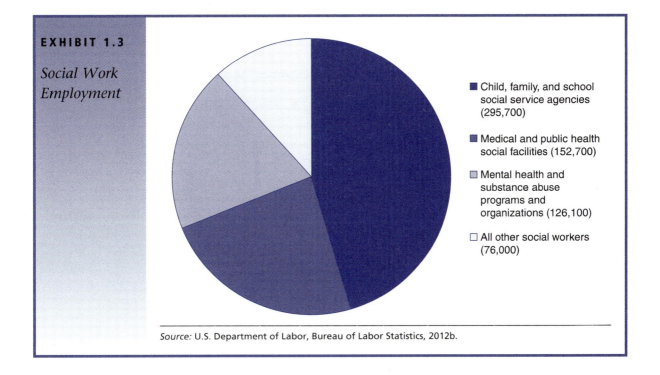

EXHIBIT 1.3

Social Work Employment

■ Child, family, and school social service agencies (295,700)

■ Medical and public health social facilities (152,700)

■ Mental health and substance abuse programs and organizations (126,100)

☐ All other social workers (76,000)

Source: U.S. Department of Labor, Bureau of Labor Statistics, 2012b.

to the NASW website (socialworkers.org) provides an illuminating listing of areas in which you may work as a social worker, including schools, hospitals, mental health clinics, senior centers, elected office, private practices, prisons, military installations, corporations, and in numerous public and private agencies that serve individuals and families in need. They often specialize in one or more of the practice areas listed in Exhibit 1.4.

Social workers also have a choice of working in the private or public sector. Between one-half and two-thirds of all social workers are employed in the private social service sector (BLS, 2010; Whitaker & Arrington, 2008). A majority work in nonprofit settings such as social service agencies, hospitals, residential care facilities, home health agencies, health centers, and criminal justice programs. These privately funded agencies are administered by boards of directors, and their profits are retained or reinvested in the programs to enhance service delivery. These agencies raise funds through individual and corporate donations, grants, fundraisers, and public sector contracts. In addition, an increasing number of social workers (over one-quarter) are working in for-profit settings such as corporations (for example, in employee assistance programs) and private schools (Whitaker & Arrington, 2008). The private social service delivery system in the United States consists of approximately 94,700 organizations—75,700 (two-thirds) serve individuals and families; 9,500 provide food, housing, and other relief services; and 9,500 focus on vocational rehabilitation (BLS, 2010).

Although a majority of social workers are employed in the private sector, public or governmental settings remain an important source of jobs for social workers.

			EXHIBIT 1.4
Mental health therapy	Disaster relief	Military social work	
Rural social work	Adoption and foster care	Child welfare services	*Areas of Social*
Family preservation services	Homeless family assistance	Eating disorders	*Work Practice*
Genetics	Hospital social work	Crisis intervention	
School violence	Hospice and palliative care	Depression	
Institutional care	Chronic pain	Outpatient treatment	
Development disabilities	International social work	Advocacy, consulting, and	
Community mental health	Employee assistance	planning	
Veterans services	Child abuse and neglect	Private practice	
Political development	Parent education	Domestic violence	
HIV/AIDS	School alternative programs	Family planning	
Gerontology services	Community-based services	Difficulties in school	
Alzheimer's disease and	Addictions prevention/	In-home services	
other dementias	treatment	Criminal justice	
Housing assistance	Public welfare	Employment services	

They provide services in the areas of case management and determining eligibility for services in a wide area of services, including mental health, social services, child welfare, housing, education, and corrections (BLS, 2010). The overwhelming majority of social workers in the public sector are employed at state and local levels, with a smaller number working in programs at the federal level. Of all persons employed in state and local agencies, approximately 6% are engaged in community and social services areas (BLS, 2010).These publicly funded local, state, and federal settings include state-funded public welfare/human service departments; mental health agencies; child welfare agencies; housing programs; veterans' and military programs; local, state, and federal court/justice systems; public schools; hospitals; and policy-making organizations.

PATHS TO BECOMING A SOCIAL WORKER

Emily's path to becoming a social worker is her own, but it is typical for many social workers. It began with a significant personal experience. Emily married shortly after graduating from high school, and she clearly did not expect that domestic violence would occur in her marriage. But when it did, Emily ended the marriage in a relatively short time. With her family's support, Emily headed off to college. She had no idea what she wanted to major in, but she was influenced by her past life experiences.

Emily was intrigued by a psychology course she took to fulfill her university's general education requirement. She liked the idea of trying to understand the ways that people think and behave. She had often been the person among her friends in whom others confided—maybe because she was a good listener. Next, Emily took sociology and anthropology courses. She was drawn to the idea of thinking about people within their societies, but she also liked the possibility of being able to help people.

One of Emily's instructors commented that she seemed to enjoy these classes, and she asked if Emily had considered social work. Emily had never met a social worker, but she began to investigate the social work program. The rest, as they say, is history. Emily went on to get her bachelor's and master's degrees in social work, and she has worked in a variety of settings. And yes, she has worked in many situations that involved domestic violence. Because of her training as a professional social worker, Emily recognized the importance of exploring her own life experience in relation to her professional work, and she has continued to do just that throughout her career.

Emily's story is not an uncommon example of a social worker's journey into the profession. Many social workers come to the profession through interest in helping people, a psychology or sociology course, or past personal experiences. Emily happened to have all three. The psychology course helped her to find a connection with one of her strengths—an interest in helping people. Her personal experience as a survivor of domestic violence helped her tap into a reservoir of empathy to help others. Knowing your strengths and developing skills for working with people are essential for considering a career in social work.

You might wonder, though, why Emily decided to major in social work instead of psychology or sociology. Had it not been for that insightful faculty member, Emily would likely have graduated with a psychology degree. Having a degree in psychology could have taken Emily down a different career path. She might have gone on to complete a graduate degree in psychology, which would have led her to focus primarily on psychological testing. A doctorate in psychology could have taken her into private practice, research, or academic life. You can see how psychology can overlap with social work, but there are differences, too. Emily can become a therapist with a master's degree in social work and a clinical credential (license). In psychology, she would have needed a doctorate.

SOCIAL WORK EDUCATION

To practice social work, social workers need the proper credentials. Professional social work can be performed only by a person who has been awarded a bachelor's or master's degree from a college or university social work program that is accredited by the CSWE. NASW has issued a policy statement that conveys the importance of the title of social worker being used only for persons who hold social work degrees (NASW, 2012–2014b) and actively lobbies state legislatures to uphold that policy. In fact, many states have passed legislation stipulating that only persons with social work degrees from CSWE-accredited programs may refer to themselves as social workers. In addition, all states have enacted legislation that enables degreed social work practitioners to obtain a license or certification to practice social work. The specifics of these laws vary from state to state and by area of practice.

U.S. social work programs grant three types of degrees:

1. Bachelor of Social Work (BSW) prepares the graduate for generalist social work professional practice.

2. Master of Social Work (MSW) prepares the graduate for advanced professional practice in an area of concentration.

3. Doctorate of Philosophy in Social Work (Ph.D. or DSW) is typically considered a research-oriented degree with a focus on preparing the graduate for a teaching or research career. However, several programs offer a doctorate degree in social work that emphasizes clinical practice.

The BSW curriculum exposes students to a wide range of content areas. A liberal arts background provides students with basic knowledge and skills that are an asset in social work practice, including an appreciation for scientific methods and historical developments; skills for effective communication and critical thinking; awareness of the human condition and the contribution of the arts to society; openness to diversity, difference, and improvability; and knowledge of human biological function. For their elective coursework, many undergraduate social work students gravitate to courses that will strengthen their knowledge of human behavior or social policy development. A growing number of BSW students seek fluency in a second language, such as Spanish or American Sign Language (ASL). As our society becomes increasingly diverse, bilingual skills and knowledge of global issues will become more important within the social work profession. Within the BSW program, an array of courses covers the areas that have been identified as essential competencies for the professional social worker (CSWE, 2008), as shown in Quick Guide #1.

QUICK GUIDE #1   Essential Competencies for Professional Social Workers (Council on Social Work Education)

✓ Identify as a professional social worker and conduct oneself accordingly.
✓ Apply social work ethical principles to guide professional practice.
✓ Apply critical thinking to inform and communicate professional judgments.
✓ Engage diversity and difference in practice.
✓ Advance human rights and social and economic justice.
✓ Engage in research-informed practice and practice-informed research.
✓ Apply knowledge of human behavior and the social environment.
✓ Engage in policy practice to advance social and economic well-being and to deliver effective social work services.
✓ Respond to contexts that shape practice.
✓ Engage, assess, intervene, and evaluate with individuals, families, groups, organizations, and communities.

Source: Council on Social Work Education, 2008. Available at: http://www.cswe.org/Accreditation/2008EPASDescription.aspx.

Among the helping professions, social work is the leader in preparing graduates with a bachelor's degree to work effectively in social services. The BSW permits such quick entry into professional practice for three reasons:

1. Students in the BSW program are required to participate in two or three service-learning experiences in a social service agency.

2. The BSW program is accredited by a professional body.

3. States have already determined that BSW graduates have the required education to obtain a license or certification (Hopps et al., 2008).

The distinction between the BSW and the MSW is primarily in the areas of content, program objectives, and depth, breadth, and specificity of knowledge and skills (CSWE, 2008). According to one NASW survey, nearly 80% of practicing social workers who responded possess an MSW degree, while 12% of respondents had the BSW as their highest degree (NASW Center for Workforce Studies, 2005). Social workers with BSWs and MSWs often work in the same settings and with the same client systems, but each functions at different levels and performs different tasks.

At the BSW level, Emily worked directly with women and children in the domestic violence program. She helped them gain admittance to a safe-house program and to obtain legal, financial, health, and mental health services. Once she had reached the MSW level, Emily provided mental health treatment for the women and children in the shelter.

FIELD EXPERIENCES

Whichever level of social work education you might pursue, you can expect the theory learned in the classroom to be integrated with practice. The field education experience promotes the application of knowledge, skills, and values through at least 400 hours of supervised practice in a social work setting. Members of the profession feel strongly that social workers should be mentored and supervised by other social workers. This training enables social workers to work competently, effectively, and ethically with people facing real challenges.

Actual experience is invaluable. In fact, one strategy for determining if social work might be the profession for you is to gain exposure through a volunteer or service-learning experience. Whether or not you have previously engaged in community service, now is an excellent time to work with and observe social workers as they perform their activities. Seek out a population or setting that interests you and imagine yourself as a social work professional in that setting. If you are not required to engage in a community or service-learning project as part of your introductory coursework, do it anyway. Take full advantage of this opportunity to challenge yourself.

In addition to providing an opportunity for you to gain experience, your community service can be an asset in other ways (Dale, 2001):

- Helping you to identify interests (or areas in which you are not interested) and goals.

- Enhancing your résumé, future marketability, and social work network.

- Building self-confidence and guiding your career directions.

Most social service agencies welcome—and actually rely on—the contributions of volunteers. Here are some suggestions for learning about service opportunities in your community:

- Consult with faculty members or the field education department in the social work program or your academic advisor.

- Contact your state's NASW chapter office.

- Contact your local United Way.

- Check your university's community service or volunteer clearinghouse office.

Like Emily, you may find yourself unexpectedly drawn to the profession of social work. And, like Emily, you will find that every little bit of experience helps. In each of the jobs in which Emily has worked, she has used the skills that she learned during her training and in previous jobs. Each job led to the next, and each job built on the last.

CONCLUSION

In this chapter, you have been introduced to the definition of social work, areas in which social workers practice, and the education required for becoming a social worker. I hope you are beginning to perceive the diversity and breadth of the profession. Like others, you may have entered this course with stereotypes about the social work profession (e.g., social workers only "steal babies and hand out food stamps"). It is the intent of this book not only to dispel those myths, but to open up the broad and exciting world of social work in which you will learn that social workers work with individuals, families, communities, and organizations using a multitude of skills and practice methods. As you have already begun to learn, social workers work with individuals and families in crisis, but we also work with groups of people to become better parents, neighborhoods to enhance the safety for the residents, and communities to influence legislation to improve services to persons with autism. I hope at the end of this book you will review the misconceptions you may have held as you began this course and that you will find they no longer exist.

In the remaining chapters we will explore the history of social work, current challenges that influence social work, areas of practice, cultural competence, values and ethics, theoretical frameworks for guiding practice, fields of practice, and the possibilities for the future of the social work profession.

As you proceed, keep in mind the following, written by an MSW student (Walton, 1996, p. 63). Her words not only capture her enthusiasm for her new profession, but they also provide a sense of the work that social workers do.

Social work is a career you can't leave at the office. You are committed to facilitating change in people's lives and the environment in which they live. You often work with, or on behalf of, individuals who have difficult problems and lack the resources with which to cope. It can be inspiring to see your clients help themselves out of a crisis using skills you helped them find within themselves.

I hope that you, too, can be inspired and that you are now beginning to consider whether you want to be a social worker. Check out the top 10 reasons for being a social worker in Exhibit 1.5 for some insight into a profession whose mission is to help others, make the world a better place, and perform meaningful work.

10. Help People
9. Do What Counts
8. Practice Your Principles
7. Foster Success Stories
6. Match Skills with Life's Challenges
5. Change the Future
4. Make the World a Better Place
3. Satisfaction Guaranteed
2. World-Class Peers
1. Career of Champions

EXHIBIT 1.5

Top 10 Reasons for Being a Social Worker

Source: National Association of Social Workers, n.d.

MAIN POINTS

- Social work is a professional activity that provides the opportunity to work with individuals, families, groups, organizations, and communities. Over a half-million people in the United States are practicing social workers.

- Other professions, such as psychology and sociology, have contributed to the development of social work, but the profession of social work also has unique values, knowledge, and practice skills.

- Social workers provide an ever-changing array of services such as counseling, advocacy, case management, education, prevention, support, and crisis intervention.

- Social workers work with persons throughout all areas of our society, including children, adolescents, and adults experiencing life changes or crises; persons who are struggling with an illness, disability, addiction, or homelessness; persons who are the victims of oppression, discrimination, or social injustice; and persons who have survived a disaster who have emigrated from their home country.

- Social workers work in a variety of settings, including schools, hospitals, mental health facilities, addiction treatment programs, advocacy programs, and residential facilities for children, youth, persons who are homeless, and older adults.

- Social workers can obtain degrees at bachelor's, master's, and doctoral levels. The NASW and the CSWE have defined the criteria for competence in a degreed social worker.

EXERCISES

1. Visit one of the following websites to obtain information about the social work profession:
   a. NASW: www.naswdc.org or www.socialworkers.org. Click on "State Chapters" to get information about NASW programs in your state, including student resources. You may also want to check out the NASW Twitter at www.twitter.com/nasw to learn more about NASW. Consider reviewing the General and Issue Fact Sheets that are available on the NASW Press Room (http://www.socialworkers.org/pressroom/features/genfactSheets.asp) and the Occupational Profiles available through the NASW CWS to learn about social work employment options (http://workforce.socialworkers.org/whatsnew.asp#profiles).
   b. CSWE: www.cswe.org. Review information regarding the accreditation process and the many resources provided by CSWE.
2. Personal reflection: Describe yourself (character, traits, and values) in terms of how you perceive the world and human nature. Then, reflect on a time that you asked for help for yourself. Discuss how these qualities and experiences may impact your professional work.
3. In this exercise, you will meet the Sanchez family. Go to: www.routledgesw.com/cases and click on the Sanchez family case. Read the introduction to the case and explore how the interactive program can be used. Activate each button to familiarize yourself with the presentation of information, the questions and tasks, and the Case Study Tools.

   Go to the Engage tab and complete Tasks 1 and 2 to understand better the needs of the Sanchez family. Use My Notebook to reflect on the roles that a social worker can play; describe the types of things a social work professional might be able to do to help the Sanchez family.
4. In this exercise, you will review the RAINN National Sexual Assault Online hotline case. Go to: www.routledgesw.com/cases and click on the RAINN. Read the introduction to the organization and explore how the interactive program

can be used. Activate each button to familiarize yourself with the presentation of information, the questions and tasks, and the Case Study Tools. After reviewing the information on the two client scenarios, Sarah and Alan, respond to the following:

a. Summarize your concerns about each of the clients.
b. Discuss the ways in which RAINN may prove to be a helpful resource for both clients.

CHAPTER 2

History of Social Work and Social Welfare

The exact beginnings and origins of the profession of social work are difficult to determine, but ample evidence throughout history suggests that what has come to be recognized as social work has been performed for thousands of years. This work, often performed by persons affiliated with religious institutions, usually took the form of providing tangible goods and services to impoverished people confronted with health problems. As you will learn in this chapter, this "charity" work evolved over the centuries to include the provision of mental health services, community organization and development work, and advocacy for groups of people experiencing oppression whose voices are not heard by decision makers.

Imagine what it was like, though, to be one of the pioneers who began to practice social work before it had a name. What would it have been like to pursue social work before much of society acknowledged the idea that we should care for all our citizens? Imagine that you are in 17th-century England trying to help poor families obtain enough food to eat; in 18th-century America trying to gain support to open that first orphanage; in 19th-century America working in one of the new settlement houses helping immigrants adjust to their new home. In the 20th century social work was identified as a profession, and its activities included many of those that had been undertaken in previous centuries as well as working for school desegregation and elimination of domestic violence. In the 21st century we are still working in the same areas—new challenges, but the same areas—along with new areas of social problems and needs.

As we begin this discussion of the history of social work and social welfare, clarifying the difference between the two is important. Although the terms are often used synonymously, they are not the same. As you learned in Chapter 1, social work is the professional practice that involves helping individuals, groups, and communities. In contrast, social welfare is a system aimed at creating social and economic justice. Social welfare services and programs have been part of society for centuries, and they provide the cornerstone for the emergence and development of the social work profession.

Our discussion here will include a chronicle of the history of social welfare programs and services in which many social workers are active as well as the history of the social work profession. It will end with an overview of the development of social work education. Two informative references are used here as the primary sources for compiling this historical perspective: National Association of Social Workers (NASW)'s *Milestones in the Development of Social Work and Social Welfare* (1998) and the 20th edition of Mizrahi and Davis's *Encyclopedia of Social Work* (2008).

DEVELOPMENT OF SOCIAL SERVICES

The roots of the social work profession lie within the religious community. For many centuries, the provision of charity (or alms) was entirely within the purview of religious groups. As early as 1200 BC, religious leaders urged Jews to help the poor of their communities. Historical Jewish documents describe charitable services that actually resemble modern-day mediation and casework (Senkowsky, 1996). For examples of the influence of religious doctrine on modern-day social services, see Exhibit 2.1.

EXHIBIT 2.1 *Early Cornerstones of Modern-Day Social Services*	• 1750 BC—In a code of justice, King Hammurabi of Babylonia decrees that his subjects must help others in time of need. • 1200 BC—Jewish faith embraces the tenet of helping the poor and those in need. • 500 BC—The Greek concept of philanthropy (i.e., acts of love for humanity) is incorporated into daily life as people begin donating money for the good of others. • 300 BC—Followers of Confucian philosophy promote the belief that humans have an obligation to help those in need. • 30 AD—The teachings of Christ focus on helping others. • 313 AD—Money donated by Christian converts is used by the church to help the poor. • 400–787 AD—"Hospitals" are established in India to care for those who are disabled or homeless. This movement expands into Europe, being first developed in France and later moving into Italy, with staffing provided by the religious community. • 650 AD—Islamic beliefs specify that taxes be directed to help the poor. • 1100 AD—Catholic canon law mandates that the rich have legal and moral obligations to help the poor. *Source:* NASW, 1998.

A man named Stephen has been called the "first" social worker. In the 1st century, seven Jewish deacons were selected by Christian leaders to see to the needs of Jews who had been enslaved. One of these seven men, Stephen, was particularly effective in this mission. Along with his six peers, he collected food and money for distribution to the "needy." These activities themselves were not innovative; however, designating specific persons to do the work was innovative. Stephen was commended by many for his work, but the leaders of Jerusalem did not support it.

He was tried by the High Court of the Great Temple and executed by the religious leadership for his values and beliefs (Marson & MacLeod, 1996).

Beginning in the 14th century, social changes in Europe began to transform attitudes toward the poor and the provision of charity. The feudal system of paying for services with land was beginning to shift to a more wage-based economic and social system, and increased trade within the towns and cities created a new middle class (Reid, 1995). In 1349, the Statute of Labourers was established in England to create a distinction between the "worthy" and the "unworthy" poor. Under this law, only older adults and people with disabilities were deemed worthy to receive charity.

Two centuries later, this concept was expanded into the Henrician Poor Law of 1536. King Henry VIII of England created even more restrictive categories of persons eligible to receive aid. He also developed government regulations for the collection and disbursement of mandatory donations (taxes) from the general citizenry. One effect of this law was to transfer the responsibility for charity from the church to the state. Together, the Statute of Labourers and the Henrician Poor Law established the precedent for public social services and provided the framework for the enactment of the Poor Laws of 1601.

Elizabethan Poor Laws of 1601

A defining point in the history of social services was the passage of the Elizabethan Poor Laws of 1601, during the reign of Queen Elizabeth I. These English laws are thought to have defined the social service and welfare delivery system for the next 300 years. Many historical accounts of the development of the social work profession actually begin with the institution of these history-making laws.

Advancing the philosophy of Henry VIII toward caring for persons in need, the Poor Laws of 1601 were aimed at placing responsibility for charity with the government and categorizing levels of charity based on worthiness. The Poor Laws employed the concept of mandatory local taxation to fund social and financial assistance (Corbett, 2008). Public assistance was provided to persons deemed eligible in three distinct categories:

1. Monetary help for poor people who were deemed unemployable (older persons and persons with disabilities).

2. Work for persons of limited income who were not older or disabled.

3. Apprenticeships for orphaned and dependent children.

In order to receive assistance, recipients were often required to live in residential institutions known as workhouses, poorhouses, or almshouses for adults and orphanages for children. Known as "indoor relief," this practice continued well into the 19th century, and in some areas of Europe and the United States could be found into the mid-20th century.

The Poor Laws arose during a time of profound change in the European social and political climate. Due to what were called the Enclosure Laws, an increasing number of persons were being denied their rights to farming land and thus being displaced from rural areas. The result was increased unemployment and homelessness. Such changes served as the impetus for the creation of the Poor Laws. These laws were an attempt to:

- Extricate the church from the delivery of social services.

- Eliminate begging and criminal behavior.

- Centralize assistance within the government.

- Standardize the types and amounts of assistance provided for the growing class of workers.

The Poor Laws made a significant, long-term impact on policies for providing aid to persons in need by creating a clear-cut distinction between persons deemed worthy of receiving assistance and those deemed unworthy of receiving help. Persons deemed unworthy of aid were considered to be responsible for their situations. This belief continues to be at the core of the debate regarding funding for social programs. The Poor Laws also represent a clear shift away from private-sector involvement in social service (that is, by the church) to governmental responsibility for the poor. This controversy over private versus public responsibility also continues to the present day.

Social Services in the 17th and 18th Centuries

The basic principles of the English Poor Laws can be seen in other events and advances that occurred during the next two centuries. They had a profound effect on social services in Europe and, later, in North America. During the 17th and 18th centuries, social services expanded in scope and reach.

For example, in the early 1600s, Father Vincent de Paul founded charity and religious organizations in France that established formalized structures for providing food, clothing, and financial support for persons in need. The St. Vincent de Paul Society operated solely on voluntary contributions from parishioners, a model that prevails in the social service delivery system today. You might recognize the name, as the Society itself is still active in many communities.

Also during the 1600s, the **Protestant work ethic** was gaining popularity in England and other parts of Europe. This belief system and way of life emphasize self-discipline and frugality. It has had a significant influence on societal attitudes toward the poor. Many people now believe that all persons, through hard work and discipline, should be able to care for themselves at all times without help from others. Such thinking often translates into opposition to funding for social service programs.

Further efforts in 17th-century England to restrict access to aid by the poor took the form of the 1662 Law of Settlement, which stipulated that aid was based on one's place of residence. This law discouraged aid recipients from moving to other areas where they might find work (Reid, 1995).

Meanwhile, in England's North American colonies, the colonists began formulating social welfare policy fashioned after the Poor Laws in England. By 1657, Boston was home to the first private social welfare agency, the Scots' Charitable Society. In the same year, New York was the site for the first almshouse, with others following soon thereafter in Plymouth (1658) and Boston (1660). In 1729, the first residential facility for orphans was opened in the French colony of New Orleans by the Ursuline Sisters, and the first psychiatric institution was established in 1773 in Williamsburg, Virginia. Most of these newly created organizations were private and often religiously affiliated. As you can see, even while the colonists were focused on expanding into new territory, establishing themselves in a new world, and grappling with the issue of colonization versus independence, they also devised plans to care for poor, sick, and disadvantaged persons.

Soon after independence, the government of the United States made its first major efforts to create public social and health services. A governmentally funded orphanage opened in Charleston, South Carolina, in 1790, and the U.S. Public Health Service was established in 1798 by a legislative act aimed at creating a health care system for merchant seamen. The Public Health Service still exists today to provide health care and mental health care to underserved populations around the world, to prevent and control disease, and to conduct research.

Although the primary focus of most charitable programs was the alleviation of poverty by providing financial aid, they also established the importance of addressing other aspects of the individual's life in order to facilitate a move out of poverty. Helping those living in poverty to gain economic stability was the seed for modern-day social casework and clinical treatment. A social system was literally built from scratch in the American colonies, becoming institutionalized as the country gained independence from England. However, as you will see, the belief in public responsibility for social and health services among American citizens would wax and wane from this point on—and it continues to be a source of controversy in the 21st century.

The 19th Century, a Defining Era in the United States

The 1800s were a boom time for the development of social welfare programs and the social work profession, particularly in the United States. This century witnessed progress in areas such as the creation of public and private agencies and organizations to address the country's growing social problems. During this century, the United States grew substantially in both size and population. In addition, the population became more diverse due to increasing rates of immigration. Following the Civil War, the United States experienced a fluctuating economy that produced many periods of depression. Thus, the time was ripe for the formation of a more organized system of social service delivery. With the growth of the social service system came a dawning awareness that qualified and trained persons were needed to provide these services and to work with the increasingly diverse populations.

Exhibit 2.2 highlights some of the advancements that were made in our country's burgeoning system for taking care of all our citizens. Most important was the emerging belief that certain groups within our population need help in having their voices heard. The new United States was becoming more humane toward citizens living in poverty.

EXHIBIT 2.2

19th-Century Advances in Social Services

- Societies for the Prevention of Pauperism were founded in New York, Baltimore, and Philadelphia aimed at providing aid to those who were suffering as a result of the War of 1812.
- 1824—The Bureau of Indian Affairs was created as well as the House of Refuge—the first program for juvenile delinquents that was state-funded.
- 1835—Boston followed other cities by establishing the Society for the Prevention of Pauperism, which became the forerunner of the Charity Organization Society (COS) movement.
- 1836—Passage of child labor laws in Boston.
- 1841—The first investigations of services provided to "insane people" were conducted by Dorothea Dix (1802–1887), who went on to help create 32 state and federal hospitals for persons with mental illness.
- 1845—The first public mental health facility (or "asylum") was opened in Trenton, New Jersey.
- 1853—Children's Aid Society (CAS) (still in existence in many states today) was organized in New York.
- 1863—First oversight organization for social services programs was founded in Massachusetts.
- 1865—As a partnership between the federal government and private philanthropies, the Freedmen's Bureau was created as the first federal welfare entity to help freed slaves find new lives, gain education, and be protected from abuse and violence (ceased services in 1872).
- 1868—Public monies were used to pay "foster" families in Boston for housing children (New York followed in 1875).
- 1870—A forerunner to the modern-day long-term care facility, the Home for Aged and Infirm Hebrew of New York City, was established.
- 1877—Society for the Prevention of Cruelty to Children is organized in New York. The first COS began serving clients in Buffalo.
- 1880—The Salvation Army was expanded to the United States (began in 1878 in England).
- 1886—First U.S. Settlement House opened in New York followed by the now famous Hull House in Chicago in 1889.
- 1896—Public education became available to the "mentally deficient" in Providence, Rhode Island.

Sources: Corbett, 2008; NASW, 1998; Quam, 2008a, b.

Source: Quam, 2008b.
Photo: Corbis.

Dorothea Dix

Dorothea Lynde Dix first worked as a teacher but later focused her attention on improving conditions for persons living in prisons and almshouses. An ardent advocate for legislative change, Dix lobbied in the United States and abroad to gain support for public and private funds for hospitals to house persons with hearing loss and mental illness.

Still, children, African Americans, widows and children of war veterans, persons with mental illnesses, and people devastated by disasters were just a few of the groups whose voices were then—and are now—often not heard by the majority of society. Advocates faced considerable adversity as they defended the rights of these

Ida Wells-Barnett

Ida B. Wells-Barnett (1862–1931), born in Mississippi to parents who were slaves, was able to attend high school and college and then work as a teacher. Her teaching career ended when she was fired for drawing attention to the poor school conditions for Black children. She turned her passion and talents for social justice to a career in journalism where she was able to raise awareness about her community. Her newspaper in Memphis was burned by a mob in 1892. Undaunted, Wells-Barnett went on a crusade for justice for Black men and women through her work with the Negro Fellowship League, Anti-Lynching Bureau of the National Afro-American Council (which later became the National Association for the Advancement of Colored People (NAACP)), and the Alpha Suffrage Club of Chicago.

Source: Peebles-Wilkins, 2008.
Photo: Getty Images.

marginalized groups. They often risked their reputations, safety, and personal funds to start programs to enhance the quality of life for these groups. Ida Wells-Barnett was one such pioneer who championed the rights and needs of the African American community, particularly in being able to gain access to services that were typically open only to Caucasians. Instrumental in the founding of the group that became the National Association for the Advancement of Colored People (NAACP), Wells-Barnett's contributions are noteworthy.

Although indoor relief was still considered by many authorities to be the preferred method for providing aid, it eventually gave way to "outdoor relief," the provision of services outside the institutional setting. From this paradigm shift came the founding of two movements that are of particular importance in the 19th-century history of social work and social welfare. The settlement house and **Charity Organization Society (COS)** movements, similar in intent but different in function, changed the nature of social service delivery and are considered responsible for the birth of the social work profession. Both movements share a philosophy that has become synonymous with American culture—individualism and personal freedom—even if they were not always compatible with the prevailing individualistic stance of the era. Nonetheless, settlement houses and charity organizations became the cornerstone of the American social service delivery system, despite the contradictions.

Settlement House Movement   A settlement house is a facility based in a geographically bound neighborhood whose purpose is to provide a center for the neighbors to come together for educational, social, and cultural activities. Settlement houses also provide social services and financial assistance. A key belief of this movement is that the social structure and society overall are responsible for individual problems. The settlement house idea is based on three concepts: (1) social change can occur; (2) social class distinctions can be narrowed through information and education; and (3) change can come only when the settlement house workers immerse themselves in their clients' community (Blank, 1998). Simply stated, settlement houses were created as an attempt by socially minded persons to engage in "friendship with the poor through sharing their lives" (Kendall, 2000, p. 16).

The first settlement house, Toynbee Hall, opened in London in 1884. It was not long before this model spread across England and the United States. In fact, just 2 years later, rooted in the Progressive Reform movement, the first American settlement house began operation in New York under the leadership of a former resident of Toynbee Hall, Stanley Coit. By the early 20th century, the number of settlement houses in the United States had grown to over 400 (Hopps et al., 2008). The best-known U.S. settlement house is Hull House, opened in Chicago in 1889 by Jane Addams and colleagues. Sadly, after several years of financial challenges, Hull House closed its doors on January 27, 2012.

Originally aimed at serving the growing immigrant population, the early settlement houses focused on education and socialization into the American culture of

Jane Addams

Widely considered the originator of social work in the United States, Jane Addams (1860–1935) opened Chicago's Hull House in 1889. Partnering with Ellen Gates, Addams established Hull House after visiting the original settlement house, Toynbee Hall, in London. Ever the activist, Addams fought for improved sanitary conditions in Chicago and, as a result, was appointed neighborhood sanitation inspector.

Many organizations had their roots among the activism of Hull House. One example is the organization that later became the Children's Bureau. Quaker and staunch pacifist, Jane Addams' contributions go far beyond the work of Hull House. She was a community organizer, peace advocate, 1931 co-winner of the Nobel Peace Prize, and one of only two social workers inducted into the Hall of Fame of Great Americans. In 1909, Addams was elected president of the National Conference of Charities and Correction (later to be called National Council on Social Welfare), the first woman to hold this post. A prolific writer, Addams' works include six books on her life and her views. Addams' dedication to the issue of world peace resulted in her active involvement in a number of peace organizations, including the Women's Peace Party, the National Progressive Party, and the Women's International League for Peace and Freedom. She accomplished all of this despite the fact that as a woman she did not acquire the right to vote until 1920.

Sources: Barker, 2003; Corbett, 2008; Hopps et al., 2008; NASW, 1998; L. Quam, 2008. *Photo:* Getty.

the time (Blank, 1998). Jane Addams described her approach to the settlement house movement this way:

> Teaching in a Settlement requires distinct methods, for it is true of people who have been allowed to remain undeveloped and whose facilities are inert and sterile, that they cannot take their learning heavily. It has to be diffused in a social atmosphere, information must be held in solution, in a medium of fellowship and good will . . . It is needed to say that a Settlement is a protest against a restricted view of education.
>
> (Urban Experience in Chicago, available at http://uic.edu/jaddams/hull/urbanexp/contents.htm)

Settlement house workers are thought by many to have been in the forefront of the social work profession's long history in social action and policy practice. They were typically young, well-educated adults (mostly women) interested in social issues and the arts. Because settlement house workers chose to live in the same neighborhoods as those with whom they worked, they could not ignore the mounting social concerns: living and sanitary conditions, housing, child care, education, and worker exploitation. The settlement house workers soon were often instigators of controversial and much-needed social change and advocacy for marginalized groups. They played roles in the development of social entities such as juvenile courts, mothers' pensions, child labor laws, and workplace protections (McNutt & Floersch, 2008, p. 3). They also instituted training programs that would later become a component of the social work profession.

The settlement house concept is still in existence today, but it has undergone considerable reconstruction. The centers where idealistic, youthful volunteers lived and made efforts at teaching the arts and literature have been replaced by neighborhood-based community centers that provide a wide array of goods and services, including food and clothing, health care, after-school and summer recreation, crisis intervention, and counseling. However, the basic ideal on which the settlement houses were founded still exists today: change is most effective if it comes from within the community itself. One example, Grace Hill Settlement House in St. Louis, MO, provides an array of services for children, older adults, and low-income persons and families (Exhibit 2.3).

Charity Organization Society During the same period that the settlement houses were improving life for immigrants and influencing the formation of social welfare services in the United States, another movement that would impact the future of social work was under way. The London-based Society for Organising Charitable Relief and Repressing Mendicity provided the framework for the first North American COS in Buffalo, New York, in 1877.

The philosophical underpinning of the charity society movement was a morally based belief that the person was responsible for his or her own difficulties but could be rehabilitated through individual sessions with a "friendly visitor" as opposed to

EXHIBIT 2.3

Grace Hill
Settlement
House

GRACE HILL SETTLEMENT HOUSE

Grace Hill Settlement House, located in St. Louis, Missouri, can trace its origins to a decision in 1844 by leaders of the town of North St. Louis to donate land for a church. Grace Episcopal Church was built in a neighborhood in which most residents were Episcopalians. As wealthier residents moved out of this neighborhood, it became home to a middle-class and then a low-income population, including many recent immigrants. In response, Grace Episcopal Church founded the Holy Cross Mission in 1903 to meet the changing needs of the neighborhood.

To expand their mission into the delivery of health care services, the Episcopal Diocese began the Holy Cross Dispensary in a nearby location in 1906. In 1914, Holy Cross Mission was incorporated. In 1923, the organization joined with the Community Fund (now United Way) to provide kindergarten, health clinics, recreation, and classes in crafts, dance, athletics, and music. From 1938 to 1944, Grace Hill gained recognition as a settlement house and instituted such changes as accepting African Americans and replacing religious staff with social workers. By 1965, Grace Hill had established its first Head Start program for preschool education. Shortly thereafter, Grace Hill, using neighbors (residents of the neighborhood) as advisors to program operations, began a meal program for older adults and developed a 10-year neighborhood improvement plan that resulted in the construction of low-cost apartments and the rehabilitation of existing housing stock.

By the 1980s, the philosophy of the agency was that the neighbors should be involved in developing training programs, forums, a resource bank, self-help groups, and communication centers. Keeping the settlement house model alive, services are now provided in the areas of child and older adult care, housing for low-income persons and families, self-help, job skills training, and community and economic development.

a financial handout (Brieland, 1995). "Not alms but a friend" was the motto of the early COS workers, who believed that extending friendship and sympathy would enable persons living in poverty to feel better about themselves and rise out of poverty (Kendall, 2000). The principles on which the COS was founded include: (1) detailed investigation of applicants; (2) a central system of registration to avoid duplication; (3) cooperation between the various relief agencies; and (4) extensive use of volunteers in the roles of "friendly visitors" (Corbett, 2008, p. 7). The concept of a charitable service that did not involve living with the persons being served quickly spread throughout the country; by 1892 there were 92 such societies in operation (Brieland, 1995).

The first workers in the movement, the "friendly visitors" that would eventually become modern-day social workers, were primarily middle-class women who voluntarily ventured into neighborhoods in which persons of low income lived in order to share their wisdom and advice on good and moral living. The COS entities engaged in such activities as individual assessments and registration of those "worthy" of receiving charity and, ultimately, employment and legal services (Brieland, 1995).

Although the COS movement has been criticized for being shortsighted and judgmental, and this attitude became a pervasive part of social work for many decades, the work of these well-intentioned volunteers laid the groundwork for advancements such as social casework and the formation of family and children's service agencies. Together with the settlement house movement, the COS movement was a key part of the evolution of the social work profession, enabling society to move forward in our treatment of poor, abused, and oppressed groups. Exhibit 2.4 summarizes the contributions of these two developments.

Social Services in the 20th Century

The dawning of the 20th century brought with it even more changes in our society, in general, and the social services community, in particular. Economically, the country

	SETTLEMENT HOUSE MOVEMENT	CHARITY SOCIETY MOVEMENT	**EXHIBIT 2.4**
Central Vision	Reform of systems and environment	Relief for clients	*Contributions of the Settlement House and Charity Society Movements*
Contributions to Social Work Profession	• Assessment and understanding of the conditions and cultures in which clients live • Impact of environmental conditions on the quality of people's lives • Client empowerment through education, information, and group work	• Assessment of each individual situation • Intervention specific to the individual • Knowledge that money alone does not always facilitate change	

Source: Hopps et al., 2008.

was emerging from the depression of the late 1800s. The first two decades of the 1900s were a time of economic prosperity, and leaders in the social service movement had the opportunity to focus on coordinating services and organizing coalitions to enhance service delivery. Socially and politically, the 1890s and early 1900s, known as the Progressive Era, were a time of significant reform in far-ranging areas such as women's rights (specifically suffrage), health care and social service programs, education, political practices, occupational and consumer safety, child and social welfare laws, environmental preservation, and socialization for immigrants. The leaders of the progressive movement successfully advocated for changes in social insurance, government regulation, and the professionalization of helping professions (Reid, 1995, p. 2212).

By this time, social work was established as a profession that responds to current economic, political, and social events and trends. The Progressives, a group of social and political activists that included Jane Addams, gained national recognition for the need to establish a federal infrastructure for financial assistance, public health interventions, and social work professionalization that would concretize the delivery of social services for many years to come (Reid, 1995).

Three organizations that grew out of the progressive movement and had an impact on the work of social workers were the National Urban League, the Children's

Signing of Social Security Act

President Franklin Delano Roosevelt signed the Social Security Act of 1935.

Source: Getty Images.

Bureau (first headed by Hull House alumna, Julia Lathrop), and the Child Welfare League of America. Despite social workers having a role in the founding of these organizations, the influence of such organizations on social work may not be readily apparent. The endorsement of governmental agencies and the merging of smaller groups into larger groups strengthened the position and voice of those committed to serving the poor.

Of particular importance during this period was the implementation of social policy and programming aimed at workers, women, and children. Workers' compensation legislation was first passed in 1910, and within 10 years most states had followed suit. The Mothers' Pensions program that provided assistance for women and children was launched. Recipients of the Mothers' Pensions were typically Caucasian widowed mothers. While this program was modeled after traditional charity programs in which the financial benefits were minimal and the goal was moral reform, the Mothers' Pensions program was the first nationwide public program that actually did provide financial assistance to women who were rearing families on their own and attempted to destigmatize recipients (Seccombe, 1999).

Also of importance during the early part of the 20th century was the emerging presence of social service departments within institutions. The Massachusetts General Hospital in Boston was the first to create a department to serve patients' social and psychiatric needs. Soon there would be over 100 hospital social service units. The term "psychiatric social worker" was, in fact, first used in Boston in 1914.

Developments During the Depression and the New Deal   The stock market crash of 1929 sent the country spiraling downward into an economic and social depression that would last through the next decade. The Great Depression of the 1930s was a time of suffering and unrest. Nevertheless, as had become the tradition for the profession, social workers once again rose to the occasion. One particularly prominent social worker of this era, Frances Perkins, was the first woman appointed to the U.S. Cabinet, serving as Secretary of Labor in Franklin D. Roosevelt's administration.

When Franklin D. Roosevelt, a Democrat, was elected to the presidency in 1932, nearly one-third of Americans were living in poverty, manufacturing and agriculture had been devastated, and the breadlines were long and getting longer. In response, the Roosevelt administration instituted a number of programs, collectively called the New Deal, that would have a lasting effect on our society.

Probably the most important New Deal legislation was the Social Security Act of 1935. Championed by members of the progressive movement since the early years of the century, the Social Security Act was passed to alleviate the poverty of older adults, widows and widowers, the unemployed, persons with disabilities, and dependent children. The legislation became the foundation of our public welfare and retirement systems. Social worker Jane M. Hoey was appointed by the president to direct the Federal Bureau of Public Assistance, the entity that oversaw distribution of aid through this legislation.

Frances Perkins (1882–1965)

Frances Perkins earned a master's degree in social work from Columbia University in 1910 and went on to have an illustrious career as an administrator, leader, and author. She served in a number of leadership roles, including the New York Consumer's League, New York Committee on Safety, New York State Factory Commission, New York Council of Organizations for War Services, Council on Immigrant Education, and New York State Industrial Board. She then became U.S. Secretary of Labor, the first appointment of a woman to the U.S. Cabinet. Following her service as the Secretary of Labor, she spent her final working years on the U.S. Civil Service Commission.

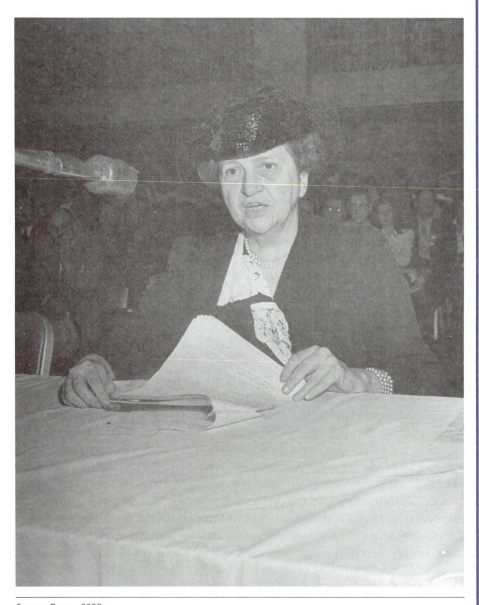

Source: Quam, 2008c.
Photo: Getty Images.

In addition to providing a retirement income for older adults, the Social Security Act ultimately resulted in the development of public assistance programs that would include services such as health care, employment services, transportation, and child day care for persons living in poverty and with disabilities, as well as impoverished women and children (known as Aid to Dependent Children, then, Aid to Families with Dependent Children—AFDC and now, **Temporary Assistance to Needy Families (TANF)**). The Social Security Act and other New Deal reforms served to affirm the role of the federal government in the administration of social services. This development would later serve U.S. society well, because structures were in place during times of economic crisis.

Other important social and economic programs implemented during the New Deal include the following:

- *Federal Emergency Relief Administration (FERA)*: Headed by social worker Harry Hopkins, FERA formed a system of state grants to provide financial assistance. FERA later became the Works Progress Administration, an agency that created employment from 1935 to 1943 for over 8 million people in such diverse areas as construction of roads and bridges to development of cultural programs. To read more about Hopkins, see page 38.

- *Civilian Conservation Corps (CCC)*: In existence from 1933 to 1942, the CCC was designed to conserve and develop the nation's natural resources, while creating employment opportunities for unemployed men.

- *National Youth Administration (NYA)*: Out of concern for ensuring that the country's high school and college students be able to complete their education, the NYA provided funding for part-time employment.

Developments During World War II and the 1950s   As often occurs during wartime, the United States experienced an economic recovery during the 1940s. World War II had a significant impact on the social work profession as well. For example, social workers developed and administered mental health programs for military personnel. This activity ultimately led to the creation of the nationwide, community-based mental health system that remains the basis for the provision of mental health services (Reid, 1995).

Nevertheless, there was little expansion of the social welfare system during the latter half of the 1940s. The focus during these years was on the returning veterans, 1 million of whom used the 1944 GI Bill of Rights to acquire a college education and purchase homes. In 1946, the group now known as the Baby Boomer generation made its debut. This period provided a segue into the 1950s, which was clearly a strong economic period as well as a relatively conservative era in politics.

One of the most important events for social welfare and social work in the postwar period was the creation of the cabinet-level Department of Health, Education, and Welfare in 1953, during the administration of Republican president Dwight D.

Harry Hopkins (1890–1946)

Known best for his work during the New Deal era, social worker Harry Hopkins led the newly created Federal Emergency Relief Administration (FERA). Committed to the social work profession early on, Hopkins had first worked with boys at a New York settlement house and later for the Bureau of Family Rehabilitation and Relief. Appointed by then New York Governor Franklin D. Roosevelt, Hopkins served as the executive director of the Temporary Emergency Relief Administration. Having gained the respect of the future president, Hopkins went on to serve Roosevelt in the Works Progress Administration and as the Secretary of Commerce.

Source: Longres, J.E., 2008.
Photo: Getty Images.

Eisenhower. This was the first acknowledgment by the federal government that the well-being of all people in the United States was a high priority. This department—which in 1979 was divided into the Department of Health and Human Services and the Department of Education—has been instrumental in formulating and administering virtually every federally funded social welfare program in existence in this country.

Otherwise, the 1950s, like the 1940s, is an era not well known for advances in the social service arena. Historically, the combination of Republican presidential administrations and prosperous times means little attention (and funding) is devoted to the social service community; the 1950s are a prime example of that historical pattern.

Developments During the 1960s and 1970s   The 1960s have become well known as a tumultuous time on many fronts. In 1960, the nation elected a Democratic president, John F. Kennedy. The civil rights movement was heating up. The war in Vietnam would soon take center stage, bringing with it civil unrest here at home. The youth were headed in a different direction from those of the previous decades. Many young people opposed the Vietnam War and military service in general, participated in the sexual revolution, and experimented with illicit drugs.

From the social work perspective, the 1960s were an interesting time, indeed. Many social workers feel that the 1960s were one of the most significant times for the profession due to the creation of a number of social programs, advances in civil rights, and the willingness of U.S. citizens to confront injustices in a public way. The Kennedy administration established the Peace Corps in 1961 and encouraged Congress to pass the 1963 Community Mental Health Center Act. Kennedy's successor, Lyndon B. Johnson, another Democrat, oversaw passage of the Civil Rights Act of 1964 as well as the Economic Opportunity Act of 1964—an array of social welfare legislation known collectively as the Great Society. Designed to build on the "welfare-oriented" initiatives that emerged during the administration of Franklin D. Roosevelt in the 1930s, Johnson's efforts specifically focused on creating safety nets for those living in poverty and on the racial dynamics, particularly as they existed in inner cities (Terrell, 2010). The War on Poverty was a "unique anti-poverty experiment . . . that powerfully influenced the character of community policy-making and administration in subsequent decades" (Terrell, 2010, p. 1061). Although some critics consider Johnson's War on Poverty and the Great Society to have been a failure, the 1964 legislation was responsible for the creation of numerous social programs, many of which still exist in some form today: Job Corps, Head Start, Volunteers in Service to America (VISTA—the domestic version of the Peace Corps), and the Neighborhood Youth Corps. Proponents of the War on Poverty efforts advocate that the programs are responsible for decreasing the number of individuals and families living in or near poverty and that erosion of such supportive programs results in increasing the number of persons struggling to survive (Rank, 2008). Although halted due to increasing program costs and the escalating war in Vietnam, the War on Poverty produced two significant, long term outcomes: (1) the voices of more people, particularly those with low incomes and persons of color, were heard for the first time in policy-making activities; and (2) in the form of contracting for service delivery, partnerships were formed between public and private institutions (Terrell, 2010). Both practices continue to this day.

Five major social programs were enacted during the Great Society that enhanced—and perhaps saved—the lives of the people they serve and, as many contend, decreased the number of persons living in poverty:

1. *Food Stamp Act (now referred to as Supplemental Nutrition Assistance Program (SNAP))*: This Department of Agriculture program, enacted in 1964, provides food assistance to people living on limited incomes.

2. *Medicare*: Passed in 1965, national social insurance program that provides health insurance for older adults and younger persons experiencing a disability.

3. *Medicaid*: Health insurance for those who receive public welfare benefits, also passed in 1965.

4. *Older Americans Act*: A nationwide system of community-based services for older adults, created in 1965.

5. *Elementary and Secondary Education Act*: In 1965, federal funding was directed for the first time in history toward the goal of providing students in the public school system with an array of services and support.

While protecting the civil rights of U.S. residents had been on the forefront of certain segments of the population for hundreds of years, the 1960s saw some of the most significant strides of our history in the passage of legislation aimed specifically at protecting the rights of more Americans. The Civil Rights Act of 1964 provided protection against discrimination based on race, color, religion, or national origin, leading to the desegregation of public schools and equal employment opportunities (Pollard, 2008). Numerous laws have since been enacted to protect the civil rights of many of our underrepresented and oppressed residents, including persons with disabilities, the gay, lesbian, bisexual, and transgender community, and immigrants and refugees. Social workers have always been, and will continue to be, on the front lines of these activities, ensuring that the voices of our clients are heard.

Although not as glamorous and exciting as the 1960s, the 1970s was a decade of progress in social services. Despite the ultimate downfall of the Republican administration of Richard M. Nixon, a significant number of programs were created under his leadership. The focus of his administration was a traditional Republican one in that "charity" was not endorsed, but work incentives were supported (Reid, 1995). The laws passed during the administrations of Nixon and his successor, Gerald Ford, that had far-reaching effects on social service delivery include:

- *Supplemental Security Income (SSI)*: Additional benefits were made available in 1972 for older persons and people with disabilities whose income was still well below poverty standards.

- *Comprehensive Employment and Training Act (CETA)*: This 1974 program provided educational and job opportunities for persons of limited income.

- *Child Abuse Prevention and Treatment Act*: Enacted in 1974, this measure created a comprehensive approach to the prevention, investigation, and treatment of child abuse, and it was expanded in 1978 to address inadequacies of the adoption system.

- *Education for All Handicapped Children Act*: This 1975 legislation required all public schools to provide educational experiences for children with disabilities that are comparable to those available to children without such disabilities.

- *Title XX amendment to the Social Security Act*: In 1975 funds were provided for the purchase of social services, training, and housing for persons who qualified based on their income.

Developments During the 1980s and 1990s   Those in the social work community do not typically view the 1980s with favor. The Republican administrations of Ronald Reagan and George H.W. Bush followed the traditional pattern of decreased spending on domestic and social programs. Specifically, two legislative acts passed during Reagan's first term severely cut social service funding: the Omnibus Budget Reconciliation Act (OBRA) of 1981 and the Tax Equity and Fiscal Responsibility Act of 1982. OBRA gave more authority and less funding to states for administration of public assistance programs and made it more difficult for those living in poverty to access services, as states could individually determine eligibility and access. The 1982 law resulted in decreased Medicare, Medicaid, AFDC, SSI, and unemployment funds.

Continuing in his predecessor's footsteps, George H.W. Bush advocated for increased privatization of the social service system based on a belief that the public should not be responsible for the welfare of the general population. Enacted in 1988, the Family Support Act was an attempt to impact the welfare system positively by providing improved employment and training programs, child support enforcement, and child care services. Ironically, it may be argued that the attempts of Reagan and Bush (senior) to disempower the social welfare system resulted in a strengthening of sorts. Increased funding and management options at the state level and a renewed interest in the nonprofit sector helped bring the attention of the general public to the need for a centralized social service system (Reid, 1995).

President Bill Clinton's campaign platform in the early 1990s was designed to redirect the public's attention to domestic issues. Clinton's presidential years focused on reviewing and revamping a number of domestic programs. His administration took on such intractable social issues as health care, family health and well-being issues, abortion, discrimination against gays and lesbians in the military, welfare reform, and distressed communities (Green & Haines, 2002). With a

Republican-controlled Congress, the effort to embrace universal health care failed. Yet the Clinton administration made significant strides in revitalizing the economy, increasing the minimum wage to $5.15/hour, creating new jobs, and eliminating the budget deficit (Hopps et al., 2008).

For social workers, the most significant issues addressed during the 1990s were welfare reform and community development. The 1996 Personal Responsibility and Work Opportunity Reconciliation Act (PRWORA) became law, replacing Aid to Families with Dependent Children with TANF. TANF continues to provide cash assistance to low-income women and their children, but with greater restrictions, mandated work requirements, and a 5-year lifetime cap on the receipt of benefits. Proponents believe that the welfare-to-work programs created by this welfare reform are responsible for positive changes, while others (mostly those on the front lines) believe they are a deterrent to getting out of poverty. Many former welfare recipients gained employment during the prosperous 1990s, but many critics questioned whether this trend could be maintained during weaker economic times (Green & Haines, 2002). In addition, many persons working full-time for minimum wage still lived in poverty without health care and other resources.

The 1990s saw an array of new legislation aimed at protecting the rights of certain populations and ensuring access to services. Passed in 1990, the Americans with Disabilities Act guarantees that persons with disabilities can have access to public facilities and live without fear of employment discrimination. Originally established as the Education for All Handicapped Children Act of 1975, the Individuals with Disabilities Education Act, last revised in 2004, addressed the gap of services to children with disabilities who attend public schools. The Mental Health Parity Act (1996) mandates that insurance companies must provide coverage for mental health services as well as physical health services.

In spite of changes pursued and achieved by the Clinton administration, critics question whether real change occurred and, if so, who benefited from that change. For example, homosexuality was publicly addressed for the first time by the military with the creation of the "don't ask, don't tell" policy. This policy, which meant that the military could not officially inquire about a service member's sexual orientation, and service members could not offer that information, was viewed as a setback by the gay and lesbian rights movement.

Social Services in the 21st Century and Beyond

The new millennium saw the inauguration of a Republican president whose campaign platform let us know that he was not a supporter of increased funding for governmental social programs. In fact, one of George W. Bush's early efforts in this area was to make federal monies available to faith-based social services instead. In many ways, this was a continuation of the agenda promoted by his father, George H.W. Bush, who launched the 1,000 Points of Light project that showcased private-sector agencies. Through the two terms of the 21st-century Bush presidency, social services experienced continued and increasing privatization and decreased governmental responsibility for funding. The 2005 Deficit Reduction Act, which tightened funds for many social services, was passed to offset deficits due to tax cuts, the Iraq war, and natural disasters such as Hurricane Katrina (Hopps et al., 2008).

The 2008 presidential elections marked a dramatic shift on several levels. We elected Barack Obama, the first African American president in our history, whose candidacy was focused on turning the economic, educational, and social tide in our country. Within the first month in office, the new president's history-making economic stimulus package was an effort to stabilize the country's economy by creating new employment and opportunities. In the early days of his administration, the president also made a commitment to tackle other areas of crisis within our country, to include housing, educational, and social services. He has fulfilled his promise through the introduction of the "Affordable Care Act," the repeal of the "don't ask, don't tell" policy related to sexual orientation in the military, increases in aid and employment opportunities for veterans, extensions of unemployment benefits, and programs for persons in danger of losing their homes due to foreclosure. The economic crisis which began in 2008 has made sweeping changes both challenging and necessary.

Although historical trends can be a guide, predicting what will happen in the coming years would still be speculation. However, we can predict which issues among the current social, economic, and political challenges that confront our social service system will affect social work practice. While there are a myriad of social and economic issues on the forefront of societal concerns, a sampling of the more pressing areas include: welfare reforms, changing population and family demographics, restricted access to benefits, an aging society, the need for greater understanding of global issues, improving services to active duty military and veterans and their families, expanding college access, unemployment rates (particularly among young adults), and the implications of the economic crisis on all citizens (minority groups, in particular). These are all expected to provide opportunities for social workers to test their skills. Here are some observations from current research:

- Approximately two-thirds of our population will use public assistance benefits at some point in their adult life (Rank & Hirschl, 2002). In fact, over a 3-year period, approximately one-third of Americans spent at least 2 months or more living in poverty (DeNavas-Walt, Proctor, & Smith, 2008). More funding will be needed to support welfare-to-work programs, particularly for single, female-headed households.

- Both domestically and internationally, the population will continue to become older, creating new challenges for older adults, their families, and their societies.

- Immigrants and refugees are at higher risk for living in poverty, particularly those who enter the United States as undocumented persons. Coupled with a growing anti-immigrant sentiment that can result in racial/ethnic profiling, arrests, and prosecutions, social workers must be prepared to confront these challenges.

PROFESSIONAL EDUCATION IN SOCIAL WORK: A HISTORICAL PERSPECTIVE

As you have seen, the social work profession has been evolving for centuries. However, the term "social work" was not commonly used and formalized social work education did not exist until the late 1800s and early 1900s. In a sense, social work education began in the early settlement houses, which served as "social laboratories" for university students. A charity organization worker in England, Octavia Hill, is credited with introducing group discussions by caseworkers. Thus some of the training originated "in the field" and not at university.

Despite the fact that social work was not fully recognized as a profession until the 1930s, the term social work was first used in 1900 by an educator, Simon Patten, to refer to the work of friendly visitors and settlement house workers. This bit of social work trivia indicates that the emergence of the profession coincided with the growth of these two movements during the late 1800s. In fact, the volunteers who were prominent in the early movements were motivated to "address the 'social question,' the paradox of increasing poverty in an increasingly productive economy" and recognized the need to move their voluntary efforts to an occupation and then to a profession (Hopps et al., 2008, p. 1).

Educating Social Workers

As in England, U.S. social work training emerged from the COS and settlement house movements, taking the form of apprenticeships and in-house training. The leadership of the burgeoning profession quickly determined that more formal training was needed. By 1893, a call had been issued for "formal education in applied philanthropy" because the "on-the-job" training offered within the agency setting was deficient in the provision of principles and theory (Leighninger, 2000, pp. 1–2). In 1894, the first social welfare textbook, *American Charities*, was published. Two decades later, in 1917, Mary Richmond developed the book *Social Diagnosis*, which became the primary textbook for the emerging profession.

The idea of formalized social work training quickly gained appeal throughout the United States. These early educational ventures were agency-based, but, within a brief period, the training programs were increasingly located in university settings, with input provided by agency personnel (Frumkin & Lloyd, 1995). Many people believed that the early British approach was more advanced than U.S. methods

Octavia Hill (1838–1912)

A little-known charity organization worker from an upper-middle-class English family, Octavia Hill entered the "charity" world by working with young girls in a toy-making project under the guidance of her mentor, social reformer John Ruskin. Hill soon became aware of the appalling conditions in which the girls lived.

By 1869, she had moved from the toy project into recruiting and training other volunteers to help improve housing for low-income persons. These female volunteers, known as housing estate managers, collected rents and engaged in individual work that would later be known as social casework.

Hill's contribution to the development of the social work profession around the world is that she trained the volunteers to work with tenants on an individual basis in a caring, respectful manner, affirming their dignity and autonomy—the cornerstone of what we now know as social work. In fact, Hill's group discussions about cases, facilitated by a mentor, were the origins of organized social work training. Hill is also credited with establishing an organization that became the model for the Charity Organization Society movement.

because the training was entirely university-based. Many English social workers, however, considered the slower-developing American system—with its independent schools of social work heavily influenced by community agencies—to be superior to their university-based system (Kendall, 2000).

What is considered to be the first social work training program in the United States was founded in 1895 at the Chicago School of Social Economics. By 1903, the program was known as the Chicago School of Civics and Philanthropy (which later became the University of Chicago School of Social Service Administration) and was offering a year-long training program. By 1918, 17 social work training programs had been established (Frumkin & Lloyd, 1995)—an average of one new program per year. Most programs emphasized a casework curriculum, thus carving out a niche for clinical social work. Despite the rapid growth of educational endeavors, however, the profession was still in its infancy, and it was generally unorganized and fragmented.

Abraham Flexner, an educator and not a social worker, made a major contribution to the growth of the social work profession, although his efforts initially were viewed as devastatingly negative. His 1915 critique on the profession resulted in some of the most important advancements in the profession's history. Flexner's report states that a profession must:

- Involve intellectual operations with large responsibility.

- Derive raw material from science and learning and apply it to a practical and definite end.

- Possess educationally communicable techniques.

- Have self-organization.

- Be altruistic in motivation.

Flexner recognized that social work at the time possessed character, practicality, a tendency toward self-organization, and altruism, but he stated that it was not yet a profession due to deficits in individual responsibility and educationally communicable techniques (Syers, 2008).

Social work professionals of the time rallied in an effort to strengthen the profession. Social work training programs became more formalized, and social workers began to conduct their own research and generate their own theories. Finally, the profession began to articulate its own methods of practice and focused on organizing social workers into a professional group. One response to Flexner's concerns was Mary Richmond's 1917 book, *Social Diagnosis*, which outlined assessment techniques for use with clients (Exhibit 2.5).

EXHIBIT 2.5

Mary Richmond

The "foremother" of American professional social work, Mary Richmond (1861–1928) was a social activist and prolific writer on social issues. Starting out as a treasurer for a Maryland Charity Organization Society, Richmond also served as a friendly visitor.

In 1897, Richmond, then secretary of the Charity Organization Society of Baltimore, delivered a speech at the National Conference of Charities and Corrections, in which she said: "we owe it to those who shall come after us that they shall be spared the groping and blundering by which we have acquired our own stock of experience." Richmond

EXHIBIT 2.5

continued

argued that workers needed training as "relief and child-saving agents" with "shoulder-to-shoulder contact which makes cooperation natural and inevitable" (p. 181). She went on to state that theory and practice should be concurrent, with students beginning in a general area of study and moving into a specialization—the model still used as the basis of social work education today. Richmond's definition of social casework set the stage for the future of social work practice.

Richmond's call for the formalized training of "charity" workers had previously been made by a Massachusetts community activist, Anna Dawes, but it was not acted on until 1898 when the New York School of Philanthropy (now the Columbia University School of Social Work) offered a 6-week summer school session that was extended in 1910 to 2 years. Richmond went on to become a faculty member in this program.

She is best known for her 1917 book, *Social Diagnosis*, which was a compilation of her own lectures and interdisciplinary reading. This book became the primary text used by early social work educators. Interestingly, Richmond debated with Simon Patten (who coined the use of the title "social worker") on the issue of the focus of social work, whether it should be working with individuals or serving as advocates.

Source: Barker, 2003; Brieland, 1995; Kendall, 2000; Longres, J.F., 2008; Richmond, 1897.

By 1917, 17 of the social work education programs that were in operation in the United States and Canada came together to establish the Association of Training Schools for Professional Social Work. Reorganizing later, the group became known as the American Association of Schools of Social Work (AASSW). By 1952, the AASSW joined forces with the National Association of Schools of Social Administration to become the Council on Social Work Education (CSWE)—the organization that now accredits bachelor and master of social work programs. In addition, the National Association of Social Workers was established in 1955 when seven previously separate professional social work organizations joined to form one national organization that could represent the interests of the profession.

Expanding Professional Boundaries

Establishing social work education was not the only activity of the social work profession that was occurring during the late 19th and early 20th centuries. Professional social work was gaining recognition in three fields of practice: medical social work, psychiatric social work, and child welfare. In 1905, the first hospital social work department was organized at Massachusetts General Hospital, and just 2 years later, the same institution offered psychiatric social work services. The title "psychiatric social worker" came into use in 1914.

In the realm of child welfare services, a variety of practice activities were emerging. Social workers were being trained in the area of mental health diagnosis at the same time that juvenile court systems were being established to address the issue of juvenile crime and delinquency (Brieland, 1995). Social workers were also making their presence felt in the public school systems, where they worked with children whose home lives were dysfunctional. These areas remain a central part of social work today.

While much of the early period of the profession's formation focused on developing knowledge and skills for working with individuals and families, other concepts and areas of practice have emerged. By the 1930s, group work and community organizing were gaining recognition as areas of practice (Hopps et al., 2008). Since the 1960s, we have seen an expansion of these areas as well as the introduction of generalist practice, ecological and systems theory and, most recently, evidence-based practice (McNutt & Floersch, 2008). As you will learn throughout this book, each of these areas has found its place in contemporary social work practice.

In 1977, a special issue of the journal *Social Work* was devoted to defining, describing, and discussing conceptual frameworks that were pertinent to social work practice at that time. This effort to refine further the definition of the profession of social work addressed issues such as the mission, objectives, professional oversight, knowledge and skills, and educational implications associated with the profession (Minahan, 1981). This special issue generated such attention that a second special issue appeared in 1981. This second effort to frame social work as a strong profession included a working statement on the purpose of social work and a list of its objectives. The complete statement, which is reproduced in Quick Guide #2, is a point from which to build our collective understanding of the social work profession.

QUICK GUIDE #2   Working Statement on the Purpose, Principles, and Objectives of the Social Work Profession

The purpose of social work is to promote or restore a mutually beneficial interaction between individuals and society in order to improve the quality of life for everyone. Social workers hold the following beliefs:

- The environment (social, physical, and organizational) should provide the opportunity and resources for the maximum realization of the potential and aspirations of all individuals, and should provide for their common human needs and for the alleviation of distress and suffering.
- Individuals should contribute as effectively as they can to their own well-being and to the social welfare of others in their immediate environment as well as to the collective society.
- Transactions between individuals and others in their environment should enhance the dignity, individuality, and self-determination of everyone. People should be treated humanely and with justice.
- Clients of social workers may be an individual, a family, a group, a community, or an organization.

Social workers focus on person-and-environment in interaction. To carry out their purpose, they work with people to achieve the following objectives:

- Help people enlarge their competence and increase their problem-solving and coping abilities.
- Help people obtain resources.
- Make organizations responsive to people.
- Facilitate interaction between individuals and others in their environment.
- Influence interactions between organizations and institutions.
- Influence social and environmental policy.

Source: Minahan, 1981, p. 6.

An additional area of activity for the social work profession was the creation of professional associations. See Exhibit 2.6 for some of the highlights of the profession's organizational efforts.

- 1898—New York Charity Organization Society offers the first social work training course (later becomes the Columbia University School of Social Work)
- 1905—Massachusetts General Hospital establishes a social services department
- 1917—Social workers organize for the first time in a group called the National Social Workers Exchange (later the American Association of Social Workers)
- 1924—The first social work program for African Americans is established at the Atlanta School of Social Work
- 1934—Social work regulation is passed for the first time in Puerto Rico
- 1937—The 2-year Master of Social Work degree is determined by the American Association of Schools of Social Work (AASSW) to be the required degree for professional social services
- 1952—Through a merger of the AASSW and the National Association of Schools of Social Administration, the Council on Social Work Education (CSWE) is formed and becomes the accrediting body for social work education
- 1955—National Association of Social Workers (NASW) is established after a merging of seven social work organizations
- 1962—NASW creates the first social work credential, the Academy of Certified Social Workers (ACSW). Prior to the introduction of state licensure laws in most states, the ACSW was the primary credential for social workers, and it is still widely recognized today
- 1962—NASW passes the first professional *Code of Ethics* (later revised in 1990, 1996, 1999, and 2008)

EXHIBIT 2.6

The Professionalization of Social Work

Continued

EXHIBIT 2.6

continued

- 1969—Baccalaureate social workers are invited to join NASW, previously open to master-level social workers only
- 1979—American Association of State Social Work Boards (AASSWB) is established to coordinate state licensure of social workers
- 1983—CSWE officially recognizes the Bachelor of Social Work (BSW) degree as the first level of social work education
- 1987—NASW publishes the first social work dictionary (Barker)
- 1991—NASW establishes the Academy of Certified Baccalaureate Social Workers (ACBSW)
- 1998—The social work profession celebrates its first century
- 2000—Every U.S. state has social work licensure or certification
- 2005—Comprised of 400+ social work leaders, the first Social Work Congress meets and develops 12 imperatives for the future of the social work profession
- 2008—CSWE develops the Educational Policy and Accreditation Standards (EPAS) to emphasize a competency-based social work education in baccalaureate and master's programs

WHERE WE HAVE COME FROM AND WHERE WE ARE GOING

The history of social work and social welfare began more than 3,000 years ago with the concept that we have a moral obligation to help others. Throughout the centuries, those early hints of altruism have blossomed. However, the social work profession did not come into existence until the 19th century, out of a need to respond to the "social question" of the time, specifically, how could poverty and social need exist in a country of prosperity (Hopps et al., 2008)? In just over 100 years, the definition of a social worker has evolved from "anyone involved in activities with a social purpose" (Kendall, 2000, p. 93) to a professional who completes a degree from an accredited social work program and who is engaged in a theory-based practice of helping others to optimize their potential in life. As a profession, social work has moved from a belief system that blamed the individual for creating her or his pauperism to an understanding that environmental conditions are the precursors for poverty. In addition, both social action and individual casework are now recognized parts of the profession (Kendall, 2000).

Social work education has also evolved from informal apprenticeships to a three-level, accredited professional education built on a framework of knowledge, skills, and values. While Flexner's 1915 report may have spurred the profession into a critical review of our educational and practice models, it is through the work of many educators and practitioners that our educational system has continued to stay abreast of the needs of our society. A 2008 overview of social work education noted that our focus is, and should be, strengthening our accountability to those we serve, specifically by developing key competencies for students and practitioners (particularly in the area of multiculturalism—the ability to work with diverse populations), determining appropriate outcomes for education and interventions, and evaluating our practice (Hoffman et al., 2008; Hopps et al., 2008). To remain on the cutting edge of human service education and delivery, members of the social work profession continuously review our educational programs and explore ways to make them more available and effective. Providing distance education programs in alternative formats and venues is just one example. Having made the journey from the origins of the profession to the present day, you can see that a long and rich history will guide social workers into the future.

CONCLUSION

This chapter has described the history of social welfare and the social work profession. Many innovative and courageous women and men helped shape the profession that is so integral to our modern-day society. I hope that their experiences provide a meaningful context for learning about the values and ethics of the profession, the fields of practice in which social workers engage, and some of the skills needed to be a professional social worker.

The history of social work and social welfare has been and continues to be linked to the events of the time. As social workers respond to the changing needs of the clients that they serve, new knowledge and skills are developed. To be effective practitioners, we must be acutely aware of the constant changes that occur in economic, political, and social policies while, at the same time, being mindful of adhering to our professional values and ethics.

Our profession was founded on a need to help people who are impacted by a changing environment, and we are still engaged in that quest today. While definitions of the social work profession have evolved over its history, a common theme of commitment has been woven throughout. That is, social workers have long been committed to perceiving clients within the context of the environment in which they live and to interventions targeted at individuals, families, groups, communities, and societies.

MAIN POINTS

- Social welfare is the system of programs and services that respond to social and economic needs and injustices. The first organized attempt at mandating the provision of social services was the 1349 Statute of Labourers that designated categories of need in England.

- The Elizabethan Poor Laws of 1601 established an approach to the delivery of financial and social aid that continues today. Intended to transfer the authority for charity from the church to the government, standardize aid programs, and decrease criminal activity, these laws dictated that public aid could be given to the unemployable, but that the employable must work and children who were orphaned or dependent would serve as apprentices.

- The roots of the U.S. social service system can be found in the British system's settlement houses and charity organizations. In the settlement house movement, young people lived and worked in poor neighborhoods to help improve living conditions; in the charity organization movement, caseworkers focused on helping individuals overcome their problems.

- The 20th century saw the formalization of the social work profession and growth in the social service delivery system. The Depression of the 1930s prompted a shift of services from the private to the public sector. The civil unrest of the 1960s and 1970s prompted new social initiatives created to address issues of poverty and the needs of women, minority groups, children, and older adults.

- Demographic changes in the 21st century are creating a society with widening economic gaps and an older, more diverse population with greater social, economic, and physical needs.

- In existence for a century, social work education has continued to change in response to societal needs. Flexner's 1915 report on the profession had the effect of solidifying social work as a profession.

EXERCISES

1. Go to the Sanchez family interactive case (www.routledgesw.com/cases). You will note from Celia Sanchez's history that Celia uses the food bank at her church as a resource for her family. The Catholic Church has a long and venerable history of caring for the poor in its communities. Describe a faith-based organization in your community that offers services to persons with limited incomes. How does it differ from sectarian institutions that offer the same or similar services?

2. Select one of the concerns or needs identified in the Sanchez family case. Citing examples from this chapter, speculate on the ways that the concern or need would have been addressed in different eras.

3. Review the case file for Hector Sanchez. You will note that Hector was given amnesty under a 1986 federal amnesty program. Conduct an online search to learn about the history and current policies associated with federal amnesty programs.

4. Go to the Carla Washburn interactive case at www.routledgesw.com/cases and familiarize yourself with the case. You will note that the social worker is employed by the Area Agency on Aging (AAA). The AAA was established through the Older Americans Act. Develop a brief report on the history and current focus of the Older Americans Act, specifically as it relates to the Area Agency on Aging. Identify those services provided by the AAA that Mrs. Washburn could receive.
5. Go to the RAINN interactive case at www.routledgesw.com/cases. Upon familiarizing yourself with the history of the development of RAINN, research the history of services to victims of sexual assault at the federal level or in your state or local community.

CHAPTER 3

U.S. Poverty and the Implications for Social Work

How did I get to be eighty
    And
        Never
            Get over
                Being
                    Poor?
When I was little
    I was poor.
        But playing
            And
                Dreaming
            Kept some of the pain
                Of
                    Being poor
                        Away
            And my folks
                Kept
                    Lots of the worries from me.
When I was a teenager
    I just knew I'd marry a good man
        With work
            And
                Things would be all right.
And I did.
But he was poor, too.

Work was steady for a while,
    But so were the children.

There were good days
    And warm times

But there were lots of times
When his work died off

And
   His worrying
      Brought pain.
He worked any kind of job
   In
      Any kind of weather
         Till
      The fever got him
         And
      The Lord took him
         And I had to go to welfare.
   Then
         They cut that—some.

Reverend,
   Do people born poor?
      Have
   To stay that way—always?
Ain't there any other way—
                  Even when we get to be eighty?
Does "poor" always have to be
      A
         Life sentence?

From *If . . . A Big Word With the Poor* by Don Bakely, Faith & Life Press,
Newton, Kansas. Used by permission.

This 1976 poem, composed by social activist Don Bakely, focuses on the plight of an impoverished 80-year-old woman. At the same time, the poem raises a number of issues that continue to plague our society more than 35 years after its publication. The woman in this poem contacted Bakely for help one Thanksgiving Day because she was out of food and fuel. His powerful words move us as we read this poem because they address the issues of lifelong poverty, being an older adult and poor, and the inadequacy of the public welfare system. His words, however, also capture the hope and resilience that this woman continued to have throughout her life—a phenomenon we do not usually associate with chronic poverty and advanced age.

The social issues raised in this poem provide us with a beginning point for a discussion of the needs of many persons in our society and the approaches that have been devised to address those needs. Specifically, we will continue our investigation of the social work profession by discussing the issues of poverty along with the historical responses of both society and the social work profession to eliminating poverty. Understanding poverty, public assistance programs, and social services are critical for all social workers. This chapter covers the origins of poverty, the ways in which the public and private sectors have attempted to minimize poverty and its effects, and the role of a social worker in optimizing clients' capacities within a context of poverty.

DIMENSIONS OF POVERTY

Emily did not have much experience with or knowledge of poverty before deciding to be a social worker. Actually, Emily had no personal experience with poverty. She certainly knew there were people in the world and in her community who lived in poverty, but she did not think about their situations, so they were not real for her. She had no insight into the realities of living in poverty. She had heard people say that poor people could escape poverty simply by "pulling themselves up by their boot-straps." Not being sure about the truth of that adage, Emily found herself wondering about the reasons for so many people to become impoverished and wondered if it was a matter of work ethic.

Emily's first experience with persons living in poverty came during her community service for her introductory social work course. She believed that, as a social worker, she needed to gain insight into the lives of persons living in poverty. Therefore, she opted to complete her service learning experience at Oasis House, a shelter for families who are homeless. There, she began to gain insight into poverty and the ways in which living in poverty affected people. As she worked with children on their homework, they shared with her stories about having utilities cut off, being hungry, getting evicted, and living in the car—all because a parent was laid off from her or his job. Emily learned that poverty is not simple or just, and it is not caused by a lack of motivation or work ethic. Rather, poverty is a complicated phenomenon with many contributors and has many faces that range from young children to older adults.

If asked such questions as what does being poor mean, who are the poor, how do people get to be poor, what keeps people in poverty, many people in our society would have opinions, but those opinions are often not fact-based. The definition of poverty, profiles of those who live in poverty, and the causes of poverty have been and continue to be emotional and value-laden issues with which our society struggles in the political, social, religious, and public and private social service arenas.

What Is Poverty?

A simple definition of **poverty** would be having inadequate financial resources or means of subsistence to meet basic needs (Barker, 2003). Stated more poignantly:

Poverty is hunger. Poverty is lack of shelter. Poverty is being sick and not being able to see a doctor. Poverty is not being able to go to school and not knowing how to read. Poverty is not having a job, is fear for the future, living one day at a time. Poverty is losing a child to illness brought about by unclean water. Poverty is powerlessness, lack of representation and freedom. (Worldbank Group, 2003)

The quantification of poverty was first documented in 1795 in England when the government subsidized wages that fell below a designated level. Known as the Speenhamland system, the amount of the subsidy was determined by the current price of bread and the number of members in the family (Barker, 1999).

It was not until 1964 that the U.S. federal government devised the **poverty line as** an official measure of poverty. The poverty line is the amount defined by the federal government as the minimal income level at which a family or individual can meet their basic needs. The measure was originally based on research from 1955 that suggested that people spend one-third of their post-tax income on food (Sherraden, 1990). For what was known as the Thrifty Food Plan, the government calculated the poverty line by identifying the amount needed for the minimum subsistence diet and then multiplying that number by three. Based on this formula, in 2011, a family of four living in the contiguous United States with a total household income of $23,018/year ($1,918/month) or less meets the poverty guidelines (U.S. Department of Commerce, Bureau of the Census, 2012). This is known as the poverty threshold or "poverty line." Beginning in 2008, the economic recession has resulted in the second highest numbers of persons living in poverty since the mid-1960s (Trisi, Sherman, & Broaddus, 2011). Moreover, the number of persons living below the halfway mark of the poverty line (e.g., an annual income for a family of four of $11,157 or less) is the highest in recorded history of 6.7% of the U.S. population (Trisi et al., 2011).

Many consider the poverty line, as it is currently calculated, to be an inadequate measure of poverty. Current spending patterns differ dramatically from what they were in 1964. Today families spend a smaller percentage of their income on food and a much larger percentage on transportation, housing, and medical care. Moreover, poverty is measured on income before taxes are deducted, and some nonmonetary supports (such as **food stamps**) can be considered a part of income. Thus strictly economic measures of poverty (though still used) are considered outdated by welfare rights advocates. Many social workers think that poverty can best be understood in social, political, economic, and emotional terms. Economically, "absolute" poverty occurs when an individual's income is less than the amount needed to obtain the minimal necessities for living. On an emotional level, "relative deprivation" is the perception that an individual does not possess as many assets as others (Hopps & Collins, 1995). Both types of poverty are real and interrelated, and both can be devastating for the individual and the family.

Who Are the Poor?

Many people believe the stereotype that people who are poor are nonwhite unemployed single mothers with lots of children, who subsist on welfare and are homeless or live in dilapidated housing in "bad" areas. Most unfortunate is the widespread myth that people who live in poverty are lazy and unmotivated to change their situations. Many people living in poverty are employed, have two or fewer children, and are very motivated to move out of poverty.

The 21st century, particularly the years since the economic recession of 2008, created households that constitute the "new face of poverty." The new faces include women, children, persons of color, and older adults. As the U.S. population becomes more diverse, so do the "faces" of those living in or near poverty. In 2010, 15.1% of individual Americans, or 46.2 million people, were living in poverty. That is about 1 in 7 Americans (U.S. Census Bureau, Statistical Abstract, 2012).

The percentage and number of Americans living in poverty fluctuates, as Exhibit 3.1 shows. Earlier in the century, the greatest increases occurred in the Midwest and southern states and among immigrants (Rank & Hirschl, 2001a; Sherman, Greenstein, & Parrott, 2008), but in the most recent Census analyses, the highest numbers of persons living in poverty are primarily in the southern United States (averages at or more than 16% in 17 states) (Bishaw, 2011a).

At-Risk Groups   Although many of the stereotypes of poverty are unfounded, the reality is that certain groups are vulnerable for living in poverty:

- *Women* are disproportionately represented among the ranks of those living in poverty, particularly when they are the single heads of households. Overall,

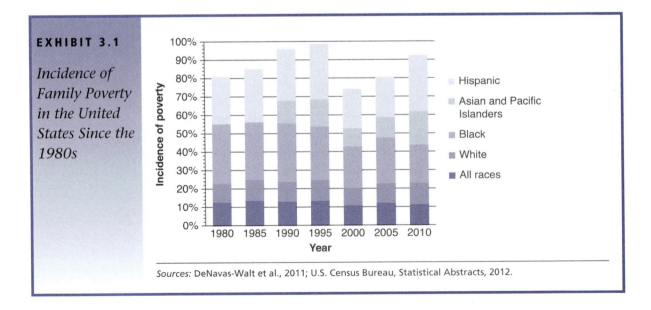

EXHIBIT 3.1

Incidence of Family Poverty in the United States Since the 1980s

Sources: DeNavas-Walt et al., 2011; U.S. Census Bureau, Statistical Abstracts, 2012.

one-fifth of adult females live below the poverty line (Kaiser Family Foundation, 2012a). Poverty rates for female-headed households rose in 2010 to 34.26% (from 32.5% in 2009) (Albelda, 2012). For those female-headed households located in higher-income geographic areas, the poverty rate is 14%, while those in lower economic regions experience poverty rates as high as 46% (Bishaw, 2011b). Women at each end of the age continuum are particularly at risk for living in poverty, with 15% of women aged 18–44 and 11.5% of women aged 75 and over living in poverty. Nonwhite women are at the greatest risk for poverty among all groups, with rates ranging from 20.2% (Hispanic women) to 23.4% (African American women) to 27.6% (Alaska Native/American Indian women) (U.S. Department of Health and Human Services Health Resources and Services Administration, 2008).

- *Racial and ethnic minorities.* Being African American and having limited education places one at higher risk for poverty (Rank, 2004, 2008). In 2010, 36% of African Americans and 35% of Hispanics/Latinos were reported to have incomes below the poverty line as compared to 14% of non-Hispanic whites (Kaiser Family Foundation, 2012b).

- *High school dropouts.* By age 75, 98% of African American women and 96% of African American men with less than a high school education will have spent at least 1 year of their lives living in poverty, compared to 65% of white women and 74% of white men lacking a high school diploma (Rank, 2004; Rank & Hirschl, 2001b).

- *Children.* Approximately 22% of all children in the United States (up from 20% in 2009) live in poverty (DeNavas-Walt, Proctor, & Smith, 2011). Many of them have at least one working parent (Annie E. Casey Foundation, 2011). While children make up one-quarter of the population, they are over one-third of those living in poverty and have the highest levels of poverty of any other age group (DeNavas-Walt et al., 2011). African American and Hispanic children are more likely (38.2% and 32.3%, respectively) to live in poverty than their white and Asian counterparts (17% and 13%, respectively) (McCartney, 2011).

- *Older adults.* Within the older adult population, approximately 9% have incomes below the poverty line (DeNavas-Walt et al., 2011). By age 65, some 64% of Americans will require assistance from at least one form of a social welfare or "social safety net" program (publicly funded programs that prevent people from falling below the poverty line) such as Medicaid, food stamps, and cash assistance (Rank & Hirschl, 2002).

Others who have a higher risk of long-term poverty are those who have physical or mental health disabilities or live in an economically disadvantaged area (Rank, 2008). Poverty of this type may continue through multiple generations. Experiencing poverty as a child places individuals at greater risk for experiencing poverty in adult-hood (Fass, Dinan, & Aratani, 2009). Clearly, age is a factor in influencing one's risk for experiencing poverty, with the risk being greatest during one's 20s and in one's 60s and 70s and the risk being the lowest during the decades of the 40s and 50s (Sandoval, Rank, & Hirschl, 2009).

While there are some new faces among those living in poverty, single female-headed families, particularly in the non-Caucasian community, continue to experi-ence economic struggles, even when the mother is employed outside the home. The majority of single mothers are employed (67.8%), but their unemployment rates still surpass that of the general population (Albelda, 2012). Despite the fact that employment rates and wages for single mothers have both increased, these families are living on resources that are comparable to those of the 1990s. Women are employed, but frequently in low-paying jobs without consistent schedules and benefits (e.g., health insurance and vacation and sick leave), but are often still unable to move out of poverty or near-poverty (Albelda, 2012).

Some relief may be on the horizon. Signed into law in 2010, the Patient Protection and Affordable Act expanded health insurance coverage and covers pre-existing conditions. This legislation is a beginning, but should not be considered to be the sole strategy to eliminate poverty. The Act is aimed at ensuring "quality, affordable health care for all Americans," which includes improving health care access, quality, and efficiency and focusing on expanding health prevention and workforce resources (Responsible Reform for the Middle Class, 2010, p. 1).

Providing full-time employment opportunities with wages above the minimum wage and ensuring that those positions include benefits to support the workers are two interventions that can make a difference. To achieve these necessary changes, social workers can advocate for policy and regulatory changes. To learn more about poverty-related legislation and to examine legislators' voting records, visit the Sargent Shriver National Poverty Law Center website at: http://www.povertylaw.org/.

The Working Poor Employment is no guarantee that a person will escape poverty. The **working poor** are defined as "persons who spent at least 27 weeks in the labor force (working or looking for work) but whose incomes still fell below the official poverty level" (U.S. Department of Labor, Bureau of Statistics (BLS), 2011, p. 1). In 2009, nearly one-quarter of the U.S. population experienced poverty for at least 2 months (DeNavas-Walt et al., 2011). The percentage of the population considered to be in the working poor category has steadily been climbing in recent years, from 5.1 (2006) to 7.0 (2009) for individuals and 6.1 (2006) to 7.9 (2009) for families (U.S. Department of Labor, 2009a). Persons more likely to be categorized as "working poor" are African and Hispanic Americans, those lacking a high school diploma, families with children under the age of 18, and female-headed households (BLS, 2011). The total income for a family of four in which one member is earning minimum wage still falls nearly $8,000 under the poverty line. Clearly, working full-time in a minimum-wage position does not raise a family above the poverty

Annual income from full-time employment at $7.25/Hour	$14,372.40
Plus tax credit	$3,090.00
Food stamps (SNAP)	$6,696.00*
Total annual income	$24,158.40

EXHIBIT 3.2

Profile of the "Working Poor"

*As Supplemental Nutrition Assistance Program (SNAP) benefits are state-based, the amount presented here is based on Missouri.

Original source: Furman & Parrott, 2007; updated by author 2012, utilizing Internal Revenue Services (http://www.irs.gov/individuals/article/0,,id=130102,00.html) and U.S. Department of Agriculture (http://www.snap-step1.usda.gov/fns/).

line. In fact, at 130% of the poverty level, the income for a family of four is $28,665 and, at 185% of the poverty level, the same family has an income of $40,793 (World Hunger, 2012).

Consider the situation for the family of four represented in Exhibit 3.2. The "breadwinner" is working full-time at the minimum wage. As you can see, if $23,018 is the poverty line for a family of four, this family would be considered to have an adequate total income, although they will probably struggle to make ends meet. However, that income includes earned income tax credit (EITC), child tax credits, and food stamps (now called the Supplemental Nutrition Assistance Program (SNAP)). Without those additional benefits, the family's income would place the family approximately $1,000 above the poverty line (adapted from Furman & Parrott, 2007).

The wage earner in this example is making $7.25 per hour, the federal minimum wage (effective July, 2009). While the median hourly wage in the United States is $9.06, a minimum wage of approximately $11.00/hour would enable this family to live above the poverty line. Although six states do not have any minimum wage, 27 states and the District of Columbia have enacted laws that require minimum wages above the federal standard, with the highest being $8.55 in Washington (U.S. Department of Labor, 2009b). The purchasing power of the federal minimum wage has decreased by nearly one-third in the last 40 years (National Law Project, 2012).

Lifetime Chances of Temporarily Living in Poverty   People who do not consider themselves to be among the poor may nevertheless live in poverty at some point in their lives. Over half of Americans will live in or near poverty at some point between the ages of 20 and 40 (Rank, 2004). By the age of 70, over half of U.S. citizens have lived in poverty at some point during their lives (Exhibit 3.3), and over half will have received food stamps (Rank, 2004). Prior to the most recent economic recession, many of these families were living in the middle-income category, but were forced to utilize food pantries in order to make mortgage payments to avoid losing their homes.

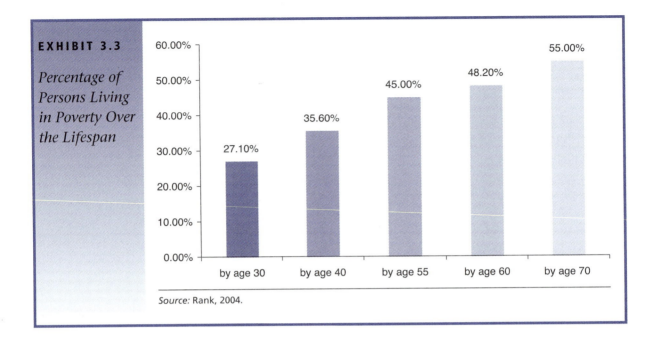

EXHIBIT 3.3

Percentage of Persons Living in Poverty Over the Lifespan

Source: Rank, 2004.

For African Americans, living in poverty is not only more likely to occur than for U.S. residents who are Caucasian, but they are less likely to own a home, accumulate assets, or reach a level of financial affluence (Rank, 2009). In fact, over 90% of African Americans will experience poverty, while only 13% will reach financial affluence.

Living in poverty is typically short-term (fewer than 3 years) (U.S. Department of Health and Human Services, 2006b), but can be chronic, lasting for years or across generations. Those living in poverty for briefer periods of time can also move in and out of poverty depending on their life circumstance. For example, a person may be laid off from her or his job or have a short-term disability. Recent immigrants may also fall into this category. Individuals in these situations may receive public assistance until they are able to rejoin the labor force.

What Causes Poverty?

One of the most controversial issues in U.S. society today concerns the causes of poverty. Most opinions will be in one of two directions: (1) the individual is responsible; or (2) societal structure is responsible. We will examine both arguments.

Individual Differences Even before the Charity Organization Society movement, individuals have been considered by some to be responsible for their inability to earn an adequate income. This philosophy, which is sometimes referred to as "blaming the victim," is rooted in the belief that all individuals can and should be self-sufficient and should not require any outside assistance for themselves or their families. This belief is consistent with the national narrative that contends that, with hard work, anyone can be rich. A related belief is that persons living in poverty are "different from mainstream Americans," with poorer motivation and life choices, and this difference explains their poverty (Rank, 2006, p. 22).

This belief system presents an ongoing challenge for those who advocate for the poor, particularly when funding decisions are at stake. Voters and policy makers who adhere to the "pull yourself up by your bootstraps" philosophy are typically less supportive of spending tax dollars on programs to combat poverty. Interestingly, these views fall neatly along political lines. Historically, Republicans have typically believed that lack of hard work and an unwillingness to be employed are the major causes of poverty, whereas Democrats more often cite external circumstances as the cause of poverty (National Public Radio, 2001).

Research findings consistently confirm that those living in poverty are not all that different from "mainstream Americans"; the attitudes and values of those living in poverty mirror those of mainstream society. What does seem to play a significant role in determining one's earning potential is "human capital" (Rank, 2008). One's "capital" is related to factors such as parental income, education, health, and accumulated wealth.

Social Structure   The alternative view places the blame for poverty on societal structures. Much like the founders of the settlement house movement, proponents of this approach believe that a number of external factors over which the individual has no control make certain individuals vulnerable to a life of poverty. In the United States, being female, nonwhite, disabled, too old, or too young—none of which a person can control—may reduce opportunities. Other factors over which a person has little control include being a victim of domestic violence as a child, an adult, or both; being a victim of institutional oppression; discrimination based on disability or social class; or growing up in an economically disadvantaged neighborhood with poor-quality schools, few mentors/role models, or little opportunity for higher education.

That is not to say that our social system prevents disadvantaged individuals from finding any work. Rather, structural vulnerability occurs when the opportunities for employment, child care, and housing are not adequate (Rank, 2008). Low-income persons cannot achieve financial stability when the only jobs available to them pay low wages and do not offer adequate benefits or the possibility for advancement. Even in economic boom times, there is no guarantee that good jobs will be accessible to those who lack a high school diploma and/or higher education, or the required training and technical sophistication.

Rank (2006) offers a new paradigm for understanding poverty from a structural perspective:

- Poverty occurs when the structure, not the individual, fails.

- Over a lifetime, people move in and out of poverty.

- Poverty creates deprivation that goes beyond income and includes quality of life, health, and opportunities.

- Poverty is an injustice because it can be prevented.

- Poverty affects everyone through creating problems in the areas of health, education, and crime.

Viewing poverty as a societal issue moves the discussion away from holding the individual responsible for both the cause and the solution and makes all citizens responsible.

In a recent 14-year study of social work students' perceptions of the causes of poverty, findings suggest that the causes of poverty are structural and students believe poverty can only be eliminated through societal change. Further, social work students also believe that those living in poverty are the best determiners of their own lives (Clark, 2007). These findings suggest that the focus of an intervention should be targeted at the intersection of both ability and opportunity.

CHALLENGES AND BARRIERS TO MOVING OUT OF POVERTY

Living in poverty can become chronic and cyclical for those individuals who begin their lives in poverty. Throughout their lives they may move in and out of poverty, particularly with changes in employment or partner status, health, and child care status. To understand this concept, consider the lives of these individuals:

- Recall the older woman in the poem at the beginning of the chapter. She was born into poverty, a life that probably did not provide adequate opportunities for health care, education, or career choices. She probably did not complete high school. She and her husband worked in a series of low-paying jobs that did not offer opportunities for upward mobility or even stability and certainly not for saving for old age or their children's education. Her children grew up in an environment of deprivation and lack of choices, thereby creating another generation of a family who will rear their children in poverty. Thus, the cycle continues.

- Consider the lifelong struggles of a teenage girl who experiences an unplanned pregnancy and applies for public assistance as a single parent. As a result of her pregnancy, she may not be able to complete high school or pursue any post-high school education. If she obtains full-time employment, she will lose the financial assistance that she receives from the government or other agencies for child care. Even with her salary, she may be unable to pay for child care and other basic needs. If her car breaks down, she may not be able to afford the repairs. Without a car, she could lose her job due to absenteeism and may consequently be forced to reapply for public assistance. Thus, the cycle continues.

- Consider the woman who married at a young age and had several children. Her husband insisted that her job was to take care of the children, so she did not work outside the home. The husband's occasional outbursts of violence devolved into physical abuse, and the woman decided she and the children had to leave. She sought safety for herself and the children in a shelter for survivors of intimate partner violence, applied for public assistance, and filed for divorce. The court ordered her husband to pay child support, but payments were erratic at best. Because the woman had never held a full-time job, she had no work history or discernible skills to market to potential employers. She found a few minimum-wage jobs, but she was always the first worker to be laid off. Even when she was able to survive without public assistance, she could never move herself out of poverty. Thus, the cycle continues.

- Imagine the man who dropped out of high school and has struggled throughout life to "make ends meet." In an ill-advised effort to gain economic stability, he becomes involved in drug trafficking which lands him in prison. While in prison, his wife divorces him and is awarded child support for their two children, which, of course, he is unable to pay. As a paroled felon, he finds it difficult to secure employment, cannot obtain credit, and is faced with a return to prison for not paying child support. Thus, the cycle continues.

These are just four examples of the challenges of moving out of the cycle of poverty. These are the types of people who benefit most from social work services. Social workers can both help people living in poverty to receive services to meet basic needs and work toward change in society to alleviate poverty. Let us now turn to a review of the approaches that have been adopted in the United States to address the issue of poverty.

APPROACHES TO POVERTY IN THE UNITED STATES: SOCIAL WELFARE

The best strategy for addressing poverty has long been a hotly debated issue in the United States. Strategies for raising people's incomes above the poverty line are controversial because tax dollars are the primary funding source for public assistance programs. Public debate often includes rhetoric that providing a safety net for the poor discourages work and rewards laziness. Helping the poor is a value-laden and emotional decision, further complicated by the fact that all U.S. taxpayers have a vested interest in the way their money is spent. For this reason, funding for social programs is a consistently volatile issue for politicians, special-interest groups, and those agencies responsible for implementing the programs.

Let us not forget, though, the group that has the most vested interest in the ways in which public funds are spent: the persons themselves who are living in poverty. Unfortunately, this group often has the least influence over the decisions that affect their well-being. There are far fewer lobbyists to speak for those living in poverty, thus they are less organized than other advocacy groups, resulting in their views not being well represented in the decision-making process.

Another group that has a keen interest in social welfare programs is social workers. It is much easier for social workers to fulfill their mission of empowerment if they have adequate funding and support to do so.

Before reviewing the strategies that have been employed here in the United States, it is important to understand the philosophy that underpins the strategies. Let us start by reviewing definitions that are relevant for our discussion of social welfare. As you review the following pages, keep in mind the words offered by Rank (2006): "how we view poverty is critical to guiding how we will address it. Part of America's ineffectiveness in reducing poverty during the past three decades stems from a skewed and incorrect perception of impoverishment (p. 19)."

Definitions and Connotations of "Social Welfare"

In its literal interpretation, the word *welfare* means "good health, prosperity and social respect" (Albelda, Folbre, & the Center for Popular Economics, 1996). However, in the context of our discussion, **welfare** is a societal effort to help people achieve and maintain physical, emotional, and financial well-being.

Since the early 1900s, when social services were being formalized in the United States, the term welfare has come to have a negative connotation and has become synonymous with poverty and the public assistance programs that provide cash assistance to single mothers and their children. However, the term welfare, if taken in its literal sense, also comes in the form of corporate and realty investor tax benefits, corporate bailouts, home mortgage deductions, tax abatements for home ownership in economically depressed areas, and farm and low-income housing development subsidies. These benefits and subsidies are dollars that otherwise would be paid in taxes, and contribute to the amount of public funds available to meet public needs in our communities and at the federal level.

The term social welfare has also taken on a dual meaning. Social welfare describes a group's level of stability. However, social welfare also refers to our country's system of programs, benefits, and services that supports those in need of financial, social, and health care support. The term **public welfare**, often used synonymously with public assistance, also refers to the policies that a country develops to provide for the well-being of its citizens.

Social welfare programs are guided by **social policy**, defined as governmental rules and regulations that are used to develop and guide the practices and procedures related to social issues. These policies guide social workers' practice. Social policies address programs in areas such as education, health, corrections, and social welfare, but are aimed at creating resources needed to meet the basic needs of society. The work of the social work profession is inextricably linked to the social policies (perhaps even dependent on the policies) that underlie the laws, funding, insurance reimbursements, and authority to enact, implement, and oversee the programs.

Social policies can be of two types: residual and institutional. **Residual social policies** address a social need that is specific to a population and will continue to exist regardless of the policies' effectiveness or ineffectiveness. Services for pregnant women and disabled persons are examples of programs that result from residual social policies. In contrast, **institutional social policies** address a social need that is universal within our society. Social Security, which provides retirement insurance for all older adults who have invested in that system, is an example of an institutional social policy.

A subset of social policies, **social welfare policies**, allocate financial, social, and health resources. Social workers' activities are impacted by social policies, in general, and social welfare policies, in particular.

Now that you have acquired a basic understanding of the terms that are so integral to any discussion of social welfare issues, let us examine the historical underpinnings of our modern-day social welfare system. The social welfare system in the United States is based on the English model but adapted by the United States. As the country was founded on the principle of independence and autonomy, it is not surprising that the basis of the welfare system is "competitive individualism and the validity of market-based economics" (Hopps & Collins, 1995, p. 2268). The historical review that follows targets the important events that led to the creation of our contemporary programmatic approaches to social needs.

Social Welfare in the 17th–19th Centuries

Although considerable progress was made in social service-related areas in the first two centuries of our country's history, much of the accomplishment was in the private sector. Before 1862, all welfare benefits provided by the government were administered at the local, rather than the federal, level. However, the widespread disability and death caused by the Civil War created the need for a comprehensive national response. Therefore, in 1862, the federal government enacted legislation to provide pensions for Union soldiers and their dependants or survivors in the event of a soldier's death (Albelda et al., 1996). Other public assistance programs triggered by the Civil War included the Freedmen's Bureau, which provided help for freed slaves from 1865 to 1872, and an 1890 law that awarded pensions to all veterans who served in the Union army.

Social Welfare in the 20th Century

During the late 19th and early 20th centuries, in addition to the emergence of the settlement house and Charity Organization Society movements, public programs were being created to combat the results of the economic depression that had beset the country in the 1890s. Many of these programs were initiated at the state level and spread from state to state. However, groups such as orphaned or fatherless children and older adults were being marginalized by the lack of a comprehensive approach. Exhibit 3.4 provides the chronological highlights of social welfare programs during this century.

EXHIBIT 3.4 *20th-Century Advances in Social Welfare*	• 1910—Workers' Compensation legislation passed • 1911— Mothers' Pensions programs established first in Illinois (by 1934, 46 states had initiated statewide programs for supporting mothers and children) • 1914—The term "psychiatric social worker" was first used in Boston • 1916—Keating–Owen Child Labor Act was passed • 1935—Under Roosevelt's administration, the Social Security Act was passed to address the Depression-era needs of older adults, widowed persons, the unemployed, persons with disabilities, and dependent children • 1944—GI Bill of Rights legislation enabled returning veterans to purchase homes and attain college educations • 1953—Department of Health, Education, and Welfare established (name changed to Department of Health and Human Services in 1979) • 1961—Peace Corps created by the Kennedy administration • 1963—Community Mental Health Center Act passed • 1964—Civil Rights Act and Economic Opportunity Act legislation passed • 1964–1965—A number of programs were created as part of the War on Poverty and Great Society, including: Job Corps, Head Start, and Volunteers in Service to America (VISTA: 1964), Food Stamp Act (1964), Medicare and Medicaid (1965), Older Americans Act (1965), and Elementary and Secondary Education Act (1965) • 1972—Supplemental Security Act enacted for older adults and persons with disabilities whose financial means were the most limited • 1974—The Child Abuse Prevention and Treatment Act formalized intervention in child abuse and neglect. • 1975—Title XX services were established as an amendment to the Social Security Act, enabling purchase of income-based social, training, and housing services • 1988—The introduction of the Family Support Act was aimed at strengthening programming for children and families in employment, training and child support and care • 1990—The landmark Americans with Disabilities Act ensures access and equity for persons with disabilities • 1996—As part of welfare reform, the Personal Responsibility and Work Opportunity Reconciliation Act (PRWORA) created Temporary Assistance to Needy Families (TANF), replacing Assistance to Families with Dependent Children • 1996—The Mental Health Parity Act expanded insurance coverage to include mental health services *Sources:* Corbett, 2008; NASW, 1998.

In addition, a new paradigm for assisting the increasing populations of children, single mothers, and older adults was introduced during these years. In 1909, a White House Conference on Children recommended that children should remain with their parents whenever possible (Albelda et al., 1996). As a result, public funds were shifted toward providing services in homes versus automatic institutionalization. One law that reflected this new approach was the 1921 Sheppard-Towner Act, the first federal program to fund maternal and child health care for low-income women and children, thought by many to be the forerunner to modern-day public assistance for single women and their children.

New Deal Welfare Reforms   The drastic times of the Great Depression of the 1930s called for drastic measures. To alleviate the suffering of millions of Americans, the administration of Franklin Roosevelt created a number of public welfare programs. With nearly one-third of the workforce unemployed at the height of the Depression, a stronger, more comprehensive federal response was necessary. Perhaps the most famous federal initiative from this period is the Social Security Act of 1935. However, under the umbrella of Roosevelt's New Deal, a number of welfare programs were established (see Exhibit 3.5).

Most of these interventions were repealed or discontinued following the Depression. Programs developed to address crisis situations are typically intended to exist only for the duration of the crisis. Social Security is the exception. This program created a comprehensive system for providing an income for older adults and later for the children of deceased workers and workers who suffered disabilities.

Social Welfare from World War II Through the 1970s   Welfare programs established during the economically prosperous late 1940s were primarily aimed at war veterans and their dependants and survivors (although it is doubtful whether many people considered these programs to be welfare).

- *Federal Emergency Relief Act (FERA) 1933* provided temporary financial support to unemployed persons.
- *Civilian Conservation Corps (CCC) 1933* was an early federally funded employment program that became the forerunner to the Job Corps program of the 1960s.
- *Social Security Act 1935* provided assistance to fatherless families through the Aid to Families with Dependent Children (AFDC) program. AFDC became the cornerstone of the public response to poor families and remained essentially unchanged until the 1990s.
- *Works Progress Administration (WPA) 1935* was aimed at creating employment opportunities and employed 8 million workers in the building of parks, bridges, and roads.

EXHIBIT 3.5

A Sampling of New Deal Programs

Civilian Conservation Corps

Tree-planting crews within the Civilian Conservation Corps (CCC), one of the New Deal social welfare programs, are believed to have planted some 3 billion trees between 1933 and 1942. The CCC not only put unemployed young men to work but also helped to mitigate forest degradation and soil erosion, as in the Dust Bowl states; preserve and improve watersheds; and build recreational facilities such as well-appointed campgrounds.

Source: Getty Images.

The 1950s continued to be a prosperous decade for the United States, with moderate growth in the development of social welfare programs. The Social Security Act was expanded in 1950 to include benefits for low-income children and the disabled. The U.S. Housing Act of 1954 prompted urban renewal projects across the country. In 1953, the Department of Health, Education, and Welfare was created as a cabinet-level department to oversee funding and programs in these three areas.

From a public welfare standpoint, the 1960s were a boom time. As part of Lyndon Johnson's War on Poverty, new programs were established through the Economic Opportunity Act of 1964. The Economic Opportunity Act funded training and community action programs such as the Job Corps, which provided employment training for youth; Volunteers in Service to America (VISTA), which sent volunteers into poor neighborhoods; community action programs, community-based antipoverty programs; and Head Start, the program that provides early childhood development services to low-income children. Additional efforts that were outgrowths of the War on Poverty include the food stamps program, which helped low-income people to purchase food, and the Older Americans Act of 1965, which dispersed funds to communities to develop programs for older adults. While perception of the impact of many of these programs has been questioned, one program, Head Start, has consistently been deemed to have had a positive impact on children. With decades of data available on outcomes for children who participated in Head Start programs, the evidence clearly indicates that Head Start benefits outweigh the cost of delivering the program in the areas of educational attainment, performance, and decreased arrests (Society for Research in Child Development (SRCD), 2007).

Despite the fact that new programs were being created to decrease the numbers of persons receiving public assistance in the 1960s, the welfare rolls increased in both size and composition. Aid to Families with Dependent Children (AFDC) recipients were increasingly families headed by single mothers and families of color. Opponents of welfare programs called for making the benefits more restrictive and requiring welfare recipients to work.

In an effort to respond to the criticisms of public assistance programs, the Work Incentive Program was established to provide training, job placement, child care, and transportation. But the program failed due to lack of adequate funding to provide the comprehensive services that were intended.

In contrast to the 1960s, during the 1970s few new programs were introduced. Rather, adjustments were made to existing programs. For example, the 1975 Title XX amendment to the Social Security Act provided additional funding for personal social services for low-income persons, including services to promote economic independence (for example, employment training and placement), child and elder abuse and neglect prevention, and community-based services to prevent institutionalization of older adults and persons with disabilities.

The exception is the Supplemental Security Income (SSI) program, established in 1972. This publicly funded program provides financial assistance for persons who are older, visually impaired, or have disabilities and live on limited incomes. Unlike Social Security, assistance is not based on previous employment, but on current income.

Following the demise of the Nixon administration, Presidents Ford and Carter endeavored to continue the "welfare revolution" begun in the 1960s but had only moderate success. The number of recipients of welfare programs was reduced, but social welfare program funding was increased. Proponents of the work-ethic school of thought perceived that these programs were only increasing the dependence of the poor on public assistance and were not reforming them (Reid, 1995). The "revolution" as such ended with the election of Ronald Reagan in 1980.

Social Welfare in the 1980s and 1990s Reminiscent of the Nixon era, the Reagan and George H.W. Bush administrations of the 1980s and early 1990s focused on a supply-side economics approach, known as "Reaganomics." Tax policies were designed to benefit corporations and citizens at the higher socioeconomic level, and their prosperity was supposed to "trickle down" to the middle and lower economic levels. Both administrations subscribed to the philosophy that welfare should be a private business, not a public responsibility. To implement this philosophy, Reagan proposed, and Congress passed, the 1981 Omnibus Budget Reconciliation Act (OBRA), which eliminated public-service jobs, decreased benefits for low-income workers and AFDC recipients, and granted authority for resource distribution to the states (Albelda et al., 1996). The Family Support Act of 1988 established work requirements and supported the perceived need to make welfare benefits more punitive and restrictive by making eligibility more limited. Issues such as children living in poverty, homelessness, and AIDS took a backseat to support for corporate America and military spending (Segal, 2007). Many critics contend that the policies adopted by the Reagan and Bush administrations constituted a significant setback for the gains that had been made in social welfare policy throughout the 20th century. They were thought to have encouraged anti-welfare sentiments and increased tensions between the social service and political communities (Hopps et al., 2008).

The 1990s brought a renewed focus on public responsibility for social needs. Clinton's election strategies focused on returning the nation's attention to domestic issues, specifically, health and education. During the 1990s, Congress passed several laws that had economic implications for impoverished families, people with disabilities, and minority populations. For example, the 1990 Americans with Disabilities Act, the Civil Rights Restoration Act, the 1993 Family and Medical Leave Act, the Brady (gun control) Bill, and the Anti-Crime Bill were all aimed at enhancing the quality of life for large groups of Americans and, in many cases, their economic well-being (Segal, 2007).

The tides soon shifted again, however. Promoted by Newt Gingrich, then a member of the House of Representatives, the Republican-based Contract with America was introduced in the mid-1990s. The Contract was an effort by political conservatives to reverse the more liberal social welfare policies of earlier decades (for example, Lyndon Johnson's Great Society programs). Responding to the economic recession and the increased number of people living in poverty, the political community reconceptualized welfare as temporary and strengthened states' control over allocations (Gibelman, 2004).

After numerous revisions, the Clinton administration agreed to support the Personal Responsibility and Work Opportunity Reconciliation Act (PRWORA) in 1996, which replaced AFDC with Temporary Assistance to Needy Families (TANF). The PRWORA was intended to decrease dependence on welfare. Moreover, because the federal government would fund TANF through block grants to the states and would not provide a uniform set of guidelines, the PRWORA authorized each state to determine: (1) the ways that funds would be allocated and the amounts that would be awarded; (2) time limits for cash assistance; and (3) eligibility requirements for Medicaid health coverage. States that did not comply with general federal regulations regarding the restrictions for receiving TANF benefits jeopardized continued funding. One condition of the PRWORA was a 5-year lifetime cap on public assistance benefits. In addition, TANF recipients are required to be engaged in a work-related activity for at least 30 hours per week.

Despite the lack of any major positive strides being made in social welfare policies and programs, the Clinton administration was generally viewed as more supportive than his predecessors of the social work profession and those people served by social workers (Gibelman, 2004). Nevertheless, welfare reform required the social work profession to reconceptualize the way in which programs were delivered.

Social Welfare in the 21st Century   The 2000 election of George W. Bush returned the country to an earlier era of decreased public funding for social welfare programs and increased reliance on nonprofit and faith organizations to carry the burden for meeting societal needs. In fact, the first executive act of the new President was to create the White House Office of Faith-Based and Community Initiatives, which continued the shift from public to private responsibility. A commitment to "compassionate conservatism" and a supply-side economic philosophy continued the shift toward political and social conservatism and decreased governmental support—a move that historically means fewer resources for social welfare programs (Gibelman, 2004; Hopps et al., 2008).

The 2006 elections brought a change of legislative leadership as the Democrats gained control of Congress. This shift resulted in enactment of several more progressive moves: a voluntary prescription drug plan through Medicare (2006) and legislation to raise the minimum wage from $5.15 to $7.25 by 2009.

Concern for the well-being of TANF recipients who would have difficulty gaining and maintaining employment motivated welfare rights advocates to lobby state legislatures to reauthorize TANF benefits. While the Deficit Reduction Act of 2005 served to reauthorize TANF, more stringent requirements were placed on states and, ultimately, the recipients themselves (Hagen & Lawrence, 2008). The Final Rules of TANF went into effect in 2008 with a loosening of the activities that "count" as work. Critics, however, remain unconvinced that the TANF requirements are sensitive to employment barriers for all TANF recipients, particularly those with disabilities (Schott, 2008). Although many people agreed that the welfare system was in need of reform, opponents of TANF continue to view it as coercive regarding work requirements, inflexible time limits, and shortsighted as the approach is one focused on the labor force as opposed to investing in human capital (Hagen & Lawrence, 2008). Critics object to the assumption that poverty is a temporary situation that can be rectified by a stable national and global economy (National Association of Social Workers, 2009–2012a). Other critics point out that TANF recipients have been unable to obtain employment with wages high enough to lift them out of poverty.

Increasing dissatisfaction with governmental spending priorities created an environment for the election of Barack Obama, who campaigned on a platform of social and economic reform. Entering office in the throes of a major economic crisis, President Obama's first focus was to stabilize the economy. After an extended period of time with unemployment rates hovering near 10%, the U.S. Department of Labor, Bureau of Labor Statistics (2012a) reported a lower rate of 8.3% at the beginning of 2012. At any point in time, those hardest hit are those on the lowest end of the socioeconomic spectrum (e.g., high unemployment rates for African Americans). To revitalize the economy, Obama introduced the American Recovery and Reinvestment Act (ARRA) within his first month in office. Aimed at restabilizing the nation's economy, the Economic Stimulus Bill has infused $840 billion into the economy to strengthen the infrastructure, support state and local governments, provide tax assistance, and invest in health care, energy, the environment, and education (Council on Social Work Education, 2009). Recent reports suggest that the ARRA was, in fact, successful in staving off the most dire of the consequences of the economic recession with an estimated 0.7 million to 3.6 million individuals being employed as a result of the initiative (Leachman & Mai, 2011). These and other safety-net programs have kept many out of poverty, including recipients of unemployment insurance (3.2 million), Social Security (20.3 million), SNAP (3.9 million), and EITC (5.4 million) (Trisi et al., 2011). In fact, during the period of 2000–2009, for those persons receiving SNAP benefits there resulted a 4.4% reduction in poverty while the depth and severity of poverty were reduced even more. Overall depth of poverty decreased by 10.3% and 15.5% for children, while overall severity declined 13.2% and 21.3% for children (Tiehen, Jolliffe, & Gundersen, 2012, p. 1). Related areas of positive impact include tax relief, including expansion of the Child Tax Credit, support to educational and health programs, weatherizing federal buildings and private homes, strengthening road and bridge infrastructure, and support for scientific research and technology advancements (Recovery Act, 2012). To learn more about specific and ongoing ARRA spending, visit: www.recovery.gov.

In the intervening years of the Obama administration, social welfare programming has primarily been negatively impacted by the increased attention on the state of the economy. In 2012, the priorities of the presidential administration are, not surprisingly, focused on the budget. While public assistance benefits should be increased as compensation for years of not keeping up with rates of inflation, few states are responding in this way (Danziger, 2010). To the contrary, sweeping cuts are being proposed that, if passed, will inevitably result in decreases to many programs, including Social Security and Medicare (Sawhill, 2012). Many states are following suit by enacting major budgetary cuts in TANF that will decrease by one-third the number of families eligible to receive benefits, decrease the lifetime cap on eligibility, and decrease support for working families (Schott & Pavetti, 2011). With the median TANF benefit currently at $429/month, family income is stalled at 27% of the poverty level. With the addition of the food stamp (SNAP) benefit, that level is raised to 68% of the poverty line (Schott & Pavetti, 2011).

As we continue our efforts to decrease the number of persons living in poverty, we must consider new ways of understanding poverty within the context of contemporary issues. Based on the premise that our previously unrealistic understanding of poverty can be used to guide us to a more realistic intervention for addressing it, Rank (2006) offers a new paradigm for allowing people to live a life without poverty. Rank's new paradigm is based on five assumptions related to poverty, including: (1) poverty is a result of structural failings; (2) poverty is a conditional state that people move in and out of; (3) poverty creates deprivation in multiple areas (e.g., health, education, and employment); (4) poverty is an injustice; and (5) poverty affects and undermines all of us. To operationalize the new paradigm, the following steps are needed:

- Ensure a minimum wage that will enable individuals and families to work full-time and expect to live above the poverty line.

- Better utilize the taxation system to support low-income persons through EITC and other tax credits.

- Ensure that basic goods and services are available to all—education, health care, affordable housing and child care.

- Create a culture and structure for developing individual assets through Individual Development Accounts.

Although antipoverty programs come and go with political and funding changes, a core group of programs have seemingly weathered the political and economic storms. Those programs (e.g., Head Start) that have been able to establish a base of evidence to support their effectiveness have been more sustainable. Quick Guide #3 is a brief listing of the enduring programs with which social workers need to be familiar.

QUICK GUIDE #3   Current U.S. Social Welfare Programs

- **Social Security:** Retirement income (based on amount "invested") for all workers who have paid into the system during their years of employment. Income to survivors (spouses and children) of deceased workers and to workers who become disabled, if they have worked long enough to qualify.
- **Medicare:** National social insurance program that provides health insurance for older adults and younger persons experiencing a disability.
- **Temporary Assistance to Needy Families (TANF):** Monthly cash assistance to eligible low-income families with children under age 18. Within the first 2 years of benefits, TANF recipients who are able-bodied must be engaged in work or work-related activities (for example, job training or seeking) or lose benefits. Over a lifetime, an individual can receive benefits for a total of 5 years only.
- **Social Security Disability (SSD):** Cash assistance for persons deemed to be unable to work for at least 1 year for reasons of physical or mental disability. Not available to workers who become disabled due to drug or alcohol addiction.

- **Supplemental Security Income (SSI):** Cash assistance to low-income adults, older adults, and persons with disabilities or visual challenges who meet income and health standards.
- **Medicaid:** Health coverage available to some recipients of eligibility-based programs (TANF, SSI, and SSD). May also be provided to Social Security recipients who are eligible based on need.
- **Supplemental Nutrition Assistance Program (SNAP):** Formerly known as food stamps but now an electronic card that can be used to purchase food items. Provided as an income supplement to low-income individuals and families.
- **Women, Infants, and Children (WIC):** Eligibility-based benefits for mothers and their children, aimed at enhancing their physical health. Can be used to purchase certain foods.
- **General Assistance (GA):** Sometimes called general relief. Small, short-term cash benefits for low-income adults who do not qualify for any other cash assistance programs. Currently not available in most states.
- **Earned Income Tax Credit (EITC):** Refundable tax credit for low-income ($36,000–$49,000 annual income) workers paying federal taxes (additional tax credits available in some states). Benefits based on number of children and total household income.
- **Head Start:** Child development program for low-income children, which includes preschool, health, and nutrition programs.
- **Individual Development Account (IDA):** Matching funds available to low-income savers. Funds can be used for purchasing a home or business, education, or other investments that will help the individual achieve financial well-being. Funded by nonprofit organizations, with legislative support from the federal government and a majority of states.

SOCIAL WORK AND THE CHANGING APPROACHES TO POVERTY

One of the roles of an effective social worker is to facilitate a client's access to all the resources for which the client is eligible. For example, a social worker may be helping a family locate in-home services to avoid placing their family member suffering from early-onset dementia in a long-term care facility. To fulfill that objective, the social worker must have a working knowledge of relevant social welfare programs and keep herself updated on the ever-changing policies, eligibility requirements, application protocols, and benefits associated with these programs. In this example, possible programs would include Social Security Disability, Medicare, Medicaid, and SSI, that could augment any pension and/or retirement income, savings, and/or retiree health care benefits. For information on Social Security benefits, the American Association of Retired Persons has developed Social Security State Quick Fact Sheets, accessible at: http://www.aarp.org/work/social-security/info-12-2011/social-security-quick-facts-2012.html.

However, as you have learned, sentiments regarding public welfare resources and programs are complex and closely linked to political, economic, religious, and social trends in U.S. society. Our discussion raises the question: what are the implications of this changing tide for the social work profession? Social and economic needs inevitably prompt a societal and political response. This response, in turn, determines the amount of money that politicians, bureaucrats, private foundations, and individual donors will spend. This availability of funding determines the extent to which social workers will be funded to provide social work services. Let us consider three areas in which social work practice is currently being affected by current societal and political trends and issues: (1) public child welfare; (2) **food insecurity**; and (3) services for persons experiencing mental illness.

The public child welfare system provides an example of this sequence of events. When the political climate is unfavorable for public social services, funding is decreased, and the number of social work positions is lowered. Although the demand for social work services may remain high, the funding is not adequate to support all the positions required to meet this demand. The result is fewer workers with larger caseloads. During these times, politicians often suggest that the private sector should fill the gap created by decreased public funding. Social workers can become involved by documenting the need-for-use funding decisions and engaging in advocacy and fundraising efforts.

A startling 15% of persons living in the United States in 2010 suffered from "food insecurity" (lack of adequate nutrition resulting from limited or inconsistent access to adequate amounts and types of food), with 5.4% of these experiencing severe food insecurity (Coleman-Jensen, Nord, Andrews, & Carlson, 2011). Moreover, over one-fifth of children in the United States are defined as being food-insecure. This number increased from 17.6% in 2007 (SRCD, 2011a). Having insufficient nutrition can negatively impact the child's physical health, school performance, and psychosocial stability (SRCD, 2011b). Social workers can address this concern in several areas: (1) ensure that our clients are accessing relevant programs for which they are eligible (e.g., SNAP, Women, Infants, and Children, school breakfast and lunch, and summer feeding programs); (2) advocate for appropriate funding for public programs such as SNAP; (3) work to improve overall participation rates and access to available food programs; and (4) advocate for additional resources for nongovernmental food programs to reach those families that are not eligible for the public programs (Feeding America, 2011; SRCD, 2011a).

Yet another example is the treatment of persons with mental illness. Research indicates that persons experiencing mental illness, specifically personality disorders, utilize social welfare programs and services at higher levels than other groups in the population (Vaughn et al., 2009). While current funding of prevention and treatment programs for those experiencing mental illness has not been consistently sufficient, making prevention and treatment programming a funding priority could, in fact, reduce the burden on the public welfare system.

There will always be a role for social workers regardless of the political and economic climate. However, social workers' jobs may become more or less challenging depending on the political group that is in power, the state of the economy, and the prevailing sentiments regarding safety-net programs, in general, and social welfare programs, in particular. But remember that, regardless of the area of social work in which you specialize, you are responsible for staying current with the myriad changes made to social welfare programs every year. Your awareness and understanding of the myriad of ever-changing policies and programs are key to your ability to be an effective social work practitioner and advocate for your clients. Your knowledge may prevent your client from becoming homeless or unemployed; may enable your client to gain access to public assistance or employment or disability benefits; or provide access to health or educational programs. Social workers should have a clear understanding of the eligibility criteria for social welfare programs.

In the most recent policy statement, the National Association of Social Workers (2012–2014o) calls for social workers to advocate for an array of policies and plans, regardless of climate, some of which include:

- Create a safety net for persons who are experiencing poverty through comprehensive child support for all single custodial parents, universal health care, meaningful employment and training, education, increases in EITC, and livable wage.

- Help persons living in poverty to build personal and financial assets through programs such as individual development accounts.

- Enable those persons living in poverty to integrate work, education, and family life.

- Promote services to focus on the underlying economic causes of poverty, including the impact that factors such as domestic violence, sexual abuse, mental health issues, substance abuse, and literacy problems play in preventing an escape from poverty (pp. 353–354).

Like many social work students, Emily questioned the value of studying social welfare history and the myriad government programs. After all, she just wanted to help people, and spending time reading about policies had nothing to do with helping people, or did it? One day at Oasis House, Emily and her social work supervisor, John, met with one of the shelter's residents, Tonya. Tonya and her two children had fled from her violent husband. Tonya's TANF and Medicaid benefits were about to be terminated because she was not currently employed full-time. Instead, she was enrolled in a full-time licensed practical nurse program and working part-time at a skilled nursing facility. She had only 3 months until graduation, and her only income was the public assistance she received. In addition, Tonya had to make frequent medical visits related to her older child's cerebral palsy. She had held several part-time jobs while she was in the licensed practical nurse program, but she either had to quit each one or she was fired due to absenteeism because her child was hospitalized or had medical appointments.

In his role as an advocate, John telephoned Tonya's income maintenance caseworker to request that Tonya be scheduled for a hearing at which she could request a work waiver to complete training. He also requested that the agency allow him to accompany Tonya to the hearing and present photographs verifying that she was a survivor of domestic violence. As a result of John's knowledge of governmental benefits and Tonya's rights, Tonya obtained a waiver to allow her to finish training. John also helped Tonya apply for SSI for her child, who had a disability.

Through her experience with Tonya and John, Emily learned the importance of being knowledgeable about policies and programs if she intends to become an advocate for people in need.

CONCLUSION

The arrival of a new millennium provided us with an opportunity to look both to the past and to the future. While our social services continue to be delivered by both public and private entities, governmental sources provide the majority of the funding. That funding is periodically at risk, however, because some members of our society continue to explain poverty and need as being individually based.

The need only grows during crises like the one that gripped our economy, starting in 2007, and the question is whether our society can shift from an individualistic perspective to one focused on the community to help those in need. When a middle-class wage earner is laid off and the family's home is lost to a foreclosure and they have no health insurance coverage, suddenly they are living below the poverty line. Although social welfare policy and, subsequently, programs may change to strengthen the safety net, there is also a possibility that the dynamics of political, social, and economic factors will not stretch far enough to relieve this family's need—much less the need of the chronically poor.

Understanding the historical roots of contemporary social welfare philosophy and programs is essential for a practicing social worker. Social workers' knowledge, skills, and values give them valuable insights into the systemic impact of poverty on those with whom they work.

To help people achieve economic stability, social workers can also advocate for policy changes in areas such as TANF, health care and insurance, the minimum wage, tax structures, and educational benefits. But you cannot advocate for your position unless you know the varied positions of others involved. Social workers have long been at the forefront of advocacy efforts, and they will continue to use their knowledge of systems, organizations, and communities to advocate for and with others to alleviate poverty.

Even in this era of uncertainty, another of Don Bakely's poems captures a sense of optimism and hope:

> *When I was a kid,*
> *I looked to the day when*
> *I would stop dreaming those wild hopes*

and
     I'd be old enough
       to make real life
         out of
           unreal dreams.
But I still catch myself
      hanging onto dreams—
    and I'm forty.
Sometimes I catch myself thinking
    maybe today
      a big, beautiful car is going to pull up out front
        and
          the rich man is going to get out
          and say,
"I heard about you,
   that
     you are a good man
       and work hard
         and love your kids
          and are down on your luck.
Here's a check.
Come by the office. I've got a good job for a man like you.
By the way, keep the car.
   I see you need one.
   I'll catch a cab back."

Of course,
   he never comes.
I really know
   he
     never
       will.

But, see,
   with poor folks
     even wild hopes
       are
         hopes worth thinking.
          Kind of fun, in fact.

Then, too
   if we can't have some glimmer
     in

> *tomorrow*
> *even a*
> *long-shot,*
> *never-happen*
> *glimmer.*
> *Then each today*
> *is always*
> *only*
> *darkness.*

Excerpt from "The family of poor: Part three," from *If . . . A Big Word
With the Poor* by Don Bakely, Faith & Life Press, Newton, Kansas.
Used by permission.

MAIN POINTS

- Poverty is a complex political, economic, and social issue, but essentially is not having enough money to live adequately.

- The poor are not just the stereotype of the homeless man or woman sleeping in a doorway or pushing a shopping cart on the downtown streets of a city; those groups at highest risk for living in poverty are women, persons of color, high school dropouts, older adults, and children (who cannot work).

- The causes of poverty continue to be hotly debated. Some people believe that the individual is responsible for her or his economic plight, while others believe that external factors (such as employment opportunities and economic conditions) place people at risk for living in poverty.

- Poverty can be short-term or episodic, in which the individual is working but cannot earn enough money to move out of poverty; or chronic, in which the individual's poverty is long-term.

- Understanding both the literal meanings and societal connotations of terms such as welfare, public assistance, and social policy helps in understanding society's perception of poverty.

- Societal responses to poverty tend to reflect the current political climate, with conservative political administrations restricting social programs and more liberal administrations expanding social programs.

- A variety of federal, state, and local government agencies are involved in the administration of social welfare programs.

- Social welfare programs fall into two categories: universal (Social Security and Medicare) and selective (for example, TANF, SSI, and SNAP). Social workers are responsible for being familiar with these programs and staying current with the myriad changes made every year.

EXERCISES

1. Respond to the following questions:
   a. What is poverty?
   b. What causes poverty?
   c. How do we end poverty?
   Then interview friends, family members, co-workers, and/or others and ask them the same three questions. You may also ask your interviewees about their definitions of and attitudes toward "welfare." Reflect on the similarities and differences in their responses and the way in which their definitions and attitudes compare with the definitions described in this chapter.

2. As you learned from this chapter, Tonya is a single mother with two children. Her son, William, is 3 years old and her daughter, Erica, is 6 years old. Develop a budget that would be required for Tonya and her two children to live for 1 month. You may want to have a calculator available to help you in this exercise.

   This budget should not reflect a luxurious lifestyle or a life at bare minimum, but rather should show what you believe are essentials for living and their costs for 1 month. For each basic human need, enter an amount that you think is a true monthly cost regardless of who would pay for it. For example, the cost of food will be the same if the family receives food stamps or not. In actuality, the family may not have the resources to purchase that amount of food, but it is still a cost. As you are creating this budget, identify your reasons for deriving that particular amount.

   Once you have developed a picture of Tonya's needs for 1 month, you can compare your amounts with the actual amounts required if this family lived in your state by calculating a family budget at the Economic Policy Institute Basic Family Budget Calculator located at www.epi.org/content/budget_calculator.

   As you progress with this exploration, consider Tonya's situation from two different perspectives. First, assume that Tonya and her children receive TANF benefits and compare your budget with the amounts of benefits that they will receive. Second, consider the scenario in which Tonya is employed full-time in a minimum-wage job. Decide if she receives health/dental benefits for herself and/or her children. In order to make these comparisons, you will need information on living costs in your community.

   Questions to consider as you complete this exercise:
   a. What information do you need to know to be able to develop a monthly budget?
   b. What categories of expenses would a single mother with two children have during the month?

    c. What is the amount of TANF provided by your state for a mother and two children?

3. As you have learned from the Sanchez family interactive case (go to www.routledgesw.com/cases), the family has struggled financially throughout the years. Hector has prevented the family from taking advantage of many of the resources available to them. Complete the following two exercises:

    a. Using the information provided in this chapter, along with information from your state government, identify benefits that may be appropriate for various members of the Sanchez family. You may use resources in the community in which you reside or where your social work program is located.

    b. Reflect on the reasons that Hector may feel resistance to using social services. Additionally, reflect on how you think Hector and the members of his family may feel in the client role.

4. Review the case file for Junior Sanchez in the Sanchez family interactive case (www.routledgesw.com/cases). Answer Junior's Critical Thinking Questions.

5. To test your knowledge of poverty, complete the quiz "How Much Do You Really Know About Poverty?" located at: http://halfinten.org/issues/articles/how-much-do-you-really-know-about-poverty-2011/.

6. Go to www.routledgesw.com/cases to familiarize yourself with the case entitled, Hudson City: An Urban Community Affected by Disaster. Click on the Engage button to review the details of the case. Natural disasters often affect all individuals and families in negative ways, but the impact on persons of limited resources can be particularly devastating as they may not have adequate insurance coverage, financial savings, or a support network that can help in significant ways. Additionally, when disasters strike, many individuals lose their employment when businesses are affected. Utilizing the information included in the Hudson City case, this chapter, and online sources, develop a list of resources that may be of value to an individual or family who has experienced a disaster. From your research, identify those services and resources that are based on means testing (i.e., based on income).

CHAPTER 4

The Social Work Environment

The social work profession's helping mission places it in the center of people's lives and the societal issues that influence their lives. Therefore, social workers must be knowledgeable about the makeup of society in general and the populations who use social workers' services in particular. Social work "is created within a political, social, cultural, and economic matrix that shapes the assumptions of practice, the problems that practice must deal with and the preferred outcomes of practice" (McNutt & Floersch, 2008, p. 4:138). Fortunately, the political, economic, and sociocultural issues that present obstacles for persons served by social workers also provide opportunities for growth and social change. In this chapter, you will gain an understanding of the diversity of the U.S. population and then examine the challenges that confront social workers in contemporary society.

CHANGING POPULATION PROFILES

As of 2012, the world is comprised of over 6.9 billion people, over 312 million of whom live in the United States. The world population is slated to surpass 7 billion in 2012 and 9 billion by 2044, while the U.S. population is expected to reach 400 million by 2039. In 2012, a new American is born every 8 seconds, one dies every 12 seconds, and one immigrates every 46 seconds, which results in an overall population increase of one person every 17 seconds (U.S. Census Bureau, Statistical Abstract, 2012). The period from 1990 to 2000 saw the largest U.S. population growth (32.7 million people) than during any other 10-year period in history, with the largest growth occurring in the western states and metropolitan areas. During the next decade (2000–2010), the United States experienced a smaller rate of growth of 9.7%, which is comparable to the growth of the 1980s. As with the growth of the 1990s, the population increased in the southern and western regions of the country (Mackun & Wilson, 2011). While impacted by environmental, political, and social changes, the world population typically grows at a rate of 1.5–2% per year. The growth in the current century is anticipated to occur at a slower rate due to increasing age at both marriage and having children.

The distribution of the world's population and growth, however, is skewed toward the developing countries. The majority of the world's people live in developing countries and a number of these countries (e.g., sub-Saharan Africa) are experiencing increases in fertility rates in recent years but are also struggling with economic, health, governmental, and poverty crises (Williamson, 2010).

The world population as a whole is incredibly diverse. Some of the dimensions on which people differ are race or ethnicity, age, sex or gender, income level, and religion. Some societies, such as North Korea, are relatively uniform (at least as far as race/ethnicity, income level, and religion are concerned). Others, like the United States, are quite diverse. The global profile is shifting toward an older, non-Caucasian population which is and will continue to impact the economic, political, health care, and migratory realities of the world arena (Williamson, 2010). In fact, recent **demographic** shifts (changes in the makeup of the population) have made the U.S. population more diverse than at any previous time in history and continuing to become even more diverse.

Social workers' clients reflect this diversity, although some groups have fewer opportunities and resources than others and thus may be overrepresented. In addition, government policies are not always supportive of all these segments of the population, making it necessary for social workers to lobby specifically for particular groups.

To highlight the diversity of the U.S. population, this chapter uses data from four primary sources—the U.S. Census Bureau, Statistical Abstract (2012), *Women's Health USA 2008* (U.S. Department of Health and Human Services Health Resources and Services Administration, Maternal and Child Health Bureau, 2008), *Income, Poverty, and Health Insurance Coverage in the United States: 2010*, and the *2009–2012 Statistical Abstracts of the United States*. The discussion focuses on five demographic characteristics: race and ethnicity, age, gender, income, and religion. Exhibit 4.1 highlights some of the major changes expected by the demographers of the U.S. Census Bureau, Statistical Abstract (2012) between now and 2050.

Changes in Race and Ethnicity

A racial and ethnic profile of the United States is shown in Exhibit 4.2. From 1995 to 2050 the U.S. population is expected to increase by 50%, with the largest growth occurring within the Hispanic/Latino and Asian populations, primarily due to immigration. Thus, racial and ethnic diversity clearly is increasing, particularly among older adults, in general, and older adults of color, in particular. One reason for this trend is that persons of color are gaining better access to health care and are therefore living longer. At the same time, fertility among this group is expected to remain constant.

One consequence of this increased diversity is that the U.S. population will include greater numbers of people whose first language is not English and who identify with more than one racial or ethnic group. Over 6,000 languages exist

EXHIBIT 4.1

Demographic Changes in the United States in the First Half of the 21st Century

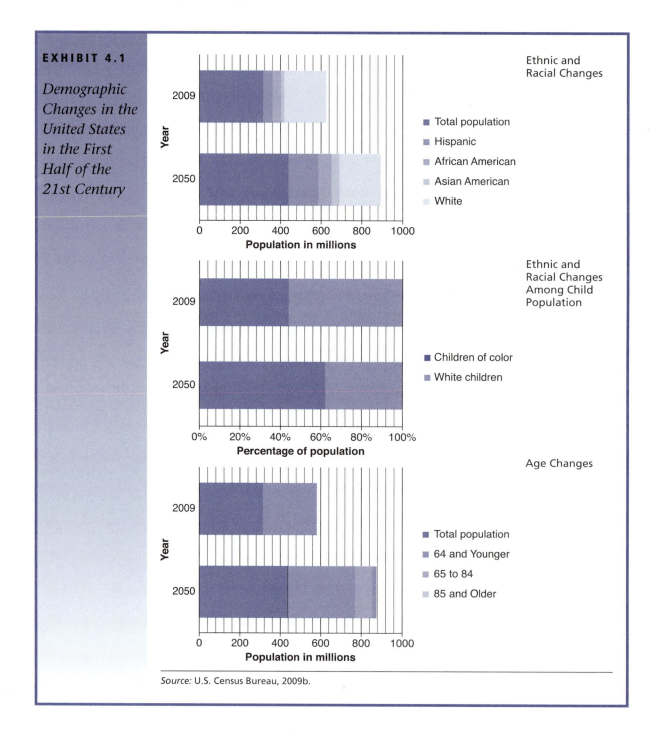

Ethnic and Racial Changes

■ Total population
■ Hispanic
▨ African American
▨ Asian American
▨ White

Ethnic and Racial Changes Among Child Population

■ Children of color
■ White children

Age Changes

■ Total population
▨ 64 and Younger
▨ 65 to 84
▨ 85 and Older

Source: U.S. Census Bureau, 2009b.

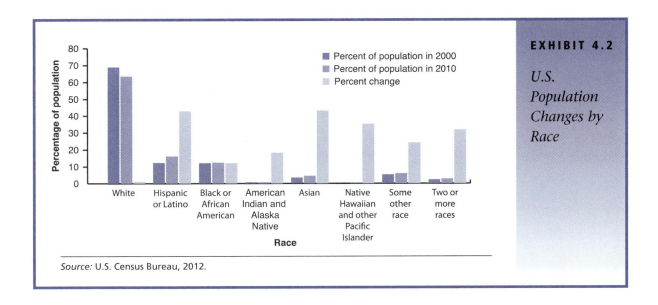

EXHIBIT 4.2

U.S. Population Changes by Race

Source: U.S. Census Bureau, 2012.

across the globe, and nearly 400 of them are represented within the U.S. population, largely because of immigration. Nearly one in five residents of the United States speak a language other than English when they are in their homes. This rate is significantly higher for those residents from Mexico and the Dominican Republic (97%), with over half of the overall foreign-born population reporting they are not fully fluent in English (U.S. Census Bureau, 2009a).

Another outcome of America's increasing diversity is the increase in the number of marriages between persons of different races. Once illegal in many states, one in 12 marriages now includes spouses from different races (Pew Research Center, 2012).

Over 1.3 million persons immigrated to the United States in 2010—a number that will rise to an annual rate of over 2 million by 2050. These numbers do not include those persons who are in the United States in an undocumented status. Over 73,000 of those immigrants are **refugees** (persons who seek refuge from danger or persecution in their home country) who were resettled in the United States in 2010 alone (U.S. Department of State, 2011).

For social workers, increased racial and ethnic diversity requires better-developed cultural competency. Clients whose experiences, perspectives, cultural heritage, language, values, and traditions are so different have different needs.

The Aging Population

Not only is the U.S. population becoming more diverse racially and ethnically, but it is also aging, as Exhibit 4.3 shows. Since 1990, the median age has increased from 32.9 to 36.6 years, and it is expected to increase to 38.1 years by 2050. Significantly, a greater percentage of the population of persons of color falls within the under-18

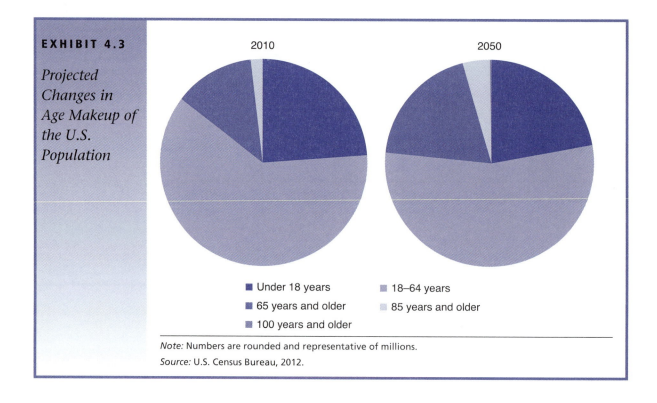

Note: Numbers are rounded and representative of millions.
Source: U.S. Census Bureau, 2012.

category, whereas whites make up the largest percentage of older adults. Based on current demographic projections, by 2030 more than 40% of the total U.S. population will be either under age 17 (21%) or over age 65 (22%). As children and older adults tend to be the most vulnerable segments of the population, such increases will result in a greater need for social work competence in working with these groups. While more males are born than females, females outrank males over the course of the lifespan, making older women particularly vulnerable (Howden & Meyer, 2011).

Life expectancy is currently expected to be 78.3 years for all groups. Men and persons of color have lower life expectancy (75.7 and 73.8 years, respectively), and women and white persons tend to have a higher life expectancy than the overall average (80.8 and 78.9 years, respectively) (U.S. Census Bureau, 2012). However, longevity is on the increase for all groups; by 2050 life expectancy is projected to be as high as 83.9 years overall, although still lower for persons of color and men. The fastest-growing segment of the population will be those over 85—this group will reach 19 million in 2050. While our population is living longer, median incomes are not keeping up with longer lifespans. Median incomes for both older men and women have decreased, with 9% of older adults living below the poverty line (U.S. DHHS, 2011).

Social workers need skills to work with the entire continuum of ages, particularly in multigenerational family situations. More older adults are rearing grandchildren as a result of the children's parents being unavailable for a variety of reasons, including substance abuse, incarceration, and divorce. Current trends suggest that multigenerational families will reside together more often. In addition, more older adults will live in congregate living situations such as retirement communities, assisted living facilities, and long-term care facilities, which will give social workers many opportunities to work with older adults.

Trends in Sex Ratios

Today, women make up nearly 51% of the U.S. population, although the male population experienced more growth than the female population between the 2000 and 2010 Censuses (9.9% and 9.5%, respectively). Men outnumber women until age 24, but for the 65-and-older segment, women make up 58% of the population. By age 85, women outnumber men by two to one. Exhibit 4.4 depicts how the gender ratio changes with age. As men age, mortality begins to increase, initially due to professional and recreational activities and later due to chronic fatal illnesses such as heart disease and cancer. These patterns are expected to continue. The exhibit also shows how the age and sex distribution will change by 2050.

As older women become a larger segment of the population, social workers need to be increasingly aware of the issues that confront this population. Compared to older men, older women are more likely to live alone, to have lower incomes, to experience more chronic health problems, and to assume more caregiving responsibilities

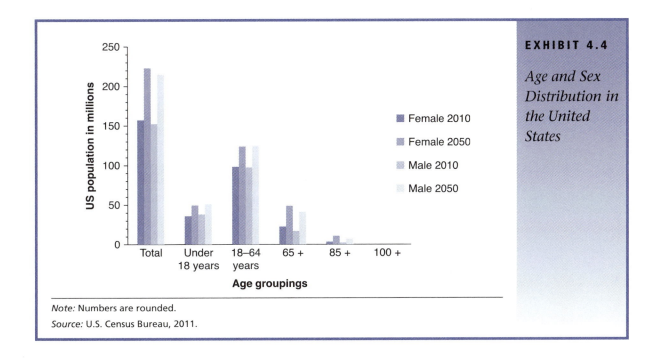

EXHIBIT 4.4

Age and Sex Distribution in the United States

Note: Numbers are rounded.

Source: U.S. Census Bureau, 2011.

(for example, for spouses or grandchildren). With the changes that have occurred in recent decades regarding women's roles in society, social workers also need to be preparing proactively for the new generations of older women who have participated in the workforce for most of their lives. This new and emerging group of older women may differ from their predecessors as they may have greater financial independence, fewer children, be unavailable to serve as family caregivers as they are still employed, and have different expectations for their older adult years.

Increasing Income Inequality

In 2010, the median household income for all Americans was $49,445/year with a range of $32,068/year for Black Americans to $64,308/year for Asian Americans. Incomes varied considerably state by state, from a high of $68,854/year in Maryland to $36,851/year in Mississippi. Household income has declined over 6% since 2007, the year prior to the beginning of the 2008 economic recession and, in 2012, is still 7% below the 1999 all-time high level (Bishaw, 2011a). Poverty rose at all levels, with 32 states experiencing increases in the rates of poverty and no state reporting a significant decline.

Over the past 30 years, as the population increased, the number of persons living in poverty has climbed steadily and is now at the highest rate (46.2 million) in the 52 years that such data has been tracked. Due to the recent economic crisis, one of the most significant changes in the current social work environment is the increase in both the number and percentage of people living in poverty. For the third consecutive year since 2009, the number of people living in poverty rose. Increasing by 1.0% from 2009 to 2010, the number living in poverty climbed from 14.3% of the population to 15.1%. Non-Hispanic whites, Hispanics, urbanites, southerners, and children were most affected. Many of the states in the southeast and southwest region of the U.S. report 16% or more of the residents living in poverty. Only New Hampshire has a poverty level below 10% (Bishaw, 2011a).

As Exhibit 4.5 shows, the poverty rate for the non-Hispanic white population is now approximately 9.9%, while the rates for African Americans and persons of Hispanic/Latino origin are over 27% and 26%, respectively (Bishaw, 2011a). Only Asian Americans did not experience an increased rate of poverty. For those U.S. residents who immigrated to this country, nearly 20% live below the poverty line, ranging from a high of 28% for Mexican immigrants to a low of 9.8% for European-born residents.

A much-noted fact in the past few years is that the gap between rich and poor has increased. The per capita income of those living in poverty has remained unchanged over the past two decades, resulting in a decreasing income share for the poor and a widening gap between rich and poor (Buss, 2010). Between 2009 and 2010, overall median household incomes fell 2.3%, while median household incomes decreased for African Americans by 3.2%, Asians by 3.4%, and Hispanic/Latino households by 2.3%. Despite the economic recession that began in 2008 and

EXHIBIT 4.5	RACE/ETHNICITY	2009	2010	PERCENT CHANGE
Increases in U.S. Poverty Rate by Race and Ethnicity	TOTAL	14.3	15.1	0.8
	White	12.3	13.0	0.7
	White, non-Hispanic	9.4	9.9	0.5
	Black	25.8	27.4	1.6
	Asian	12.5	12.1	−0.4
	Hispanic (any race)	25.3	26.6	1.3

Source: U.S. Census Bureau, 2011.

negatively impacted U.S. citizens at all economic levels, the small elite at the highest levels have not experienced the same devastation as the majority of the population. While the bottom 90% of the U.S. population experienced a 4% decrease in income from 2002 to 2008, the top 1% enjoyed a 30% increase in income (Shaw & Stone, 2010). Exhibit 4.6 provides a more detailed look at this issue. To place the gap into perspective, the richest 20% of the population receive almost 50% of household incomes, while the poorest 20% receive 3.5%.

A related issue is the "wealth gap." Wealth is the accumulation of financial resources. Two people may be earning the same income, but if one owns a home and has a 401(k), that person has more wealth than the other. Wealth often reflects the passing-along of property and financial resources from one generation to the next. A financial setback, say the loss of a home due to foreclosure, may affect the family's wealth for generations. Exhibit 4.7 shows that the bottom 90% of Americans have a much smaller share of national wealth than of national income.

A longer-term trend has been a discrepancy in the poverty rates between women and men. Over 20% of women and 18% of men currently live in poverty (Kaiser Family Foundation, 2012a). One reason for the discrepancy is that, despite the Equal Pay Act being passed in 1963, women's incomes still lag behind their male

	2002–2008 INCOME GAINS	EXHIBIT 4.6
Top 0.1% of the U.S. population	68%	*The Growing Income Gap, 2002–2008*
Top 1% of the U.S. population	30%	
Bottom 90% of the U.S. population	−4%	

Source: Shaw & Stone, 2010.

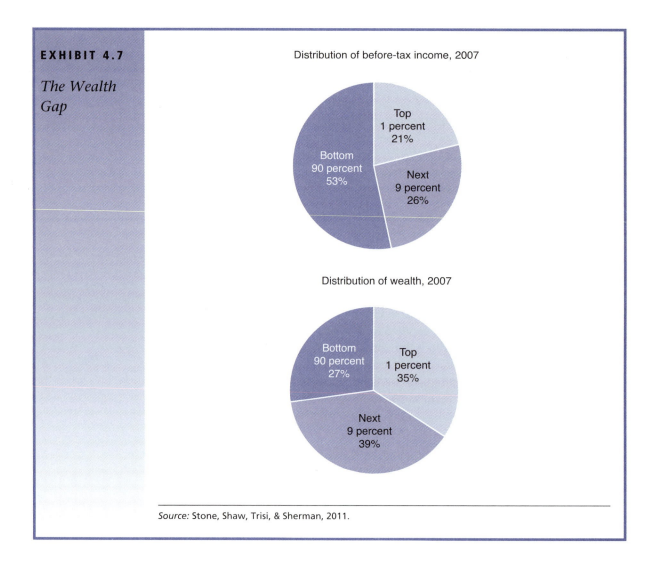

EXHIBIT 4.7

The Wealth Gap

Distribution of before-tax income, 2007

Top 1 percent 21%

Bottom 90 percent 53%

Next 9 percent 26%

Distribution of wealth, 2007

Bottom 90 percent 27%

Top 1 percent 35%

Next 9 percent 39%

Source: Stone, Shaw, Trisi, & Sherman, 2011.

counterparts (Bishaw, 2011a; U.S. Census Bureau, 2008b). Interestingly, overall incomes for women rose (5%) during that time, bringing the female-to-male earnings ratio to an all-time high of 0.78 (women earn 78 cents per every dollar earned by men). While the "wage gap" has closed somewhat since the 1960s from 59 cents/dollar to its current level of 78 cents/dollar, the discrepancies for women of color is lagging behind (National Committee on Pay Equity, 2011). Compared to all males in 2010, African American women earn 62.3% and Hispanic women earn 54% of male counterparts. Only Asian American women fare better, earning 79.6 cents/dollar (Hegewisch & Williams, 2011).

Despite some gains for women, the trend over the past few decades has been toward the "feminization" of poverty. Higher divorce rates and more households headed by single women have contributed to this trend. Since 2009, poverty in female-headed households with no second wage earner has increased nearly 2%, while poverty rates for male-headed households with no second wage earner have not changed (Bishaw, 2011a).

Social workers can help to close that gap by addressing the structural causes of poverty and lobbying to increase women's (and other minorities') opportunities for education, health coverage, child care, and employment that provides a **living wage** (National Association of Social Workers (NASW), 2012–2014i). Also, as poverty rates increase, more people will need assistance with finances, health, employment, food, housing, utilities, and child care. In addition, family crises and violence often increase when families are experiencing stress. Therefore, social workers increasingly need the skills to work with diverse families in crisis.

Trends in Religious Affiliation

At the beginning of the 21st century, approximately 1,600 different religions and denominations were being practiced in the United States, almost half of which have been established in the past 40 years (Mindell, 2007). Conducted each decade, the U.S. Religion Census cites that nearly half of U.S. residents report membership in a religious institution (Briggs, 2012). The majority of members practice a form of Christian denominations, but non-Christian-based (e.g., Judaism, Islam, Buddhism, and Hinduism) and nondenominational/independent religious institutions are increasing. Membership appears to be decreasing among mainline religious organizations (i.e., approximately 13% for Protestant and 1% for Catholic) (Briggs, 2012) but increasing by one-third for non-Christian groups and nondenominational churches (now the third largest religious group in the United States) (Briggs, 2012). Although people who self-identify as Muslim are a small percentage, their number, and the number of people who self-identify as members of other religions, is increasing. Increases reported include Islam—109%; Buddhism—170%; Hinduism—237%. A portion of this change can be attributed to increases in immigration from the Middle East and Asia. Exhibit 4.8 depicts this growth.

Social workers need to be aware of their own religious and spiritual beliefs as well as those of others. They can then more effectively incorporate spirituality into their practice and promote religious acceptance and understanding. Because the population is aging and religious affiliation increases with age, social workers will also benefit from sensitivity to the role of religion and spirituality in the lives of older adults. Integrating religious and spiritual information into the information-gathering process can expand your perspective of the client's situation. For example, being aware of a client's religious involvement can be a resource in the social work intervention whether the client is an older adult, an immigrant, or a refugee (Sheridan, 2002).

EXHIBIT 4.8

Changing Religious Affiliation in the United States

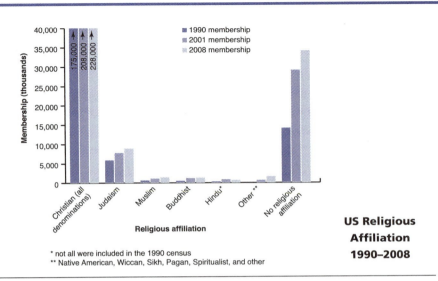

US Religious Affiliation 1990–2008

* not all were included in the 1990 census
** Native American, Wiccan, Sikh, Pagan, Spiritualist, and other

Source: U.S. Census Bureau, 2011.

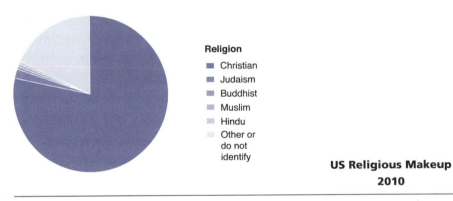

US Religious Makeup 2010

Source: U.S. Census Bureau, 2011.

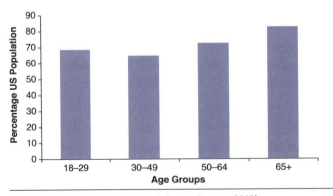

US Religious Affiliation by Age

Source: Kosmin & Mayer, 2001; U.S. Census Bureau, 2009b.

OPPRESSION AND DISCRIMINATION

A major issue that has long confronted social workers is the **oppression** and **discrimination** faced by those groups with whom practitioners work. Oppression occurs when the actions or beliefs of individuals, groups, or institutions are controlled or repressed by other persons or groups within a society. Oppression can be formalized and overt, as in the historical treatment of gay, lesbian, bisexual, and transgender persons in society. However, it can also be informal and covert, such as the continued mistreatment of these groups following passage of hate crimes legislation. In contrast, discrimination is the behavior that results from possessing a bias toward an individual or group based on characteristics such as race, ethnicity, gender, religion, age, sexual orientation, mental and physical conditions, class, and lifestyle (Barker, 2003). Both concepts involve actions, and in both cases an individual or group exerts power over a less-powerful group, often through force, violence, or restriction of resources (Van Soest, 2008).

In spite of the fact that many people come to the United States to escape oppression and discrimination in their homelands, U.S. history has been fraught with devastating and longstanding examples of both. We can see this in the ways in which persons of color, women, homosexual, transsexual, or transgender persons, persons living with a disability, and many immigrant, refugee, and religious groups historically have been mistreated. If such treatment goes unchallenged, both the oppressed and the oppressors can rationalize oppression and discrimination, which in turn perpetuates these behaviors. For example, both the oppressed and the oppressors may come to believe that those in power are superior to or protective of those being oppressed or have control of needed resources (Van Soest, 2008).

Regardless of the form that oppression takes, four commonalities can be found in all instances (Van Soest, 2008, p. 323):

1. Those perceived to be "normal" are perceived to have power and those who are different are viewed as being lesser.

2. Violence or the threat of violence is at the root of the oppressive acts.

3. The oppression persists because it is institutionalized—that is, built into the policies and practices of institutions.

4. Oppression becomes a part of the fabric of the oppressing group, and those being oppressed become devalued or invisible.

Oppression is thus a deep-seated and persistent element of the social world. The Social Work *Code of Ethics* (NASW, 2008) calls for social workers to work to fight oppression. As Martin Luther King Jr. said: "Injustice anywhere is a threat to justice everywhere" (King, 1963).

Cycle of Oppression

Oppression is self-perpetuating. The cycle of oppression is a three-step process:

1. Everyone is born into a social group. Oppression develops when we take in stereotypes, misinformation, biased history, and missing facts about both our own group and other social groups.

2. We are socialized by people we know, trust, and love to follow certain rules about how to be, think, and behave. The misinformation we receive about other groups is reinforced by the people and entities within our individual environments.

3. Continued socialization then becomes internalized, and we come to accept societal values. Persons being oppressed begin to believe the stereotypes that the dominant culture has about the group, resulting in the inability to distinguish truth from misinformation.

Each phase of the cycle of oppression can elicit one or more of the following reactions from both oppressors and the oppressed:

- *Emotional reaction:* The emotions that one feels about oppressive attitudes and behaviors can range from anger to guilt, sadness, confusion, and alienation. The individual must determine the behavior or action that is going to result from one or a combination of these emotional responses.

- *Internalization:* Rooted in stereotypes, felt emotions can evolve into attitudes and behaviors that can then become part of the person's mindset and be expressed through actions at either conscious or unconscious level.

- *Dissonance:* When the emotions, attitudes, and behaviors that occur through socialization come up against contrary evidence about the group, individuals often respond by examining and exploring their feelings about the oppression they have observed, which can result in a newfound understanding of the oppression experienced.

- *Collusion:* Individuals may simply accept the oppression they encounter and thus act in ways that perpetuate the cycle of oppression.

As this list of reactions implies, the only way to break the cycle of oppression is to confront stereotypes, prejudices, and discriminatory or submissive tendencies. Strategies for promoting social justice practices and behaviors may include legal mandates and changing social interactions (Society for Research in Child Development, 2011b). There will always be diversity and difference, so we must learn to understand, accept, and value diversity. Social workers have a lead role to play in breaking the cycle.

Social Work and Oppression

Throughout the history of the profession, social workers have played an active role in working to eliminate social injustices that arise from oppression and discrimination. For example, they have helped vulnerable groups organize, as in the case of welfare rights organizations, and they have advocated for change in the legislative arena at both federal and state levels. Social workers have lobbied and, in some cases, sought elected office to work for justice for victims of domestic violence and hate crimes. They have campaigned for access to housing and public facilities for older adults and persons with disabilities.

As they work to reduce oppression and discrimination, social workers need to keep in mind the following points:

- People are not born with prejudice; they learn it—and can unlearn it.

- We all make assumptions about others, which can lead either to prejudicial attitudes and discriminatory behaviors or to cultural insight and appreciation for diversity.

- Devaluation and disempowerment are the preconditions for prejudice and oppression.

- All people have prejudices, but not all people can enforce their attitudes through institutions and systems of power.

- Discrimination and oppression create real problems of living for those in an oppressed group.

- Those who are not oppressed enjoy a privilege that is a social and economic (or political) benefit.

- Guilt over discrimination and blame for oppression immobilize individuals and groups; social workers must focus on issues and solutions.

As a profession, we have the opportunity and obligation to recognize and attend to the fact that privilege and oppression are present in our own and our clients' lives, listen to the experiences of our clients, and be willing to take action to eliminate oppression and discrimination (Johnson, 2010). Now that you understand the role of social workers in combating oppression and advocating for social justice, let us consider some of the political, economic, and social challenges and opportunities that will confront society and, in particular, the social work profession in the coming years. We will also explore the knowledge and skills that social workers will need to acquire in order to practice competently in an ever-changing society. Current changes in the demography of our country are particularly challenging. Social workers must remain aware of the social forces that face society so that they can respond to the needs of diverse and changing client groups.

CHALLENGES AND OPPORTUNITIES FACING SOCIAL WORKERS

Emily began to notice that the domestic violence shelter program where she worked was serving an increasing number of women whose first language was not English and who frequently had limited English-speaking skills. The community in which Emily worked was experiencing an overall increase in the number of refugees and immigrants from Eastern Europe, Russia, African countries, and several Spanish-speaking countries. The women in the shelter were being identified primarily through hospital emergency rooms where they were seeking emergency medical treatment.

Emily and her co-workers realized that their understanding of domestic violence within other cultures was limited. They also realized that the domestic violence program staff and volunteers spoke only English and therefore had to rely on the women's family members (often their children, who were more proficient in English) or the on-call interpreters engaged by the hospitals. Providing services to non-English-speaking women in crisis without regular interpreters hampered Emily's ability to establish rapport, gather information, and develop supportive and helpful interventions with this client group. Consequently, Emily and her co-workers were growing increasingly concerned that their non-English-speaking clients were not being effectively served by their agency or other agencies that provided services to victims of intimate partner violence and their children. Having identified this gap in the agency's service delivery system, the shelter staff developed a twofold plan to enhance services. The plan included gaining increased knowledge of the cultures represented by the clients to improve their cultural competence and creating a pool of volunteer interpreters. Having more competence in working with a diverse population and ready access to an interpreter who is not related to the client or based at the hospital enabled the staff to develop more accurate and appropriate assessment and intervention plans for the clients.

As you have learned, social work practice is often shaped by current political, economic, and social philosophies and events. Although the specific issues may be different from those that affected past generations, the social work profession must be prepared to influence and respond to the effects of such changes on the individuals, families, organizations, and communities that it serves. Changes will bring new and controversial issues for social workers, but it will be the profession's "values and mission that will anchor the profession in the sea of change" (Allen-Meares, 2000, p. 179).

Political Environment

Because funding for social services is often a volatile and controversial political issue, the political climate in the United States has always had a significant impact on the social work profession. As you saw in Chapters 2 and 3, the political climate of the early part of this century shifted to a more conservative direction, resulting in decreased political and financial support for many social service programs and resources. The end of the 20th century, much like its beginning, was known as a "period of increasing political tension" with issues of race, culture, diversity, civil rights, immigration, religion, abortion, gun control, and nontraditional families at the forefront of the political scene (Austin, 1997, p. 398). Rooted in an antigovernment stance, the 21st century appears to be shaping up much the same with an antisocial service sentiment. Because the issues with which practitioners work have long been "politicized," social workers cannot view their work as apolitical. As we have long known, social workers must assume responsibility for understanding and participating in the political process (Haynes, 1996).

In 2008, the American voting public called for a change. With the election of Barack Obama came a shift in the political climate and, optimistically, a commitment to bipartisan collaboration aimed at enhancing the quality of life for Americans, particularly those in need. For example, the passage of the American Recovery and Reinvestment Act of 2009 (known as the economic stimulus package) was a result of a cooperative effort on the part of politicians from both parties in the House of Representatives, the Senate, the Obama transition team, and the newly appointed Administration (Council on Social Work Education, 2009).

The 2008 elections provided considerable hope for those working in the social service arena. President Obama's campaign agenda and his economic stimulus package and health care reform have been shown as evidence of his administration's strong commitment to strengthening not only the economy but also the social infrastructure of our society. In the economic stimulus package, hundreds of millions of dollars were allocated for services for health, children and families, older adults, Native Americans, education, persons with disabilities, employment, and housing. Elements of the economic stimulus package were specifically focused on those with low and moderate incomes, as evidenced by the infusion of new funds into Temporary Assistance to Needy Families, employment and educational programs, unemployment insurance, child care and support, Supplemental Nutrition Assistance Program, emergency shelter, and tax credit programs—Child Tax (up to $1,000/child) and Making Work Pay ($400/worker) (Center on Budget and Policy Priorities, 2009).

The initial optimism that surrounded the Obama administration quickly gave way to the political and economic realities of the end of the decade. The economic recession, the bipartisan divisions, and mounting concerns about the federal budget became the focus of the political environment.

Challenges in the Political Environment   Social workers can initiate change by working inside the political system (Reisch, 2000). More than 15 years ago, Reisch challenged the profession to consider the following, which remains relevant today:

We have long operated under the illusion that compassion alone will produce change. Although compassion motivates some people to act and think differently, it is insufficient to transform the deep-rooted institutional indifference of our society. (Reisch, 1997, p. 90)

In these politically and economically turbulent times, the continuation of many social service programs will require social workers to integrate both their work with individuals, families, groups, organizations, and communities, and political activism to ensure that adequate funding and resources continue to be available for those services.

Conservative political trends in the 21st century have already had considerable impact on social policy. We began this new century with a large-scale transfer of policy making from the national to state level, thus creating widespread inequities in the way that individual states administer social policies and programs (Schneider, 2002). Additionally, the government is increasingly contracting with outside agencies for the provision of services. These changes resulted in the role of the federal government shifting from service provider to monitor of services (Reisch & Jarman-Rohde, 2000).

Another political development has been hyper-partisanship. The hyper-partisan political environment has created an ongoing debate and dissension regarding the funding of social service programming, resulting oftentimes in the decrease or cessation of funding for needed health and social service delivery. Among the programs that are now threatened are energy assistance, reproductive health services (specifically, through Planned Parenthood), and housing programs. President Obama, in his 2012 State of the Union address, called for change in this era of hyper-partisanship:

We need to end the notion that the two parties must be locked in a perpetual campaign of mutual destruction; that politics is about clinging to rigid ideologies instead of building consensus around common-sense ideas.

While Obama's words are motivational, change in this longstanding partisan climate will be slow to occur. Social workers who are engaged on the frontlines of the social service delivery system can strive to put the president's challenge into action by serving as the voice for their clients through advocacy at local and agency, state, national, and international levels. Social workers are well poised to document and draw attention to the impact of political decisions on clients. Social workers have firsthand knowledge of their clients' inability to maintain economic stability, much less progress to a higher level of economic security.

A final challenge for social workers in the political environment encompasses the global political climate. While there is an array of global issues that should be of concern to us all, a list of those that have reached crisis proportion include, but are not limited to: poverty, HIV/AIDS, hunger and malnutrition, trade issues, and government corruption (Borzutzky, 2010). With nearly half of the world's population living in poverty, the number of AIDS and malnutrition-related deaths on the rise in developing countries, and an increasing number of countries experiencing military and governmental corruption that negatively impacts productivity and

equality, international support, and credibility, social workers working both internationally and domestically will witness the impact of these global challenges.
Social inequities through lack of access to adequate food, health care, education,
and government protection have led to an increase in people motivated to leave
their home countries. For instance, the "Arab Spring" (the wave of political demonstrations in the Middle East) and resulting civil wars around the globe have led to
decreased access to the basic services needed to survive and many individuals and
families fleeing their homes, often to live in temporary situations lacking adequate
support and stability.

Opportunities in the Political Environment   Strategies that social workers employ
to effect political change can involve both education and participation. From an
educational perspective, social workers have long been encouraged to raise the
awareness of client systems, community residents, organizational staff, and policy
makers regarding the realities of the impact of the political system that result in the
inadequacy of the social service systems to meet the needs of people (Reisch, 1997).
From a participant perspective, social workers can engage in the electoral advocacy
and lobbying process by becoming candidates for political office, encouraging
candidates to support issues that are important to the clients served by social
workers, supporting candidates who may be excluded from political office due to
the exorbitant costs of contemporary political campaigns, and working to promote
governmental monitoring of the social service delivery system (Reisch, 2000).

NASW has long been committed to helping social workers be involved in
political activity. Through Political Action for Candidate Election (PACE), national,
state, and local candidates from any party whose political platforms are consistent
with the NASW agenda are endorsed and financially supported. To learn more about
PACE and the candidates supported by this important social work organization,
visit the NASW website at: http://www.socialworkers.org/pace/default.asp.

One of the elected politicians endorsed by PACE is Edolphus "Ed" Towns, a
Democratic Congressman and social worker from New York. In addition to introducing legislation to enact the Dorothy I. Height and Whitney M. Young Jr. Social
Work Reinvestment Act, Towns worked with 53 Congressional colleagues to launch
the Congressional Social Work Caucus. The objectives of this bi-partisan congressional caucus (i.e., a political group or meeting focused on a specific issue) are
(http://www.socialworkreinvestment.org):

- Initiate and support legislation to address the unique challenges and
  opportunities for professional social workers.

- Monitor and evaluate programs and legislation designed to assist and support
  individuals, families, and communities at all income levels who are coping
  with economic, social, and health problems, particularly those with limited
  resources.

- Provide Congressional staff members with educational tools and resources directed toward improving the social work profession and the people social workers serve.

- Assist in education and awareness efforts on the breadth and scope of the social work profession.

At the inaugural event of the Caucus held on World Social Work Day 2011, Congressman Towns shared these inspiring words:

> I am excited about the possibilities for our newly created Congressional Social Work Caucus. This Caucus will provide a platform in the House of Representatives where social workers' voices can be heard, social workers' concerns can be addressed and social work's best and brightest can serve their fellow Americans in meaningful ways. Whitney M. Young spoke many times about how important it is for social workers to tell our story. We want to have a stronger voice in the national conversation about what needs to be done to strengthen families, protect the elderly, and make sure children have the opportunity to prosper. The Congressional Social Work Caucus plans to host a series of public briefings this year to explore the impact professional social workers have on health care, mental health, aging, and child protection outcomes. We want to educate legislators, their staffs, and the public on issues that challenge the social work profession.

To learn more about the work of Congressman Towns and the Caucus, visit the Social Work Reinvestment Initiative website at: http://www.socialworkreinvestment.org.

Social workers can embrace opportunities to influence political decision making through a variety of strategies, including working to increase voter registration and participation, advocating for legislation that supports clients and services, and getting involved in the political process through campaigning, joining PACE or other groups and coalitions working for policy change, and even running for political office. Many social workers organize client groups to engage in advocacy efforts at local, state, and federal levels. Strengthening the role of social work in the public sector can help political leaders understand better the needs of client systems. Such understanding is beneficial when social workers advocate for policy changes.

The ever-changing relationship between the social work profession and the political environment is both frustrating and exhilarating, but the relationship is worth tending. It provides our profession with the opportunity to develop knowledge and skills to serve our clients better (Gibelman, 2004). The Occupy Movement that sprang into being across many U.S. cities during 2011 has now become a new part of the political dialogue for our country that has raised the issue of the wealth gap and provides an opportunity for social workers to engage in the political practice process. The "Occupiers" are challenging the leadership of our country to invest in ecological reforms, electoral changes, and changes to the American infrastructure (Mason, 2012, p. 3). As a voting public, we are being called upon to demand examination of economic inequalities, particularly the causes and economic and social realities of poverty. Policy change begins with a public discussion. Similarly, understanding the impact of global events on social work practice can enable social workers to serve increasingly diverse client systems better. Supporting political efforts to increase international aid for addressing poverty, hunger, and health care access and eliminating government corruption are all strategies consistent with the values of the social work profession.

Economic Environment

Inextricably linked to the political climate, the economy has a powerful influence on the social work profession. Social workers need to understand the U.S. and global economies as they relate to daily work with clients. For example, assisting persons with securing a job depends on overall employment opportunities in a community.

The U.S. economy in recent years has created many difficulties for most of the populace, although the wealthy have continued to do well. Increased social and economic inequities (the rich becoming richer, the poor becoming poorer, and the middle class disappearing) have increased poverty rates for persons of color, children, women, immigrants, and older adults. The severe economic downturn that began in 2007 and continues into 2012 has led many employers to lay off workers, consolidate jobs, use temporary workers who do not receive costly employee benefits, and move companies out of the country to less expensive work environments. Employment instability, particularly in the current period of economic recession, typically results in increased unemployment and underemployment (e.g., temporary workers and working at lower-level positions) and has forced employees to become more flexible, have no assumptions about long-term commitments from employers, and be prepared for longer durations of unemployment, once they are unemployed (Hollister, 2011). Men working in the private sector have been particularly hard hit in the current climate, while employment stability for women has remained somewhat unchanged (likely due to the increase in numbers of women in the workforce) (Hollister, 2011). For social workers, these trends mean more persons with greater economic needs, individuals seeking employment for longer periods of time, families who have lost their homes due to foreclosures, and families living apart due to employment and/or homelessness. Individuals and families who have never previously utilized social services are finding themselves seeking the services of social workers. The U.S. economy in the beginning of the second decade of the 21st century is an unfortunate, but accurate, depiction of this historical trend.

Challenges in the Economic Environment   Economic turbulence has pervasive and challenging implications for social work practice. It seriously affects both the lives of clients and the social worker's ability to provide services. An unstable economy can generate financial, social, and emotional difficulties for clients. Women and persons of color may be particularly vulnerable, as these two groups often have the least stable employment histories and are the first to be laid off in times of economic hardship. Many military veterans returning from serving in overseas deployments are facing challenges in adjusting to civilian life, particularly in the areas of finding employment and reintegrating into their families and communities. President Obama has initiated a plan to create more jobs specifically targeted at military veterans. This program will employ post-9/11 veterans in conservation-related employment, building roads and levees as well as increasing the forces of the country's fire and law enforcement departments.

Social workers whose agencies are experiencing downsizing as a result of decreased funding and private contributions can be faced with larger caseloads and thus have less time to devote to clients. An increased emphasis on cost-effectiveness in social service delivery can result in fewer resources being allocated to clients. The current economic recession has resulted in the majority of state governments proposing to decrease their 2012 state budgets, with most being cut to pre-recession level—cuts will average 10% (adjusting for inflation) (Leachman, Williams, & Johnson, 2011). The overwhelming majority of states that plan to cut public funding have targeted pre-kindergarten through post-secondary education, health care-related programs that will primarily impact persons living on limited incomes, and public welfare programs (Leachman et al., 2011).

A nation's economic policy is key in determining the availability and type of employment, the amount of salaries paid, and the role of the government in employment areas (NASW, 2009–2012a). In the years immediately prior to 2008, there were signs that the economic policy of the previous administration was not working. Increases were seen in the unemployment rates for those with limited income and education levels, food stamp applications, and those living in "deep poverty" (income less than half of the poverty line). The recession that began in 2008 has been doubly challenging due to weakened safety nets in unemployment insurance (despite unemployment benefits being extended to 96 weeks) and cash assistance for families who are poor (Parrott, 2008). At the outset of the current recession, analysts speculated that the number of people, including children, living in poverty would increase. Now that we are several years into the 2008 economic recession, the earlier predictions have, in fact, come true. While the number of children in the United States increased only 3% from 2000 to 2009, the number of children living in poverty increased 18% during the same time period and over 40% of children living in economically struggling families (Annie E. Casey Foundation, 2011). The 2011 Casey Foundation report emphasizes that children growing up in poverty experience problems in a multitude of areas, including school, behavior, and health and, over the course of their lives, they accumulate less education and earnings.

Recent concern about the national debt has further constrained the ability to implement and improve—even to continue—social programs. Some economic experts argue that, along with the economic recession, the tax cuts and military spending perpetuated by the previous presidential administration are responsible for the current and continuing economic deficit (Ruffing & Horney, 2011). Even with the economic recovery and stimulus programs initiated by the Obama administration, the national deficit is the largest the United States has seen since the 1940s (Ruffing & Horney, 2011), poverty rates are at a near-record high, the number of persons lacking health care coverage is at its highest level in recorded history, and those living in deep poverty (annual incomes less than $11,157 for a family of four) are at extremely high levels (Trisi et al., 2011). Never more present than in budgetary debates is the chasm that has emerged between the political conservatives and liberals. Considerable controversy and tension have arisen in the 2012 presidential campaigning regarding the ongoing cost of funding of such social programs as Social Security and Medicare. A longstanding political and economic conflict has surrounded the support of the military conflicts in the Middle East. The economic impact of the billions spent on the second war in Iraq and the U.S. military presence in Afghanistan and the rebuilding efforts in those countries can affect areas ranging from social service funding to the availability of employment for returning service personnel. President Obama's 2011 withdrawal of troops from Iraq and the revamping of the Defense Department budget have further fueled the heightening economic and political maelstrom. Despite slight improvements in the post-recession economic climate, poverty is expected to continue to rise through 2012. With the impact of budget cuts continuing to filter down through the programs, decreases in poverty rates will be slow to emerge (Trisi et al., 2011).

Opportunities in the Economic Environment   A first step in understanding and participating in the economic process is to develop a working knowledge of economics. Understanding economic trends and implications can improve the social worker's ability to serve and advocate for social service resources. Armed with knowledge of social work and economics, social workers can influence the economic system by advocating for **economic justice**—"an ideal condition in which all members of society have the same opportunities to obtain material resources necessary to survive and fulfill their human potentials" (Barker, 2003, p. 137). One example of a political intervention to remedy an economic injustice is the first legislation enacted by the Obama administration. In 2009, the Lilly Ledbetter Fair Pay Act was passed. This law holds employers responsible when they have discriminated against employees in the area of wages.

We can also call for employers to pay a living wage to promote self-sufficiency, which can, in turn, decrease the need for a number of social services (such as financial assistance, housing, and health care). Living wage is defined as the amount needed to ensure that the standard of living for a person/family does not fall below the poverty line. Community-based advocates across the country have equated that amount to be an hourly wage ranging from approximately $7.00 to $12.00 an hour, with many advocating for at least $8.20 an hour in most areas of the country. To learn more about the amount that is considered to be a living wage in your state and county, visit the Pennsylvania State University "Living Wage Calculator" developed by Glasmeier at: http://www.livingwage.geog.psu.edu/. The Calculator will also provide information on the poverty and minimum wages in those areas, taking into consideration the cost of living in that region.

During challenging economic times, social workers have the opportunity and an obligation to develop and learn new practice methods to meet people's needs (McNutt & Floersch, 2008). We can advocate with policy makers to increase opportunities for employment, education, and tax credits and allocations for food, housing, and cash assistance—all areas that can buffer the impact of a recession (Parrott, 2008). For example, in the current economic downturn, social workers can advocate for such large-scale economic changes as the expiration of the tax cuts for the wealthiest of our society, against the dissolution of many workers' rights, and the sustained role of government in social programs, particularly safety-net programs. First, tax cuts that were implemented in 2001 and 2003 by the Bush Administration are set to expire in 2012. The termination of these tax cuts that primarily benefit individuals and couples on the upper end of the economic spectrum would help to offset the national debt and help to restore social spending that has been reduced without stifling the economic recovery process (Ruffing & Horney, 2011). Second, many state legislatures are pursuing legislation that will decrease workers' rights, resulting ultimately in antiunion laws and fewer protections for employees. The role of government in the provision of social programs is a third area in which social workers may serve as advocates and change agents. With many in our country calling for decreased spending for safety-net programs, social workers can attest to the fact that such programs are not just helpful, but necessary for many of those served by our agencies. A sampling of safety-net programs includes: Medicare, Medicaid, school breakfast and lunch programs, and earned income tax credit programs. Once thought to benefit those with the lowest incomes, the majority of persons receiving such benefits are not living at the lowest levels. In fact, nearly half of U.S. households received some form of government help, up from 37% in 1998 (U.S. Census Bureau News, 2010).

In the area of public welfare policies, social workers can embrace a true multicultural vision and point up the failures of policies that separate and isolate ethnic groups. Advocating for interventions that will address issues of foreclosure prevention, health care coverage, and financial and educational interventions is key to tackling some of our current economic struggles, particularly as they relate to children (Annie E. Casey Foundation, 2011). Educating others regarding the relationships among economic instability, decreased resources, and social stressors (such as chemical dependency and addiction, domestic violence, child/older adult abuse and neglect, and mental illness) is another strategy for positively impacting the lives of the clients served by social workers.

Social Impacts of the Environment

Inequality and social justice are continuing themes for social work practice and social policy. A few of the major issues facing those served by social workers include: the aging of the U.S. population, access to adequate health care, lack of upward mobility, housing inadequacies, reintegration of military veterans, increasing issues with substance abuse, lack of tolerance seen through the increase of hate crimes and bullying (in person and digital), and the need for increased knowledge of multicultural issues. The political and economic environments of this decade have introduced a great deal of uncertainty into social life. It is not only politicians who are affected by the hardening of political positions: families and neighbors are finding themselves at odds over issues of social policy, such as reproductive rights (sometimes referred to as "sexual politics") and responsibilities and the role of government in people's lives. In addition, budgetary problems in government, organizations, and households are creating anxieties about spending priorities and economic mobility or lack thereof. Political and economic realities have created considerable uncertainty for people and have led to changes in the way in which we live and relate to one another and the priorities that we establish.

Challenges in the Social Environment   While the social environment is constantly and historically in flux, the current economic and political turbulence has presented social workers with several new and unique challenges. As previously highlighted, the U.S. population is expected to experience considerable growth within the populations of persons of color and older adults over the next several decades. This has significance for the future of social work practice in the area of health care, in particular. Projections suggest that health care needs, particularly for persons of color and older adults, will increase, but the available resources will decrease. The number of older adults living in long-term residential care facilities will increase, requiring considerable increases in both financial support and staff trained in gerontological care areas.

While the early years of the 21st century saw improvements in the number of persons and families with access to health care coverage, the economic recession has resulted in some decreases. Currently, the number of people who have health care coverage through private or employer-based plans has decreased, while coverage through government programs has increased (Bishaw, 2011a). Due to continued workplace downsizing and increasing use of part-time, temporary, and contract workers (who typically do not have employee benefits), these numbers are likely to continue to rise.

Housing inadequacies are also a casualty of the economic turbulence that impacts the social environment. An increase has been reported in the 2010 Census in household "doubling up" (i.e., having at least one additional adult living in the household who is not a spouse or partner). Increases have occurred particularly in adult children living with parents, nearly half of whom would be living below the poverty line were they not living in their parents' homes (Bishaw, 2011a). Mortgage defaults and foreclosure rates have skyrocketed, causing record numbers of families to lose their homes and be forced into living with family or friends, in rental properties, or being homeless. Since 2007, foreclosure rates range from 1% to 13% of the population. The ability to move upward in one's economic standing is virtually impossible when the limited resources available to a family are devoted to acquiring the most basic of needs. Without stable employment, health care coverage, and/or housing, it becomes a challenge to maintain, and virtually impossible to achieve, any level of upward mobility.

While previously mentioned, the reintegration of military veterans presents challenges to social workers in a wide range of settings. Certainly, those social workers working in programs and agencies that serve the military and veteran populations are experiencing increased numbers of clients and, in many cases, are seeing more severe injuries and cases of posttraumatic stress disorders. Social workers in other settings, however, must also be prepared to work with this population and their family members. Social workers working in mental health facilities, domestic violence programs, child welfare, educational and employment programs, programs serving the homeless population, and substance abuse treatment facilities are all seeing increased numbers of veterans seeking their services. Social workers have an obligation to gain knowledge and skills for working with veterans and their families so they may understand better the experiences and the appropriate and effective interventions that will best serve our returning soldiers and their families.

While certainly not a new social problem, substance abuse continues to be a significant challenge for our society and the social work profession, in particular. Approximately 6% of adults living in the United States are thought to have substance abuse addiction (Substance Abuse and Mental Health Services Administration (SAMHSA), 2012). Oftentimes, an addiction co-occurs with a mental illness. Of persons diagnosed with a mental illness, nearly 20% also struggle with an addiction (SAMHSA, 2012). Over one-third of youths (ages 12–17) who report experiencing major depression also report abusing drugs and/or alcohol. While these numbers affect a staggering number of individuals, that is only part of the full picture. Substance abusers are members of families, employees, and friends and their addictions negatively and profoundly impact many who care about and depend on them. Social workers working in essentially every setting are confronted on a regular basis with the challenges of addiction; therefore, they must be competent to address the issues, for both the substance abuser and her/his support network.

As our society becomes more diverse, it stands to reason that we should be more accepting of others. While this statement is true for the most part and we, as a society, have made many strides in our treatment of one another, there are glaring and tragic exceptions. In 2010, the Federal Bureau of Investigation received reports from over 8,200 victims of nearly 7,000 incidents of hate crimes based on race, religion, sexual orientation, ethnicity, or disability. We have to assume that only the most extreme incidents are reported, leaving the vast majority unreported. It is likely those cases that are not elevated to the level of law enforcement that present to social work practitioners. Our responsibilities are not only to act in culturally competent ways ourselves but to support those who have been victims of intolerance and to educate others in understanding diversity.

Each of the social issues described in this section can lead to a host of social and mental health issues that present for social work intervention. Decreased social relationships, which in turn can result in increased isolation, morale problems, and reduced productivity, are just a few of the implications of challenges in the current social environment. Increases in single-parent (mostly female and many persons of color) households will result in greater financial and social service needs. Related to increases in single-parent households, decreases in average household incomes will lead to more households, particularly those with children, being considered "poor." Social workers must have the skill set and the competence to practice effectively in any and all of these areas.

Opportunities in the Social Environment Social workers have the knowledge, skills, values, and the vantage point for creating changes in the social service system to address conditions in the social environment. In building on the earlier discussion on challenges in the current social environment, there are multiple areas in which social workers have had and continue to have the opportunity to engage in change, including:

- We must first consider the demographic makeup of the profession itself. The social work profession continues to be comprised primarily of white and female practitioners. This profile does not adequately reflect the population of the United States or the clients who are served and the profession must strive to recruit a workforce that encompasses greater ethnic, racial, and gender diversity so that we may better serve our clients through service delivery and advocacy (NASW Center for Workforce Studies, n.d.).

- The profession has made a significant commitment to preparing its members for culturally competent practice. Being well trained and receiving ongoing professional development in working with and advocating for diversity is considered essential for all social work professionals (NASW, 2007). Through cultural competence, we have an opportunity to gain insight into our clients' lives.

- Advocating for legislative actions that will address the current social issues that impact clients, whether that is in the areas of reducing poverty, confronting racial/ethnic intolerance, improving access and services for specific client groups, or creating mortgage foreclosure prevention programs. Social workers have the opportunity to help the voices of our clients be heard. Facilitating the passage of legislation and policies to create legal regulations, programs and policies, and interventions are all strategies for strengthening the social service delivery system and enhancing the quality of the lives of those served by the profession.

- Related to cultural competence is the need for social workers to be informed about the needs of specific populations. As discussed throughout this chapter, social workers, regardless of their place of employment, will work with diverse people with a range of needs. Being comfortable and competent to address the issues of persons who are older, veterans, homeless, struggling with addictions and financial issues, or who have been victims of discrimination, bias, crime, or oppression are all required of the social work practitioner.

- Becoming more globally sophisticated in order to intervene successfully with the increasing numbers of clients who live in or have emigrated from other countries. Changes may include self-assessment and expansion of global awareness as well as developing knowledge and skills related to cultural norms, beliefs, behaviors, language, values, culture, and policy (Hoffman et al., 2008).

- Creating more ethnically sensitive social and health care programs that focus on localized community building. Such efforts can help to develop services for the diverse and changing client populations. Such enhancements can help reduce the lack of coordination and communication that currently exists among agencies in the social service delivery system. Clients must often travel to multiple agencies in varying locations to complete applications for services.

Although the future of the social service delivery system seems fraught with challenges, and many social workers currently have diminished resources with which to respond to these challenges, the profession can look to its strengths. The social work profession has always worked to build and strengthen the system for those who count—clients and their communities. Social workers will be participants in shaping the future.

Emily's and her co-workers' concern about communicating effectively with the increasing number of women appearing in emergency rooms who did not speak English led them to face one of the challenges of the changing profile of U.S. society. They saw this situation as an opportunity to assess their own cultural competence and the need for interpreters, develop an in-service training program for staff, determine the availability of interpreting resources, and develop a network of interpreters who could supportively and accurately translate for this client population during times of crisis.

In addition to seeking out training to enhance their knowledge and skills for working with this new population, the staff conducted interviews with agencies that typically provided services to victims of domestic violence—public welfare, health care organizations, schools, mental health agencies, and housing programs—to determine their needs and resources for translation services. Following this assessment, Emily's agency contacted other agencies and organizations that had access to the ethnic communities that spoke the languages of the women who were being abused. As a result, the staff created a database of volunteer interpreters who spoke a variety of languages, and they sent the list to all the organizations that provided services to victims of domestic violence.

As a result of having identified the need for additional training and a new service, Emily and her co-workers became aware of the need for yet further change to support their non-English speaking clients better. Through the coalition that was formed to address the need for interpreters, the group engaged in legislative advocacy at the state level with the aim of seeking legislation that would enable the creation of interpreter services throughout the state.

CONCLUSION

Social work is a profession that functions within the context of the larger society; therefore, social work practitioners must have a comprehensive understanding of the political, economic, and social environment in which their clients live. In addition, our position on the frontlines of social issues creates an obligation to share insights about the political, economic, and social environments with decision and policy makers.

The projections related to shifts in the U.S. demographic profile included in this chapter give you insights into the knowledge and skills that you will need in order to practice social work in the coming decades. You have seen how understanding diverse racial and ethnic groups and their languages and cultures, the needs of older adults and their families and caregivers, and the impact of religious and spiritual beliefs on behavior will be critical in the coming years. These are just a sampling of those competencies needed for effective social work practice.

Social workers must also be vigilant in their efforts to maintain up-to-date knowledge of the political, economic, and social issues that impact their work and their clients' lives. Social work is built on the premise that we can respond to societal needs; therefore, it is our "capacity to change that gives hope for the profession's future" (Kindle, 2006, p. 17). It is for this reason that social work students must take coursework in such areas as economics, political science, and philosophy along with sociology and psychology. Regardless of the path that you pursue in your social work career, responding to contemporary societal issues and advocating for social and economic justice and participating in the political process are going to be a part of virtually every social worker's professional life.

MAIN POINTS

- The demographic profile of the United States is becoming more diverse. To be effective social workers, professionals need to be aware of the trends and to develop the knowledge and skills to work with diverse client systems.

- The largest population growth in U.S. history occurred between 1990 and 2000, with the largest increases being the Hispanic/Latino and Asian populations. The following decade (2000–2010) saw a decreased growth in the population, reminiscent of the 1980s' growth.

- By 2030, nearly one-fourth of the U.S. population will be 65 years or older, with the fastest-growing segment of the older-adult population being in the 85 and older group. Women make up the majority in this age group, and social workers will need to be aware of gender-related issues.

- Religious diversity is increasing and in some cases means increased religious discrimination.

- Social workers remain advocates of social and economic justice while working with individuals and groups that continue to experience discrimination and oppression.

- Both challenges and opportunities exist for the social work profession, specifically within the context of the political, economic, and social changes.

- The political and economic environments, which are fraught with contentious issues and hard choices, are making the social environment more difficult.

- The social work profession has an obligation not only to serve clients but also to advocate for more helpful programs and more equitable policies.

EXERCISES

1. Using the Sanchez family interactive case (www.routledgesw.com/cases), respond to the following:
   a. What are the political, economic, and social issues that are present in this case?
   b. Identify the information from the case that helped you to determine the political, economic, and social issues.
   c. Select one of the policy areas identified and examine the evolution of that issue throughout the case. Identify the relevant societal, economic, political, or religious implications of the policy.

    d. Hector may be laid off from his job at the construction company. Reflect on the implications for Hector and his family if he were to be laid off. What benefits will he/they be eligible to receive? What strengths does Hector possess that will enable him to obtain employment? What barriers exist that may present challenges for Hector in obtaining employment?

2. Understanding the environment in which social workers practice can be complex. Go to the Riverton interactive case at www.routledgesw.com/cases. Upon familiarizing yourself with the community, particularly the Alvadora neighborhood, choose a social, political, or economic perspective and respond to the following:

    a. Describe the community from the perspective that you have chosen.

    b. What are the issues and challenges that exist within the Alvadora neighborhood?

    c. Describe your perspective on the reasons for the presence of the issues and challenges you identified.

    d. Within the perspective that you have selected, identify the opportunities for the Alvadora community.

3. Go to the RAINN interactive case at www.routledgesw.com/cases and take the virtual tour of the RAINN organization. Investigate the resources in your community/region that are available for survivors of sexual assault and molestation. Reflect on your thoughts regarding the benefits and drawbacks of an online versus community-based resource.

4. In an effort to gain insight into the societal and legal protection for gay, lesbian, bisexual, and transgender individuals, search the internet to identify a city or municipality in your state that includes sexual orientation in its city or municipal codes. Write a reflection paper on the number of communities that have included protection for sexual orientation. Are you surprised by your findings?

5. From a recent issue of your local newspaper, identify the key political, economic, and social issues. Reflect on your thoughts regarding whether these issues are consistent with social work concerns.

6. Describe the social class with which you identify and respond to the following:

    a. Do you believe your class influences your attitudes toward others in society?

    b. Do you believe your class influences your behaviors and life choices?

    c. If so, how? If not, explain.

CHAPTER 5

Diversity in Social Work Practice

As a result of increased globalization, enhanced communication, and greater access to transportation, the world in which social workers function has expanded. The population of the United States has become more diverse in the areas of race, ethnicity, culture, age, and sexual orientation. Diversity is a concept that is woven throughout every facet of social work practice. Since practitioners work with the entire spectrum of society, they must possess knowledge and skills to be effective in working with all people, whether they are similar to or different from themselves. Through the accreditation standards for social work education programs, the Council on Social Work Education (CSWE) (2008) requires that students learn about diversity and use knowledge and skills that demonstrate their understanding of and appreciation for diversity.

Competent practice requires social workers to learn continually about other cultures and aspects of a diverse society. The first step in becoming an effective social worker is to embrace **cultural competence** as a vital social work skill. Culturally competent social workers understand the need to address diversity and examine individual awareness and experiences. The social work profession defines cultural competence as:

> the process by which individuals and systems respond respectfully and effectively to people of all cultures, languages, classes, races, ethnic backgrounds, religions, and other diversity factors in a manner that recognizes, affirms, and values the worth of individuals, families, and communities, and protects and preserves the dignity of each. (National Association of Social Workers (NASW), 2007)

Achieving **linguistic competence** is also critical. Linguistic competency is commitment by individuals and organizations to communication that can be understood by all and encompasses strategies such as multicultural staff, language and sign interpreters, multilingual written and electronic materials, and information that is sensitive to a diverse audience (Goode & Jones, 2006). In two policy statements issued by the NASW (2006–2009a), the social work profession is called to view language as one expression of an individual's culture and to promote and support the "implementation of cultural and linguistic competence at three intersecting levels: the individual, institutional, and societal" (p. 81).

In this chapter, we explore the reasons that diversity is a key facet of the profession of social work and the roles that language plays, both negative and positive. We also review the areas of diversity that have presented challenges for social workers and the practice skills necessary for working effectively with diverse client systems.

DIVERSITY AS A COMPONENT OF SOCIAL WORK EDUCATION

One of Emily's child protective service cases provided her with a new perspective on the meaning of culture and family. Emily was assigned to investigate the alleged neglect of Shanté, a 6-year-old African American child who lived with her mother, Jerilyn. Shanté had missed a number of days of school and often came to school unkempt and hungry. During her investigation, Emily learned that Jerilyn had sustained a head injury during a car accident several years earlier and was now living with a physical disability. Until recently, the two had lived with Jerilyn's mother, who had been the primary caregiver for both Jerilyn and Shanté, but the mother had recently died following a stroke. Recognizing that she was unable to care for Shanté, Jerilyn agreed to award custody to her sister Roberta. Roberta lives in the house next door to them.

The case went to court to finalize the custody arrangement, and during Roberta's testimony, the fact emerged that she was not Jerilyn's biological sister. The two women had been lifelong friends and belonged to the same church, one whose members referred to one another with the honorifics of "sister" and "brother." Emily had assumed that sister meant a familial connection because her cultural experiences had not included indepth knowledge of the African American culture or the religion practiced by the two women. From this experience, Emily learned some valuable lessons related to making assumptions, particularly when working with persons whose cultures are different from her own. Ultimately Roberta was awarded custody of Shanté, who was well cared for and saw her mother on a daily basis.

In the United States and other multicultural societies, social workers must learn about the history, beliefs, family structure, religion, dress, food, and lifestyles of all groups with whom they are likely to interact. The NASW *Code of Ethics* (2008) calls for social workers to respect the inherent dignity and worth of a person, to be sensitive to cultural and ethnic diversity, and to work toward ending discrimination, oppression, poverty, and social injustice. The *Code* further directs social workers to understand human behavior within the context of culture. In 2008, language was added to the *Code* that calls on the profession to respect and protect gender identity and immigrant status as well. The *Code* thus binds all social workers to practice without discrimination.

Over 40% of social workers providing direct services work with a caseload that is largely non-Caucasian. Findings from the NASW Center for Workforce Studies (2005) survey of licensed social workers report that groups represented in social work caseloads include clients who are non-Hispanic white (99% of social workers report working with this population); African American (85% of social workers report working with this population); Hispanic (77% of social workers report working with this population); Asian (49% of social workers report working with this population); and Native American (39% of social workers report working with this population). Given that the majority of social workers surveyed report that they serve a racially and ethnically diverse group of clients, it is critical for social workers to possess knowledge of multiple cultures and their values and have the skills to work with individuals from those cultures.

As an extension of the *Code of Ethics*, the NASW membership, in 2001, developed a set of 10 Standards for Cultural Competence in Social Work Practice. Culturally competent practice requires more than knowing about diversity; it requires the ability and skills to take action (Simmons, Diaz, Jackson, & Takahashi, 2008). As an acknowledgment of this premise, in 2007 the profession added indicators for demonstrating the achievement of cultural competence to those standards. The standards and indicators are shown in Quick Guide #4.

QUICK GUIDE #4   Standards and Indicators of Culturally Competent Social Work Practice

STANDARD	INTERPRETATION	INDICATORS
Ethics and values	Within the context of the client system's culture, the profession's values mandate that social workers respect the individual and her or his right to self-determination, and confront any ethical dilemmas that result from conflicts.	Knowledge of the NASW *Code of Ethics* and social justice and human rights principles. Ability to recognize and describe areas of conflict and accommodation in values. Awareness of differences and strengths.
Self-awareness	Culturally competent social workers are responsible for being aware of their own cultural identities as well as "knowing and acknowledging how fears, ignorance, and the 'isms' have influenced their attitudes, beliefs, and feelings."	Examine and describe cultural and social heritage and identities, beliefs, and impacts. Ability to change attitudes and beliefs and increase comfort. Demonstrate understanding of limitations. Work with others to enhance self-awareness.

Cross-cultural knowledge	Baseline and ongoing knowledge of cultures other than one's own is an expected component of culturally competent practice.	Gain knowledge of: client groups, dominant and nondominant groups, privilege, and interactions of cultural systems.
Cross-cultural skills	Because culturally effective social workers intervene with a wide range of people who are different from them, they must remain open to learning new knowledge and skills.	Gain skills to communicate, interact, assess, intervene, and advocate with diverse groups. Effectively use clients' natural supports.
Service delivery	Interacting with co-workers, agencies, and the community to maintain awareness of cultural diversity and to ensure the provision of culturally competent services is critical to effective practice.	Utilize formal and informal community resources. Advocate for and help to build culturally competent services.
Empowerment and advocacy	Within the context of the client system's culture, social workers advocate for and with client systems toward consciousness raising, development of personal power, and social change.	Advocate for culturally respectful policies. Utilize appropriate methods and interventions. Be aware of own values and their impact on client systems.
Diverse workforce	Social workers advocate for maintaining the diversity of the social service delivery system.	Advocate for and support a diverse workforce that reflects the needs of the client systems being served.
Professional education	Social workers advocate for cultural-focused education and training for the social work profession.	Advocate for and participate in education to ensure culturally competent knowledge, skills, and values.
Language diversity	Social workers are obligated to ensure that services are provided in a linguistically competent manner.	Advocate for and implement use of culturally competent written, electronic, and verbal communications.
Cross-cultural leadership	The profession is committed to sharing the profession's values and ethics training knowledge with others.	Social work leaders model cultural competence through interactions, communications, policies, and hiring.

Source: Adapted from NASW, 2007.

As the information in Quick Guide #4 demonstrates, to practice social work with cultural competence, you need an extensive knowledge of persons different from yourself, an awareness and understanding of yourself, and skills that are appropriate for application with persons and groups different from yourself. In essence, cultural competence is the ability to examine your own attitudes, beliefs, and values and to gain knowledge and skills that will enable you to adapt your practice to the unique needs of all clients. Being culturally competent "can mean the difference between a person making it or falling through the cracks" (NASW, n.d.). It is important to note that cultural competence extends beyond racial and ethnic differences to include gender, sexuality, socioeconomic status, place of origin, religious affiliation, and other aspects of diversity.

SELF-AWARENESS: AN EXPLORATION

For those who are members of a majority group in the United States, there is not a "lived experience" of being in a minority group. Think of a time when you felt you stood out or were a minority in a group. What emotions does that memory evoke? Why did you feel different—was it race, gender, age, economic level, religion, sexual orientation, or maybe your dress or speech? What was the outcome of that situation? Getting in touch with the experience and feelings of being different can help you develop empathy for others and their experiences of difference.

While raising your self-awareness about issues of diversity, oppression, discrimination, and social justice is critical for effective social work practice, it can be exhilarating and liberating as you learn more about your own culture and heritage. At the same time, however, delving into your own culture, your place in society, and the impact of your behavior on others can be a painful process, as you may discover biases about which you were unaware.

To understand the meaning of social justice, it is important to identify the ways in which you knowingly or unknowingly speak or act in ways that can result in the discrimination of other persons. You may come to terms with the fact that you have biases (we all do) or that you or others have engaged in or supported behaviors that have been disrespectful or hurtful to others. Recognizing these facts will likely be painful and difficult, but it is an important step toward achieving cultural awareness and sensitivity and, ultimately, cultural competence.

Another useful strategy to heighten your self-awareness is to examine your own diversity and its impact on your life. To identify issues related to your own culture and experiences, consider the questions posed in Exhibit 5.1. Compare your culture to other cultures by considering the similarities and differences in the ways in which you celebrate special occasions, interact with others, and use language to describe your group and other groups, for example.

Having strategies for broadening your awareness of other cultures is also useful in achieving cultural competence. You can use these strategies to acquire knowledge about the practices of other cultures, compare and contrast these practices with those of your own culture(s), and develop an understanding of the culturally competent skills that are needed to be an effective social worker with specific groups. Some suggestions for exposing yourself to new experiences are listed here. Each of these experiences will be most educational and meaningful if you are with other people with whom you can compare observations and feelings.

EXHIBIT 5.1

Self-Awareness of Cultural Identity

Who are you?

With which racial, ethnic, religious, gender, age, social class, and sexual orientation groups do you identify?

Into which of these groups were you born, and which have you joined since birth?

What unique characteristics do your affiliations have that other groups do not?

What do you like about your culture(s)? What do you not like about your culture(s)?

Have you ever experienced discrimination as a result of your affiliation with one or more of the cultures to which you belong?

What was the nature of that discrimination?

Consider the language that you use. What terms do you use to refer to other groups? How do others refer to you?

- Seek out interactions with persons or groups who are different from you. For instance, engage someone you see on a regular basis but have never talked with.

- Attend international festivals, museums, or arts events, and ask questions about the culture. It is ideal to attend an event with someone familiar with that culture or heritage.

- Read a magazine or newspaper targeted to a specific group with whom you are not familiar.

- Attend a service in a religious institution that is new to you. This experience will be even more meaningful if you attend the service with a member of that religious group.

- Read a book that portrays a culture with which you are not familiar.

- Watch a television show or movie in a language other than your first language or one that portrays a culture with which you are not familiar.

- Visit a restaurant or eat food that is new to you (or better yet, organize a potluck gathering in which people bring food of their culture).

- Identify a controversial issue that is currently plaguing society or your community and identify your thoughts and feelings about the issues. Talk with others, seek out information from credible sources on the issues, and reflect on strategies for resolving the dilemma on the individual, community, or societal level.

- Observe the conversations of others: Do they use discriminatory language, make inappropriate jokes, or engage in offensive behaviors? If so, what is your response (or lack of response)? Are you silent and, if so, why?

- Volunteer with an age or a cultural group with whom you have little experience. Senior centers, skilled nursing facilities/adult day care, child day care centers, and programs for persons who are developmentally disabled, new to this country, or experiencing poverty or homelessness are all good choices.

Moving out of your "comfort zone" and having new experiences is a positive step toward understanding more about yourself and your cultural origins. It also serves to expand your comfort zone so that you can be effective with others who are different from you. Gaining cultural competence will be a lifelong endeavor, but one to which we are all obligated.

THEORY THAT HELPS US UNDERSTAND DIVERSITY

In order to practice competently with diverse populations, social workers understand issues related to diversity from multiple perspectives. Having explored these issues from the historical and demographic perspectives in earlier chapters, we will now consider working with diverse populations from social justice and theoretical perspectives.

The social work profession is deeply committed to ensuring social justice for all persons, thus making it important that we utilize the concepts of social justice to guide our work, particularly our work with diverse populations. As we discussed in Chapter 4, many of the clients served by social workers experience oppression and discrimination. Considering oppression as a social justice issue within a theoretical context enables us to view the lived experiences of our clients as a hierarchical dynamic in which one group dominates or disempowers another group (Bell, 2010). Guided by theory, oppression as experienced by our clients can be viewed as "a fusion of institutional and systemic discrimination, personal bias, bigotry, and social prejudice in a complex web of relationships and structures that shade most aspects of life in our society" (Bell, 2010, p. 22). Understanding the ways in which clients' rights and capacities are compromised through oppressive acts and practices can provide the social worker with insights into the cultural, social, and educational experiences that come together to shape clients' lives. Through the use of culturally competent knowledge and skills, social workers can incorporate clients' history of oppression into the assessment and intervention planning.

Let us now consider oppression within the context of two theoretical frameworks that serve as the cornerstones of social work practice: ecological perspective and strengths perspective. These theoretical approaches sensitize social workers to the need to consider cultural information. For example, when working with persons with diverse backgrounds, along with the lived experience related to oppression and discrimination, social workers should note differing home environments and family cultures and identify culturally related strengths in these environments.

The ecological and strengths perspectives are strategies that can guide social workers in providing services to and recommending policies for all clients, but they are particularly helpful in working with clients whose cultural experiences are different from their own. As you come to appreciate the way in which theory can help in conducting an engagement, assessment, intervention, and evaluation, you can focus on the language and challenges of multicultural social work practice.

Ecological Perspective

A longstanding theoretical approach to social work practice that views the client within the context of the environment in which the client lives is known as the **ecological perspective** (Germain & Gitterman, 1980)—also the person-in-environment perspective. The concept of "environment" includes family, work, religion, culture, and life events (for example, developmental issues and life milestones and transitions). This perspective directs the social worker to consider each aspect of the client's life when establishing rapport, conducting an assessment, and developing an intervention plan with the client. It emphasizes the fact that clients' beliefs, emotions, behaviors, and interactions are influenced by their past and present life experiences as well as the larger society in which they live. Within each client encounter, the social worker must be aware of the influence of cultural factors such as race, ethnicity, place of origin, age, gender, social class, religion, and sexual orientation. Culturally competent practitioners incorporate any societal, cultural, and personal influences that impact the client's experience.

A fundamental component of the ecological perspective is recognition of the impact of oppression on the client's life experiences. As an example, imagine that you are a social worker working with a client who is Native American and you are not Native American yourself. Native Americans have long been oppressed by society in areas such as resource allocation, education, and employment. They have been victims of exploitation, abuse, segregation, open hostilities, and violence. In working with the client, you would be remiss if you did not consider the historical, political, and societal issues related to Native Americans, in general, and to individual tribes, in particular. Clients who have experienced institutionalized oppression are likely to feel powerlessness and mistrust, particularly regarding members of the oppressing group. As social workers, we are bound by our *Code of Ethics* not only to oppose such oppression, but to understand its origins and impact, to advocate against it actively and develop interventions that will combat it (Van Soest, 2008).

In building rapport, the effective social worker will gain knowledge of the client's experiences of discrimination and strive to understand the client's values, beliefs, and cultural practices. All of these things impact the client's perspective and interactions with her or his environment. Such sensitivity conveys to the client the social worker's respect for the client's cultural heritage and experience. For example, the social worker assigned to work with a Native American family can be more effective if armed with knowledge about that client's tribal affiliation, history, traditions, and current issues.

Strengths-Based Perspective

A concept embedded within the ecological perspective is the **strengths-based perspective**. Viewing the client's cultural experiences and beliefs as strengths on which to build is an extension of the ecological model. The strengths-based perspective is particularly important for practicing social work with cultural competence (Saleebey, 2006). Using a strengths perspective, the social work relationship is built around the experience and life of the client, thus demonstrating respect for culture, lifestyle, and client right to self-determination. Framing cultural diversity issues as part of the client environment provides the social worker with additional resources for understanding the stressors being experienced by the client, aids in building rapport and trust, and contributes to culturally appropriate intervention plans.

Too often in the past, practitioners have seen culture, ethnicity, religion, and sexual orientation as irrelevant, different (a deficit), or an area for change, rather than as an asset or resource in problem solving. Incorporating the client's cultural characteristics and experiences into the intervention strategy as a strength is consistent with the social work value of respecting each individual's uniqueness and worth. Applying the knowledge and skills of the strengths-based perspective along with those of culturally competent practice, social workers can promote a multicultural environment.

Consider a scenario in which you are a social worker working with an older Jewish woman who, as a child following World War II, immigrated to this country from Europe. She is a widow and a retired teacher who lives alone and has no immediate family nearby. Since the death of her husband, she has become more withdrawn, and you are concerned that she is depressed. While conducting an assessment, you learn that she is a survivor of the Holocaust and the concentration camps. You help her to see her life experiences as a resource for educating others about the atrocities committed during the Holocaust, and you arrange for her to join a speaker's bureau for the local Jewish Community Center. She travels to schools to share her story with children, most of whom have never met a Holocaust survivor. Her depression dissipates; she is now feeling useful because she is using her skills as a teacher and her life experiences as a survivor.

While client disempowerment as the result of oppression and discrimination is certainly not viewed as a strength, consider, however, this paradigm shift. Your client's negative and, likely, painful experience can become an opportunity for growth. Utilizing the strengths perspective as the basis for reframing the past as experiences from which the client can identify ways in which she or he endured and grew can help the client view her- or himself as a competent person who has the capacity to achieve goals and can, in fact, be immensely empowering.

THE "ISMS"

Throughout history, social workers have been on the forefront of challenging certain ever-present "**isms**"—doctrines, causes, or theories that motivate behavior. Although "isms" can be positive or neutral belief systems (for example, patriotism or romanticism), to social workers they typically imply negative attitudes or beliefs regarding a specific population of people. The "isms" that social workers most frequently encounter are **racism**, ageism, sexism, classism, ableism, and heterosexism, and religious discrimination.

Once a person has been identified as a member of a vulnerable group, society tends to view that person only by her or his membership in that group. For example, a person with a physical disability is often viewed only as a person with a disability and not in light of other roles and memberships, such as parent, teacher, or employee. As you read the following sections, keep in mind that each group comprises individuals who are also members of other groups. We are more than our race, age, gender, social class, abilities, sexual orientation, or religious affiliations. Known as intersectionality, an issue related to the theoretical approaches to working with marginalized populations is the intersection of the multiple dimensions of diversity (e.g., race, class, and gender). This concept helps us gain insight into the fact that most diversity encompasses a complex range of issues, not just one, and they come together to create the lived experience.

The following discussion is not intended to be an all-inclusive list of "isms" but rather a sampling of those areas that social workers encounter on a routine basis. Awareness and knowledge of these isms are part of becoming a culturally competent social worker. Because the demographic characteristics of the United States are changing, social workers are also responsible for keeping abreast of changing attitudes and preferences among the population as a whole and among their clients.

Racism

Probably the most common "ism" challenging modern-day society is racism, which results from the categorization and stereotyping of groups by racial characteristics or ethnic origins. Whether on a personal or societal level, racism is defined as the belief that one group is superior to another group(s) based solely on race. Racism in its most extreme form is typically perpetrated by a majority or dominant culture and serves to segregate, isolate, and disempower a minority or less powerful group of people. In the United States, the Caucasian population has historically held the majority position due to population composition, but as demographic trends indicate, the population ratios are changing. However, that change has not resulted in the end of racism (NASW, 2012–2014k). Anti-immigrant sentiment, which is often based on racism, continues to exist in areas such as access to social services, education, and housing. Whether it is perpetrated at a conscious or unconscious level, racism has consequences for both the dominators and those persons being oppressed (Bell, 2010).

Racism has permeated essentially every aspect of U.S. society. Racism exists on two levels: **institutional racism** and individual racism. Institutional racism refers to discrimination against persons of color in accessing resources such as employment, education, financial assistance and credit, organizational membership, and home ownership. It is built into the system and becomes nearly invisible to those who benefit from the status quo. Institutional racism can be difficult to change for a host of reasons: it typically is longstanding; individuals do not feel empowered to affect an actual change; institutions are slow to change; and institutional racism is usually complex and reinforced by society (Diller, 2007). Discriminating against a group (e.g., African Americans or Hispanic Americans) in mortgage lending to prevent ownership in certain communities is one example of institutional racism. In contrast, individual racism is abuse or mistreatment propagated by a person or group. For example, the uttering of a racial slur by one person to another is individual racism.

Over the past 50 years, U.S. society has dramatically modified its definitions of and approaches to race-related issues. During the mid 20th century, a "melting pot" approach, in which sameness among the races was emphasized, aimed at creating a society in which all cultures become blended into a single culture without the distinctions of diversity. Not all segments of society embraced such an approach; for example, most southern U.S. states embraced a forced segregation approach, and many members of minority racial and ethnic groups, such as Latinos, wanted to retain elements of their own cultural identity. Then, during the late 1950s and 1960s, support grew for an approach that embraced a "world of difference" focused on racial uniqueness. However, others within the civil rights movement advocated for total racial integration.

The decades of the 1970s and 1980s began to emphasize a multiculturalist perspective that valued individual ethnicities. This perspective met with intense intellectual and political opposition from persons and groups that wanted to maintain racial separateness. For some, this view again shifted during the 1990s to a pluralistic conceptualization in which people exist within a society of groups that are distinctive in ethnic origin, cultural patterns, and relationships. As evidenced by the NASW's 2012–2014 policy statement, the social work profession embraces an "inclusive, multicultural society in which racial, ethnic, class, sexual orientation, age, physical and mental ability, religion and spirituality, gender and other cultural and social identifies are valued and respected" (NASW, 2012–2014k, p. 285). At the end of the first decade of this century, the social work profession has continued to refine the approach to gaining cultural competence. This is guided by an ethnocultural framework that recognizes that culture shapes us and competence evolves from the client's opportunity to develop a narrative that tells the story of her or his lived experience (Kohli, Huber, & Faul, 2010). To this end, NASW has also developed a policy statement that calls for human service programs to work to preserve cultural and linguistic diversity through policies, printed materials, and services (NASW, 2012–2014f).

Racial issues can evoke intense emotional reactions. Most people have been either a victim or perpetrator of racist thoughts or behaviors, and many people have been both at one time or another. Some students, both white students and students of color, report being uncomfortable in a classroom in which racism is discussed because of shame related to the behaviors of their racial group, anger regarding the treatment of persons of color, or resentment toward students who have not experienced discrimination. However, when students agree to create a safe environment in which issues, and not people, are confronted, they can initiate stimulating and meaningful discussions. As long as we remain open to expanding our cultural awareness and sensitivity, the social work classroom can be an excellent environment in which to learn and grow. Known as critical multiculturalism, this approach goes beyond race to include education on culture, oppression, multiple identities, power, whiteness and privilege, historical context, and social change (Daniel, 2008).

The status of racial justice at the beginning of the 21st century remains controversial and is, as yet, undetermined. While considerable strides have been made by society and the social work profession in recent years to eradicate racism, we are reminded to continue our efforts (Blank, 2006). Social workers can confront racism in many ways. The most obvious strategies include advocacy, education, and, sometimes, mediation (for example, serving as an agent to promote effective communication). To be effective in any of these areas, social workers must be willing to recognize areas in which their own knowledge and skills are lacking. (Exhibit 5.2 presents many of the terms that must be used correctly in discussing racism.) We must ask ourselves if we are

EXHIBIT 5.2

Terminology Related to Race and Ethnicity

- **Accommodation:** Efforts of a dominant group to make changes to enable another group to live within society—for example, offering printed materials in multiple languages to enable persons whose first language is not English.
- **Acculturation:** Socialization of the dominant culture into the values, beliefs, and behaviors of another culture.
- **Assimilation:** Adoption of the dominant group's cultural practices (including values, norms, and behaviors) by another group—for example, the "Americanization" of refugees when they immigrate to the United States.
- **Bias (prejudice):** Positive or negative prejudgments or attitudes toward a person, group, or idea, typically based on misperceptions and not on fact or evidence.
- **Color:** Despite political, social, and emotional connotations, literally the pigmentation of a person's skin.
- **Culture:** Social construct encompassing issues such as race, ethnicity, and group membership; defined by the many characteristics and components possessed by a group, such as values, beliefs, religious and political tenets, rituals and other behaviors, and artifacts; and used in interacting, communicating, and interpreting information (Okun et al., 1999).
- **Ethnicity:** Aspect of one's identity characterized by national origin, culture, race, language, and religious beliefs and practices.
- **Ethnocentrism:** Belief that one's culture is the norm (and thus, typically, superior) and that other cultures with different practices or beliefs are therefore outside the norm (Okun et al., 1999).
- **Integration:** Bringing together of diverse groups as equals in institutions such as public schools, the military, and the workplace.
- **Marginalization:** Subordination of individuals or groups who possess less power, due to the perpetuation of stereotypes and oppression.
- **Multicultural competence (multiculturalism):** Practice of understanding, recognizing, and respecting the cultural values, beliefs, and behaviors of others.
- **Pluralism:** Belief that all groups have value and a basis for understanding the way members of a society interact with one another and the environments in which they live (Logan, 2003).
- **Race:** Human characteristics that can be determined by physical traits (such as skin color or hair texture).

- The 2010 Census uses five racial categories for the U.S. population:

  o **White**—origins in Europe, the Middle East, or North Africa.

  o **Black or African American**—origins in any of the black racial groups of Africa.

  o **American Indian or Alaska Native**—origins in any of the original peoples of North, Central, or South America and who maintains tribal affiliation or community attachment.

  o **Asian**—origins in any of the original peoples of the Far East, Southeast Asia, or the Indian subcontinent, including Cambodia, China, India, Japan, Korea, Malaysia, Pakistan, the Philippines Islands, Thailand, and Vietnam.

  o **Native Hawaiian or Other Pacific Islander**—origins in any of the original peoples of Hawaii, Guam, Samoa, or other Pacific Islands.

- **Segregation:** Racial and religious segregation—the separation of one group from other groups; institutionalized racial and religious segregation is currently unlawful but many other forms of segregation, whether institutionalized or informal, are not.

- **Social class:** An individual's or group's standing in the social hierarchy based on characteristics such as income, status, and education.

- **Stereotype:** Assumption that a person possesses the same characteristics as all other individuals within his or her group.

EXHIBIT 5.2

continued

implementing approaches that take into consideration the culture of the client (Golden, 2008). Social workers confront racial injustices at any and all levels and areas of practice, and we must all ask what our role is in promoting justice.

Ageism

When most people hear the term *ageism*, they immediately think of the mistreatment of older adults. In fact, ageism refers to discrimination based on *any* age. The two groups most at risk for age bias and discrimination are children and older adults. Being on the two ends of the age spectrum places these groups in vulnerable positions regarding access to resources. Moreover—and perhaps even worse—the two groups are sometimes pitted against each other when resources are allocated.

The sheer number of older persons has risen and will continue to rise dramatically. Their collective "voices" are increasingly being heard, in part because they have become highly organized and are diligent advocates for their own rights and benefits. Even so, older adults continue to need support from social workers and others who will advocate on their behalf. Children have a difficult time being heard by policy makers and funders and must depend on adults to champion their causes.

While we all have experienced being on the youthful end of the age spectrum, most of us have yet to experience life as an older adult. Therefore, we rely on our perceptions of older adults, which may be biased and stereotypical. In one study of social work students' perceptions of themselves at age 75, most students expected to have health and memory problems, but would still be attractive, valued, and active (Kane, 2008). To better understand the needs of older adults whom you will encounter in your social work practice, consider how you see yourself as an older adult and how you would like to be perceived.

Dealing effectively with ageism begins on a personal level. Conduct an inventory of your ageist experiences:

- Have you ever purchased a greeting card that lamented the fact the person was over the hill?

- Have you ever been dismissed by someone because you were too young (or too old) to understand something?

- Have you heard or made stereotypical remarks about the driving abilities of either young or old people?

- Have you ever referred to a person's age in a derogatory manner—"geezer" or "baby," for instance?

As a part of any diversity self-awareness campaign, checking ourselves and our society on ageism issues is our obligation as social workers. In social work specifically, all practitioners are ethically bound to acquire knowledge and skills that will enable them to be effective in working with persons of any age.

Sexism

Sexism is typically defined as the belief that men are superior to women as a result of gender. Based on that concept, sexism occurs when women are discriminated against because they are women. While sexism or gender bias is usually male-to-female, men can be the victims of sexism as well. Consider the online interactive case in which Hector Sanchez is disapproving of his son's desire to engage in cooking, which he considers "unmanly." Despite the fact that men can be the targets of sexist acts, the majority of sexism is directed toward women, which will be the focus of our discussion here.

Historically, there are numerous examples of institutionally enforced sexism that have been directed toward women: Women could not own property, vote, run for public office, or divorce their husbands, and they were prevented from being trained in many professions. Although our nation has made considerable strides toward improving the status of women, significant gender-based inequities remain:

- Women's earnings continue to be lower than men's for the same positions.

- Women are still in the minority in most traditionally male-dominated professions (such as medicine, engineering, and politics), and when women achieve a major presence within a professional discipline, the salaries of both men and women tend to decrease.

- The majority of persons who are victims of violence or living in poverty (particularly for female-headed households) continue to be women.

Although equal employment and sexual harassment policies have eradicated institutional sexism, other forms of sexism continue to exist but appear to have gone "underground." For example, both genders continue to make sexist remarks, particularly in the areas of domestic and sexual violence, clothing, and behaviors. When women engage in traditionally male activities, they may be criticized, particularly when the women excel in the activity. Women continue to function as the primary caregivers for the family, even when they work full-time outside the home.

An interplay of characteristics makes many women doubly vulnerable to discrimination and oppression (Worden, 2007). Consider the female client who is also a woman of color, a religious minority, or economically disadvantaged and the way in which those factors impact her life experience and self-perception.

Social workers have an ethical responsibility to address issues of gender equality for all women. Gender is significant in the areas of employment, public assistance programs, education, health and mental health, and global women's issues. NASW, in the 2012–2014 policy statement, calls for equity and social and economic justice in these areas (NASW, 2012–2014p). Social workers can work to prevent sex discrimination by dispelling stereotypes and myths about women's rights and abilities. Social workers can also empower women by informing them that they do not have to let a sexual assault go unreported or remain in a violent relationship. Social workers can work at the policy level to ensure that policies are crafted to guarantee gender equity. Every social worker can write letters to the media when women are portrayed unfairly, stereotypically, or as inferior to men. You might take a minute to consider other types of activities that you can do to combat sexism.

Classism

Although some philosophers have claimed that the United States should be a classless society, the reality is that our society has distinct classes that have evolved over time to include class-related values, expectations, beliefs, and lifestyles (Okun, Fried & Okun, 1999). Classism, or discrimination based on social class, can occur as a result of occupational status (for example, blue collar or white collar), educational achievement (for example, high school diploma or college graduate), or income (for example, working class or middle class).

Social class is used prejudicially as a mechanism for labeling people. Some people believe that membership in a particular socioeconomic class is based on the person's willingness to work hard—the philosophy of pulling yourself up by your bootstraps. They tend to characterize people on the low end of the economic continuum as simply lacking ambition, without consideration for factors such as race, ethnicity, gender, disability, and access to resources and opportunities. As described in Chapter 4, the distinctions between the richest and the poorest in our society continue to become more extreme. With the overwhelming majority of resources being held by a small percent of the population and the middle socio-economic class shrinking, those on the lowest end of the economic spectrum have less and less opportunity to affect their financial status positively.

Your experiences with and views on socioeconomic class are yet another issue to consider as you conduct your diversity self-assessment. Consider the following messages that you have received throughout your life regarding social class and income:

- Have you ever thought about the socioeconomic class into which you were born? If not, in which class does your family of origin belong?

- Do you continue to be a member of that class? If you have changed socioeconomic class, how did that occur?

- What does membership in your socioeconomic class, or any other socioeconomic class, mean in terms of your education, resources, opportunities, place of residence, and employment?

- Have you been a victim of classist remarks, or (be honest here) have you made classist remarks?

- Do you perceive a difference between those students whose parents pay for college and those students who must take out loans?

As with all the isms, the social worker's role in combating classism is often one of advocacy and education. Countering the "bootstrap" myth, empowering people to reach their optimal functioning and quality of life, and confronting classist language are just three anticlassism activities in which social workers can engage proactively.

Ableism

Ableism is discrimination against individuals who have disabilities in the areas of intel-lectual/cognitive, emotional, and physical functioning. Disabilities can be perceptual, illness-related, physical, developmental, psychiatric, psychological, mobility-related, or environmental (for example, allergies). Unfortunately, U.S. society has oppressed this population for centuries, from the language used to refer to a person with a disability, to the restriction of access to schools and buildings, and to the penchant for "warehousing" people with disabilities in institutions and separate schools.

Despite the fact that many in our country will experience a disability within our lifetime, it has only been in recent years that ableism has been considered in areas such as policy making, funding, and public sensitivity. Over a dozen major legis-lative acts have been passed since the 1970s (NASW, 2012–2014h). In particular, two legislative mandates, the Rehabilitation Act of 1973 and the Americans with Disabilities Act of 1990, established institutional support for the civil rights of, and supportive accommodations and services for, persons with a wide range of disabilities.

Throughout history, society has used and misused a variety of terms to describe groups that are different from one another. Think for a moment of all the disability-related terms you have heard throughout your lifetime. Exhibit 5.3 lists some common terms and provides alternative language, or "words with dignity," that is less likely to offend people with different abilities. You should also be aware that some disability advocates are challenging the use of some of the entries in the exhibit (Mackelprang, Patchner, DeWeaver, Clute, & Sullivan, 2008). They contend that

WORDS WITH DIGNITY	AVOID THESE WORDS	**EXHIBIT 5.3**
Person with a disability, disabled	Cripple, handicapped, handicap, invalid (literally, invalid means "not valid")	*Substitutes for Ableist Terms*
Person who has, person with (e.g. person who has cerebral palsy)	Victim, afflicted with (e.g. victim of cerebral palsy)	
Uses a wheelchair	Restricted, confined to a wheelchair, wheel-chair bound (the chair enables mobility; without the chair, the person is confined to bed)	
Non-disabled	Normal (referring to nondisabled persons as "normal" insinuates that people with disabilities are abnormal)	
Deaf, does not voice for themselves, nonvocal	Deaf mute, deaf and dumb	
Disabled since birth, born with	Birth defect	
Psychiatric history, psychiatric disability, emotional disorder, mental illness	Crazy, insane, lunatic, mental patient, wacko	
Epilepsy, seizures	Fits	
Learning disability, mental retardation, developmental delay, ADD/ADHD	Slow, retarded, lazy, stupid, underachiever	

Other terms which should be avoided because they have negative connotations and tend to evoke pity and fear include: abnormal, burden, condition, deformed, differently abled, disfigured, handi-capable, imbecile, incapacitated, madman, maimed, manic, moron, palsied, pathetic, physically challenged, pitiful, poor, spastic, stricken with, suffer, tragedy, unfortunate, and victim.

Preferred terminology: blind (no visual capability), legally blind, low vision (some visual capability), hard of hearing (some hearing capability), hearing loss, hemiplegia (paralysis of one side of the body), paraplegia (loss of function in the lower body only), quadriplegia (paralysis of both arms and legs), residual limb (post-amputation of a limb).

ADD/ADHD, attention deficit disorder/attention deficit hyperactivity disorder.

Source: Paraquad, n.d.

disabilities are a form of diversity, not a pathology. Generally, using **person-first language** is considered most appropriate; for example, saying, "he is a person with a disability," instead of "the disabled man."

In striving to eradicate ableism, the social work profession has long championed equity, respect, and physical accommodation. Although our society has made strides in many areas—particularly education, accessibility, employment, and benefits—the professional challenge is to continue to draw attention to the abilities and strengths of persons with different abilities. The following are principles of practice to keep in mind when working with persons with disabilities (Mackelprang & Salsgiver, 2009, pp. 436–438):

- All people are capable or potentially capable.

- Disability does not imply dysfunction; persons with disabilities do not need to be "fixed" in order to function in society.

- Disabilities are a social construct, and interventions therefore must target the political barriers that exist within the environmental, attitudinal, and policy arenas.

- Despite having different disabilities, persons living with disabilities have a common history and culture resulting in a shared experience.

- Persons with disabilities should be viewed as different, not dysfunctional.

- Persons with disabilities have a right to self-determination.

As with other isms, social workers are ethically obligated to be on the cutting edge of services and resources for persons with disabilities. They must also combat both the use of inappropriate language and discrimination in the provision of services. Finally, they should fight to ensure the rights of any person with a disability.

Heterosexism

Heterosexism, the belief that heterosexuality is the only acceptable form of sexual orientation, exists at all levels of our society and is perpetuated formally and informally. A nonheterosexual orientation continues to be considered by many people to be a choice, a defect, or a perversion and therefore "curable." As a result of heterosexism, lesbians, gay men, bisexuals, and transgender persons (persons whose gender identity is counter to their presumed biological sex) (LGBT) have been prohibited in the not too distant past from employment in many areas, from legally marrying, from adopting children as a couple, from receiving partner benefits, from serving in the military if they disclose their sexual orientation, and from making legal and medical decisions for their partners. The LGBT community has often been the victim of hate crimes that range from verbal harassment to physical assaults, or "gay bashing," and to murder. As a result of the overwhelming biases that have prevailed in our society, these groups have historically been highly reluctant to disclose their sexual orientation in any but the safest places, often not even "coming out" to their families, co-workers, or some friends.

Recent years have seen significant progress in the area of gay rights. Same-sex households were counted in the 2010 Census, numbering approximately 600,000 (Lofquist, 2011). The recognition of same-sex partners and marriages by some states and employers is one example of the progress made. At the beginning of this century, same-sex marriage was not recognized in any state, but in 2012, seven states and the District of Columbia have legalized same-sex marriage, five states support civil unions, and 13 states are addressing the issue either through legislative proposals or lawsuits. In 2011, the U.S. military ended its "don't ask, don't tell" policy and thus made the burden of being identified as homosexual less onerous for members of the military. Despite these gains, there are still areas in which members of the LGBT community face discrimination. Over 30 states have laws defining marriage as legal only between men and women.

More than with most of the other isms, talking about homosexuality makes some people uncomfortable. Talking about sexuality, in general, is awkward for many of us, but a lack of knowledge, fear of offending the person, deep-rooted religious beliefs, or even fears about our own sexuality make talking about homosexuality particularly difficult for some of us. In fact, for some students, their first social work course might also be the first time that they engage in a discussion in which homosexuality is not framed as deviant. Social work classrooms can be a safe place to share thoughts and feelings about working with sexual orientation issues.

As it has for other social work issues, the NASW formally took, in two separate policy statements, a stand against LGBT discrimination and prejudice in areas such as inheritance, insurance, marriage, child custody, employment, credit, immigration, health and mental health services, and education (NASW, 2012–2014g, n). To become culturally competent to intervene successfully with LGBT clients, social workers must be mindful of the historical issues that surround the oppression of this population. Adhering to the values of the social work profession, social workers' stance should be a "celebration of the strengths of this largely invisible minority," not just an acceptance or tolerance of them (Boes & van Wormer, 2009, p. 938). Social workers must also (Gates, 2006):

- Learn and use appropriate language.

- Be open to understanding differences.

- See beyond the person's sexual orientation.

- Confront organizations' heterosexist policies and eligibility criteria and ensure LGBT-inclusive language and materials.

- Advocate for equality and respect in legislation, policies, service delivery, and practices for these groups.

Religious Discrimination

Religious oppression and discrimination have existed for thousands of years, largely because of religionism (religious zeal or the belief that religions other than one's own are inferior). People have been persecuted for practicing a variety of religions by being segregated from the rest of the population, denied employment, and even tortured and killed. Religious discrimination has taken the form of formally and informally restricted educational and employment, political, and social opportunities. The Holocaust, which targeted primarily people of the Jewish faith, is the most notorious example of religionism in the recent past.

Despite the U.S.'s constitutional value of freedom of religion and a population adhering to a wide variety of religious affiliations, the United States is far from being free of religious segregation and discrimination. The events of September 11, 2001, for example, prompted a rash of discrimination directed toward Muslims. The terrorists who led the attack were Muslims. Although their actions were vehemently criticized by many Muslim faith leaders, Muslims in the United States have been subjected to physical, verbal, and written assaults, threats against their lives, and damage to their businesses and homes. Muslims are an example of the "racialization" that has occurred for various groups who identify themselves primarily by their religious affiliation as opposed to their race or ethnicity (Adams & Joshi, 2010, p. 232). This attitude has led to a need to separate religion from political, ideological, and cultural conflicts.

Although religion has always been a part of the lives of the people served by social workers, religion has not always been included in mainstream social work education and practice. Another strong American value, secularism (broadly, the separation of church and state), has led many social workers to avoid the topic of religion, with the positive goal of reducing discrimination based on religion. However, in recent years social workers have recognized the important role that religion and spirituality play in their clients' lives. Consequently, they have begun to incorporate these issues into their assessments and intervention plans. Along with knowledge of biological, sociological, cultural, and psychological development across the lifespan, knowledge of spiritual development is now required content in CSWE-accredited programs.

The profession recognizes that the "faith life" of a client can be an important component of the social worker–client relationship. Considering the client's religious and spiritual beliefs within the context of the strengths-based perspective can enable both the client and the social worker to utilize these aspects of the client's life in a positive way (Casio, 2012). Exploring, supporting, and connecting the client's spiritual beliefs and faith life can lead to a more effective intervention strategy. For example, when working with persons around death and dying issues, it can be important for the social worker to view the client's faith beliefs as a source of coping. As the profession continues to integrate faith beliefs into social work practice, social workers are exploring issues of religion and spirituality on both personal and professional levels. Although social workers cannot possibly be knowledgeable about all of the world's religions, they are professionally bound to consider each client's faith life as part of the client's environment and to learn the influence of faith, religion, and spirituality.

Intersectionality

This review of "isms" has provided insights into an array of challenges faced by the clients served by social workers. As noted earlier, these experiences often encompass multiple and complex types of oppressive and discriminatory experiences. Having the lived experience of intersecting dynamics has the potential to influence multiple aspects of clients' lives, but does not need to be immobilizing. As an example, we need to understand the complex interrelationships that occur when intersections occur between religion and ethnicity, class, gender, and nationalism and the impact this has on the individuals and groups involved (Adams & Joshi, 2010). Collins (2010) offers the following strategies for creating social change through intersectionality:

- Acknowledge that personal experiences with power and privilege (regardless of the experience) contribute to challenges in relating to others, but are responsible for the individuals we have become.

- Building alliances with others who have common experiences that cut across boundaries and differences can promote feelings of empathy toward others.

- Based on individual experiences with oppression and discrimination, we can develop empathy for individuals and groups by assuming responsiblity for our own actions. Building empathy for others can contribute to becoming a more knowledgeable and culturally competent social work practitioner.

THE CULTURALLY COMPETENT SOCIAL WORKER

During the time Emily worked in the domestic violence program, she encountered a particularly challenging cultural dilemma that involved ethnicity, religion, and gender issues. Through the intervention of a neighbor, a woman who was a recent immigrant from South Asia and had limited English-speaking skills sought protection from the shelter. When she was presented with the option of pursuing an Order of Protection through the court system, she stated that a legal order would have little to no influence with her husband. She told Emily and the staff that the only person who could help influence her husband would be the local leader of her faith community. She believed that her husband would be more responsive to the faith leader's rule than a court judge.

Emily's responsibilities in this situation were to conduct an assessment, offer the services of the domestic violence program, explore options for safety, and develop an intervention plan if the woman would agree to it. Being unfamiliar with the client's religion and customs, Emily was uncertain how to proceed. She consulted with her supervisor and together they contacted the religious leader, who then intervened on behalf of Emily's client.

Consider for a moment the cultural competency skills that Emily was required to demonstrate in this situation:

- Knowledge of the client's faith beliefs, traditions, and values, particularly as they relate to women, marriage, and domestic violence.

- Ability to communicate with a reluctant person in crisis through an interpreter.

- Ability to relate to a woman whose values and religious beliefs differed dramatically from Emily's views on women, marriage, and violence.

- Willingness to affirm the woman's right to self-determination when she opted not to pursue legal intervention and to return to the violent situation.

As Emily's experience depicts, culturally competent practice comprises skills at multiple levels: cognitive (knowledge of diversity history and issues), affective (emotional), and behavioral (language and communication skills) (Schlesinger & Devore, 1995). An effective practitioner possesses a high level of awareness in each area as well as a commitment to the idea that cultural competence is a lifelong learning process that can be both challenging and rewarding. You may want to begin your journey to cultural competence by acknowledging that you are feeling fear or anxiety about the process of becoming culturally competent. An array of challenges lie ahead, including the fact that much of the information you need to gain is unknown, you will make mistakes, your old beliefs will require examination, and the work may take an emotional toll on you (Diller, 2007). Rest assured that, while these fears are legitimate, the journey will be worth the effort if you are honest and realistic about your feelings and beliefs and make a commitment to gaining competence.

The following discussion is intended to heighten your sensitivity regarding the basic practice skills in awareness, language, and communication that are critical for a multiculturalist approach to social work. This approach is based on the premises that cultural reality is socially constructed and unique to the individual experiencing it, worldviews should be appreciated, people experience multiple cultural realities, and the role of the social worker is to identify client strengths so the client may be empowered to overcome painful experiences (Kohli et al., 2010, p. 266). The skills offered here are not specific to any particular group, because diversity within client populations does not allow a "cookbook" approach to social work practice (Congress, 2009; Colon, Appleby, & Hamilton, 2007; Dunn, 2002).

Cultural Awareness

Increased self-awareness and knowledge of your own identity are the first steps in cultural awareness. Key skill areas include:

- Every social worker–client relationship is a cross-cultural experience in that everyone has distinct cultures and backgrounds.

- Recognize that cultural characteristics and differences can be a resource in the helping process.

- Do not assume anything based on the client's membership in a particular group. You can assume there is as much diversity within a culture as there is between cultures.

- If you share membership in a cultural group with the client, do not assume that you have anything else in common. Likewise, do not assume that you have nothing in common with a client who is in a different group than you.

- Recognize that the client with whom you work may be uncomfortable with your cultural differences.

- Stay in touch with your own beliefs at all times—your biases and lack of knowledge as well as feelings of comfort.

- Before you encounter a client or situation, identify the knowledge and skills that you may need. For instance, do you need to arrange for an interpreter, do you need information on religious practices, or do you need to ensure that the meeting location is accessible for the client(s)?

- If interpretation is needed, try to find someone other than a family member, particularly a child, to provide interpretation unless it is appropriate or necessary.

- Approach your assessment from a cultural diversity perspective and include topics such as place of origin, reason for relocation, language(s) spoken, and beliefs about health, illness, family, holidays, religion, education, and work. The **culturagram** (Congress, 2009) is one tool that can be used to conduct a culturally focused assessment. Designed as a strategy for engaging and assessing the experience of immigrant families, in particular, the culturagram provides information useful for developing interventions by highlighting the family's past and current experiences, values, and family strengths (Congress, 2009). See Exhibit 5.4 for more information on the culturagram.

EXHIBIT 5.4

Culturagram for Immigrant or Refugee Family

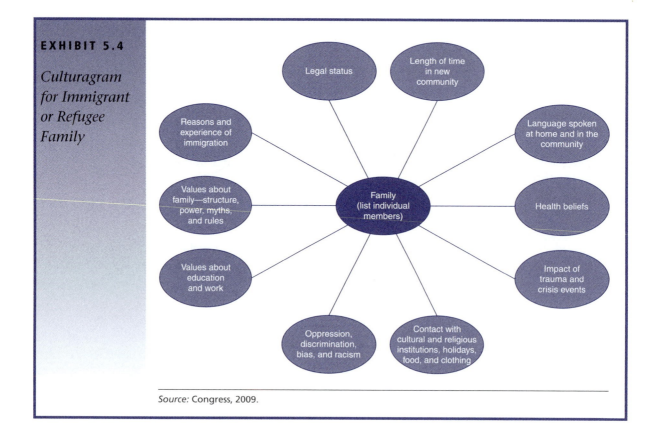

Source: Congress, 2009.

• Monitor your communication style and the ways in which your verbal and nonverbal behaviors could be interpreted. For example, do you speak too quickly to be clearly understood by a person who is just learning English? Are you uncomfortable when people you do not know well get too physically close to you?

• Know that you will make mistakes, and be open to the possibility that the client can teach you about diversity and help you learn from your mistakes. When you make a mistake, do not attempt to cover it up. Rather, acknowledge the mistake, and take the opportunity to learn a better way to interact.

Your level of awareness may be different in certain areas of diversity, such as sexual orientation, age, or social class. While each area of diversity requires specialized knowledge and skill, working with clients who identify as being multiracial may challenge your cultural competence. With approximately 3% of the U.S. population reporting one or more racial categories (Humes, Jones, & Ramirez, 2011), social workers need to expand traditional approaches which do not include multiracial awareness. Using a culturally attuned ecological approach, the social worker can work with clients to identify gains and challenges of being multiracial and connect with their multiracial legacy (Jackson & Samuels, 2011).

If you wish to work toward more cultural awareness, you might find the action continuum, shown in Exhibit 5.5, a useful tool. Ask yourself these questions: (1) Where are you on the continuum now? (2) Where would you like to be? (3) What will help you move to the next step?

Language and Communication Skills

As you have observed throughout this chapter, language and communication are particularly challenging areas of culturally competent practice. Language is intricately tied to the culture of any group. It is a powerful mechanism for imparting positive and negative messages, and for this reason it can serve both to perpetuate oppression and discrimination and to demonstrate respect and sensitivity. Therefore, social workers are responsible for using appropriate and culturally sensitive language and communication whenever they refer or speak to any group.

Social workers must always be mindful of using language that is preferred by the group being addressed. Doing so helps to create a safe environment for the client that will foster trust and build rapport. Although slang may be acceptable in certain settings, society and, in particular, social workers often struggle with using slang appropriately. More mainstream language is a safer alternative. Slang terms change, they have regional connotations, and they are heard differently depending on the speaker.

Effective multicultural practitioners also possess practice skills that enable them to communicate sensitively with diverse groups. When in doubt regarding the most appropriate language, you have several options for obtaining more information. You can ask other professionals who work with the population or persons who are members of the cultural group with whom you are working to serve as your cultural guide. In cases in which you have established a rapport with the client, you may ask the client for help in understanding appropriate language. In addition, pay particular attention to the opening of any encounter with a client by introducing yourself by name and title, referring to an adult client using an honorific that is respectful and culturally appropriate (for example, Mr., Mrs., or Ms.), and clarifying the pronunciation of the person's name and desired address. Then inquire about the person's culture, specifically the preferred name of the group in which the person is a member (for example, Indian versus Native American).

Here are further suggestions for communicating sensitively:

- Balance the use of professional language and language that is familiar to the client. Clients may misunderstand or be offended by professional jargon (particularly medical or legal terminology or acronyms), slang, or colloquialisms.

- Be genuine in your use of language and style of communication, particularly avoiding words or behaviors with which you are not familiar.

EXHIBIT 5.5

*Action
Continuum:
From
Discrimination
to Respect*

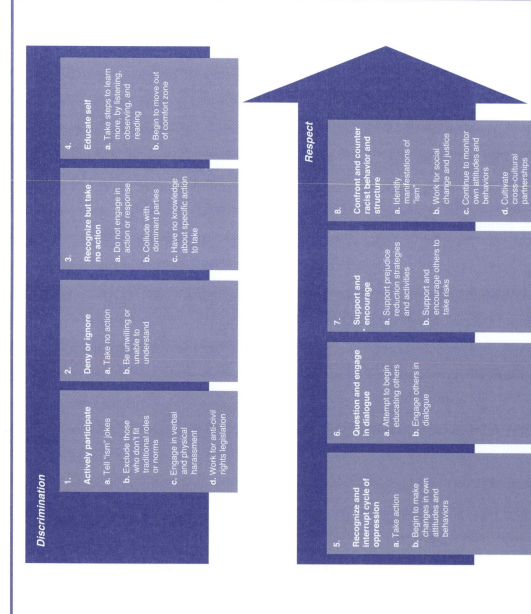

Discrimination

1.

Actively participate

a. Tell "ism" jokes

b. Exclude those who don't fit traditional roles or norms

c. Engage in verbal and physical harassment

d. Work for anti-civil rights legislation

2.

Deny or ignore

a. Take no action

b. Be unwilling or unable to understand

3.

Recognize but take no action

a. Do not engage in action or response

b. Collude with dominant parties

c. Have no knowledge about specific action to take

4.

Educate self

a. Take steps to learn more, by listening, observing, and reading

b. Begin to move out of comfort zone

Respect

5.

Recognize and interrupt cycle of oppression

a. Take action

b. Begin to make changes in own attitudes and behaviors

6.

Question and engage in dialogue

a. Attempt to begin educating others

b. Engage others in dialogue

7.

Support and encourage

a. Support prejudice reduction strategies and activities

b. Support and encourage others to take risks

8.

Confront and counter racist behavior and structure

a. Identify manifestations of "ism"

b. Work for social change and justice

c. Continue to monitor own attitudes and behaviors

d. Cultivate cross-cultural partnerships

e. Work for anti-civil rights legislation

Source: Adapted from the National Conference for Community and Justice—St. Louis Region. Developed by Roni Branding, 2002.

- Be aware of the meanings that different cultures attach to certain nonverbal behaviors. These meanings may be assigned or interpreted based on traditions, thus resulting in a misunderstanding (Okun et al., 1999). For example, eye contact may be interpreted as an invitation to continue speaking or as a sign of sexual interest, aggression, respect, or disrespect. Similarly, silence and facial and physical expressions convey different messages depending on the individual's culture, ranging from discomfort to anger to respect. Finally, space and physical touch can be interpreted as intimacy, aggression, or dominance based on cultural definitions.

- Be sensitive and aware of a person's culture, but do not discuss it unless it is relevant to the situation. For example, a disability or sexual orientation may not be pertinent to the reason for your encounter. Therefore, there is no need to focus the professional relationship on that aspect of the person's life.

- To avoid labeling, use person-first language, which refers first to the person and then to the situation (for example, "person with a disability" instead of "disabled person" or "person from the Middle East" rather than "Middle Easterner"). Referring accurately to the client's cultural background may include, for example, Asian American (citizen or born in the United States) or Asian (international person or non-U.S. citizen).

- Check regularly with a person whose culture is different from your own to ensure that she or he has understood what you have said or meant. Ask the person to repeat her or his understanding of the content of the conversation. This strategy will prevent you from assuming that you are being understood simply because the person nods in assent.

- If you are unsure of the meaning of a word, phrase, or behavior used by the client, ask the client in a nonjudgmental, nonpatronizing way to explain the meaning.

CONCLUSION

We have explored a range of issues related to diversity and culturally competent social work practice. Like other aspects of social work practice, cultural competence requires that you continually seek out knowledge, skills, and self-insights. Being an expert in all areas of diversity is impossible, but social workers are obligated to acquire as much information as possible about the populations that are living in their communities and to whom they are providing services. Culturally competent practice means being proactive and assertive in your efforts to understand other cultures. Clients bring a rich and inspirational history of diversity and can serve as teachers for the social worker who views that diversity as a strength.

Let us end this chapter with William M. Chace's 1989 perspective on diversity:

Diversity,
Generally understood and embraced, is not casual liberal tolerance of anything and everything not yourself. It is not polite accommodation. Instead, diversity is, in action, the sometimes painful awareness that other people, other races, other voices, other habits of mind, have as much integrity of being, as much claim upon the world, as you do. No one has an obligation greater than your own to change, or yield, or to assimilate into the mass. The irreconcilable is as much a part of social life as the congenial. Being strong in life is being strong amid differences while accepting the fact that your own self can be a considerable imposition upon everyone you meet. I urge you to consider your own oddity before you are troubled or offended by that of others. And I urge you, amid all the differences present to the eye and mind, to reach out and create the bonds that will sustain the commonwealth that will protect us all. We are meant to be together.

MAIN POINTS

- Culturally competent social work practice is the ability to work respectfully and effectively with all persons. A key element is developing insights into your own beliefs and values regarding culture—your own and that of others—and continually learning about others.

- Social workers must routinely conduct a "reality check" regarding their beliefs and actions related to working with persons different from themselves as well as persons from similar backgrounds as themselves.

- Within the context of the theory of oppression and social justice, two theoretical frameworks, the ecological and strengths-based perspectives, help social workers understand and work with clients who are different from themselves.

- Understanding the isms and the dimensions of intersectionality faced by many cultures in our society helps social workers to be more sensitive to people of different races, ages, and abilities.

- Language and communication in all forms play a major role in both oppression and the work of building respect for diverse groups.

EXERCISES

1. Using the Sanchez family interactive case (www.routledgesw.com/cases), review the case file for Vicki Sanchez. Answer Vicki's Critical Thinking Questions. Next,

review the case file for Hector Sanchez and answer Hector's Critical Thinking Questions.

2. Using the Sanchez family case, imagine that you are a social worker newly assigned to work with Hector and Celia on the adoption of their grandson, Joey. Based on your own cultural heritage, select a description from the general list below:

- You are not of Hispanic or Latino origin and have had little experience with this population.

- You are not of Hispanic or Latino origin, but have had some experience with the Hispanic population and have limited Spanish-speaking skills.

- Your ethnic background is of Latino origin, but you have not lived in or near a Latino community.

- Your ethnic and cultural background is Latino. You speak fluent Spanish and your upbringing is similar to that of the Sanchez children.

Having identified your personal characteristics as they relate to the Sanchez family, consider the following social work skill issues:

a. What are the differences that you may encounter?
b. What are the similarities that you may encounter?
c. What are your feelings about working with the Sanchez family, including stereotypes, biases, feelings of familiarity, or anxiety?
d. Given your knowledge of the Latino culture (or lack of knowledge), what information, knowledge, or skills do you need to acquire before meeting with the Sanchez family?
e. How might you respond if you make a cultural mistake (speak or behave in such a way that you offend the person(s))?
f. What might you ask the Sanchez family to help you in establishing a rapport?
g. Who or what resource can be helpful to you in preparing for your meeting with the Sanchez family?
h. If you do not speak Spanish, how will you communicate with Celia? If you are bilingual, will you speak in Spanish or English? How will you determine which is appropriate?

Although your responses to the above questions are speculative at this point, you have engaged in an exercise that is critical to becoming an effective and culturally competent social worker.

3. Using the Carla Washburn interactive case (www.routledgesw.com/cases), write a narrative description of Mrs. Washburn and her current situation. Review your narrative for any evidence of ageist terms or attitudes. If evidence of ageism is noted, rewrite your description of Mrs. Washburn from an ageist-free perspective. Lastly, write a brief reflection on this experience (i.e., how were you ageist, what are the origins of your ageist attitudes, etc.).

4. In order to understand better the origins of your thoughts, feelings, and stereo-types about the diverse range of persons in our society, consider each of the social groups listed in Exhibit 5.6 and the sources of your information about each group. List the specific information you gained from each of the sources in the two categories on the right of the table.

5. Consider an experience that you have had with diversity at any point in your life. This experience may be one in which you were the recipient or perpetrator of discrimination or oppression, or an experience in which you felt uncomfortable

EXHIBIT 5.6

Things I Have Learned About Diverse Groups

SOCIAL GROUP	LEARNED FROM FAMILY, TEACHERS, AND FRIENDS	LEARNED FROM MEDIA*
African Americans		
American Indians		
Asian Americans		
European Americans		
Hawaiians and Pacific Islanders		
Hispanics and Latino Americans		
Persons of dual racial heritage		
Men		
Women		
Young adults		
Older adults		
Persons with disabilities		
Persons who are economically disadvantaged		
Persons who are affluent		
Persons who are gay, lesbian, bisexual, or transgender		
Persons who practice religions other than my own		
Muslim Americans		
Other†		

* Media can include television, radio, internet, magazines, and advertisements.
† Fill in other groups you have learned about.

Source: Adapted from the National Conference for Community and Justice—St. Louis Region.

due to your lack of familiarity with the situation or person(s). After you have identified the experience, write a narrative that includes the following:

a. A description of the experience.
b. What was uncomfortable, awkward, or painful about this situation?
c. Which of the "isms" is relevant to this situation? Why?
d. How did you respond to the experience?
e. If you were to encounter this situation again, would you respond differently? Why? How?
f. How might this experience influence your future professional life?

Now that you have completed this portion of the exercise, stop and read the narrative that you have written and answer these questions:

g. Did you learn anything new about yourself?
h. Have you changed since this experience? How?
i. What would you say to someone else who has had this experience?
j. What culturally competent skills did you use? If you were to encounter this situation again, which culturally competent skills would you use?

You have begun a lifelong journey of self-reflection that is essential for culturally competent social work practice. You can continue to use this exercise as you encounter future issues of diversity.

6. In an effort to gain further insight into yourself, respond to the following:

a. When you see an older adult in a wheelchair, what are your thoughts?
b. When you see someone who is cognitively impaired, what is your reaction?
c. When you are on public transportation and you are sitting next to a person with a developmental disability or a possible mental illness, how do you react? What are your feelings in this situation?
d. When you see a person with Down syndrome, what is your reaction?
e. When you see two persons of the same gender walking down the street holding hands, what is your reaction?
f. Can you think of other situations that have made you feel uncomfortable about the other person's differences from you or from those with whom you interact most frequently?

Once you have considered your responses to the above questions, identify the culturally competent skills that you feel you possess. How did you gain these skills? What skills do you lack?

7. Personal reflection: Identify an area, event, or situation related to diversity (racial, ethnic, religious, economic, gender, age, sexual orientation) that has challenged you. Describe your response, how you might respond differently in the future, and how this experience may impact your professional work.

CHAPTER 6

Values and Ethics in Social Work Practice

Emily faced a difficult situation while completing the community service requirement for her introductory social work course at Oasis House, a shelter for persons who are homeless. She was in the recreation room of the shelter talking with one of the residents, Lorinda, a single mother with two young children. Emily had talked with Lorinda on several previous occasions and felt a special bond with her. Lorinda and Emily were the same age and had many similar interests. They had both been on their high school track teams and had competed in the same events. During one conversation, Lorinda asked Emily for money. Lorinda told Emily that she needed the money to help her boyfriend get bus money to get back home. He had gone to another city to look for work so he could earn money and send for Lorinda and the children. He had not found a job and had no money for the trip back. Lorinda assured Emily that she would repay the money as soon as she and her boyfriend had jobs.

Emily did not know what to do. She liked Lorinda and wanted to help her, but was not sure that she should give Lorinda her own money. What would you do in this situation?

The situation that Emily encountered is considered an **ethical dilemma**, a commonplace occurrence in the social work profession. An ethical dilemma exists when the social worker "must choose between two or more relevant, but contradictory, ethical directives, or when every alternative results in an undesirable outcome for one or more persons" (Dolgoff, Loewenberg, & Harrington, 2012, p. 10). A dilemma can occur when a social worker experiences a conflict between at least two of the profession's ethical principles and standards. Areas of practice challenges can include the birth of a child, loss of a loved one, natural disasters, child or older adult abuse, neglect, or exploitation; mental or physical illness; financial or housing needs; discrimination; and domestic violence. Such value-laden issues create the potential for an ethical dilemma to occur because the social worker may have to involve authorities, challenge the client's choices, or confront an injustice.

When a social worker intervenes in a situation, several value systems and ethical practices are already in place. Specifically, the values and ethics of the social worker, client, agency, and society are all present, and they impact the social work intervention and outcome. In this chapter, we focus on values and ethics and the ways in which they relate to social work practice. We will begin our exploration of this topic by defining the terms and highlighting the reasons that values and ethics are central to competent social work practice. As part of this process we will consider the National Association of Social Workers (NASW) *Code of Ethics* (2008). You will have an opportunity to examine your own values and to apply social work values and ethics to challenging social work practice.

SOCIAL WORK'S COMMITMENT TO VALUES AND ETHICS

National events determine our ideals, as much as
our ideals determine national events.
—JANE ADDAMS

Values can be defined as a society's system of beliefs, principles, and traditions that guide behaviors and practices. You might also think of values as the ideals by which we live. For example, the social work profession believes that all people have a right to access the resources needed to optimize their quality of life. Values are important because they are implanted in us so thoroughly and, in turn, the impact of our values is significant for those we encounter and for society as a whole. To rephrase the quotation from Jane Addams, our values are shaped by society and society is shaped by our values.

The definition of **ethics** is somewhat different. Ethics are defined as: "a system of moral principles and perceptions about right versus wrong and the resulting philosophy of conduct that is practiced by an individual, group, profession, or culture" (Barker, 2003, p. 147). Ethics are a critical part of the social work profession as they provide the professional moral compass for social work practice. In a sense, values are the inner beliefs and ethics are the guidelines for action and behavior. Each of us possesses a personal value system (i.e., beliefs) that informs and shapes the way in which we interact with the world around us (i.e., our ethical standards and behaviors). As we develop into social work practitioners, we incorporate the values of the profession, and commit to complying with the ethical standards established and endorsed by the members of the profession. In essence, the relationship between values and ethics is one that begins at the intellectual and emotional level where we develop our value systems and is operationalized through our attitudes, words, behaviors, and practices as we act out our ethical standards and responsibilities.

Values and ethics are different but closely related. As one example, the social work profession has turned the value regarding access to resources into a professional ethic by advocating with policy makers for groups marginalized by society.

For example, social workers advocate for families living on limited incomes to gain better access to resources.

Value and ethical issues are present in every encounter that a social worker has with a client. The role of the social worker may be to advocate for a client's rights, to help the client access information and resources, or to assist the client in enhancing her or his quality of life. Therefore, at this level, a competent social work practitioner is aware of value and ethical issues and the implications of those values and ethics on the social work intervention. In the area of policy practice, social workers may advocate to ensure that policies are ethically administered to all eligible recipients. For example, a number of states have recently cut Temporary Assistance to Needy Families benefits, resulting in hundreds of thousands of individuals losing their access to benefits. Social workers can advocate with their states' legislatures to prevent the decreases in state spending for children and families living in or near poverty.

In order to approach an ethical dilemma or value conflict, social workers need to understand the value systems of all involved: themselves, clients, agency of employment, profession, and the larger society. Although social workers are not expected to *share* the value systems of their clients, they are ethically bound to *respect* the value systems of others. In fact, experiencing a "gap" between your values and those of your clients is a common occurrence and likely to be unavoidable (Dolgoff et al., 2012, p. 109). Having insight into the client's value system can help to ensure that social workers do not unknowingly discriminate against a client through inappropriate language or behavior. Moreover, it helps social workers to understand the client's decision-making processes, choices and behaviors, and patterns of functioning and dysfunction.

This is the first step toward a resolution of an ethical challenge. The social worker does not attempt to change the client by imposing her or his values on the client, but instead strives to understand and respect the client's values.

VALUES IN SOCIAL WORK

Every client with whom a social worker interacts is different, and each conflicted situation is unique. Therefore, a social worker cannot formulate blanket responses to ethical dilemmas or value conflicts. Instead, social workers are mindful of the client's values as well as any ethical implications that may result from the social worker–client relationship. The social work profession has also developed several ways of looking at values. These frameworks may help you understand the types of issues that you may encounter.

One approach to understanding the importance of values in the social work profession is a historical perspective. In response to changes in the political, economic, and social environment, the profession's values moved through four phases (Reamer, 2009b):

1. *Morality period* of the late 19th century, in which the client's morals were of primary interest.

2. *Values period* of the 20th century focused on the profession's development of core values.

3. *Ethical theory and decision-making period* of the latter 20th century emphasized the development of guidelines and protocols for responding to ethical dilemmas.

4. *Ethical standards and risk management* period, in which conduct and malpractice are currently emphasized.

This evolution has enabled the profession to establish a core set of values, processes for ethical practice, and guidelines for protecting clients. In these early years of the 21st century, the evolution of the social work profession still encompasses aspects of the ethical theory and decision-making period and has, by necessity, incorporated a risk management perspective. We continue to look to ethically based theoretical frameworks and our ethical code to guide practice, but we are obligated to adhere to ethical standards that will provide legal safeguards for both our clients and ourselves.

More than a century of focus on values and ethics has also highlighted awareness of the complex nature of social work. Social workers are knowledgeable about values at several levels. One popular model delineates values by level of involvement (Dolgoff et al., 2012):

- *Individual or personal values:* the values of one person.

- *Group values:* the values of groups within society (for example, religious and ethnic groups).

- *Societal values:* the primary values of the larger social system.

- *Professional values:* the values of a specific discipline or professional group.

Having a conceptual basis for understanding your own, your client's, and societal values can help you to interpret the inevitable value conflicts that you will encounter as a social worker.

Value Conflicts

After Emily graduated with her BSW degree, she secured her first social work position. Finally, she was going to be in a position to really help people. Her first social work job was in the adult social service unit of a multiservice public community agency. When she interviewed for this position, she was told she would be working as a case manager with older adults to help them maintain their independent living situations.

Emily enjoyed this position for 3 years, until the agency overhauled the structure of its social services. All workers became "generic" workers, handling both child and adult services. Emily found herself being assigned child protection cases, in which she investigated allegations of abuse and neglect, testified in court, and often recommended that the child be removed from the home and placed in foster care. For the first time in her career, Emily felt conflicted regarding her role as a social worker. She felt her lack of knowledge about and interest in working with children and their parents would hamper her ability to serve the best interests of the clients.

Emily experienced a **value conflict**—a situation in which a social worker's values (or "shoulds") clash with the value system of a client, agency, co-worker, or society in general. In this case, Emily's dilemma was the result of her adherence to both the social work value and ethical principle of practicing only in her areas of competence.

Value conflicts present themselves in many different forms and may have no easy, clear, or acceptable resolution. You cannot possibly anticipate all the potential conflicts that await you, but you can anticipate that such conflicts will arise, and you can prepare yourself by developing a set of skills to respond to them when they do. When personal and professional values conflict, we are obligated to apply our professional values and ethics to all practice situations (Comartin & Gonzáles-Prendes, 2011).

Recognizing that value conflicts are an inevitable part of the social work intervention, developing a plan for your response can be helpful. Here is one possible approach (Dolgoff et al., 2012, p. 109):

1. Identify the conflicting values and consider the impact of the conflict on your client and yourself.

2. If possible, frame the problem so that the value conflict is not relevant.

3. Clarify the connection between the value differences and the reason the client has presented to you.

4. Begin the intervention by addressing issues that do not include the value conflict.

5. Engage in a discussion with the client regarding the difference so a joint decision can be made to determine if the differences will negatively affect the working relationship.

6. Determine if you can continue to work with the client or if you should refer the client to another professional.

The following sections describe some value conflicts that you may encounter as a social work professional.

Job-Related Value Conflicts   Emily's conflict is one example of a situation in which the social worker's value system comes into conflict with the duties that she or he has been hired to perform. Because social workers intervene in settings in which they assume a position of authority over the client, such conflicts are not uncommon. Possible settings for value conflicts include the public welfare system, the criminal justice system, for example, an incarceration facility, a residential care facility, or an agency to which clients are mandated for social work services by the judicial or legal system. Social workers working in host settings (organizations whose primary service is not social work, such as schools, hospitals, or the court system) can find that their values are in conflict with that of their employer. While all professionals who work in these settings are there to serve the client or patient population, the avenues for fulfilling that goal can come into conflict with those of their co-workers' disciplines.

Value conflicts can also arise when social workers find themselves in the role of an authority or "pseudo-cop" (Baldino, 2000, p. 25). Pseudo-cop social workers may be torn, for example, between their duty to comply with the court's directives and their obligation to support their client. For social workers who find themselves in such a dilemma, observing and seeking the wisdom of other experienced workers in similar settings can be an effective strategy for gaining perspective and competence in this role.

Unethical or impaired behavior on the part of a co-worker may also create value conflicts. Consider a scenario in which you learn that a co-worker's drug or alcohol use is beginning to impair his ability to perform his job duties. Consider also the co-worker who defames or discriminates against clients and co-workers. What is your personal and professional obligation in these situations? Is it acceptable for you to look the other way? Do you confront the co-worker or report your suspicions to a supervisor? As a social work professional, you consider the potential conflict between your personal loyalty to a co-worker and the profession in the area of unethical or dangerous behavior (NASW, 2008).

Value Conflicts Related to Religion or Spirituality and Belief   Many people are drawn to the social work profession out of a sense of religious or spiritual calling or obligation or as a result of experiences related to their religious or spiritual beliefs. A number of social work practitioners are employed by faith-based organizations that espouse a religious mission and philosophy. Ideally, social workers in these situations will work with clients and colleagues who share their religious beliefs. Although many social workers find that practicing social work and their religion or spirituality go hand in hand, others experience conflicts between the two.

In reality, religious differences are common, even in situations in which the client or colleague is of the same faith as the social worker. A value conflict can occur when the religious beliefs of the client and the social worker impede their ability to work together effectively or when the religious beliefs of the social worker and the agency conflict. For example, consider a situation in which the worker's position on abortion is pro-life and the client is seeking an abortion.

Although social workers are trained to maintain emotional objectivity, issues related to religious beliefs and practices are areas in which the social worker's experiences may be an asset for effective practice. For example, consider a situation in which a client appears to be resistant to the professional's suggestions for intervention. If the social worker is familiar with the client's religious or spiritual beliefs, she is more likely to understand that the client's lack of cooperation is not resistance at all, but rather an expression of the client's religious beliefs, which make it impossible for the client to comply (Williams & Smolak, 2007).

Value Conflicts Over Limited Resources The social work profession values each person's right to have access to resources to optimize her or his quality of life. Although society as a whole supports this value, heated debates occur at the personal and policy levels regarding the distribution of those resources, most of which are limited.

One example is the value held by many people that persons living in poverty do not deserve a "handout" but instead should have to work "like the rest of us" for their living. This value can be translated into an anti-poor attitude and further into supporting political candidates who oppose welfare. Social work students may struggle with this particular issue, which actually may be a conflict between values to which they have been exposed and different value systems that they are encountering in social work classes.

The Social Worker's Values

Although social work training emphasizes being nonjudgmental and objective, the reality is that you cannot "check your values at the door." Your value system reflects the influences of the family who reared you; your friends and peers; your educational, religious, spiritual, social, and professional experiences; and your formal social work training. You bring your value system into each and every social work situation. Before you can begin to determine strategies for understanding and working with the value systems of clients, agencies, or society, you must consider your own value system, its origins, and the implications of your values for your life and your future practice.

Throughout the history of social work, some social workers have espoused the views that social work practice should be value-free and that values do not affect social work practice (Dolgoff et al., 2012). Over time, however, most social workers have recognized that personal, group, and societal values do influence their work. The challenge for the profession then becomes to enable social work students and practitioners to explore and clarify their own values, understand the profession's values, and acquire skills for ethical social work practice.

An important step in understanding values and their impact on ethical behavior is to clarify your own values. **Values clarification** is the process of exploring your values and comparing them to others for the purpose of developing an appreciation and respect for your values and the values of others (Barker, 2003). Clarifying your values does not mean that you automatically change them. In fact, taking the risk to learn other perspectives may confirm your commitment to your values. Sometimes, however, as you are exposed to new and different ideas or provided with different information, your previous perspective can be expanded or altered. The key is your willingness to risk change by exposing yourself to other views and value systems that may differ from your own. An ongoing commitment to developing self-awareness regarding your values and biases can help to reach clarity regarding practice approaches and interventions. Without some level of resolution by the social worker, the client may be negatively impacted (Comartin & Gonzáles-Prendes, 2011)

Some people might go so far as to argue that attaining a social work degree is, in fact, an ongoing exercise in values clarification. As a social work student, you will find that your value system will constantly be challenged through your discussions with faculty and fellow students, readings, assignments, and field experiences. You can begin the process of clarifying your values by starting with casual conversations or issues that arise in your classes. Part of the process of understanding your own values is taking the risk of hearing ideas that are different from your own. Although that may not be a comfortable situation, it is an important process to engage in during your training so that you will be more comfortable and aware once you become a practitioner. Although you will continually encounter new situations throughout your career, you will eventually develop a strategy and a comfort level for these situations. Valutis and colleagues (2011) report that learning about and clarifying value and ethical beliefs is related to one's age as opposed to academic class standing; therefore strategies for promoting effective learning and practice include being proactive in learning about the range of others' values and planning to engage in learning throughout one's career. Utilizing your support system of colleagues, supervisors, and mentors can aid in exploring and processing values conflicts.

When you are involved in a conversation regarding ethics, you can initiate the process of clarifying your values by asking yourself these questions:

- What do I think about this issue?

- What are the origins of my values on this issue?

- What are the other person's values on this issue? Are our values similar or different? If they are different, does this difference create a dilemma for me? For the two of us?

ETHICS IN SOCIAL WORK

> *Action indeed is the sole medium of expression for ethics.*
> —JANE ADDAMS

As you read this book, I hope that you have questioned why the social work profession needs to dictate appropriate professional behavior. After all, do we not all become social workers because we are altruistic and giving persons? If this is true, then why should we require a formal document to guide and monitor our practice? The fact is that, as the complexity of the social worker's job has increased, so has the potential for ethical dilemmas. When faced with multiple alternatives, directions, or potential contradictions of ethical principles, social workers can use a set of guidelines in establishing an intervention that serves the best interests of the client and the system in a manner that is consistent with present-day cultural demands (Dolgoff et al., 2012).

Many professions have developed a standardized approach, or a code of ethics, to guide their members in establishing a competent and effective practice. By definition, a **code of ethics** is a document, created by the members of the profession, that provides specific guidelines for appropriate and expected professional behaviors. These behavioral expectations are rooted in the values and ethical standards deemed acceptable by the profession.

The social work profession's current interest in codifying values and ethical practice has been formalized largely since the 1960s and 1970s. This emphasis on a formal code of ethics may be due, in part, to societal changes that have affected the clients served by social workers. Advances in areas such as medicine (for example, treatments, technology, and disease awareness), electronic technology, global awareness, resource management, and the social work mission continue to prompt social workers to consider the impact of these developments on their clients (Reamer, 2008b).

The social work profession has several codes aimed at promoting ethical practice. The most widely known, the NASW *Code of Ethics*, referred to many times in this book, was developed to specify clearly expected professional conduct for the members of the association. Other social work organizations have developed codes of ethics that are similar in intent to the NASW's but are specific to their organizational mission and membership. For example, the *Code of Ethics* of the National Association of Black Social Workers (NABSW) embraces a commitment to "protect the security of the Black community, and to serve as advocates to relieve suffering of Black people by any means necessary" (NABSW, n.d.).

Most social workers view the codes as guides for their professional behavior, but many practitioners also recognize that even a well-developed, professionally binding code has its limitations. The standards are broad in nature and leave particular situations open to interpretation. Nevertheless, the NASW code remains the best resource to consult when you are faced with an ethical dilemma.

NASW *Code of Ethics*

The NASW Delegate Assembly, a body of NASW members elected by their state chapters, meets once every 3 years to debate and vote on NASW policies, including the *Code of Ethics*. The initial NASW *Code of Ethics*, accepted by the membership in 1960, emphasized the primacy of professional responsibility over personal interests, the client's right to privacy, obligations for service during public emergencies, and a duty to contribute to the knowledge of the profession (Reamer, 2008a). Recognizing that social work changes as society changes, NASW has revised the *Code* several times since its inception in 1960, most recently in 1999 and 2008. The current version mirrors the earlier documents, although it is longer and uses more legal terms.

Organization of the *Code of Ethics*   The NASW *Code of Ethics* addresses a range of broad but important—and sometimes controversial—behaviors and practices. It consists of four sections: preamble, purpose, values and ethical principles, and ethical standards.

The preamble outlines the mission and core values of the social work profession. As stated in the 2008 *Code of Ethics*:

- The mission of the social work profession is to enhance human well-being and help meet the basic human needs of all people, with particular attention to the needs and empowerment of people who are vulnerable, oppressed, and living in poverty.

- A historic and defining feature of social work is the profession's focus on individual well-being in a social context and the well-being of society.

- Fundamental to social work is attention to the environmental forces that create, contribute to, and address problems in living.

- Social workers promote social justice and social change with and on behalf of clients. "Clients" is used inclusively to refer to individuals, families, groups, organizations, and communities.

- Social workers are sensitive to cultural and ethnic diversity and strive to end discrimination, oppression, poverty, and other forms of social injustice.

- Social work activities may be in the form of direct practice, community organizing, supervision, consultation, administration, advocacy, social and political action, policy development and implementation, education, research, and evaluation.

- Social workers seek to enhance the capacity of people to address their own needs.

- Social workers also seek to promote the responsiveness of organizations, communities, and other social institutions to individuals' needs and social problems.

- Social work's **core values** are service, social justice, dignity and worth of the person, importance of human relationships, integrity, and competence.

Following the preamble, the second section outlines the six purposes of the *Code*:

1. Identify core values on which social work's mission is based.

2. Summarize broad ethical principles that reflect the profession's core values and serve as the basis for a set of specific ethical standards to guide social work practice.

3. Help social workers identify relevant considerations when professional obligations conflict or ethical uncertainties arise.

4. Provide ethical standards to which the general public can hold the social work profession accountable.

5. Socialize practitioners new to the field to social work's mission, values, ethical principles, and ethical standards.

6. Articulate standards that the social work profession itself can use to assess whether social workers have engaged in unethical conduct.

The statement of ethical principles, the third part—highlighted in Quick Guide #5—is based on the six core values identified in the preamble. These ethical principles are the "ideals to which all social workers should aspire" (NASW, 2008). These help provide a guide for social work practice in challenging ethically laden situations.

QUICK GUIDE #5   Ethical Principles Based on Core Social Work Values

CORE SOCIAL WORK VALUES	SOCIAL WORK ETHICAL PRINCIPLES
Service	Help people in need and address social conditions and concerns.
Social justice	Challenge social injustice.
Dignity and worth of the person	Respect the inherent dignity and worth of the person.
Importance of human relationships	Recognize the central importance of human relationships.
Integrity	Behave in a trustworthy manner.
Competence	Practice within areas of competence, and develop and enhance professional expertise.

The final part of the *Code* includes six sections that list ethical standards or categories of ethical responsibilities:

1. Clients.

2. Colleagues.

3. Practice settings.

4. Professionalism.

5. Social work profession.

6. Larger society.

Considered to be the substance of the *Code of Ethics*, these six standards include 155 specific items that stipulate social workers' ethical responsibilities within each standard (see Exhibit 6.1 for a summary of these ethical concerns). The standards are intended to guide the conduct of social work professionals and serve as the basis for evaluating violations of the *Code of Ethics*.

EXHIBIT 6.1

Ethical Concerns for Social Workers

Ethical concerns with clients

- Client's right to self-determination
- Client's decision-making capacity
- Informed consent
- Competence
- Appreciation of diversity
- Conflicts of interest
- Privacy and confidentiality
- Access to records
- Sexual relationships and harassment
- Physical contact
- Derogatory language
- Interruption/termination of services
- Payment for services

Ethical concerns with colleagues

- Confidentiality
- Interdisciplinary collaboration and consultation
- Disputes involving colleagues
- Referral for services
- Sexual relationships and sexual harassment
- Impairment or incompetence of colleagues
- Unethical conduct of colleagues

Ethical concerns with practice settings

- Supervision and administration
- Education and training
- Performance evaluation

- Confidentiality and completeness of client records
- Client billing
- Continuing education
- Commitment to employers
- Labor management disputes

Ethical concerns with professionalism

- Practice that is ethical, competent, fair, and honest
- Interference of private conduct with professional responsibilities
- Dishonesty, fraud, and deception
- Impairment of ability
- Misrepresentation
- Solicitations
- Failure to acknowledge colleagues' contributions
- Discrimination

Ethical concerns with social work profession

- Commitment to the entirety of the social work community
- Integrity of the profession
- Evaluation and research

Ethical concerns with larger society

- Social welfare
- Public participation
- Public emergencies
- Social and political action

As you may have noticed, a number of themes recur throughout the *Code*. Possibly the most important theme is respect for the client, as reflected in standards such as the social worker's commitment to clients and client **self-determination**. Part of demonstrating respect for the client is the commitment and ethical responsibility to practice culturally competent social work (NASW, 2007). Another underlying theme is responsibility for the profession, as evidenced by those standards that address colleagues with impairments and unethical colleague behaviors. The *Code* also articulates the responsibility of the social work profession for society, which is attained through efforts such as advocacy, education, and political action. Buila (2010) notes that the ethical code of the social work profession is unique among professional codes through the inclusion of ethical responsibility for social justice, social activism, and confronting the discrimination of specific oppressed populations.

Application of the *Code of Ethics*   The application of social work ethics evolves over time as social problems and issues emerge and change. For example, mandated reporting of suspected child abuse, neglect, and exploitation is an ethical practice issue that emerged in response to the changing social climate. Until the 1970s, social workers were not legally required to report incidents of suspected abuse. However, as society focused attention on this issue, the social work profession followed suit by supporting mandated reporting.

Although the *Code of Ethics* is intended as a guide, it also serves as a mechanism for monitoring social workers' competency and ethics. Violations can be reported to a state chapter or the national office. A committee of NASW members then reviews the complaint and can recommend any number of actions if the complaint is substantiated. Such actions may include corrective action (such as suspension from the organization, mandated consultation, or censure), notice of unprofessional conduct to the regulatory board of the state in which the social worker practices, or public sanction. Social work licensure or certification, which exists in every state, requires ethical practice. Social workers can risk being sued for malpractice in civil court if ethical practice is violated.

Critics of the *Code of Ethics* argue that, to be ethical, social workers need only "practice wisdom" (the knowledge, skills, and values that a social worker collects over the course of a career), instincts, and virtuosity and that being governed by a code is time-consuming, coercive, and a wasted effort (Dolgoff et al., 2009, pp. 34–35). Now that you have reviewed the *Code of Ethics*, what do you think?

Ethical Dilemmas

During one of her practicum experiences, Emily was invited by her field instructor at a mental health center to co-lead with two male colleagues a group for men who had been perpetrators of intimate partner violence. You will recall from Chapter 1 that Emily was a victim of intimate partner violence several years earlier. She did not share that reality with her field instructor or her co-workers at the practicum site because she was afraid they would view her as inept and too emotional about this issue. After all, if she were a competent individual, would she have allowed herself to become involved in a violent relationship? Nevertheless, Emily agreed to participate in the group, feeling that she would disappoint her supervisor if she rejected the invitation. She also believed that she had put the experience behind her and that because of her personal e xperience and social work training, she would bring a valuable perspective.

Unfortunately, Emily's experience was less than successful, to say the least. She was extremely uncomfortable as she listened to the men rationalize their violence against their female partners. Based on her value system, Emily viewed violence as reprehensible, and she was now solidly entrenched in that belief because of her own experience. Emily's belief system had evolved to believing that batterers could not be rehabilitated. She soon realized that she probably had not "put the experience behind her," and she was faced with a couple of ethical dilemmas:

- *In her current state of discomfort, she was not fulfilling her commitment to be a co-facilitator.*
- *If she left the group, she would be leaving her colleagues without a female co-facilitator.*

The agency was strongly committed to having a male/female team for this group. Because she had not told her supervisor or her colleagues of her past experience, Emily was fearful they would think she was hiding this information. This belief might lead them to question her ethical behavior. She questioned whether her personal values were impeding her practice obligations. She was especially fearful of her reactions if she continued in the group: Would she "lose it" during a group session, or would she continue to be immobilized? What would you do in Emily's situation: leave, stay, or seek help?

An ethical dilemma is most challenging when personal values and professional ethical obligations conflict. Most practitioners agree that the "best interests" of the client should take precedence, but your personal values may override your professional duty in some situations. Consider Emily's dilemma, for example. Her experience with domestic violence made it difficult at this early point in her career for her to work with males who had battered. Nevertheless, when she was given the opportunity to co-lead a group of men who had battered a female partner, she felt she could maintain enough emotional objectivity to be an effective co-leader. Clearly, her personal experiences and values clouded her objectivity and, potentially, her professional competence. It was important for her to learn that putting personal values aside is not always an easy task. The negative group experience enabled her to confront her fears during supervisory sessions. With her supervisor's support and challenges, Emily was able to come to terms with her feelings and shift her belief to consider that treatment of violent behavior could be successful. As a result, she ultimately was able to co-facilitate the group.

The first step in confronting an ethical dilemma is to determine if the situation meets the criteria of a professional ethical dilemma. In order to be considered an ethical dilemma, three conditions must be met: (1) the social worker must decide on a course of action; (2) multiple courses of action exist; and (3) regardless of the course of action, one of the social work ethical principles will be compromised (Allen, 2012, p. 4).

Although the ethical dilemmas that you are likely to encounter in your practice will all have unique characteristics, some common areas that challenge social workers can be identified. Based on suggestions by Reamer (2008b), the ethical challenges presented in the following sections, when linked to the social values and ethical principles discussed earlier, can provide a context in which to consider appropriate responses to the situation. As you review these challenges, consider your own value system, your potential responses, and the intersection of the two. You may find that these situations prompt more questions than answers, but keep asking the questions.

Confidentiality   The social worker–client relationship is based on trust. When that trust is threatened or violated, an ethical dilemma may occur. A key to establishing a trusting relationship is for the social worker to respect the client's confidentiality. Defined as the disclosure of client-related information only with the permission of the client, **confidentiality** can be categorized as either absolute or relative. *Absolute confidentiality* means that all information is to be held in confidence; *relative confidentiality* means that some information can be disclosed.

Because the social work profession places such importance on the issues of privacy and confidentiality, these issues are addressed in two of the profession's documents: the NASW Policy Statements and the *Code of Ethics* (NASW, 2008). The current Policy Statement (NASW, 2012–2014a) on confidentiality and information utilization provides clear guidelines for obtaining, sharing, and utilizing information related to clients. Additionally, Standard 1.07(a–r) of the NASW *Code of Ethics* addresses privacy and confidentiality in great detail because social workers are privy to considerable and intimate client information. The standard, derived from the social work value of viewing each person with dignity and worth, provides guidelines for protecting information related to the client's reasons for receiving services, her or his legal and financial status, and other personal life details.

Legally, clients have relative confidentiality, and social workers must share certain information, in two situations:

1. In cases of suspected abuse of children, older adults, and persons with disabilities (must report the suspected abuse to the state agency).

2. In cases in which a person threatens harm to self or others (must report to the designated authority in that state).

Social workers are among the group of professionals mandated to report suspected abuse and neglect in every state in the United States; therefore, no violation of confidentiality has been committed should a social worker report to the appropriate state agency that she or he is concerned about an individual's safety and well-being. Social workers are also within the law and our ethical standards to share information that is mandated by a court order.

The second category noted above, reporting situations in which a person is a danger to self or others, is more complex, in part due to the fact that legal statutes vary from state to state. The Tarasoff rulings of 1974 and 1976 legally clarified that mental health professionals are ethically responsible for warning potential victims of violence that they are in danger and to take steps to protect the individual's safety.

As social workers have expanded their areas of practice over the years, the duty to warn and protect has expanded to include cases involving HIV/AIDS, domestic violence, and health care situations (e.g., end-of-life and genetic issues) (Granich, 2012). When social workers find themselves in these difficult situations, they must confront the dilemma of preserving confidentiality or fulfilling the obligation to warn and protect (Granich, 2012).

Having a plan for informing your actions can be helpful in a time of crisis. Guidelines may include being knowledgeable about state law and agency policy; having a plan/protocol to follow (including prior consultation with appropriate agency personnel) that helps you to assess danger and develop a planned response; understanding documentation requirements; and ensuring your own self-awareness and self-care (Tapp & Payne, 2011). Of critical importance is that social workers assume responsibility for knowing the policies of their agency, laws of their state, and implications for malpractice and licensure. For more information on state laws, review the information on the NASW website at http://www.naswdc.org/ldf/legal_issue/2008/200802.asp?back=yes.

Social workers can also share information when the client has granted **informed consent** through a signed release of information. Such consent is needed for the practitioner to share information regarding the information contained within the client records (e.g., assessment, intervention, and evaluation information) that is to be shared with insurance companies, other providers, and family members (Polowy, Morgan, Bailey, & Gorenberg, 2008). Relative confidentiality exists in these situations also. In order to grant a valid informed consent, the client or the client's guardian must give written permission to release information and be told the information to be shared and the reasons for sharing it, with whom the information will be shared, and the date of expiration for the information. Most agencies have a standardized informed consent form.

Additional protection of client information is included in the Health Insurance Portability and Accountability Act of 1996 (HIPAA) (U.S. Department of Health and Human Services, 2004). The HIPAA legislation is designed to protect and enhance the rights of consumers of health care services without compromising the access to or effectiveness of the provision of services. The law mandates that consumers of health care services have the following rights: to see and obtain copies of their health care records; to be informed in writing about the ways in which health information is used by the health care provider; and to have assurance that their identifiable health information is protected.

Privacy and confidentiality do, however, have limits. When the limitations of the social worker's ability to maintain privacy or confidentiality are challenged, an ethical dilemma can arise. For example, the social worker strives to maintain the client's confidentiality (and trust) but may have a legal or societal duty to divulge the information, as in the case of suspected abuse or harm to self or others (Dolgoff et al., 2012). In such situations, the social worker may face a conflict between maintaining the client's trust and recognizing the mandate to violate confidentiality.

For beginning social workers, the responsibility to maintain a client's privacy and confidentiality can become overwhelming. When do you share or not share client information? What can you write or not write in a client record? What if you accidentally breach a confidence? These are all questions that you should be routinely asking yourself. Here are recommended practices to maintain your client's privacy and confidentiality (Dunlap & Strom-Gottfried, 1998):

- Be vigilant, including taking note of your location as you communicate information to or about the client. Make confidentiality foremost in your mind as you practice.

- Protect records by keeping them in a locked receptacle, and safeguard computer files with a firewall, password, or short-delay screen saver.

- Monitor your ongoing client-related activities by gathering only the information that is relevant to the services being provided.

- Learn and understand laws and agency policies and practices regarding the protection of information.

- Monitor yourself. Use your supervisor and colleagues for consultation, not the clients or your friends or family.

- Picture yourself as a consumer of your services—how would you like to be treated?

Client Self-Determination   The right to self-determination is also derived from the social work value and ethical principle related to dignity and worth of the person. Standard 1.02 specifies that the social worker is obligated to respect the client's right to make decisions and choices and to determine her or his own goals. As with confidentiality, situations arise that limit the social worker's ability to comply with this obligation fully. As mentioned earlier, when a person has threatened physical harm to herself or himself or to others, the social worker is ethically and legally obligated to protect the person and override the right to self-determination (Reamer, 2006).

Ethical dilemmas can also occur in nonlife-threatening situations in which the social worker feels the client is making a decision that may have a negative or harmful outcome. Consider, for example, the person who resumes drinking or using drugs, returns to a violent relationship, or is mandated for services but refuses to participate even though noncompliance will result in a return to prison. In these situations, the social worker must balance the issue of respecting the client's right to self-determination with the competing obligation to help the client achieve a positive outcome (Dolgoff et al., 2012).

A useful guideline to follow in these difficult situations is to remember that the person's right to self-determination takes precedence whenever possible. Even the client who has not voluntarily come to the social worker for services has the "right" to choose nonparticipation. The social worker's responsibility is to offer or provide the opportunity to identify and examine the consequences of that choice. If social workers are truly to respect and value their clients, they must diligently respect the client's right to self-determination. The reality is that all people have the right to make decisions about their lives.

Boundaries   The parameters that define your relationship with the client system as professional rather than social are called **boundaries**. Boundaries can be difficult to delineate and maintain because clients often share intimate details of their lives with their social worker, making the relationship appear to be personal and intimate. The social worker–client relationship can involve sharing, cooperation, and even liking each other, but it is not a friendship, romance, or business partnership (Strom-Gottfried & Dunlap, 1998). Having a personal as well as a professional relationship with a client is considered to be a dual relationship. For example, dating or a business partnership is a dual relationship and is considered unethical. Conflicts of interest are addressed in Standard 1.06 of the *Code of Ethics*, which states that a social worker must maintain separateness in personal, religious, political, and business areas.

Becoming familiar with the profession's ethical standards as well as agency policies and practices will help you to avoid committing ethical infractions related to client–worker boundaries. Conducting periodic reality checks with colleagues and supervisors in cases of ambiguity can also help social workers maintain appropriate boundaries.

Despite the best precautions, it is not always possible to maintain boundaries. You could encounter a client somewhere outside the social work setting, for example. In those instances, allow the client to acknowledge you first, and if you engage with the client, ensure that you do not discuss the professional relationship during the encounter. Be prepared for the possibility that the client may not choose to acknowledge you at all, or that she or he may openly acknowledge you and discuss the reasons why you know each other. In either case, it is the social worker's responsibility to maintain professional boundaries.

Self-Disclosure   Related to boundaries is the issue of **self-disclosure**, the sharing of personal information with a client. The *Code of Ethics* states that social workers should not allow their personal issues to interfere with the best interests of the client. Although this does not specifically address the issue of self-disclosure, it implies that social workers should approach self-disclosure with caution.

Sharing personal information with clients may be done with the best of intentions. For example, substance abuse treatment programs may hire workers who are recovering from chemical dependency or addiction and encourage them to disclose their history of abuse to their clients to establish a rapport. The social worker may believe that if the client knows that the worker has had similar experiences, the client will be better able to work through the challenge. In fact, the social worker's self-disclosure may achieve that goal. The client may see the social worker as more credible or trustworthy, feel that her or his experience was normal, or feel more confident and inspired to change (Reamer, 2001).

In other cases, however, self-disclosure can sabotage the social work intervention. The client may become confused by the worker's disclosure, may try to mirror the worker's recovery, or may shift attention to the worker's life (Strom-Gottfried & Dunlap, 1998; Reamer, 2001). For example, consider Emily's experiences related to self-disclosure. In the case of the client at Oasis House, her self-disclosure prompted the client to feel comfortable asking Emily for money. In the situation with the domestic violence group, would Emily have wanted to share with the batterers her history as a victim of domestic violence?

Social workers monitor themselves closely regarding the disclosure of personal information. Here are some strategies for self-monitoring:

- Learn the agency policy and practice regarding self-disclosure.

- Determine the appropriateness, benefits, and costs of sharing the information and the client's ability to use the information (Strom-Gottfried & Dunlap, 1998).

- Remember that the social worker's responsibility is to be a support for the client; they are not in a reciprocal relationship (i.e., friendship) with the client.

- Consult with colleagues and supervisors regarding their experiences with self-disclosure.

Allocation of Resources   Particularly during challenging economic times, social workers are often faced with the dilemma of too few resources for too many clients. They may have to deny an application for assistance because the funding has been exhausted or there are no beds in a shelter or food in the pantry. As social workers are often the first contact for the clients, they typically must shoulder the burden of informing them that there are no resources to meet a request.

Resources are typically allocated on the basis of equal-sized proportions, a lottery system, or on a competitive basis using financial need or past oppression as the criteria (Reamer, 2001). Ethical dilemmas involving resource allocations can be particularly challenging because there may be little that the social worker can do to influence the outcome. Nevertheless, social workers have an ethical obligation to play a role in the allocation of resources. Social workers who work directly with client systems can be the voice for these clients. Similarly, social workers who occupy supervisory, administrative, and policy positions in both public and nonprofit organizations can advocate for equitable allocation of resources. All social workers have an ethical obligation to advocate for needed resources for clients, both on the individual client level as well as on a local, state, or federal level. On the individual level, a social worker may advocate to her or his own agency, another agency, or a funding source for resources for a client or family. Social workers can also play an important role in advocating to funding and policy decision makers for greater allocation of resources to groups of clients. Engaging in activities such as legislative advocacy, political campaigning, community organizing, and speaking out on behalf of clients can bring attention and resolution to limited resource allocations.

VALUES AND ETHICS IN PRACTICE

The potential for a value conflict or an ethical dilemma is something that social work practitioners keep in mind at all times. No matter how clear, simplistic, or mundane a situation may seem on the surface, social workers do not trivialize the situation or routinize the interpretation or the response. Instead, social workers keep in mind the values that have long guided social work practice. The knowledge and skills developed by social work professionals are deeply rooted in this set of values, which have changed little since they were first introduced.

Although the core social work values and ethical principles are widely accepted by the profession, their meanings and the implications of those meanings are routinely open to interpretation and often result in disagreements (Dunlap & Strom-Gottfried, 1998). To help in the application of ethical principles, social work theorists have developed three tools for making ethical decisions.

One such tool is the Enhanced Ethical Decision-Making Matrix (D'Aprix, Boynton, Carver, & Urso, 2001). It is based on the premise that the social worker explores all options before taking action, recognizes her or his personal values and biases, and evaluates the effectiveness of the action. The first step in applying the Enhanced Ethical Decision-Making Matrix is to identify the ethical issues using the *Code of Ethics*. Exhibit 6.2 presents a set of questions and the basis for those questions that can aid in the identification process.

EXHIBIT 6.2	QUESTIONS TO IDENTIFY ETHICAL ISSUES	BASIS FOR QUESTION
Ethical Decision Making: Identifying the Issues	1. What are the interventions and ethical issues that make it difficult to choose a course of action?	Worker is able to address all potential ethical issues to be addressed. Worker determines if any *Code of Ethics* standards or laws are involved.
	2. What are my viewpoints about these issues?	Worker is able to recognize her/his personal biases and determine any impact of the biases on client system outcomes.
	3. Which actions (interventions) might address the practice and ethical issues listed in number 1?	Worker is able to consider all potential alternatives for intervention.
	4. What are the potential consequences/ outcomes of these actions?	Worker can conduct a cost–benefit analysis of the potential intervention.
	5. How would I prioritize the intervention and ethical issues using the Ethical Principles Screen (EPS)?	Using the EPS, the worker can rank-order priorities.
	6. Based on this prioritization, which issues will I address first and which action will address this issue?	After prioritizing the ethical issues, the worker can prioritize the proposed interventions.
	7. Throughout this process, have I consulted with colleagues for their professional opinions?	Worker can benefit from the practice wisdom of other social work professionals.
	8. How will I monitor and evaluate the effectiveness of this plan of action?	Ongoing monitoring enables the worker to know when to proceed to the next priority and to assess the status of the dilemma.

Source: D'Aprix et al., 2001.

Once the ethical issues have been identified, another tool, called the Ethical Rules Screen, can help the social worker decide how to proceed (Dolgoff et al., 2012, pp. 79–80). It requires the following steps:

1. Examine of the *Code of Ethics* (2008) to determine if any of the *Code* rules are applicable.

2. If one or more of the *Code* rules apply, follow the *Code* rules.

3. If the *Code* does not apply, move to the Ethical Principles Screen.

The Ethical Principles Screen (Dolgoff et al., 2012, pp. 79–80) provides an approach for rank-ordering client-related issues using seven ethical principles. Quick Guide #6 provides the listing of the seven ethical principles that can be helpful in determining the most ethical way in which to approach a complex situation. Using these seven principles prioritizes the ethical questions and enables the social worker to determine the issues that are most important to address. While each of the principles is of significance, the principles are listed in order of their perceived importance within the client's life. For example, protecting life is considered to have greater value than preserving confidentiality and, in decision making, a dilemma that may impact the client's life would take precedence over maintaining confidentiality.

QUICK GUIDE #6   Ethical Principles Screen

Ethical Principle 1: Protection of Life
Ethical Principle 2: Social Justice
Ethical Principle 3: Self-determination, Autonomy, and Freedom
Ethical Principle 4: Least Harm
Ethical Principle 5: Quality of Life
Ethical Principle 6: Privacy and Confidentiality
Ethical Principle 7: Truthfulness and Full Disclosure

Source: Dolgoff et al., 2012, pp. 79–80.

Applying any of these decision-making frameworks does not ensure "easy answers to the tough questions," but the tools can provide an approach for analyzing the situation and devising an ethical and thoughtful response. The models prompt the social worker to ask the questions that are relevant to the ethical dilemma, to compartmentalize the information, to establish priorities, and to consider the impact of the outcome on all the parties involved.

CASE: CATHLEEN'S RIGHT TO PRIVACY AND CONFIDENTIALITY

We have explored a number of issues related to social work values and ethics. It is now time to apply the concepts and framework to an ethical dilemma. The dilemma is followed by the questions that might arise from the situation.

Here is the ethical dilemma: You are a social worker at Oasis House, where your supervisor asks you to talk with a new resident, Cathleen. Cathleen told shelter workers that she is 18 and homeless. During your talks with Cathleen, however, she admits that she is really 15 and has run away from home. She further divulges that she does not want to go home because her mother's live-in boyfriend sexually abused her. She begs you not to share the information about the sexual abuse with anyone or to contact her mother.

The questions that might arise include the following:

- Does the adolescent have a legal right to make decisions about her life without parental consent?

- What is your responsibility to Cathleen's parents?

- Would it be appropriate for you to discuss Cathleen's situation with her mother without Cathleen's informed consent?

- If Cathleen is being sexually abused, does she have a right to privacy after she has shared her secret with you?

- Was Cathleen informed that you might not be able to maintain complete confidentiality *before* she confided in you?

- What are the agency's policies and procedures related to sexual abuse and Cathleen's status as a minor and a runaway?

You can analyze this practice situation by using the decision-making matrix in Exhibit 6.2 as a guide.

Then look at Exhibit 6.3. It uses the general categories in Exhibit 6.2 to present possible ways of breaking down the problem to reach a satisfactory solution. As you can see, this ethical dilemma poignantly addresses the client's right to protection, self-determination, privacy, and confidentiality. At the heart of the NASW *Code*'s first ethical standard, Social Workers' Ethical Responsibilities to Clients, is client self-determination. Having respect for the client is based on the core social work value of "dignity and worth of the person" and the ethical principle of "respect the inherent dignity and worth of the person."

Respecting Cathleen's right to self-determination, privacy, and confidentiality is key to upholding her dignity and worth. You are ethically bound to respect her dignity and worth, behave in a trustworthy manner, and practice with competence. By asking you to keep the alleged abuse in confidence and help her with emancipation, Cathleen is attempting to exercise her right to self-determination, privacy, and confidentiality. However, although you want to maintain her trust, as a social worker you are ethically and legally bound to report the abuse because she is a minor. The ethical dilemma here is clearly between client confidentiality and mandated reporting of suspected abuse. To serve Cathleen best, you must report the suspected sexual abuse to the child welfare agency. At the same time, you must continue to respect her right to self-determination and privacy.

The challenge is to help Cathleen without losing her trust. Exploring her options and the pros and cons associated with the various options could help her to

EXHIBIT 6.3

Ethical Decision Making: Preserving Privacy and Confidentiality in Cathleen's Case

PRACTICE/ ETHICAL ISSUES	ETHICAL PRINCIPLE(S)	PERSONAL BIASES	ACTION(S) OPTIONS	POTENTIAL CONSEQUENCES/ OUTCOMES	ACTION(S) TAKEN	MONITOR/ EVALUATE EFFECTIVENESS
Client's request to not report the sexual abuse.	1) Protection of human life. 6) Privacy and confidentiality.	I think the mother is at fault.	a) Report the abuse to the public agency despite her opposition. b) Work with client to make the report together.	a) Report is made, but client's trust is lost. b) Build trust with client so report can be made.	Jointly work with client to make report.	Check with client at each step to determine her sexual safety.
Client's request to not contact her mother.	6) Privacy and confidentiality. 3) Self-determination. 1) Commitment to client.	I think her mother must be contacted.	a) By reporting to the public agency, the mother is contacted despite her opposition. b) Trust is built and mother is contacted.	a) Mother is contacted, but client's trust is lost. b) Trust is built and mother is contacted.	Jointly work with client to contact her mother.	Check with client at each step to determine her trust comfort levels with contacting mother.

Ethical Principles Screen:
1) Protection of life
2) Equality and inequality
3) Autonomy and freedom
4) Least harm
5) Quality of life
6) Privacy and confidentiality
7) Truthfulness and full disclosure

Source: Adapted from D'Aprix et al., 2001; Dolgoff et al., 2009.

feel positive about reporting the abuse. Helping Cathleen to understand that reporting the abuse is part of the helping process can help to maintain her trust.

CONCLUSION

To maintain a professional perspective and avoid feelings of being overwhelmed, remember that clarifying your own values and practicing social work in an ethical manner is a lifelong endeavor for social workers. As social workers interact with people in a changing society, new ethical challenges will continue to emerge.

The effective practice of social work means that social workers approach each situation with questions regarding the ethical implications of their actions. I hope this chapter encourages you to begin to explore and expose your own values and ethics and their origins, and that such an exploration will become an ingrained part of your social work practice. One social worker's statement sums it up:

> To practice competently, contemporary professionals must have a firm grasp of pertinent issues related to ethical dilemmas and ethical decision-making. This knowledge enhances social workers' ability to protect clients and fulfill social work's critically important, value-based mission. (Reamer, 2009a, p. 120)

MAIN POINTS

- Social work values are defined as the beliefs that we hold for ourselves and others in our communities. Ethics are the behavioral manifestations of the values that we hold about the way we and others should behave toward one another.

- Understanding values and ethics is a personal thought process that is difficult to measure, seldom has obvious or concrete solutions, may evolve and change over time as a result of culture, contemporary norms, and events, and is applicable at all levels of social work practice.

- To practice social work in an ethical manner, awareness of your own values and of the profession's code is key.

- Ethical dilemmas can occur in every aspect of social work practice. Social workers are especially likely to face ethical dilemmas in the areas of legal and health care issues, client rights and responsibilities, allocation of resources, and privacy and confidentiality.

- The NASW *Code of Ethics* serves as the guide for ethical practice. Taking advantage of the practice wisdom of your social work colleagues, consulting the *Code of Ethics*, and familiarizing yourself with the laws, policies, and practices related to your position are three "musts" for being an ethical practitioner.

EXERCISES

1. To prepare yourself for working through the exercises in this chapter, go to the Sanchez family interactive case (www.routledgesw.com/cases). In the Assess tab, complete Task 3, "A Values Inventory for Social Workers."
2. Using the Sanchez family case, review the case file for Roberto Salazar and answer his Critical Thinking Questions. Next, click on the Interaction Matrix and examine the interactions between Roberto and the other family members. Summarize your thoughts on the values and ethical implications of Roberto's situation as it relates to the other Sanchez family members.
3. The best method for clarifying your values and developing responses to the inevitable ethical dilemmas that will arise during your social work career is to practice. In this exercise, you can explore the values, ask the questions, and apply the ethical principles highlighted in this chapter. When you have read the following scenario, use the Enhanced Ethical Decision-Making Model in Exhibit 6.2 to complete the matrix in Exhibit 6.4.

MATRIX FOR ETHICAL DECISION MAKING						
PRACTICE/ ETHICAL ISSUE	ETHICAL PRINCIPLES IDENTIFIED IN THE CODE OF ETHICS	PERSONAL BIASES	ACTION(S) OPTIONS	POTENTIAL CONSEQUENCES/ OUTCOMES	ACTION(S) TAKEN	MONITOR/ EVALUATE EFFECTIVENESS
1.						
2.						
3.						

EXHIBIT 6.4

Matrix for Ethical Decision Making Exercise

Now, using the Sanchez family interactive case study, imagine that you are a social worker in a not-for-profit agency that provides crisis services over the telephone and to walk-in clients. Emilia Sanchez, a 24-year-old who is 2 months pregnant, has telephoned several times. In her last telephone call, she confided to you that she uses heroin and drinks alcohol daily. You have expressed your concern that her drug use may be dangerous for her unborn child, but she does not seem worried. She has also stated that she is unable or unwilling to give up the drugs. In this telephone conversation, she told you that she is unsure if she wants to keep "it." You suspect that she has traded sex for drugs and she is not working or attending school. Emilia tells you that her Catholic parents do not know about the pregnancy and she does not want them to know anything because they will insist she have the baby. Her mother already cares for Emilia's son, Joey, and has two younger children still living at home, and Emilia's father works long hours. They have little money and she does not want to burden them with another mouth to feed.

Finally, consider this question: If your best friend was in Emilia's situation, would your analysis change? If so, in what way?

4. Go to the Riverton interactive case at www.routledgesw.com/cases. The social worker in this case is both a professional working in the community and a resident of the community. Using the information included in this chapter, identify the potential ethical implications for the social worker and develop a response to each issue identified.

5. Go to the Carla Washburn interactive case at www.routledgesw.com/cases and consider Mrs. Washburn's right to self-determination. Using the information from this chapter, describe the issue of her right to refuse services and health care, specifically responding to the following:

    a. Does Mrs. Washburn have a right to refuse services and treatment?

    b. What is the social worker's role/option should the client refuse services or treatment?

    c. Discuss the ethical implications of the client's right to refuse services and treatment.

    d. Cite the section of the NASW *Code of Ethics* that addresses this issue.

6. To understand better where your values come from, complete the matrix in Exhibit 6.5:

    a. Identify five values that are important in your life and consider the origins of those values (first and second columns).

    b. Think about the ways in which you act on each value (third column). Do you engage in activities or behaviors that enable other people to discern your values on that particular issue, or would other people have no idea about your values?

    c. Compare those values to those of the social work profession (fourth column).

    d. Finally, consider whether this value has ever created a dilemma for you (fifth column). If so, what was the dilemma, and how did you resolve it?

PERSONAL VALUE	ORIGINS OF VALUE	BEHAVIOR	RELEVANT SOCIAL WORK VALUE	DILEMMA	NASW CODE OF ETHICS STANDARDS	**EXHIBIT 6.5** *Matrix for Values Exercise*
1.						
2.						
3.						
4.						
5.						

To help you compare your values with those of the social work profession, the six social work values are listed below:

- Service.
- Social justice.
- Dignity and worth of the person.
- Importance of human relationships.
- Integrity.
- Competence.

7. After you have completed exercise 6, reflect on your work and consider these questions:
   a. Did you learn anything new about yourself?
   b. Did you learn anything new about anyone else?
   c. Are you satisfied with the ways in which you act on your value system? If not, what changes can you make?

    d. If any of your values created an ethical dilemma for you, were you satisfied with the way in which you handled the dilemma? If not, what could you have done differently?

    e. Do you feel your value system is consistent with the values of the social work profession?

    f. Which of the social work values is the most important to you?

    g. How do you currently see that you may be exercising this value in your life?

8. Go to the RAINN interactive case at www.routledgesw.com/cases and complete the Phase 3 Critical Thinking questions.

9. When responding to a natural disaster, social workers often face complex value conflicts and ethical dilemmas. To begin the process of clarifying your values related to working with survivors of natural disasters, go to the Hudson City case at www.routledgesw.com/cases and click on My Values. Respond to the questions presented.

    After completing the questions, refer to the list of six core values of social work presented in this chapter and reflect on the ethical obligations of a social work practitioner when working in disaster response.

10. Personal reflection: Identify a value conflict or ethical question you have encountered in your life. Include your thoughts and feelings, response to the dilemma, and what you might do in the future with a similar situation. Discuss how your values related to this issue may impact your profession.

CHAPTER 7

Social Work Perspectives and Methods

Emily's BSW degree provided her with the knowledge and skills to work with individuals, families, groups, and communities. In her first job as an adult services worker in a small multiservice community service agency, she intervened on all these levels:

- *On the individual level, she worked with the older adults through the homemaker/chore program as well as with persons with visual impairments and female recipients of public assistance who were seeking employment. In each of these programs, she also worked with the clients' families.*

- *On the group level, Emily facilitated a support group for persons who had recently lost their vision.*

- *At the community level, Emily helped a community group develop a telephone reassurance program in which volunteers from the Senior Center telephoned homebound older adults each day to ensure their safety and well-being. Emily helped the Center committee oversee this program and set policy. As a result of her involvement with the Senior Center group, Emily became part of a community task force that included community agencies and older adults to create an annual community-wide resource and wellness fair.*

Emily performed all these levels of social work in just one job. Her varied activities are an example of generalist social work practice.

The social work profession has established a framework for bachelor-level social work known as **generalist social work practice**. At this level, social workers have a broad-based set of knowledge and skills that they can use for assessing and intervening competently at multiple levels. In this chapter, we define and explore the generalist area of social work education and practice from both theoretical and practice perspectives.

One of the six values included in the National Association of Social Workers (NASW) 2008 *Code of Ethics*, Importance of Human Relationships, clearly states this framework. It calls on social workers to "strengthen relationships among people in a purposeful effort to promote, restore, maintain, and enhance the well-being of individuals, families, social groups, organizations, and communities." Similarly, the 2008 Council on Social Work Education (CSWE) *Educational Policy and Accreditation Standards* required accredited BSW programs to include content on working with individuals, families, groups, organizations, and communities.

HISTORY OF GENERALIST SOCIAL WORK PRACTICE

The concept and practice of providing services to individuals, families, groups, and communities are deeply rooted in the origins of the profession. However, the framing of generalist practice is a relatively recent development.

Historically, two movements that shaped contemporary social work practice helped both to separate and to unite the profession around the concept of generalist practice. Despite their ongoing philosophical competition, the Charity Organization Society, which emphasized the individual, and the settlement house movement, with an emphasis on groups and communities, paved the way for three distinct paths: individual casework, group work, and community organization (Hernandez, 2008).

However, the social turmoil of the 1960s prompted the profession to consider an approach to social work practice that would integrate these three modalities in an effort to provide more comprehensive services (Landon, 1995). This shift of philosophy led to the emergence of the generalist perspective.

Interest in a universal approach to social work practice resulted in the emergence of the baccalaureate in social work, beginning in the 1960s and 1970s. Before this period, the only social work degrees granted were at master's level. Social work scholars and practitioners agreed that practitioners with BSWs, trained in the generalist perspective, could best fulfill the needs for professional services in an array of areas, including providing case management services in settings such as inner-city and rural agencies, and in organizations in the private and public sectors. The generalist practice model also provides a solid preparation for the graduate social work degree, which focuses social workers on an area of concentration. Thus the BSW curriculum prepares generalist practitioners and the MSW curriculum begins with a generalist perspective but offers specialization through concentration in particular areas of study, thus allowing for more depth in education and experience.

After decades of debate, a consensus has been reached regarding the definition of generalist social work. In 2007, the Association of Baccalaureate Social Work Program Directors approved the following definition:

Generalist social work practitioners work with individuals, families, groups, communities and organizations in a variety of social work and host settings. Generalist practitioners view clients and client systems from a strengths perspective in order to recognize, support, and build upon the innate capabilities of all human beings. They use a professional problem solving process to engage, assess, broker services, advocate, counsel, educate, and organize with and on behalf of client and client systems. In addition, generalist practitioners engage in community and organizational development. Finally, generalist practitioners evaluate service outcomes in order to continually improve the provision and quality of services most appropriate to client needs. Generalist social work practice is guided by the NASW *Code of Ethics* and is committed to improving the well-being of individuals, families, groups, communities and organizations and furthering the goals of social justice.

LEVELS OF GENERALIST SOCIAL WORK PRACTICE

Perhaps the greatest strength of the generalist approach is that it facilitates the application of social work skills to different types of situations and allows for influencing social change on a structural as well as personal level. Within generalist practice, the nature of the intervention is determined by the "size" of the client system.

As you know, generalist social work practice takes place at three levels:

1. *Individual and family level:* Interventions on this most basic level can include working one-on-one with an older adult and her or his family toward developing a post-hospital discharge plan, a survivor of sexual assault and her or his significant others, or individuals and their closest associates facing virtually any kind of personal issue. Consider the social worker who conducts the home study for a couple seeking to adopt a child. The social worker interviews the couple to determine their motivation and qualifications for adoption, compiles a written assessment, and guides them through the legal adoption process. Working with individuals and families can sometimes provide insight into the larger service delivery system.

2. *Group level:* Social work practice on the group level demands many of the skills developed for working with individuals. Practice at this level may include assisting a group of families seeking family therapy, instituting a support group for persons with eating disorders, or providing guidance to a group seeking to eradicate the drug problems of young people in their neighborhood. Returning to the example of the couple seeking to adopt a child, the social worker may work at the group level by engaging the couple in a support group for adoptive parents.

3. *Organization and community level:* At this level social work practice involves interventions with large groups, organizations, and communities of all sizes. The practitioner can be engaged in varied activities such as **locality or community development** (intervention targeted at enhancing living conditions in a specific geographic area or region); analysis and

implementation of policy; advocacy activities (for example, lobbying, letter writing, and public speaking); and administration (for example, personnel, supervision, budgeting, and grant writing). The adoption social worker might promote legislation that will open adoption records for adult adoptees. A social worker can work to create a community task force to address a need for improved economic stability.

Training in generalist practice enables the social worker to practice ethically and competently at all three levels. Moreover, most social work positions require the social worker to function at all three levels at some point. Most generalist practitioners develop a stronger focus on one or two of the areas, although preferences and employment opportunities result in changes over the years of practice. For example, you might begin your career working with individuals in direct service but find later that you have a desire or opportunity to move into social work administration. This is a major benefit of being a social worker: Your knowledge, skills, and values provide you with mobility.

It is important to emphasize, however, that the three levels of practice are interconnected. Social work practice knowledge, skills, and practice behaviors identified with working with groups, organizations, and communities are frequently incorporated into practice with individuals and families. The reverse is true as well—knowledge and skills used at the individual and family level are a key component of group, organizational, and community practice. Practicing as a social worker does not result in the professional selecting one level of practice over the others, but demonstrating the ability to practice competently across the multiple levels in various systems.

GENERALIST SOCIAL WORK SKILLS AND ROLES

Regardless of where or with whom a beginning social worker intervenes, she or he must acquire a basic set of skills. Exhibit 7.1 is a list of the "100 Skills of the Professional Social Worker," compiled by an executive director of a state NASW chapter. The list is a testament to the wide variety of skills that are part of the social work repertoire. This array of skills enables generalist social workers to function in a number of roles in a variety of situations.

Some of the most important roles filled by generalist social workers include (Association of Baccalaureate Program Directors, 2007; Barker, 2003):

- *Broker:* The social worker who serves as a broker helps client systems on the individual, group, organization, and community levels to link to needed resources. Broker activities could include helping an older adult apply for assistance with his heating bill, assisting a group of parents of children with attention deficit disorder to arrange a meeting with the school board to

EXHIBIT 7.1

*100 Skills
of the
Professional
Social Worker*

Activism	Fundraising	Post-discharge follow-up
Administration	Financial counseling	Political action
Adoption	Gestalt therapy	Prevention
Advocacy	Goal setting	Problem evaluation
Applied research	Grant writing	Problem-focused therapy
Assessment	Grass-roots organizing	Problem resolution
Basic skills training	Group therapy	Program administration
Behavior therapy	Health education	Program planning
Brief therapy	Health planning	Psychosocial assessment
Career counseling	Home studies	Public relations
Case management	Intake	Qualitative research
Child advocacy	Independent practice	Quantitative research
Client and family conferences	Information and referral	Rational-emotive therapy
Client and family education	Interagency collaboration	Reality therapy
Client screening	Interdisciplinary collaboration	Recording
Coaching	Intervention	Referring
Coalition building	Interviewing	Residential treatment
Cognitive therapy	Legislative advocacy	Resource allocation
Community organization	Life skills education	Role playing
Conflict resolution	Lobbying	Service contracting
Conjoint therapy	Mandated reporting	Service coordination
Consultation	Marital therapy	Short-term therapy
Continuity of care	Mediation	Social action
Coping skills	Milieu therapy	Social work education
Counseling	Needs assessment	Staff development
Crisis intervention	Negotiation	Supervision
Data collection	Networking	Support group
Direct practice	Outcome evaluation	Task-centered casework
Discharge planning	Outreach	Teach coping skills
Divorce therapy	Parent training	Team player
Empowerment	Placement	Termination
Expert witness	Planning	Treatment planning
Family therapy	Policy analysis	Utilization review
	Policy development	

Source: Akin, 1998.

improve school-based services, or working with another social service agency to streamline their application process for their clients.

- *Advocate:* In this role, the social worker can help to voice the needs of a client or group to facilitate a change that will improve the lives of the client or group. Oftentimes, social workers will strive to impact a positive change in an unjust situation. For example, the social worker can advocate on behalf of a client at the adoption hearing, or she or he can lobby the state legislature to enact laws to address the needs of foster children.

- *Direct service provider:* Social workers providing direct services work with people at all levels and in all areas, including counseling, therapy, and group work. They engage with individuals, families, and groups, and organizations, and communities to assess needs and develop plans for intervening toward the goal of desired change, either on the individual or family level or at the organizational or community level. For example, at the individual and family level, a social worker providing direct services might meet with people seeking counseling or conduct intake surveys for an organization. At the group level, the social worker may serve as a facilitator with a group of persons experiencing a life change. At the organizational and community level, social workers may collaborate with individuals to develop a plan for improving their neighborhood safety.

- *Case manager:* Within the direct service provider role, the social worker may serve as a case manager. In this role, the social worker serves as a liaison between the client and the systems needed to meet the goals of the intervention. As a case manager, the social worker may help to develop, coordinate, and mobilize a variety of health, education, and social services. For example, a case manager for a person with severe and persistent mental illness may provide suggestions or referrals regarding resources for housing, mental health, financial, employment, and transportation services for the client. A frequently sought-after job for social workers with BSWs, case managers are on the front lines of social service delivery.

- *Educator:* In the role of educator, the social worker provides information to the client utilizing a variety of strategies. In one-on-one encounters with clients, the social worker conveys information on strategies for coping, enhancing well-being, using resources, and identifying alternative behaviors. Social workers can educate through role modeling. Social workers also engage in a more traditional role of educating through making presentations, group facilitations, and lobbying efforts.

- *Organizer:* Social workers can utilize organizing skills at all levels. Having knowledge of the operations of organizations, social workers can mobilize resources to fulfill the client's needs and goals. As generalist practitioners, social workers can analyze the strengths and deficiencies of policies and programs and work toward influencing change within those systems.

In addition, generalist social workers may help to maintain service systems (as analysts or supervisors, for example), teach social work students, or conduct evaluation research. As you can see, there are roles for social workers who prefer to work directly with people as well as for those whose strengths are in working with systems and social policy.

THEORY IN GENERALIST SOCIAL WORK PRACTICE

The knowledge and skills of the competent generalist practitioner are based on a framework that is known to be effective for the client system. Theoretical frameworks that are empirically tested through research can provide the practicing social worker with a foundation for determining the type and direction of the assessment, intervention, and evaluation of the client relationship.

Theory, as it is applied in the social work profession, encompasses both the traditional scientific concept of empirical tests that are used to explain behaviors and processes and the more contemporary concept of pragmatism—explanations that emanate from practice (McNutt & Floersch, 2008). A subset of theory, referred to as **practice theory**, is this pragmatic aspect, specifically targeted at work with individuals, families, and groups (Walsh, 2010). Knowing and being able to apply current practice theory enables the social worker to: (1) predict and explain client behavior; (2) generalize among clients and problem areas; (3) bring order to intervention activities; and (4) identify knowledge gaps about practice situations (Walsh, 2010, p. 4).

Researchers test practice theory in controlled situations so that social workers have evidence that a particular approach is appropriate for specific populations. These practice methods are not speculative or performed by trial and error. The result is **evidence-based practice**, which uses research to guide the social worker in developing knowledge and skills for client system interventions. The ability to link theory with practice and to articulate the who, what, when, where, why, and how of all interactions and activities in which social workers engage differentiates the professional from the nonprofessional or the paraprofessional worker. Utilizing a multi-step process, practitioners identify the questions for which they desire answers, seek empirical evidence to answer the questions, and then apply and evaluate the outcomes (Jenson & Howard, 2008).

In the following sections, we explore several of the theoretical frameworks that have become hallmarks of the social work profession, particularly generalist social work practice. Theory provides the basis for a perspective or framework that then guides practitioners to the appropriate practice methods or approaches. Remember, however, that applying theory in practice situations can be challenging. Social workers must become well versed in a variety of perspectives so that the application of theory becomes a natural part of the delivery of services.

You have already been introduced to two of these theories in earlier chapters—the ecological and strengths perspectives. We will look at these in more detail here, particularly within the context of the systems framework. We will also examine the solution-focused perspective. These frameworks can be helpful in practicing at all levels. A final note will highlight the way that these theories work together and the way that social work draws on theory from other disciplines.

Systems-Based Perspectives

In Emily's work with the senior homemaker/chore program, she came to appreciate the importance of viewing clients within the context of their social and physical environment. The homemaker/chore service provides in-home services to older adults who are unable to perform those tasks needed to maintain independent living. The typical client is an older adult with physical health problems who lives alone. Without the support of this program, the individual would likely have to enter a residential long-term care facility.

Marietta, a 78-year-old, widowed, African American woman living alone in a rental house, taught Emily the importance of seeing the "big picture." Marietta was referred to Emily's agency by her family physician, Dr. Stephens, who was concerned about Marietta's ability to care for herself. In her initial assessment of Marietta's situation, Emily was ready to recommend that Marietta be placed in a skilled care facility due to her physical frailty, vision problems, lack of ability to cook or maintain her house, limited income, and apparent lack of social support.

Through her assessment, Emily learned that Marietta's only son had recently died and she was estranged from her daughter-in-law and adult grandchildren because she believed they had not provided her son with adequate care during his illness. Marietta's daughter lived nearby, but they were frequently in conflict because Marietta believed her daughter should leave her husband because he was abusive to her when he was drinking. Marietta's only living sister suffered from Alzheimer's disease and was no longer able to care for herself. Marietta told Emily that she did not believe her children or sister would help her, and she refused to consider moving in with any of them.

Upon conducting a more thorough assessment, Emily learned that Marietta had close ties with her neighbors, church, and several of her nieces and nephews. Although she did need in-home services to continue living independently, she was part of a large, close, and supportive network of caregivers.

The origins of the theoretical perspectives that inform and guide contemporary social work practice encompass a philosophical commitment to the concept of societal systems. Specifically, each individual, family, group, organization, or community exists within one or more larger systems with which they interrelate and are often interdependent. The following section will provide an overview of the various aspects that comprise the systems-based perspectives.

Person-in-Environment and Ecological Perspectives   As noted in Chapter 5, the social work profession has a long history of emphasizing the **person-in-environment**

perspective, now more commonly being called the **people:environment perspective**, or P:E perspective, to highlight how people also influence their environment and not are just influenced by it. The P:E perspective perceives each individual as an interactive participant in a larger physical, social, communal, historical, religious, physical, cultural, and familial environmental system (Kondrat, 2008, p. 348). The NASW *Standards for Cultural Competence* (2007) specifically mention that social workers are obligated to consider cultural factors when they use the person-in-environment framework. Had Emily not used the P:E approach with Marietta, she would not have recognized that Marietta was part of a larger, supportive system.

During the 1950s, social work scholars were urging practitioners to consider the interaction between the individual and the larger world. A landmark event in this movement occurred in 1973, during an era of heightened interest in the social environment, when social work scholar Carel Germain introduced the ecological perspective for social work (Kondrat, 2008). With its roots in the person-in-environment framework, this perspective is based on the premise that the relationship between the individual and her or his social environment determines the individual's life situation. Examining the interaction between the client system and the larger social and physical environment is the focus for understanding human behavior, rather than looking to the cause of the interaction. For example, understanding the impact of a child's relationships with her family on her ability to perform well academically is more important than explaining the cause of specific parent–child interactions.

The original ecological model encompassed 10 conceptual components, with eight concepts added later as the framework evolved (Germain & Gitterman, 1995; Gitterman & Germain, 2008). The 18 concepts are described in Exhibit 7.2. This model aided the profession in understanding that we could most effectively help clients positively interact with their environments by eliminating life stressors. It provides a strategy for identifying the client system; assessing the client's dilemma in terms of strengths, supports, resources, and previous coping and adaptive skills; and intervening with the client with a number of possibilities. The generalist social worker can intervene with the client and use different facets of the client system (for example, family, employer, or religious institution) to address the client's needs. The practitioner can then use an ecological perspective at the individual, family, group, organization, and community levels. For example, Emily used the ecological perspective to identify existing family and community resources and mobilize those resources to enable Marietta to continue living in her own home.

Systems and Ecosystems Theory Rooted in theoretical biology, the concept of viewing clients within a systems framework first emerged in the late 1950s and early 1960s and became the major guiding theoretical framework for the social work profession for several decades (Kondrat, 2008). **Systems theory**, logically enough, evolved from the concept that a system is comprised of multiple components that interact with one another to create an entire entity.

EXHIBIT 7.2	ECOLOGICAL CONCEPTS	DESCRIPTION
Basic Concepts of the Ecological Perspective	**ORIGINAL MODEL:**	
	Person–environment fit	The ability of client system to positively engage with the environment—a positive fit suggests the client system has adapted successfully.
	Adaptations	To maintain a stable person–environment fit, systems constantly adapt to changing environment.
	Life stressors	The person–environment fit may be compromised if the client system is unable to adapt to life crises.
	Stress	The individual's response to a life stressor.
	Coping measures	To maintain a desired person–environment fit, systems develop methods for adapting to life stresses.
	Relatedness	Connections that people make with others in their environment; they serve as resources for adaptations.
	Competence	Systems must have the resources to function effectively.
	Self-esteem	The person's self-perception influences her/his ability to feel competence.
	Self-direction	The client system's ability to feel control over itself impacts self-esteem, competence, and ability to adapt to life stresses.
	Habitat and niche	Referring to clients' physical space and place within that space, habitat and niche can determine the client system's well-being.
	ADDED CONCEPTS:	
	Coercive power	Poverty, "isms," and homelessness are examples of "social pollutions" that inhibit the client system's ability to adapt and fit with the environment.
	Exploitative power	Another stressor, exploitative power is the oppression of one group over another.
	Life course	Ecologically, the path of a client's life is fluid, changing, and unique.
	Individual time	The meaning that the client system attaches to life experiences.
	Historical time	The impact of historical and social change on the client system.
	Social time	The client system's transitions and life events are a product of social, biological, economic, demographic, and culture factors.
	Resilience	Protective factors enable people to thrive in spite of life stressors.
	Flexibility	In order to adapt to environmental changes, the network must have the ability to be diverse and responsive.

Sources: Germain & Gitterman, 1995; Gitterman & Germain, 2008.

In recent years, social work scholars have incorporated the concept of the **ecosystem** into general systems theory. The ecosystem perspective emphasizes the dynamic and interdependent relationships that the client system has with the surrounding environment (Kondrat, 2008).

From a social work perspective, a **system** can be a physical and/or social entity that includes individuals, families, groups, organizations, communities—local and global, and even nations. You have no doubt noticed from your reading so far that the persons or groups served by social workers are considered **client systems**, but the term is used interchangeably with **clients**.

Every system is made up of elements, which can be any physical, social, or personal entity that is orderly, interactive, and functional. For example, a person may be part of a system that is composed of physical elements such as the individual's household, neighborhood, community, city, country, and world. Social elements can include the client system's relationships with persons that make up the environment in which the client lives. A system is composed of the various parts that interact with one another to contribute to the overall functioning of the system.

To function, a system must be dynamic and flexible. A change in one element affects all of the other elements.

Systems Theory Concepts   The systems theory framework helps social workers view client systems within the context of their interactions within a larger environment and explains human behavior in terms of the reciprocal relationships among the elements in the system. Whereas the ecological model illuminates the relationship between a client system and the environment, systems theory provides a way of understanding the change process that the client system undergoes.

To understand change from a systemic perspective, consider that when one part of a system changes, the entire system must change. For example, when a family member is added or removed from a family system for any reason, the system must change because the addition or loss creates a different configuration of people, relationships, required tasks, and available resources.

Just as natural change can modify a system, a social work intervention can prompt a system to change. In fact, the mere presence of a social worker as a "change agent" means that the worker becomes part of the system and produces a change.

Viewing the person, family, group, or community as a part of a larger system has numerous implications for generalist social work practice:

- It enables the social worker to understand how interactions between the client and the environment affect the client system.

- It provides the social worker an opportunity to target multiple components of the system for intervention.

- It incorporates the unique qualities of the client and emphasizes the dynamic nature of human interactions.

There is clearly no one theoretical approach that will explain all situations, but frameworks that view the client system in terms of the environment have prevailed within the social work profession as they are most consistent with social work values and mission.

Systems Theory in Generalist Practice   Now that you are familiar with the intersecting systems-oriented person-in-environment, ecological, systems, and ecosystems frameworks, let us apply these concepts to generalist social work practice. Due to the universality of these systems-based theories, the concepts can be applied to virtually every level and type of social work relationship.

In order to apply systems concepts, social workers use tools to assess and intervene in client situations systemically. One such tool is the **ecomap**. Developed by Ann Hartman in 1975 as a strategy for systemically assessing individuals and families, the ecomap depicts the type and quality of relationships along with the dynamic nature of those relationships (Hartman, 1978). The ecomap can be used at all levels of social work practice.

An ecomap is presented in Exhibit 7.3, using Emily's experience with Marietta, described earlier in this chapter. As you can see, each component of the client system is identified within a circle. The quality of the relationships can then be coded using the various types of lines. Arrows indicate the flow of energy and resources that are invested in and derived from each relationship. The social worker and the client can review the ecomap together to identify strengths, stressors, and areas for change. An imbalance of energy either flowing into or out of a relationship may indicate an area for change and the resources that would be needed to achieve that goal. This tool can be used to establish a social work relationship at multiple levels, monitor change, and evaluate progress at the termination of the professional relationship.

The ecomap is useful not just with individual client systems but with larger systems as well (for example, neighborhoods). The organizational client would be at the center of the ecomap, surrounded by all the organizations and institutions that are part of its environment. The ecomap clearly identifies links within and outside the larger system.

Looking at the ecomap to assess Marietta's social environment, you can see that the relationships in her life are sources of both support and stress, and several are in a state of change. The relationships that Marietta has with her nieces and nephews, her neighbors, the members of her church, and her physician serve as strengths for her. Marietta's relationship with her sister is changing, as her sister's memory is deteriorating due to Alzheimer's disease. Stressors in Marietta's life include the relationships with her estranged daughter-in-law and her daughter. The new relationships that

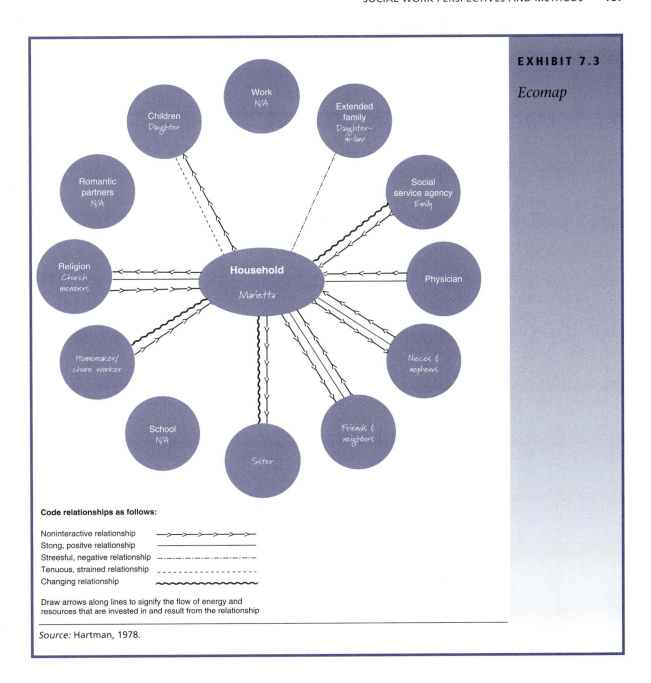

EXHIBIT 7.3

Ecomap

Code relationships as follows:

Noninteractive relationship	
Stong, positve relationship	
Streesful, negative relationship	
Tenuous, strained relationship	
Changing relationship	

Draw arrows along lines to signify the flow of energy and resources that are invested in and result from the relationship

Source: Hartman, 1978.

Marietta is developing with Emily and, later, the homemaker/chore worker have the potential to be sources of social support, but they are still being stabilized. Having the ecomap as a tool for assessment in Marietta's situation enabled Emily to identify existing resources and strengths and target areas for intervention.

Strengths-Based and Empowerment Perspectives

While working at the public welfare agency, Emily was taking her turn at "intake"— seeing walk-in or call-in clients who were in crisis. Sarah, a 16-year-old, walked into the office and explained that she found the agency address on the internet. She had her 1-day-old daughter with her, and she told Emily that she delivered the baby at her girlfriend's house (in the bathroom with only her friend present). Neither Sarah's nor her friend's parents were aware of the birth. The friend's parents were out of town. By Sarah's calculations, the baby was near full-term. Neither Sarah nor the baby had seen a health care provider. Sarah was nursing the baby, and from Emily's quick assessment, the baby appeared to be healthy. Sarah refused to identify the father, but Emily suspected the father might be her 21-year-old stepbrother. Her verbal and nonverbal cues raised Emily's suspicions.

Sarah appeared extremely distraught, asserting that she "had to do something with this baby now." However, she was also adamant that she would not involve her parents, or anyone else, in her situation. She reported that she was an above-average student, she was active in a service organization, and she worked part-time at a fast-food restaurant. She claimed to have dated casually, but denied that she was currently involved in any serious relationship. She informed Emily that her family belonged to a conservative fundamentalist religion, and she feared severe consequences if they discovered that she had become pregnant.

Initially, this case may seem overwhelming, as Emily is faced with multiple challenges: Sarah, a minor who may have been sexually assaulted by a family member, delivers her own child without benefit of health care and is fearful of being discovered by her family. However, if we look at this case more closely, we can find a number of reasons to have hope for Sarah and the baby. First, Sarah was courageous and resourceful enough to deliver the baby safely (seemingly), nurse the baby, and come to Emily's agency for help. She has a supportive friend, attends school and performs well academically, has a job, and is involved in community service. Thus, despite all the challenges Emily will face in working with Sarah's situation, there are strengths on which to build: Sarah has a history of being responsible, she is concerned for the child, and she is asking for help. Seeing Sarah through the eyes of her strengths as opposed to her deficits is the essence of strengths-based social work practice, or the strengths perspective.

Focusing the client–worker relationship on client strengths has been a relatively recent development in the social work profession, beginning in the late 1980s (Saleebey, 2006). Historically, social workers focused first and foremost on the problems, deficits, and inadequacies of the client system. To understand further the strengths perspective, it may be helpful to compare the client–social worker relationship from both a strengths and a deficit perspective. Exhibit 7.4 is a comparison of the two models (Saleebey, 1996, p. 298).

The shift to the strengths-based perspective was conceived originally as a strategy for working with persons with severe and persistent mental illness. The strengths perspective is a natural outgrowth of the systems-based perspectives because it considers both the client's own positive qualities as well as the support that exists within the environment. Using a systems framework to understand the environment in which the client system functions and then building on the available assets and resources facilitates the change process.

THE ISSUE	FROM THE DEFICITS PERSPECTIVE	FROM THE STRENGTHS-BASED PERSPECTIVE	
The person is. . .	the case, symptoms, and the diagnosis	unique and her/his traits are strengths	**EXHIBIT 7.4**
The intervention is. . .	problem-focused	possibility-focused	*Comparison of Deficits and Strengths Models*
The client's "stories" are. . .	reinterpreted by the expert	a way to know and appreciate the client	
The social worker. . .	is skeptical of the client's "stories" and rationalizations	knows the person from the inside out	
Childhood trauma. . .	predicts adult pathology	can either weaken or strengthen the client in adulthood	
The expert on the client's life is. . .	the social worker	the client	
The intervention is determined by. . .	the social worker	the client's aspirations	
Possibilities and development are. . .	limited by the client's pathology	opened by the client's possibilities and development	
Resources and skills are possessed by. . .	the social worker	the client and the social worker	
The focus of the relationship is. . .	symptom reduction	moving, affirming, and strengthening	

Source: Adapted from Saleebey, 1996.

The social work value of recognizing client uniqueness and self-worth is inherently a strengths perspective. The strengths approach is now used in every area in which social workers practice, including working with diverse populations; advocating for social justice; respecting the client system's right to self-determination; and developing interventions for individuals, families, groups, organizations, and communities (Blundo, 2008).

Strengths-Based and Empowerment Concepts   "Possibilities, not problems" is the basis of the strengths-based perspective:

> *Everything* you do as a social worker will be predicated, in some way, on helping to discover and embellish, explore, and exploit clients' strengths and resources in the service of assisting them to achieve their goals, realize their dreams, and shed the irons of their own inhibitions and misgivings, and society's domination. (Saleebey, 2006, p. 1)

Although the strengths approach is relatively simple to comprehend, it can be challenging to put into practice for both the client system and the social worker. Client systems in crisis, or with multiple challenges, may have difficulty perceiving any strengths in either themselves or their situations. Social workers will work with clients who can be hostile, resistant, or who have a history of inappropriate or illegal behavior. However, it is important to recognize and reinforce the strengths possessed by these clients in areas such as knowledge, resiliency, and goals (Blundo, 2008).

The key to the implementation of the strengths-based perspective in these cases is **empowerment,** or acting in a collaborative role with the client system and giving the clients power to participate in solving their own problems. Jane Addams exhorted her colleagues to "Do things with people, not for them." Working *with* people is to empower them.

The strengths perspective is based on six principles (also highlighted in Quick Guide #7) (Saleebey, 2006, pp. 16–20):

1. *Every individual, group, family, and community has strengths:* To discern client system strengths, the social worker must respect and value the client's "story" and knowledge of her or his situation. For example, the strength of a client suffering from severe clinical depression may be that she or he was able to get out of bed 3 days this week as opposed to only 1 day last week.

2. *Trauma and abuse, illness, and struggle may be injurious, but they may also be sources of challenge and opportunity:* Without minimizing the emotional and physical scars that come from a painful or traumatic experience, the social worker helps the client to see that she or he can use the experience to learn and grow in order to move beyond the self-defeating perception of her- or himself as victim or failure. Think of the example of a neighborhood in

QUICK GUIDE #7   **Principles of Client Strength**
1 *Every individual, group, family, and community has strengths.*
2 *Trauma and abuse, illness, and struggle may be injurious, but they may also be sources of challenge and opportunity.*
3 *Assume that you do not know the upper limits of the capacity to grow and change, and take individual, group, and community aspirations seriously.*
4 *We best serve clients by collaborating with them.*
5 *Every environment is full of resources.*
6 *Caring, caretaking, and context are key.*

which the older adult residents are afraid to leave their homes. Mobilized by the social worker, the residents are empowered to rally together and organize a community center where they can go and participate in safety.

3. *Assume that you do not know the upper limits of the capacity to grow and change, and take individual, group, and community aspirations seriously:* The social worker can empower client systems to think beyond negative life experiences, disabilities, or challenges, with the aim of expanding the client's self-vision of capacities and possibilities. Consider, for example, a middle-aged mother who dropped out of high school and receives public assistance but who goes on to finish high school, community college, and college to become a social worker.

4. *We best serve clients by collaborating with them:* Respecting clients' knowledge and expertise in their own lives or communities is the first step in developing a collaborative and empowering relationship. Collaborating with the client system creates the opportunity to use the worker's and client's strengths and resources—a strategy that diminishes the prospect for further victimization of the client. For example, consider a situation in which the social worker facilitates a meeting between police and a group of immigrants whose neighborhood is the target of hate crimes to discuss strategies for addressing the problem.

5. *Every environment is full of resources:* Regardless of the level of chaos or the sparseness of obvious strengths, the strengths-based social worker can identify resources on which to build an intervention plan with the client system. For example, a person who is experiencing homelessness, has an addiction to drugs, and is estranged from his family comes to a program serving military veterans who are homeless. The very fact that the man has come for help constitutes a strength in this situation.

6. *Caring, caretaking, and context are key:* The social work profession is deeply committed to the concept of caring for others, helping people care for

themselves, and mobilizing communities and societies to care for their members. Based on the idea that the strengths perspective is about helping people to recognize their strengths and have hope, the concept of caring for others is a natural fit for strengths-based social work interventions.

Strengths-Based and Empowerment Perspectives in Generalist Practice

The first step in applying these six principles is to develop the ability to identify strengths that will enable the client system to think and respond with a sense of empowerment. The following is a list of topics that a social worker might discuss with a client in order to discover the possibilities (Saleebey, 2006, pp. 82–84):

- Lessons learned about self, others, and the environment around the client system.
- Personal qualities, traits, and virtues.
- Knowledge of the world that surrounds the client system.
- Talents possessed by the client system.
- Cultural and personal stories.
- Resources found within the client system (e.g., the client's own pride).
- Resources found within the client system's community (e.g., people and organizations).
- Spirituality as a resource for finding meaning and hope in life.

Can you think of other areas for developing questions to add to this list—from your own life experiences or those of others?

Social workers who use empowerment strategies should keep in mind that, for many clients, this may be the first time a helping professional has prompted them to consider their life stories in terms of the successes instead of the challenges. In this sense, an empowerment-based approach can serve as a valuable learning experience for both the social worker and the client: "The formula is simple: Mobilize clients' strengths (talents, knowledge, capacities, resources) in the service of achieving their goals and visions and the clients will have a better quality of life on their terms" (Saleebey, 2006, p. 1).

One practice approach that is grounded in the strengths-based perspective is **motivational interviewing**, which was first developed for clients struggling with change. Motivational interviewing encompasses five principles: (1) the expression of empathy; (2) development of discrepancy (highlights the differences between client goals and current behaviors); (3) avoiding argumentation; (4) rolling with resistance (listening and acknowledging client's statements without engaging in confrontation); and (5) supporting self-efficacy (Miller & Rollnick, 2002). Now in use with clients who confront addictions, high-risk behaviors, and criminal charges, motivational interviewing places the client in charge of the change and employs the skills of reflective listening, empathy, and articulating the pros and cons of change (Corcoran, 2008).

Returning to Emily's experience in working with Sarah, consider the strategies she could use to empower Sarah to take action in her situation. Emily may begin by commending Sarah for being responsible, having concern for the well-being of the baby, and seeking help for herself and the infant. Acknowledging Sarah's strengths is a step toward establishing rapport and building trust so that Sarah views Emily as a partner in resolving a crisis. Emily can then explore with Sarah the options that are desired, realistic, and necessary.

From a legal and ethical perspective, it is unrealistic for Sarah's parents not to be informed about the birth and possible sexual assault by the stepbrother. Working from an empowerment approach, Emily can help Sarah develop a strategy with which she can feel safe to talk with them. For instance, Emily can offer to be with Sarah when she talks to her parents.

In addition, let us assume Sarah and Emily are in one of the 47 states that have "safe haven" laws that protect parents from prosecution if they take their newborn child to a designated site (for example, a hospital, police station, or child welfare agency) within a specified amount of time. If they are in one of these states, Emily can assure Sarah that she will have legal protection because she brought her child to a designated safe place.

Can you think of additional strategies that Emily can use to help Sarah feel empowered?

Solution-Focused Model

While working as a social worker for a home health agency, Emily was assigned to work with Charlie, a 30-year-old man recently discharged from hospital after experiencing a gunshot wound. The gunshot resulted in a spinal cord injury, leaving Charlie a paraplegic (paralyzed from the waist down). When Emily first visited Charlie, he was hostile and refused to discuss any further rehabilitation. Emily suspected that Charlie was frightened and depressed, so she began to talk with him about the aspirations he had as a child. Charlie wanted to be a minister in his church, but he strayed from that goal when he dropped out of college.

Through their conversations, Emily helped Charlie to realize that his disability need not prohibit him from returning to college and becoming a minister. Over time, Emily and Charlie reconstructed his misconceptions of his abilities, and they developed a plan for working with the occupational and physical therapists so that Charlie could reapply to college and achieve his goal of joining the ministry.

In Charlie's case, Emily is employing a **solution-focused model,** in which the social worker helps the client to construct or reconstruct her or his reality in regard to a challenging life situation. This model is based on solution-focused brief therapy, in which the client begins the intervention process by defining his or her own solution to the problem (de Shazer, 1982, 2005). This model is based on several assumptions—people are the experts about their lives; they are competent and have goals and solutions; and the change agenda must be established by the client (not the social worker) (DeJong, 2009). In that respect, the solution-focused model is closely related to the strengths perspective.

Solution-Focused Concepts Interventions using a solution-focused model are directed toward identifying client system strengths and using those strengths to encourage the client's self-perception in a more functional light. Together, the client and social worker then create an intervention plan that encompasses specific behavioral tasks aimed at the goal defined by the client. Typically, the client system has a previously successful experience on which to build for this situation. The social worker's role is to help clients modify the ways they perceive the situation and interact with others.

In her work with Charlie, Emily employed a solution-focused approach. She first listened to him talk about an earlier goal that was important to him—namely his wish to join the clergy. She then helped him reconnect with his earlier aspirations and recognize strengths he was not even aware he possessed. She and Charlie then collaborated to create several behavioral strategies to accomplish his goals, including sharing with others his desire to became a member of the clergy, researching educational options, and setting a timeframe for pursuing his goals.

Solution-Focused Model in Generalist Practice Solution-focused practice has been used primarily as a tool for working with individuals and families in clinical settings because of its emphasis on establishing individual goals and behavior change. Exhibit 7.5 lists some types of questions that can be used in a solution-focused intervention. As with all social work knowledge and skills, gaining competence to practice a solution-focused approach evolves with experiential practice inside and outside the classroom (DeJong & Cronkright, 2011).

As an example, consider the case of a student who seeks help because of failing grades in academic work. The social worker asks if this is a recent situation, and the

GOAL FORMULATION QUESTIONS
- What will your days be like when you are no longer feeling depressed?
- What would have to be different in your relationship for you to feel satisfied?

MIRACLE QUESTIONS
- What would your life be like if you were able to reach your goal of graduating from college?
- What do you need in order to accomplish the goal of graduating from college, and how can I help you?

EXCEPTION-FINDING QUESTIONS (WHAT WAS IT LIKE WHEN PROBLEMS DID NOT OCCUR?)
- What was your family life like when your parents were not fighting?
- What is it like for the rest of you in the group when Joe is not angry and hostile?

SCALING QUESTIONS (USING A NUMERIC SCALE TO RATE PAST, PRESENT, AND FUTURE STATUS)
- On a scale of 1 to 10, how motivated are you to quit smoking? Where do you need to be to actually quit smoking? What do you need to do to get from 5 to 8?

COPING QUESTIONS
- When you feel like drinking again, what do you do to stop yourself?
- You and your children were homeless last year. What did you do to change that?
- How will you know when things are going well in your life? What will you be doing, who will you be with, and how will you be feeling, thinking, and acting?

WHAT'S BETTER QUESTIONS
- What is better in your life since we last met?
- How is your life better since you started taking your medication?

Source: Dejong, 2009.

EXHIBIT 7.5

Questions for a Solution-Focused Approach

student responds that it is. The social worker using the solution-focused approach might then ask the student to describe a time when he was making better grades. Instead of focusing on things that are not going well, the social worker builds on the student's strengths. The social worker continues by asking the student to speculate as to why he was previously getting better grades. One possible response from the student is that his grades were better when he did his homework, asked for help from the teacher, and played fewer video games. In that case, the social worker may say, "So, you made better grades when you completed your homework, asked for help, and played fewer video games." Therein lies the solution.

Although it is primarily meant for therapeutic cases, the solution-focused model can be used at all levels of generalist practice. At the group, organization, and community levels, the social worker would help the group recognize its goals and its collective strengths and assets that can be mobilized to achieve its goals. In fact, the members may discover combined strengths as a group that do not exist on an individual level. The social worker can then help the group to agree on specific goals and mobilize to achieve those goals.

Integration of Social Work Theory

In this chapter we have discussed each perspective separately, but keep in mind that these theoretical perspectives are not mutually exclusive. Just the opposite: They frequently complement one another. For example, the person-in-environment perspective provides the foundation for identifying strengths and seeing the client system as part of a larger environment, while the ecological and systems frameworks influence each other and enable the social worker to compartmentalize the distinctive environmental influences that impact the client's life experiences. Similarly, thinking systemically helps the social worker to focus on the client's relationships with other elements within the system.

Moreover, the perspectives clearly flow along a path from more theoretical to more practical. The strengths-based and empowerment perspectives emanate from the ecological and systems models, while solution-focused practice is one application of these influences.

These frameworks can also be integrated with other theoretical approaches, and disciplines, to develop interventions for specific situations spanning the full spectrum of client and system issues in our society. **Eclecticism** is the practice of using knowledge and skills derived from multiple theoretical concepts that are most appropriate to the client system, population, or situation at hand. The following is a sampling of the theoretical influences that social work has gained from other professional disciplines:

- *Sociology:* Has aided the social work profession in understanding relationships between people and their environments, particularly with regard to class, culture, and inequality issues.

- *Anthropology:* Has helped social workers understand the origins and relationships of the wide diversity of groups served by social workers.

- *Psychology:* Has enhanced social workers' insights into human behavior and suggested therapeutic treatment approaches.

- *Political science:* Has been helpful in understanding issues related to government, the political process and environment, and power and control.

- *Economics:* Has helped the profession understand the ways in which the economy impacts the economic conditions in which client systems live and in the development of strategies for effecting change in the economic lives of persons living in poverty.

- *Biology:* Has been influential in several areas of social work, including human biological functioning and health and disease issues.

As social workers serve such a diverse and wide-ranging spectrum of society, multiple approaches are needed for use across populations, situations, and levels of practice. To adopt an eclectic approach, the social worker clearly must be well versed in a number of theoretical perspectives and processes.

CONCLUSION

This chapter has explored the role of the generalist social worker and the theoretical frameworks that guide and inform generalist social work practice. Applying these theoretical concepts to your practice can feel like an overwhelming challenge, particularly because there are so many theories from which to choose. Nevertheless, these constructs provide a basis on which to build your knowledge of effective and ethical social work practice.

Only a small number of the many available theoretical approaches are included in this chapter. As you continue the lifelong process of social work education, you will add other theoretical constructs to your repertoire of conceptual frameworks. For additional information on the social work profession and generalist practice, resources that may be helpful include the CSWE *Educational Policy and Accreditation Standards* (2008) and the NASW *Code of Ethics* (2008).

MAIN POINTS

- Generalist social work practice provides for assessment and intervention at three levels: individuals and families, groups, and organizations and communities. The generalist social worker employs a variety of skills and plays many roles, including educator, advocate, and mediator.

- Evidence-based practice provides the social work practitioner with empirically supported theoretical knowledge, skills, and practice behaviors to guide and inform practice approaches.

- The person-in-environment perspective views the individual within the context of the environment in which she or he lives. This perspective is the foundation of social work theoretical approaches.

- The ecological perspective is used to understand the meaning of the interactions between client systems and the environment in which they exist.

- Building on the ecological model, systems and ecosystems theories are frameworks that help social workers understand and facilitate the change process that occurs for client systems within the context of the larger physical and social environment.

- Strengths-based and empowerment perspectives help the social worker identify the client system's strengths and use those strengths to frame goals that will build on their strengths and empower the client system to make changes.

- The solution-focused perspective, which derives from the strengths perspective, has implications for practice at all levels because it enables the social worker to help clients reconstruct the ways in which they view their situation.

- At all three levels of generalist practice, these theoretical approaches can be combined to develop an intervention strategy that includes engagement and assessment of the client system, planning and implementation of the social work intervention, and evaluation of the social work intervention.

EXERCISES

1. This exercise relates to the Sanchez family interactive case (www.routledgesw. com/cases). It focuses on Gloria Sanchez.

   a. Read the following case scenario and identify the challenges and strengths that you perceive exist within the client situation. Using the Strengths Form in Exhibit 7.6, link each of those strengths to one or more of the principles of client strength, described earlier in the chapter in Quick Guide #7. Lastly, review the scenario to describe the client situation from a deficits perspective.

   You are the social worker at Our Lady of Guadalupe Church, which the Sanchez family has attended for years. During a recent church event, you noticed Gloria Sanchez wearing a long-sleeved turtleneck sweater on a

EXHIBIT 7.6

Strengths Form

CLIENT CHALLENGES	CLIENT STRENGTHS	PRINCIPLE(S) OF STRENGTHS PERSPECTIVE

particularly warm day. You speculate the reason for her attire is that she is covering up bruises. On numerous occasions, you have observed her husband, Leo, speaking to her in an extremely disrespectful manner and being demanding of her. The next time you see her you ask how things are going and she bursts into tears. She discloses to you that Leo has abused her throughout much of their marriage; she wants to leave him, but knows the teachings of the church oppose divorce. She shares that her sister, Carmen, is aware of the abuse but, for the present, has agreed not to tell the rest of the family. Carmen is very supportive, but is pushing her to "get help or get out." Gloria is terrified that her parents will learn about the abuse and blame her as they love Leo "like one of their own." Gloria has always felt close to her family and is saddened that she does not see them as often as she would like to. She visits less often out of fear that the family will suspect something is wrong.

b. In the previous exercise, you identified the strengths in Gloria's situation. Now, you will have the opportunity to consider Gloria's situation using a solution-focused approach. With your help, Gloria has identified the following areas of concern: being battered by her husband; thinking of divorce; ensuring that the rest of her family does not learn about the violence; and being concerned that her relationship with her family is becoming distant. From a solution-focused perspective, and drawing on your knowledge of her strengths, consider each of these areas in terms of the solutions that Gloria might aspire to and a behavioral strategy to help her achieve the goal. The Solutions Form in Exhibit 7.7 will help you organize your ideas.

CHALLENGE	STRENGTH/RESOURCE POSSESSED	GLORIA'S GOAL	RESOURCES NEEDED	GOAL OR OBJECTIVE
Violent spouse				
Desire for divorce				
Family learning about the violence				
Losing her relationship with her family				

EXHIBIT 7.7

Solutions Form

2. For this exercise, you will need to access the Sanchez family interactive case (go to www.routledgesw.com/cases) and familiarize yourself with situations involving several family members.

   a. Review the case file for Celia Sanchez. Then answer Celia's Critical Thinking Questions.

   b. Review the case file for Alejandro Sanchez. Then answer Alejandro's Critical Thinking Questions.

   c. Locate the Case Study Tools and click on the ecomap icon. Review the ecomap for the Sanchez family. Using the ecomap guide provided in this chapter or on the Sanchez site, create an ecomap for yourself. Provide a narrative analysis of your own ecomap, focusing on your strengths, areas for growth and change, and a future perspective on your life.

3. Go to the Riverton interactive case at www.routledgesw.com/cases and review the case information. Begin your development of an intervention:

   a. Describe the system as you perceive it from a strengths-based perspective.

   b. Identify the barriers and challenges to change.

   c. Provide your thoughts on ways in which the Alvadora residents may be empowered to address their concerns about the state of their neighborhood.

4. Through a literature search, locate a scholarly article or chapter that describes evidence-based social work practice. When you have gained some familiarity with this concept, go to the RAINN interactive case at www.routledgesw.com/cases and describe the ways in which evidence-based practice techniques are being utilized.

5. To integrate social work theory with practice, go to the Hudson City interactive case at www.routledgesw.com/cases. With the frameworks of systems theory, strengths perspective, and solution-focused model as a basis, describe the approach you would use to work with an individual or family living through a disaster.

CHAPTER 8

Fields of Social Work Practice

Like many students considering a career in social work, Emily was captivated with the range and diversity of employment possibilities. Through her social work classes, Emily learned that a BSW prepares her for generalist social work practice with a variety of persons and settings. The challenge for Emily then became narrowing her practice focus. Emily decided she needed to explore in depth the many and varied opportunities available to her as a BSW generalist social worker. In her investigation of the fields of social work practice, Emily used a number of strategies. She began by reading about fields of practice, using the internet to learn about social work organizations and opportunities, talking to fellow students and faculty at her program, interviewing practicing social workers, and volunteering in a social service setting that provided her with a range of different experiences. Even as she progressed through this exploration, Emily could still see herself working in a number of different areas, but she felt confident that she was more aware of the breadth of opportunities that lie ahead for her.

Can you relate to Emily's dilemma? Social work is a profession that offers the potential to work in an array of fields. Many social workers are drawn to a particular field of practice as a result of life experiences or a strong interest in a particular setting or population. Have you considered the field or fields of practice that interest you? To get you started in your investigation, Exhibit 8.1 provides a sampling of the many fields of practice from which to choose.

For further insights into the realities of working in the field, in this chapter, 13 social workers share their perspectives on the area of social work in which they practice. These "voices from the field" provide a window into the field of practice, the training and education required to work in that area, the rewards gained, challenges faced, and a perspective on the future of that field of social work practice. Written by the social workers themselves, these narratives are their views based on their own experiences. Each practitioner has a social work degree and is working with a different population and in a different setting, thus highlighting the

EXHIBIT 8.1	FIELD OF PRACTICE	SETTINGS
Fields of Practice and Practice Settings	Mental health services	Community-based mental health centers
		Inpatient-based psychiatric facilities
		Disaster relief programs
		Employee assistance programs
		Private practice
		Hospitals and rehabilitation programs
		Residential facilities
	Medical social work	Hospitals and rehabilitation programs
		Community-based health care programs
		Community-based health education programs
	Gerontological social work	Community-based service programs
		Hospitals and rehabilitation programs
		Residential facilities
		Adult day care programs
	Chemical dependency and addiction treatment	Community-based treatment programs
		Hospital-based treatment programs
		Prevention and education programs
	Child welfare services	Family service agencies
		Adoption programs
		Elementary and secondary schools
		Public child welfare agencies
	School social work	Elementary and secondary schools
		Alternative school programs
	International social work	U.S.-based immigrant and refugee programs
		Non-U.S.-based programs
		Disaster relief programs
		U.S.-based international programs
		Advocacy organizations
	Domestic and family violence	Shelter-based programs
		Hospitals
		Legal system programs
		Community-based mental health programs
	Criminal justice	Corrections settings
		Legal system programs
	Crisis intervention	Disaster relief programs
		Victim assistance programs
	Rural social work	Community service programs
		Hospitals and rehabilitation programs
	Military social work	Military mental health and family service programs
		Deployment support programs
	Community development	Nonprofit and public sector
	Community organizing	Community-based programs
	Advocacy	Community-based programs
	Policy development and analysis	Nonprofit and public sector programs

flexibility that social work degrees offer for working in a variety of settings with different populations throughout your career.

As you will learn in the three chapters that follow this chapter, social work interventions are built on the concept of planned change—a model that encompasses the stages of engagement of the client system, assessment of the situation to determine the strengths and barriers related to change, the planning and implementation of an intervention strategy, and the termination and evaluation of the helping relationship. As you follow the narratives contributed by the 13 social workers in this chapter, you will gain an understanding of the planned change process that each embraces as they practice in their areas of social work practice.

SOCIAL WORK PRACTICE WITH CHILDREN AND FAMILIES

Social work practice with children and families includes a range of practice areas that occur in a diverse array of settings, but all of them focus on **child welfare**, or ensuring that children are safe and protected from any harm (National Association of Social Workers Studies (NASW) Center for Workforce Studies (CWS), 2004). Child welfare encompasses child protection service, family preservation, foster care, group homes, residential facilities, adoption services, and kinship care programs (NASW CWS, 2004, p. 6). Social workers who practice in this field work in settings such as public and private child welfare agencies, residential care facilities, family service agencies, schools, mental health centers, chemical dependency and addiction treatment programs, agencies that serve persons with disabilities, and health care settings.

Working with children and families is the second largest area of practice for social workers and is particularly popular with those with BSWs. Eleven percent of social workers report that they work in the area of child welfare and with families, but an additional 5% work with adolescents and 6% work in schools (Whitaker & Arrington, 2008).

Services to children and families can be provided in settings that are publicly funded or nonprofit or in the emerging for-profit area. Nearly half of social workers who work with children and families are employed in a private nonprofit setting, with another 41% working in the public sector and the remaining 11% being in private for-profit organizations (Whitaker & Arrington, 2008). Of those social workers working in the child welfare system, two-thirds provide direct services to children and families (NASW CWS, 2004).

Policy-Practice Considerations With Children and Families

Social workers who specialize in child welfare may work in residential group homes as case managers, child care workers, and therapists. In public child welfare agencies, social workers investigate referrals about child abuse and neglect; and they work with children and families in the areas of alternative out-of-home care, prevention and adoption services, and family preservation and reunification programs. In private family service agencies, social workers also work with children and families in the areas of adoption, family preservation and reunification, alternative care, and in-home therapy programs. In agencies that provide services to persons with physical or mental illness, addictions, or disabilities, social workers complete intake assessments, develop and implement treatment plans and follow-up, provide individual and group therapy, and work with the children and/or their parents.

Greater emphasis has been given in recent years to family preservation—specifically, the prevention of out-of-home placement for children—and to strengthening the family's ability to cope and manage. As social work education emphasizes a strengths-based, systems approach, social workers are well trained to serve as family preservation professionals. Social workers provide therapeutic case management, parenting education, and life skills services to families in both the family's home and agency settings.

School social work is a related area of growth and opportunity for social workers interested in working with children and their families. In schools, social workers conduct assessments, serve as liaisons between the school and the family, facilitate groups, and participate in multidisciplinary teams to develop individual educational plans for students. Through the provision of one-on-one and family services as well as educational and prevention programs, school social workers also provide support for those students at risk for poor academic and social outcomes.

One of the most serious issues confronting social workers who intervene with children and families is child abuse and neglect. **Child abuse** occurs when a child is subjected to physical and/or emotional injury and includes sexual abuse. **Child neglect** exists when the child's caregiver does not ensure that the child's emotional, physical, nutritional, educational, or shelter needs are being met. Public education and media attention have increased awareness of child abuse and neglect and the reporting process.

Reports of child abuse and neglect are made most frequently by school personnel. Other primary reporters include professionals from social service agencies, law enforcement, and health care organizations. Many professionals who work in these settings are legally mandated to report suspected cases of child abuse, neglect, or exploitation. Nonmandated reporters (for example, family, friends, neighbors, or observers) can make anonymous reports and are protected from prosecution as long as the report is not made with malicious intent.

In 2010, over 3 million reports were made for suspected child abuse or neglect, with 436,321 of those reports being substantiated and three-quarters of the substantiated cases being cited as neglect (U.S. Department of Health and Human Services (DHHS), 2011). Involved children are evenly divided by gender, tend to be less than 1 year of age, and are most likely to be abused or neglected by a parent, slightly more often the mother. While these numbers are staggering, child abuse, neglect, and fatalities are all decreasing due to increased awareness, treatment, and parenting education (DHHS, 2011).

Even so, the number of children entering the foster care system continues to be extremely high. Of those children found to be abused or neglected, 435,000 entered the foster care system in 2010–2011, a 19% decrease from 2009–2010 (U.S. DHHS, 2010). Children of color are disproportionately represented in the foster care system. Some strides have been made in decreasing the length of time in care, although 115,000 children still await adoption (U.S. DHHS, 2010).

Working with a vulnerable population such as children who have been abused or neglected is not only consistent with the profession's mission, but children and families' outcomes are improved by working with degreed social workers (NASW, 2005a). For these reasons, NASW's *Standards for Social Work Practice in Child Welfare* (2005a) and current policy statement (NASW, 2012–2014j) provide guidelines for competent practice with children and also call for better support for the social workers who work in this area.

Angela Bratcher, BSW, MSW, LCSW, Registered Play Therapist, Great Circle

I am currently employed at Great Circle as an Assistant Director overseeing respite programs, but my position in the state Children's Division as a Social Service Worker II was the foundation of my experience in the social work field. I worked in the Department of Social Services in a Child Abuse and Neglect unit for 5 years. My primary responsibility consisted of responding to mandated reports of suspected child abuse and neglect and preventive reports made through the agency's hotline. After that, I started employment at Boys and Girls Town of Missouri as a behavior specialist in the Fostering Futures program and moved to the position of Program Manager and therapist. Two years ago, Boys and Girls Town of Missouri merged with Edgewood Children's Center and is now known as Great Circle. While working there, I am also pursuing certification as a Board Certified Behavior Analyst.

In general, child welfare workers are very focused on their role in the child protection system. It is essential to have professionals working for and with the children, since children cannot protect themselves. Social workers working in child welfare agencies emphasize the strengths of the families with whom they are working.

An emphasis on teamwork is also important within the Child Abuse and Neglect unit. Social workers support each other with resources to assist families and in the process of placing children in foster care. An increased emphasis is also being placed on activating community support for children and families. By connecting children and families to their communities, a safety net is created for them in the event of another crisis.

My work was challenging and demanding as family situations vary—from substance abuse to parenting challenges, conflict, or inappropriate discipline. One of the first challenges for any worker in this context is to engage families who become involved with the Children's Division. A family may be angry about the report, which can be an obstacle to their active involvement in the case.

Properly supporting and providing services to families is challenging enough without the ongoing challenge of handling typically large caseloads. It is

Play Therapy

Credit: Jupiterimages.

often necessary to prioritize the needs of some families over the needs of other families whose children are considered safe.

Attracting and retaining workers with social work education who want to work in the field of child welfare is challenging as well. Not all child welfare agencies require service workers to have a social work degree, but our social work training makes us well suited for the field of child welfare because we are trained to focus fully on the needs of the family. I would like to see more degreed social workers working in these positions.

Some issues cannot be addressed by providing services to families in their home. Severe physical and sexual abuse places the child's safety at immediate risk. In these cases, the child or children must either be temporarily placed with a relative with a safety plan to protect them, or the child must be taken into protective custody by the court and placed in foster care. If a child is temporarily placed

with a relative, the allegations are investigated and a decision is made based on evidence compiled during the investigation. If the child is placed into protective custody, there will be an initial protective custody hearing to determine whether the child will remain in foster care. The foster care worker and the parents will develop a service plan to work toward reunification of the parents and child.

Children who are placed in foster care often come from environments that lack structure and nurturance. These factors often result in behavior problems when a child is placed in a foster home. Children in foster care who have persistent behavior problems may have many placements over the years, which is yet another setback that children in foster care can experience. The Fostering Futures program seeks to prevent these recurring placements.

In my current position as a behavior specialist in the Fostering Futures program, my goal is to stabilize a child's foster home placement using behavior management. Disruptive behaviors may include temper tantrums, lying, stealing, talking back, difficulty following rules of the household, and substance use. Each child's behaviors are assessed through information gathered from the foster parent, case manager, and the child and by direct observation by the specialist. I then develop an individualized behavior plan to address the unique needs of each child. This plan serves as the guideline for implementing weekly home visits with the child.

Therapeutic activities that address the child's behaviors include play therapy and art therapy, which provide nonverbal outlets for feelings. Through my work with children in foster care, I have discovered that children do want to improve their behavior. Acting-out behaviors are often just an outlet for the children's feelings of anger, loss, and trauma associated with being in foster care. By teaching the children alternative strategies for dealing with their feelings, the children's behavior will eventually improve.

Another factor essential to stabilizing a child's foster care placement is the cooperation of foster parents. Although the training foster parents receive does inform them about the situations that children in foster care experience, they are often unprepared to handle the child's behaviors. I educate foster parents to understand the reasons behind the behaviors so they are more willing to work with the children instead of asking for the child to be removed from their home. By working with the foster parents on these issues and through consistency with implementation, the placement often becomes more stable. Foster parents have to be flexible and open to trying different techniques in handling a child's behavior instead of believing that one approach will work with every child. Improved education for foster parents is also needed so they understand the issues that children in foster care face and develop strategies for handling the issues.

In the respite programs I supervise, my agency also provides services that will develop the independent living skills and social skills of children with a developmental disability, which includes autism spectrum diagnosis. These programs also provide education to parents, siblings, and family members on how to address problem behavior and cope with the emotions that they are feeling. Without the continued support of these programs, many families would be unable to support their child in their community, which could result in more out-of-home placements for children with developmental disabilities.

The focus of services for children in foster care will continue to be stabilization to reduce multiple placements. Nationally, greater emphasis needs to be put on permanency for children in foster care, as stipulated by the 1997 Adoption and Safe Families Act. Many children are still lingering in foster care for several years without a permanent living arrangement.

As a Program Manager and Assistant Director, I am constantly reminded of the need to balance quality services to children and families with the budgetary challenges and accountability required of program funders. These administrative skills are increasingly needed to sustain the funding that enables programs to exist. Additionally, a leadership role requires a social worker to function as a motivator and coach for employees in the program.

Being a social worker who provides services to children in the child welfare system can be challenging and demanding, but also rewarding. As a beginning social worker working in children's services, I had a great opportunity to hone my organizational skills and learn a variety of different intervention strategies. This knowledge provided the framework for me to continue my work with children in foster care and children with developmental disabilities, by providing interventions that bring more stability to their lives and the lives of their families.

GERONTOLOGICAL SOCIAL WORK PRACTICE

Practice with older adults, or **gerontological social work**, is a field of practice that is currently undergoing dramatic changes. With the anticipated increases in the older-adult population as the baby boomers reach their senior years and people live longer, the need for more health and social services is increasing. Currently, 13% of the U.S. population is age 65 or older (Werner, 2011). This number grew by 15% from 2000 to 2009, a rate that is 6% faster than the general population. By 2030, all baby boomers will have reached age 65, making up nearly one-quarter of the U.S. population, and resulting in this population becoming larger than younger cohorts (He, Sengupta, Velkoff, & DeBarros, 2005; U.S. Census Bureau, 2008a).

More social workers will be needed to provide services to this population and their family members and caregivers, particularly in the areas of care coordination, case management, mental health services and supports, government program eligibility determination, care-giving support and counseling (U.S. DHHS, 2006a, p. 1). Currently, less than 10% of social workers identify practice with older adults as their primary field of practice (Whitaker & Arrington, 2008). However, 78% of social workers report having contact with older clients (55+ years), while one-quarter have caseloads that are largely comprised of older adults (Center for Health Workforce Studies & Center for Workforce Studies (CHWS/CWS), 2006).

Despite these statistics, only 7% of MSW students concentrate their education on gerontological social work practice, but over one-quarter of students in one survey reported taking an aging-related course as an undergraduate student and approximately 20% completed a graduate-level aging course (Council on Social Work Education (CSWE), 2006; Cummings, Adler, & DeCoster, 2005).

As the over-65 population reaches nearly one-quarter of the U.S. population, between 60,000 and 70,000 social workers will be needed in a wide range of fields, which is approximately double the number of social workers currently working in gerontological practice (CSWE/SAGE-SW, 2001). Moreover, exposure to gerontological issues during their education, positive attitudes toward older adults, and gerontological social work skills predict the likelihood of a social worker pursuing employment with older adults (Cummings & Adler, 2007). In fact, all social workers need increased awareness and skills for working with issues related to aging.

Policy-Practice Considerations With Older Adults

Through recent initiatives, social work educators have become aware of the need for increased emphasis on preparing students to work competently with older adults regardless of the setting in which they work. One such initiative, "Strengthening Aging and Gerontology Education for Social Work" (CSWE/SAGE-SW, 2001), has developed the 10 competencies shown in Exhibit 8.2 as being crucial for all social workers.

Because much of the aging-related service delivery is provided by multiple disciplines, social workers often work directly with older adults and their families in host

EXHIBIT 8.2

*Social Work
Competencies
for Practice
with Older
Adults*

1. Assess one's own values and biases regarding aging, death, and dying.
2. Educate self to dispel the major myths about aging.
3. Accept, respect, and recognize the right and need of older adults to make their own choices and decisions about their lives within the context of the law and safety concerns.
4. Understand normal physical, psychological, and social changes in later life.
5. Respect and address cultural, spiritual, and ethnic needs and beliefs of older adults and family members.
6. Examine the diversity of attitudes toward aging, mental illness, and family roles.
7. Understand the influence of aging on family dynamics.
8. Use social work case management skills (such as brokering, advocacy, monitoring, and discharge planning) to link elders and their families to resources and services.
9. Gather information regarding social history, such as social functioning, primary and secondary social supports, social activity level, social skills, financial status, cultural background, and social involvement.
10. Identify ethical and professional boundary issues that commonly arise in work with older adults and their caregivers, such as client self-determination, end-of-life decisions, family conflicts, and guardianship.

Source: CSWE/SAGE-SW, 2001.

settings. A host setting is an organization whose primary mission is the provision of services other than social services (for example, health care or education). Such settings include hospitals; rehabilitation programs; residential care facilities (for example, skilled care and assisted living facilities, and senior independent living communities); adult day service programs; senior centers with congregate meal programs; home health agencies; and hospice programs. Gerontological social workers may work in agencies that provide case management services for older adults; investigate elder abuse, neglect, and exploitation; or provide supportive services for family members and caregivers.

Another important area of practice for gerontological social workers is policy practice. Influencing the development of legislation, policy, and programming for older adults is critical to the enhanced longevity and quality of life for the burgeoning older-adult population.

Carroll Rodriguez, BSW, Alzheimer's Association Chapter

I am the public policy director for a state coalition of Alzheimer's Association chapters. I am charged with mobilizing others in an effort to bring about governmental and legislative changes that will benefit persons with Alzheimer's disease, their families, and their care partners. I work with the four state chapters, coordinating the state and national public policy activities for my state.

Alzheimer's Association

Memory Day 2012

Photo courtesy of Alzheimer's Association, 9370 Olive Boulevard, St. Louis, Missouri. Used by permission.

The route to becoming a state public policy director was not a straight one for me. Upon graduating with my BSW, I worked as a social worker in a skilled care nursing facility and an adult day program. In these positions, I was responsible for facilitating support groups, working with older adults and their families, and coordinating admissions and care planning. Following a relocation with my family, I continued my gerontological social work career in community-based services, working as a program supervisor with an area agency on aging. In this position, I supervised senior center programs in rural communities and had the opportunity to open up several new senior centers in small communities that had not previously had services. From there, it was a natural progression for me to work for the Alzheimer's Association, where I started out working in the respite program in which I coordinated access to these much-needed services that provided a break for caregivers. These varied experiences gave me both valuable skills in working with families and insight into many different facets of care needed to maintain a quality of life for our older-adult population.

In my current position, I work to improve the laws and policies that govern the services provided to persons with Alzheimer's disease. Alzheimer's disease is the most common form of dementia (the terms are often used interchangeably), a progressive, degenerative disease of the brain for which there is no cure. Alzheimer's disease affects a person's memory, judgment, and ability to reason. More than 5.4 million Americans are living with Alzheimer's disease and millions more are impacted—the families and friends that serve as their care partners. A person with dementia will live an average of 8 years and as many as 20 years after the symptoms appear. As they advance through the disease process, long-term care and support are critical but can exhaust any care partner from time to time.

My experience as a social worker working with older adults prepared me well for working at the policy level. Having direct practice experience with this population in a variety of settings enables me to understand the needs of older adults and their care partners, the gaps in the service delivery system, and the importance of ensuring that policy decision makers are well informed as they enact legislation and make policy.

The Alzheimer's Association chapters are part of the nation's largest voluntary health organization devoted to conquering Alzheimer's disease. Through a network of more than 70 chapters across the country, individuals with the disease and their care partners have access to a broad range of programs and services, and can participate in support for research and advocacy. Because the association is such a large organization that speaks on behalf of persons with Alzheimer's disease, we have the opportunity to influence state and federal policies for this population.

State public policy activities and platform development is a three-phase process:

1. *Issue identification.* As I determine the areas for advocacy, I routinely ask the following questions: What are the greatest unmet needs? Where are the gaps in services? How can we build an enhanced long-term care delivery system to meet the growing demands of an aging population? Answers to these questions can be found by listening to the voices of persons with the disease and their care partners. Through focus groups, surveys, support group visits, and other means of communication, the coalition that I direct has identified three current areas of greatest need: (1) enhanced access to a continuum of long-term care services; (2) improved quality of care throughout the long-term care continuum; and (3) a cure for Alzheimer's disease.

2. *Development of potential solutions.* Once a policy agenda is established, the next critical task is to develop potential solutions. This process involves coalition building and networking both internally, within the chapter network, and externally, with partners that have an interest in the issue. Health care providers, leaders within state agencies, researchers in the field of aging, and families with a vested interest in the issue are examples of partners that can aid in developing viable solutions and achievable goals.

3. *Creation of public policy platform.* Building on this process, I work with the coalition to outline a public policy platform that includes goals and objectives addressing the areas of focus. Some of the components that are necessary to advance a public policy initiative include drafting the language for proposed legislative bills; gaining sponsorship from legislators that are sensitive to and supportive of the issue; testifying at public hearings in front of legislators and voters; and building a broad base of supporters among voters, professionals, and legislators. Grassroots advocacy is at the core of this process. By mobilizing people that are passionate about an issue, a great deal can be accomplished.

For example, every year, I travel with other advocates to my state capital and Washington, DC, to talk with the legislature about appropriations for funding research to find a cure for Alzheimer's disease, to study the effects of this disease on individuals and their families, and to develop interventions to enhance their lives. Along with thousands of supporters, I write letters and e-mail and meet with legislators in the capitols and their home districts. As a result of these ongoing grassroots advocacy efforts, Congress has increased Alzheimer's research funding to approximately $500 million over a 13-year period. Still, this amount is far short of the federal government's commitment to combat diseases such as stroke, heart disease, HIV/AIDS, and breast cancer, which have all seen death rates decline as a result of an increased investment in research.

A current challenge for the families that I represent in my advocacy efforts is that both Medicare and private health insurance fail to address the chronic health care needs of persons with Alzheimer's disease. Medicaid is the program that serves as the safety net for long-term care services. It supports community-based programs as well as nursing home care. Access to Medicaid services has become a primary area of focus for Alzheimer's advocates. Through grassroots efforts, we have worked to maintain and at times expand options, support, and access to home and community services.

A second area of challenge in my current advocacy work is improving the quality of the care that is provided within those long-term care settings. More than half of all residents have some form of dementia. My fellow advocates and I drafted and passed legislation in my state that requires all employees caring for persons with dementia to be trained in dementia care.

Working with a coalition of Alzheimer's Association chapters to shape a public policy platform and mobilizing advocates to move that platform forward has required me to call upon a skill set acquired from both experience and education. With a BSW and 25 years of professional experience in the field of aging, I have learned the value of listening to others, the importance of negotiation and compromise, and the merits of networking and coalition building. However, of most importance is the realization that many voices can make change happen.

For the future of my area of practice, it is projected that 14 million of today's baby boomers will develop Alzheimer's disease by midcentury. Costs for persons with Alzheimer's disease will continue to increase as well. Annual public spending is projected to be an estimated $174 billion in Medicare and Medicaid costs by 2020; costs of this magnitude will overwhelm our health care system and bankrupt both Medicare and Medicaid. Succinctly stated by the Alzheimer's Association, "We are facing a race against time." Now more than ever, there is a need for social workers to engage in public policy advocacy in support of persons with Alzheimer's disease and their care partners.

SOCIAL WORK PRACTICE WITH PEOPLE WITH DISABILITIES

Throughout history, the concept of "disability" has had many connotations, many of them negative, but in the last 50 years negative perceptions have begun to shift. The 20th century saw the emergence of the disability rights movement, which culminated in the passage of the Americans with Disabilities Act (ADA) in 1990. This landmark legislation mandated easier access and less discrimination in the areas of employment, telecommunications, public accommodations, and societal services (Mackelprang et al., 2008, p. 38). The ADA has been expanded twice, in 1997 and 2004, to address educational access and equity. There has been great progress with inclusion and people with disabilities have been integrated into schools and the community.

Current estimations show approximately 10% of the world population or 650 million people have disabilities. Twelve percent of U.S. residents, or 36 million people, live with a disability (U.S. Census Bureau News, 2011). The majority of those persons who experience a disability are older adults (37%) and female (12.3%). Those who live with a disability tend to live near or in poverty and to be unable to engage in paid employment (72%).

Disabilities occur primarily in the areas of hearing, vision, memory and thinking, and mobility. Most people will experience one disability in their lifetime. Due to dramatic increases in the number of people being diagnosed with autism spectrum disorder, social workers in a variety of settings are working with more persons experiencing this disability. Recent findings by the Centers for Disease Control and Prevention (2012) indicate that one in 88 children is experiencing an autism spectrum disorder, an increase of 78% since 2008.

Given the significant segments of our population that are impacted by a disability, social workers must develop competent practice knowledge and skills to work effectively with individuals and families facing disabilities. In the most recent policy statement, NASW (2012–2014h) calls for social work curricula to include content on the history, culture, research, best practices, and civil rights issues related to disabilities and to include social workers with disabilities in the professional organization (p. 249). Whether social workers choose a practice that focuses on people with disabilities or not, they will likely know someone—a co-worker, family, friend —who has a disability.

Policy-Practice Considerations in Working With People Who Have Disabilities

Social workers have had a long history of working with and advocating for persons with disabilities. Social workers currently work with individuals within all the areas of disabilities (Mackelprang et al., 2008):

- *Neurocognitive disabilities* encompass limited capacities of intellect, memory, sensory integration, and thought processing. These conditions exist along a continuum, including autism, Down syndrome, developmental disabilities, Alzheimer's disease, and sensory integration dysfunctions.

- *Physical disabilities,* which are typically acquired after birth, create limitations in physical function or activity. They include paraplegia and other mobility limitations, speaking, hearing, and vision challenges, and chronic organ system-related disease.

- *Psychiatric disabilities* result from serious and persistent mental illness (e.g., schizophrenia, anxiety, depression, or bipolar disorder).

As societal perceptions about disabilities have evolved over time, the theoretical concepts for working with individuals with disabilities have become more focused. Contemporary thought has conceptualized disability as a "naturally occurring

EXHIBIT 8.3	
Practice Guidelines for Working With People Who Have Disabilities	• Be person-centered, involving the individual in the decision-making process regarding her or his life. • Incorporate the strengths-based perspective to build on the client's existing strengths and resources. • Facilitate access and respect in the person's environment. • Focus on helping the individual and her or his support network cope with any situation that may be challenging the person. *Source:* Mackelprang et al., 2008.

phenomenon that adds to societal diversity" (Mackelprang et al., 2008, p. 40). The problems that persons with disabilities experience are viewed within the context of society and the systems within which the individual lives. While this theoretical framework is more consistent with social work values and ethics and significant strides have been made in antidiscrimination and access policies, persons with disabilities continue to experience challenges in the areas of housing, health care, and income benefits (Mackelprang et al., 2008).

The type and extent of the disability may inform the practice approach. However, some general assumptions may guide the planning and implementation of the social work intervention. In working with any person with a disability, the practice intervention should follow the guidelines shown in Exhibit 8.3. With these practice behaviors guiding the practice intervention, the social worker may engage in crisis intervention, case management, interprofessional collaboration, and policy practice (e.g., advocacy) to support the client in maintaining the optimal quality of life.

Mark A. Keeley, MSW, LCSW, St. Louis Arc

For more than three decades, I have worked with individuals who have cognitive and developmental disabilities and their families. My first interaction with people with developmental disabilities occurred when I volunteered in high school to help with the Special Olympics in order to avoid taking a math test. I succeeded in avoiding the math test and, more importantly found my calling and career path. On that spring day, I met many wonderful individuals, from teenagers to adults, who were enjoying the thrill of victory and competition. I began speaking with them and asking them about their lives. Many of the individuals then were living in institutions and had little or no family involvement. I wondered who took care of them and advocated for their needs if they were not able to do so for themselves.

Within 2 months, I was working full-time with six adults, two women and four men, who had developmental disabilities and had just moved from an institution to a group home. Additionally, I worked in a respite facility on weekends, which gave me exposure to the support needs of families. I subsequently obtained a bachelor's and master's in social work, focusing on supporting people with disabilities.

Wasserman Family Photo

Mary, Al, and Michael Wasserman.

Photo by Jay O. Fisk. Used by permission.

Throughout my career, my primary focus has been providing holistic approaches to address the support needs not only of the individual with a disability but to the entire family. When someone is diagnosed with a disability, everyone in the family is impacted in some way. As the person ages, new challenges emerge and those too impact everyone. Addressing the individual and group needs of a family help to strengthen the family as a unit and each member individually.

From the beginning, the people I have supported who have disabilities have taught me a great deal. They have taught me to see them as the unique individual they are and to see their disability as an attribute but not something that defines them. People with disabilities rarely want someone to do everything for them but appreciate it when someone offers support so they may achieve their own goals.

People with disabilities often have a sense of isolation. When they are infants and toddlers,

people with disabilities can easily be with their typically developing peers. But as they get older, when school and sports get competitive, there is often an unnecessary divide that separates people with disabilities from those without. Inclusion has dramatically increased over the past 30 years but people with disabilities are still, too often, left out of many activities. As social workers, we must continue to work towards full inclusion in school, employment, and the community as a whole.

A challenge for most people with disabilities and their families is the Individualized Education Program (IEP) process. Any person with a disability requiring additional supports beyond the standard curriculum will have an IEP. Unfortunately, the IEP process is too often focused on a person's deficits, not strengths. Most people choose a career that suits their strengths and interests but the IEP process does not accentuate those strengths for persons with disabilities; rather, it focuses on the negatives.

People with disabilities want the same opportunities as anyone wants in life. They want to be able to live independently, away from their parents. They want to go to college, get a job, to have a social life, to have friends and someone to love. With the proper supports, people can succeed in achieving their goals.

Social workers and other professionals should never let a person's disability or diagnosis be a predictor of what they may or may not be able to achieve. Too often parents hear that their child will never be able to achieve their goals. Parents are told their child will never walk, never talk, and never be able to achieve independence. Time and time again, I have seen individuals surpass the limitations set upon them by professionals.

Sometimes we need to be creative in determining the ways in which we support someone to achieve their goals. There was a man who had significant physical and cognitive disabilities who wanted to play professional baseball. Given his physical limitations, realistically he would not qualify for a professional team. The people who supported him explored his reasons for wanting to play professional baseball. It became clear he was really interested in being part of a team and wearing a uniform; he really had no interest in actually playing the game. He is now the assistant coach of a little league team and could not be happier.

Parents learning they are about to have or have had a child with a disability face a myriad of emotions. Expectant parents dream of the perfect child. When they receive news that their child has a disability, their original dreams are shattered and they go through cognitive coping to achieve a new dream or dreams for their child's future. Young parents face a tremendous sense of isolation when they do not know any other parents who have a child with a disability. They rely on social workers and other professionals to help them navigate the ever-changing maze of services and support systems their child needs. Connecting parents with one another helps address the issues of isolation and builds natural supports for families.

Throughout the lifespan, families have to be educated about the services and supports available to them and their family members. The services that exist for infants and toddlers are different than those for school-aged children. As children become teenagers, parents face not only the typical challenges of teenagers but the additional challenges that may occur as a result of the person's disability. Parents need help to plan for the future of their son or daughter with a disability. Will they go to college, will they live independently or in a residential setting with others, will they have competitive employment or other day supports? Many parents I have talked to have the plan to always keep their son or daughter at home. They pray for the ability to always care for their family member and just need "one breath more" than their son or daughter. Social workers need to work with families to develop plans that address the long-term support needs of the individual and wishes of the family.

When taking a holistic approach to supporting individuals with developmental disabilities and their families it is important to remember siblings. Siblings bear a large responsibility when they have a brother or sister with a disability. Siblings, like parents, often have a tremendous feeling of isolation. They do not know anyone else who has a brother or sister with a disability. Siblings often excel in academics, sports, or hobbies in order to get recognition from their parents and other adults. Sibshops, a program originated by Don Meyer, offer a high-energy, fun way for siblings to meet one another and process their feelings and emotions about having a sibling with a disability.

It is important for social workers and parents to consistently give age-appropriate information to siblings so they understand the needs of their brother or sister and also so they know what the long-term plans are for the care of their sibling. I have heard children at 6 years of age talking about how they will be taking care of their brother or sister for the rest of their life. No child should feel that sense of obligation or responsibility. Parents often have plans for their son or daughter with a disability but they may not always share the plan with the siblings.

Taking the holistic approach to supporting people with disabilities and their families provides the tools they each need to achieve their individual and family goals. Social workers who support people with disabilities and their families need to offer services that address the unique needs of each individual and family while being flexible enough to address the needs of the community as a whole.

SOCIAL WORK PRACTICE WITH MILITARY FAMILY MEMBERS

Social workers have had a long history of working with military personnel, veterans, and their family members in a variety of settings. First trained to work with soldiers returning from World War I in 1918, social workers have been present throughout each military action since then as well as consistently working on the home front and abroad (CSWE, 2010). Social workers are practicing in combat zones during deployment activities, on military installations in the United States and throughout the world, in veterans' medical centers and service organizations, and in civilian public and private organizations. Services are provided by social work practitioners who are themselves on active duty and by civilian workers employed by the Department of Defense.

Just like their civilian colleagues, social workers working in military-related settings with individuals and families connected to the armed services provide an array of services, including (CSWE, 2010, p. 2):

- Direct practice, which can include prevention, treatment, and rehabilitative services, particularly related to combat experiences (e.g., traumatic brain injury, posttraumatic stress, depression, substance abuse, combat stress, readjustment issues, intimate partner violence, and polytrauma (i.e., presence of multiple injuries)).

- Policy and administration.

- Advocacy.

- Development of programs, policies, and procedures to improve the quality of life for their clients.

- Assistance and treatment for military members and families as they transition from active duty to veteran status.

Their duties can include everything from working in the field with service members to assess morale to working with retirees in a medical center intervention (Angelis, 2012). Families are an integral part of most interventions.

Policy-Practice Considerations in Military Social Work

As it relates to the military and the social work profession, the United States is in the midst of the longest military engagement in our history. As a result, social workers in a variety of settings will be working with military-related issues, regardless of their primary areas of practice. Just as with many of the other diverse areas of social work practice, it is critical that social work practitioners gain awareness of, and competence in, the culture of the military community. The military and its related institutions have a specialized language, structure, and hierarchy. Well known to the persons who are members of that community, this culture is new for most civilians.

Identifying a need for such expertise, the CSWE outlines a competency-based framework for military social work. This collaborative project calls for social workers to raise their awareness regarding the issues that are affecting the nearly 3 million individuals who have served in current military actions as well as the families and support networks. Exhibit 8.4 presents some of the CSWE's guidelines for practice in military social work.

EXHIBIT 8.4

Practice Guidelines for Military Social Work

Educational Policy 2.1.1
- Engage in lifelong learning, supervision, and consultation to enhance knowledge and skills needed to work effectively with service members, veterans, their families, and their communities.
- Practice self-reflection and continue to address personal biases and stereotypes to build knowledge and dispel myths regarding service members, veterans, their families, and their communities.

Educational Policy 2.1.2
- Demonstrate a professional demeanor that reflects awareness of and respect for military and veteran cultures.
- Recognize boundary and integration issues between military and veteran cultures and social work values and ethics.

Educational Policy 2.1.3
- Employ strategies of ethical reasoning in an environment that may have policy and value conflicts with social work service delivery, personal values, and professional ethics.
- Identify the military culture's emphasis on mission readiness, support of service, honor, and cohesion and how these influence social work service delivery at the micro, mezzo, and macro levels.
- Recognize and manage appropriate professional boundaries within the military and veteran context.

EXHIBIT 8.4

continued

Educational Policy 2.1.4
- Analyze the unique relationships among the client, the family, the military, and various veterans' organizations.
- Use professional judgment to meet the needs of all involved clients.
- Analyze appropriate models of assessment, prevention, intervention, and evaluation within the context of military social work.
- Use appropriate practice models with service members, veterans, their families, and their communities.
- Demonstrate effective oral and written communication using established Department of Defense (DoD)/Veterans Affairs (VA) professional standards and practices.

Educational Policy 2.1.5
- Manage potential conflicts between diverse identities within and among individuals and the military and veterans' organizations.
- Manage potential conflicts between personal feelings/expression and collective/institutional responsibility.
- Recognize the potential risk and protective factors among diverse populations and communities that may be the result of military service.
- Communicate with a culturally responsive approach that includes service members with varying statuses such as active duty/retired, guard/reserves, and combat/garrison.

Educational Policy 2.1.6
- Identify and analyze conflictual responses and potential consequences to conflicts between basic human rights and military life and duty experience.
- Advocate at multiple levels for service parity and reduction of service disparities for the diverse service member populations.
- Identify the needs of military and veteran individuals, families, and communities to civilian providers and workplace management.
- Teach skills to promote self-sufficiency, self-advocacy, and empowerment within the context of practice and culture.

Educational Policy 2.1.7
- Locate, evaluate, and analyze current research literature related to military social work.
- Evaluate research to practice with service members, veterans, families, and their communities.
- Analyze models of assessment, prevention, intervention, and evaluation within the context of military social work.
- Apply different literature and evidence-informed and evidence-based practices in the provision of services across the DoD/VA continuum of care and services.

Continued

EXHIBIT 8.4

continued

Educational Policy 2.1.8

- Recognize and assess social support systems and socioeconomic resources specific to service members, veterans, their families, and their communities.
- Recognize the impact of military transitions and stressful life events throughout the family's life course.
- Identify issues related to losses, stressors, changes, and transitions over their life cycle in designing interventions.
- Demonstrate the ability to critically appraise the impact of the social environment on the overall well-being of service members, veterans, their families, and their communities.

Educational Policy 2.1.9

- Communicate effectively with various veterans' service organizations to provide effective social work services and accurate benefits, entitlements, and services information to clients, their family members, and their communities.
- Apply knowledge of the Uniform Code of Military Justice.
- Use social policy analysis as a basis for action and advocacy with the chain of command and within federal agencies.
- Respond to civilian and governmental inquiries (e.g., congressional inquiry).

Educational Policy 2.1.10

- Assess service systems' history, trends, and innovations in social work practice with service members, veterans, their families, and/or their communities.
- Apply knowledge of practice within the military context to the development of evaluations, prevention plans, and treatment strategies.
- Use information technologies and organizational analysis techniques for outreach, planning multiyear projections, for service delivery to service members and the veteran populations as well as to their families and their communities.
- Recognize the unique issues and culture presented by the service member, veteran, and/or family member client.
- Establish a culturally responsive therapeutic relationship that addresses the unique issues associated with confidentiality and reporting requirements within a military context.
- Explain the nature, limits, rights, and responsibilities of the client who seeks services.
- Explain the stigma, risks, and benefits of seeking or not seeking services.
- Engage with military leadership, the unit, veteran service organizations, and/or family members.
- Demonstrate a knowledge base related to risk and protective factors associated with deployment, military service, and other aspects of life and role transitions that service members' and veterans' experience.
- Demonstrate knowledge related to health and mental health illnesses, injuries, and outcomes for service members, veterans, their families, and their communities.

- Select and modify appropriate multisystemic intervention strategies based on continuous clinical assessment of military or veteran issues.
- Use differential and multiaxial diagnoses that take into consideration signature injuries as well as other military-related illnesses and injuries.
- Use empathy, cultural responsiveness, and other interpersonal skills in completing an assessment.
- Assess coping strategies to reinforce and improve adaptation to life situations and transitions while also emphasizing ways of coping with readjustment from military to civilian life.
- Use a range of appropriate clinical and preventive interventions for various injuries, diagnoses, and psychosocial concerns identified in the assessment, including crisis intervention and advocacy strategies as needed.
- Engage clients in ongoing monitoring and evaluation of practice processes and outcomes.
- Demonstrate the capacity to reflect on one's own responses (i.e., affect and world views) that influence the progress in and the completion of treatment.
- Use clinical and program evaluation of the process and/or outcomes to develop best practice interventions and programs for a range of biopsycho-social-spiritual conditions and evaluate their own practice to determine the effectiveness of the applied intervention on military/veteran issues.

EXHIBIT 8.4

continued

Source: CSWE, 2010.

Social workers provide services to active duty personnel, veterans, retirees, and the family members of all these groups during peace time, deployments, and following the service member's time of service. Social workers can help to support military-related clients during times of transitions and crises related to military service, but also for the type of needs that occur that are not military-related (e.g., health events, end-of-life issues, or school-related problems). While military personnel and families experience the same life issues as others, there are unique challenges, particularly during times of deployment. Having a family member, particularly a parent, serving in a combat zone can result in children experiencing physical and emotional stressors and behavioral and school-related problems. Providing family-oriented interventions in which the parents learn to work with the children through play, for instance, can be an effective strategy for helping children adjust to the parent's deployment (Chawla & Solinas-Saunders, 2011).

James Allen, Ph.D., MSW, U.S. Army (Retired)

I have been practicing social work for 43 years. For 20 of those years, I served as a social work officer in the U.S. Army. During that time, I was a member of a military family and provided service to other military families. This experience shaped my understanding of the impact of military life on families and the most appropriate means of responding to their needs.

The designation "military family" may suggest that these families are significantly different than others. Understanding military families, however, begins by considering the critical dimensions that are relevant for all families. Communication is among the most important of these concepts. Effective communication enhances the ability of families to deal appropriately with the challenges they face. Families able to communicate effectively are better able to cope with challenges in a healthy manner. The ability of family members to talk and listen creates an environment in which each person feels valued. Being valued, in turn, increases the likelihood that members will actively participate in developing strategies to deal with expected and unexpected challenges. Given the importance of effective communication, it is critical that we assist all families in examining their communication patterns and finding ways to enhance them.

One of the most significant challenges facing military families is the deployment of a family member, particularly to a combat zone. This event typically generates significant feelings on the part of all members of the family and household. The social worker has no power to change the situation, but creating an environment in which members feel free to talk about their feelings helps in dealing with the reality in a healthy manner. Open communication also allows family members to talk about necessary strategies to deal with the impact of the deployment.

All families are organized in a particular manner. Individual members are assigned particular roles. Military families are no different. In some families, roles are strictly defined. Each member knows their role and the associated responsibilities. Rigidly defined roles may enable families to deal with their current situation effectively but make it difficult for them to deal with changes, such as the deployment of a family member. Family members may find themselves being called on to assume roles and responsibilities that are new to them.

Trying to address this crisis in a short time frame can be overwhelming. Failure to make the adjustment, however, can further complicate the family's ability to maintain a sense of balance. Working with families to create a more balanced sharing of responsibilities can increase flexibility and prepare them to make the necessary accommodations required by the absence of a family member.

An important dimension associated with roles is that of decision making. There are always decisions to be made. Ideally, families develop patterns that maximize the involvement of members as appropriate. Creating such an environment when all members are present increases the likelihood that the family will be able to make needed decisions in the absence of members. The crisis created by the deployment of a key decision maker further disrupts the balance of the family and exacerbates the trauma. With this in mind, families should be invited to examine their decision-making strategies carefully and consider alternative approaches that will allow them to maintain the needed balance.

Many military families include children. These children are profoundly affected by the changes in their family, both anticipated and unanticipated, but often have difficulty in communicating the impact of these events. If parents do not try to draw them into the conversation, the children's feelings go unaddressed. At times, these feelings become overwhelming and children express them behaviorally. When this happens, children's behavior may be misunderstood and labeled as "acting out." In such situations, social workers can serve as advocates for the children. We can encourage parents to recognize children's feelings and help them develop ways of encouraging children to share their thoughts and feelings. Creating such opportunities can serve to reduce the tension within the family and enable them to deal more effectively with the demands of the situation.

In working with military families, as with all families, it is important to adopt a strengths perspective. This perspective focuses on helping families to recognize their strengths and resources. It also encourages them to examine ways in which they can use these strengths and resources to confront current and future challenges. Asking families to identify those strategies that have helped them to address challenges in the past is a starting point. Recognizing that they have coped in the past helps to relieve some of the anxiety associated with the current situation.

Social workers can also help families identify resources in the community that can assist them. A sense of community among military families is a major strength. Families tend to come together, both formally and informally, to support one other as they deal with shared challenges. Encouraging families to connect with others can help to overcome a sense of isolation.

While military families may share much in common, each family is unique. From the outset, it is critical to recognize individual differences. With this in mind, social workers can view the family as the "experts" and help them to reflect on their own experience and consider lessons learned that can help them in dealing with current challenges.

Military families are more like than unlike other families. Working effectively with them requires that we apply the same theoretical and practice frameworks that we use in working with all families.

SOCIAL WORK PRACTICE WITH IMMIGRANTS AND REFUGEES

The number of current U.S. residents born in other countries exceeded 40 million in 2010 (Walters & Trevelyan, 2011). They may be in the country as a refugee or asylum seeker; be here on an immigrant, student, business, or extended visa; or live here without documentation. Exhibit 8.5 shows where they have come from. As you can see, most of them in recent years have come from Asia (Walters & Trevelyan, 2011).

Policy-Practice Considerations With Immigrants and Refugees

Social workers in the United States have always worked with an array of international issues, including providing services to people who immigrate to this country from their homelands. Social workers work with persons living in countries outside the United States as well as persons living in the United States who were born in other countries. To be a social worker with a global focus does not require that you have to work outside the United States. In the area of international adoptions, social workers assist families in applying, conduct home studies, act as liaison to the international adoption organization, and provide postadoption support services. Social workers also provide services in international emergency and disaster situations and in administering U.S.-based programs that provide services in the international community.

In addition to working with international issues, social workers play a prominent role in working with immigrants and refugees living in the United States. The settlement house movement focused originally on the provision of services to recent immigrants to the United States. Training social workers who are culturally

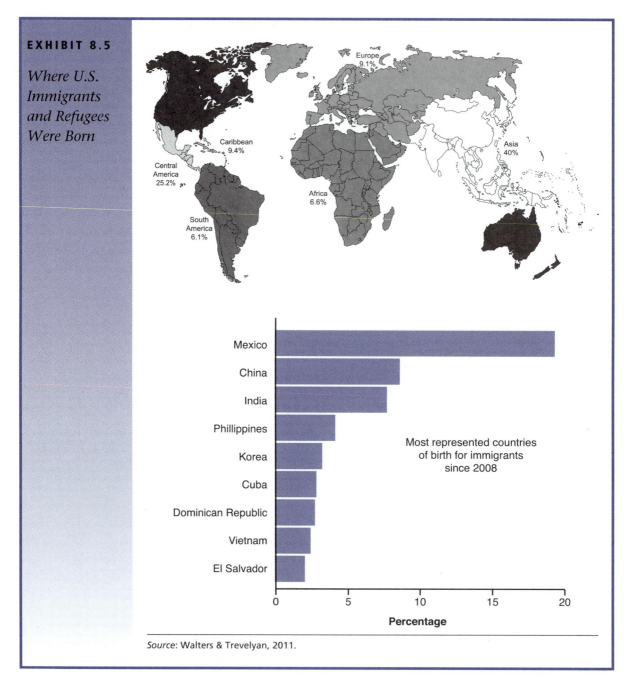

EXHIBIT 8.5

Where U.S. Immigrants and Refugees Were Born

Most represented countries of birth for immigrants since 2008

Source: Walters & Trevelyan, 2011.

competent and sensitive to the needs of the many and varied populations of persons that are new to this country is a priority for the profession. Refugee-focused legislation has been in place in the United States since 1948 when nearly a half million post-World War II refugees were admitted (Martin, 2010). Such legislation has been amended throughout the decades as needs are identified. Despite caps being imposed on the number and originating countries, refugee entry to the United States has consistently grown, with a decrease in the period following September 11, 2001 (Martin, 2010). Countries from which the largest numbers of refugees are currently beginning their journeys include Iraq, Burma, and Bhutan (Martin, 2010).

Working with persons born in other countries will span the spectrum of the social work population, thus requiring U.S.-based social workers in virtually every field of practice to have the knowledge and skills for practicing with diverse populations. Social workers may work in direct practice with individuals and families that have immigrated to this country, or they may work in the policy and advocacy arena on behalf of entire communities of persons who have relocated to the United States. Policies toward newer residents are often conflicted, thus creating a need for social workers to become the voice for this population. NASW has called for the federal government to support immigrants and refugees through enactment of legislation and programming that ensures fair and equitable actions (NASW, 2012–2014e). As an example, consider the changing demographic status of children living in immigrant and refugee families. Comprising the fastest-growing segment of the population, these children are at greater risk for living in poverty and experiencing educational and health care deficits (Society for Research in Child Development, 2008). Social workers are well positioned to advocate for improved and more culturally focused services for these children and their families. As you determine those areas of social work practice that are of interest to you, consider that internationally focused social work practice can be practiced both domestically as well as internationally and in virtually any setting.

Suzanne LeLaurin, MSW, LCSW, International Institute

I am a social worker who works with persons who emigrate from other countries to the United States. I am the senior vice president for individuals and families at an international social services agency. I oversee several departments that provide a variety of services to immigrants and their families. In the client services department, we provide case management, employment, social work, and counseling services for newly arrived refugees. The education department is responsible for teaching English to speakers of other languages. The program development and quality assurance department is responsible for continuous quality improvement and staff training on grant requirements. In the past three decades, we have served 20,000 refugees.

Social work is a second career for me. After spending over 20 years in the for-profit sector working for a large insurance company, I decided I wanted to work in the nonprofit sector, and chose to get my MSW to help others gain access to needed services and enhance their quality of life. Since completing my MSW, I obtained my license to practice clinical social work in my state.

In reflecting on my social work practice working with persons born in another country, I must emphasize the importance of advocacy. The United States is a country of immigrants, but as a society, we have conflicting views about the importance of immigrants to our country. In the mid-1990s, Congress passed legislation that restricted access by noncitizens (who enter the United States legally) to benefits available to U.S. citizens. There have been initiatives to ease those restrictions, especially since they were harming some of the most vulnerable persons in our society—seniors who had been unable to learn English sufficiently to obtain citizenship and were increasingly at risk of homelessness as well as despair (which pushed some of them to suicide).

With the horrifying 2001 terrorist attacks on the United States, many of the moves to welcome the immigrant to our shores shifted once again. Security tightened for all immigrants attempting to enter the United States. The effects were most pronounced with refugee migration—the largest population with which I work—as the number of refugees admitted dropped from almost 70,000 in fiscal year 2001 to fewer than 30,000 in 2002.

With the rise in anti-immigrant fever, advocacy became paramount in social work with immigrants. My agency worked with an advocacy group to accompany our clients to their preferred farmer's market and doctors' appointments, just to protect them from shouts of "go home, terrorist" and worse. One of my staff, a former refugee herself, slept with her clothes on and a stick and her cell phone with her, for fear of intruders. Thankfully, the panic from 9/11 has died down, but the events of that horrible day gave new impetus to the strong anti-immigration sentiment of those fighting political gains for immigrants.

Counterbalancing the political forces to keep immigrants out of our country are the needs of employers. With the baby boom generation aging and birth rates decreasing in the United States, employers and policy experts now recognize that future growth in employment forces will depend on migration into our country. During the recent recession, job opportunities were drying up for both American-born and foreign-born.

While the number of refugee numbers entering the country is close to pre-9/11 levels, we will likely continue to see fewer immigrants enter the United States. In spite of the lower numbers, we will still see those born in other countries in our midst, both to fuel our economy through a skilled workforce and because, unfortunately, we still experience war and civil unrest around the world, leading to refugees needing safe haven.

For those social workers interested in working with persons with diverse national origins, there will be many opportunities to provide a variety of social work services for refugees, those who are forced to flee their homelands due to civil unrest, persecution, and violence. These persons are considered "reluctant immigrants," as they did not choose to leave their homelands, but were forced to do so by circumstances beyond their control. Typically, they arrive here with little more than the clothes on their backs. This population needs and will continue to need our support in basic necessities (food, clothing, and shelter), learning the English language, employment, adapting to U.S. culture (while hopefully holding on to the richness of their own culture), and mental health services for coming to terms with the horrors of trauma and torture. These needs will also exist for migrant workers who come into the United States intent on making enough money to support their families, with a risk of exploitation by unscrupulous employers taking advantage of their undocumented status. Other immigrants arriving to join family also may benefit from social work support as they adjust to their new home.

There is a growing need for cultural diversity and competence training for those born in the United States that expands the definition of diversity beyond the traditional black/white/indigenous population categories into cultural diversity based on ethnicity. Our religious communities, while already pluralistic, will also shift beyond the dominant Judeo-Christian faiths, which will lead us to a need for diversity training for a variety of groups—other social service providers, employers, educators, medical professionals, and many more.

We also need to adapt our social work services to accommodate the needs of those whose cultural norms are different from those of the United States. Social workers must ask themselves questions like the ones I've asked myself. How do I, as a feminist, react to and serve a conservative Muslim woman who considers it immodest to show any parts of her body other than her hands and face; yet her clothing limits her ability to work in the only job I can find for her, such as a manufacturing job that requires clothing not get in the way of machines? How do I work with teenagers and parents experiencing family conflicts in which the teens are "Americanized" into thinking that adolescence is a time to "move away" from parents and become independent, while the parents come from a culture in which youth independence brings great shame on the family in their cultural community? How do I counsel an adult woman with an aging mother in need of long-term care, but who considers the idea of placing her mother in a skilled nursing facility a shameful rejection of her responsibilities as a dutiful and respectful daughter? Is self-esteem just a Western construct, or does it have application in a culture that is more collectivist than individualistic? As social workers, we will all be challenged to serve those with different values and beliefs from our own, and these differences will be much more pronounced with those who were born in other cultures.

The great joy—and challenge—of working with persons from diverse national origins is that they help me see the world through a different cultural and political lens, influenced by their own life experiences, cultural norms, and beliefs that are so different from my own. I am in awe of the resilience and spirit of refugees who come to this country, prepared to start building a whole new life after the one they knew was shattered and stolen from them. I am challenged to see my world through another person's eyes, and find myself questioning some of my own deeply held assumptions about my country and culture. The world has gotten so much smaller—and more exciting—for me after working with an international population for so many years.

SOCIAL WORK PRACTICE WITH SUBSTANCE ABUSE AND ADDICTION

An area of practice in which social workers have long been involved, substance abuse and addiction treatment, has undergone dramatic changes in recent years. Early substance abuse treatment efforts focused primarily on the rehabilitation of the persons addicted to alcohol, and the treatment was in the form of Alcoholics Anonymous, a model focused on mutual peer support.

Inpatient treatment programs emerged during the 1970s for the treatment of alcoholism and other drug addictions. Restrictions imposed on treatment programs by the health insurance industry regarding the amount of reimbursement for treatment resulted in the elimination of many inpatient programs because clients were no longer able to afford the cost.

In fact, of the 23 million Americans who experience an addiction to drugs or alcohol, a mere 10% receive treatment (Open Society Foundations, 2010). Reasons cited for not seeking treatment include: lack of health care coverage or existing coverage does not include addiction treatment (nearly half), not ready to seek treatment or believe treatment is unneeded (40%), lack of transportation (10%), or negative impact on employment or neighbors/community (17%).

Despite the positive results associated with substance abuse treatment (e.g., health and employment benefits and crime reductions), addiction treatment is now typically provided primarily through outpatient programs. A smaller percentage of treatment is being accessed through rehabilitation and residential programs or detoxification treatment.

Policy-Practice Considerations in Substance Abuse and Addiction

Despite the changes in the societal response to substance abuse and addiction, the prevalence of chemical dependency and other addictions has not dissipated. As a result of the shift away from large inpatient programs, a relatively small number of social workers identify substance abuse (also referred to as alcohol, tobacco, and other drugs (ATOD)) as their primary area of practice. Fewer than 5% of NASW members surveyed indicated addictions as their primary practice area (Whitaker & Arrington, 2008). Social workers who work in chemical dependency and addiction treatment programs are typically employed by private for-profit and private nonprofit organizations. Despite the relatively small number of social workers currently working in this field of practice, employment for social workers in this area is expected to increase by approximately 31% in the coming years (U.S. Department of Labor, Bureau of Labor Statistics (BLS), 2012b).

Although a small percentage of social workers practice exclusively in the field of chemical dependency and addiction treatment, knowledge of addiction prevention and intervention is critical for social workers in virtually every field of practice. Substance use and abuse and addiction issues frequently overlap in areas such as mental illness, domestic violence, and corrections; therefore, social workers in these areas must be able to identify signs of chemical dependency and addiction. Because knowledge of substance abuse and addictions is essential for all social work practitioners, NASW has developed *Standards for Social Work Practice with Clients with*

EXHIBIT 8.6

Guidelines for Practice With Clients With Substance Abuse Disorders

Screening, Assessment, and Placement: Social workers shall screen clients for substance use disorders (SUDs) and, when appropriate, complete a comprehensive assessment toward the development of a service plan for recommended placement into an appropriate treatment program.

Intervention and Treatment Planning: Social workers shall incorporate assessments into the development and implementation of intervention plans to enhance clients' capacities to address problems and needs that support an increase in productive functioning within their families, peer groups, workplaces, and communities.

Advocacy and Collaboration: Social workers who provide services to clients with SUDs shall advocate when appropriate for the needs, decisions, and rights of clients.

Continued

The social worker shall promote collaboration among service providers and seek to ensure that individuals with SUDs and their family members have access to services that support their treatment needs.

Documentation: Social workers shall document all services rendered to, or on behalf of, clients, including communications with family members, collateral contacts, and mandated stakeholders. All records should comply with applicable federal, state, and local legislation, regulations, and policies, as well as agency and/or program policies including regulations governing substance abuse treatment records (Title 42 C.F.R.) and the Health Insurance Portability and Accountability Act (HIPAA).

Privacy and Confidentiality: Social workers shall maintain appropriate safeguards to protect the privacy and confidentiality of client information, except as otherwise required by law or ethics. Social workers shall be familiar with national, state, and local exceptions to confidentiality, such as emergencies, mandates to report danger to self or others, and child maltreatment. The social worker shall advise clients of confidentiality limitations and requirements at the beginning of treatment.

Staffing: The treatment of chronic SUDs is often a complex process characterized by multiple medical, psychological, and social problems, and by frequent relapses before sustained abstinence is achieved. Workloads should reflect the amount of effort required to achieve successful outcomes with clients.

Cultural Competence: Social workers shall seek to understand the history, traditions, expectations, values, and attitudes of diverse groups as they affect the perception of SUDs and treatment planning.

Source: Adapted from NASW, 2005b.

EXHIBIT 8.6

continued

Substance Use Disorders (2005b). Exhibit 8.6, which is based on this set of standards, provides guidelines to all social workers regarding the need to understand addictions, appropriate and ethical interventions, and the role social workers can have in advocating and educating for client systems.

As you will read in the following narrative, the issue of dual diagnosis is prevalent in this area of the social worker's practice. **Dual diagnosis** or **co-occurring disorders** occurs when the person is thought to be experiencing two diseases or conditions simultaneously, and the interaction of the two diseases can impede diagnosis and treatment. Within chemical dependency and addiction treatment, dual diagnosis or co-occurring conditions is typically the presence of mental illness and chemical dependence. The current prevalence of co-occurring conditions is mounting, possibly due to increased use and/or enhanced awareness of underlying causes of mental health or substance abuse issues. Twenty percent of the U.S. adult population has experienced a mental illness in a given year, with one-fifth of those individuals also experiencing a substance dependence or abuse (U.S. Department of Health and Human Services Substance Abuse and Mental Health Services

Administration, 2012). The increasing presence of co-occurring conditions requires that social workers must develop awareness and practice skills in both mental health and addictions treatment.

Jon Hudson, BSW, Chestnut Health Systems, Inc.

I am a BSW student completing my practicum at a large agency that provides treatment for adolescents with chemical dependency. I want to practice clinical social work, and because clinical work often involves chemical dependency issues, I need to have experience in this area. I find it an honor to work with these young people as they struggle with issues of chemical dependence. Although this is my first formal social work practice experience, I gained experience through volunteering and working part-time in several social service settings before beginning my practicum. My volunteer and employment experiences helped me to determine the areas of social work in which I would like to practice and the populations on which I want to focus my practice.

The residential program at my practicum site is separated by gender. I work in the capacity of a chemical dependence counselor on the male unit. In this setting, a substance abuse counselor provides treatment to individual clients and their families, facilitates group therapy, and works in teams with other counselors to maintain the daily routine of the treatment unit. The unit where I work houses 20 boys ranging in age from 13 to 17 years. Nearly all of the residents are court-mandated to chemical dependency treatment, but the reasons for their sentences are not always related directly to use or abuse of substances.

More often, they are arrested for other crimes and discovered to be under the influence of substances during the arrest process. Most of the boys are from modest socioeconomic backgrounds, and their formal education has been interrupted as a result of their criminal activities and lack of family support. Some of the boys are dually diagnosed with a mental illness and chemical dependence. Working with persons who are dually diagnosed presents a special challenge in treatment, as both conditions must be addressed simultaneously.

Treatment of a person with a dual diagnosis usually results in a boy working with his counselor and a staff psychiatrist who provides medication and treatment for the mental illness. The counselor must be knowledgeable about the diagnosis and treatment of both conditions and balance the mental illness, chemical dependence, and, oftentimes, legal issues all at the same time.

Persons who are dually diagnosed may not be aware of the existence of a mental illness and be shocked to learn of it. The client may have been abusing drugs as a way to deal with the symptoms of mental illness and have difficulty accepting that he now has to grapple with two crises. Typically, the boy unwillingly enters the treatment program without knowing what to expect. As a result, he has no idea how to cope, and the news of a dual diagnosis puts extra stress on him. As a result, he may appear to be getting worse after the first few weeks in residence. I think the thing that touched me most was that learning that he has a dual diagnosis often makes the young man or boy feel more broken than he already feels.

A program such as the one in which I am completing my practicum provides judges with the option of sentencing alternatives that are more appropriate for developing young men and women. The fact that the boy or girl may have committed a crime, possibly several crimes, is secondary to the consideration that jail is not appropriate for everyone who commits a crime, especially children and adolescents. The program introduces the young people to treatment and healthy recovery before they have become entrenched in a maladaptive pattern of misuse of chemical substances. The longer a person is chemically dependent and actively using substances, the more difficult it is for her or him to break the cycle of dependence.

In my practicum, I am learning that there are special considerations when a client and a clinician are dealing with issues of chemical dependence. Many substances require a long time to clear the body. This can result in the person being in the treatment and recovery process longer, which increases the chances for long-term abstinence and recovery. In many parts of the world, the length of time a person is in treatment has become the leading issue in the search for new models of addiction treatment.

Traditional models of substance abuse treatment are based on the 12 steps of Alcoholics Anonymous and have complete abstinence as the primary goal. Since its beginnings in the 1930s, this model has been effective for millions of men and women suffering from chemical dependence. The model dictates that sufferers must first stop using chemicals and then admit they are chemically dependent and powerless over their substance of choice. One of the challenges that I have identified in this field of practice is that, although the 12-step model has a long-standing history, the addict must cease all drug use before she or he can move through recovery. I have observed that this approach works well for some in a self-help environment. In the framework of a treatment model, however, if the goal is to stop using and remain abstinent, cessation should not be a requirement to begin treatment.

In my practicum, I have been exposed to a new model of substance abuse treatment. The Harm Reduction model is finding success in many parts of the world, but is still controversial in the United States. Harm Reduction is based on the idea that, the longer a person is engaged in the treatment and recovery process, the better her or his chances are for long-term recovery. Harm Reduction encourages the client to prioritize goals and does not require her or him to become and remain abstinent at any point. The user may see her or his problem as cocaine and

not alcohol, for example, even though both are being used in a maladaptive pattern. The social worker using a Harm Reduction framework recognizes value in the client's theory and builds on that strength. Why does the social worker, who can clearly see that the person has a problem with cocaine and alcohol, concur with the client's theory of the problem? The social worker knows she or he can keep the client engaged in the recovery process longer by working on what the person sees as the problem, and the longer the person is engaged, the more likelihood of long-term change.

An example of a Harm Reduction program may be a needle exchange program in a city where the incidence of intravenous drug use is high. Opponents of the Harm Reduction approach claim that needle exchange does not work because it does not reduce the number of intravenous (IV) drug users. However, the incidence of new HIV infection is reduced, and this creates a safer, less harmful environment for everyone by reducing or eliminating the incidence of needle sharing. Needle exchange ensures that IV drug users are introduced to the treatment and recovery process; thus the seed is planted and the process begins.

I decided on social work as a profession because I believe in values of social justice, the dignity and worth of the person, a person's right to self-determination, and the importance of human relationships, as outlined in the NASW *Code of Ethics* (2008). Through my coursework and practicum, I have learned to engage, assess, and intervene with client systems. Also of importance are the skills of critical thinking and evaluation.

Because I have learned the value of thinking critically about my practice, I have come to understand that treatment models for chemical dependence work can vary and are more effective with multidisciplinary professional teams that include social workers as integral, working parts of the models.

As a social worker I have been educated and trained in an approach that involves not only the person and her or his disorder. The social work perspective takes into consideration the person in her or his environment over time. This multidisciplinary approach transcends and includes approaches from the fields of psychology, sociology, anthropology, biology, and history. Social work theory helps me to understand that I need to integrate the biological, psychological, and social aspects of a person to understand her or his disease. In order to help a person in a competent and respectful manner, I need to know where the person lives, the education, family history, ethnic and cultural background, spiritual beliefs, and, most importantly, the way in which the person perceives the condition or situation that prompted her or him to ask for help and the path to change.

SOCIAL WORK PRACTICE IN CRIMINAL JUSTICE

One area of **forensic social work**, social work practice in criminal justice, is a growing area for social work employment. Dating back to the Poor Laws of the 17th century, advocating for and working with those involved with the correctional system has been an area of practice for social workers throughout our entire history (Maschi & Killian, 2011). Forensic social work is the practice of social work in areas relating to the law and legal systems, including the criminal and civil legal systems. Examples include child, older adult, and spouse/partner abuse; child custody; juvenile and adult criminal issues; and corrections.

Prompted by media and political attention, society has experienced an increased focus on crime and criminals. While the number of adults in the correctional population (e.g., incarcerated or on probation or parole) declined in 2010 for the first time in over 40 years, there are still over 7 million persons or one in every 33 adults in the United States who are under the supervision of the justice system (Glaze, 2011). Half of the residents of correctional facilities are awaiting trial, and many are persons of color and of low socioeconomic status. More than half of persons who encounter the criminal justice system are under the influence of alcohol or other substances during the time in which the crime for which they are accused was committed. For these reasons, NASW calls for social workers to be trained as culturally competent, forensic professionals who can develop intervention plans to address the client within the criminal justice system (NASW, 2012–2014m).

Policy-Practice Considerations in Criminal Justice

Social work practice in criminal justice encompasses a wide range of settings and issues. Social workers in this field of practice may work in adult or juvenile correctional facilities at the local, state, and federal levels, community-based probation and parole agencies, mental health facilities, public defenders' offices, law firms, legal services organizations that represent the accused and the victims, juvenile or family court agencies, law enforcement agencies, or programs that respond to issues of domestic and family violence (Rome, 2008). Social workers may also be employed in organizations that serve ex-offenders, re-entrants, and their support networks

(Wilson, 2010). Despite the fact that social workers have been involved in social work practice in criminal justice since the 1800s, the number of social workers who identify criminal justice as a primary area of practice is small (Rome, 2008; Whitaker & Arrington, 2008). However, because of the array of settings, some social workers may identify their primary practice of focus in a related area (for example, mental health, health, or substance abuse and addiction treatment).

Due to the increasing number of persons who have been incarcerated in recent years, there is a corresponding increase in the number of individuals re-entering the community upon completion of their sentences. While numbers of persons incarcerated are higher in all categories, two areas are of particular concern—the number of women being imprisoned has increased almost twice as much as the rates for men and the re-arrest rates (Wilson, 2010). To address these increases, social workers can advocate for the provision of evidence-based biopsychosocial services for persons during and after their incarcerations (Wilson, 2010).

Practice in criminal justice is an employment option for BSW social workers. A relatively new area of focus for social workers interested in the legal system is to complete both a graduate social work and law degree.

Herbert Bernsen, MSW, St. Louis County Department of Justice Services

I am the Director for a county Department of Justice Services. I have a master's degree in social work. Through my involvement in the field of corrections, I have been designated a Certified Jail Manager by the American Jail Association. Because I have learned the importance of collaborating with others in the community whose services overlap with the criminal justice system, I am actively involved with several community organizations. I serve on the board of an Adult Basic Education program that provides General Education Development (GED) teachers for inmates and am a board member for an organization that provides services to persons with developmental disabilities who encounter the criminal justice system.

I began my career in criminal justice social work while I was a student in the MSW program. I worked as a probation and parole officer and have continued in this field for the past 40 years. I have also served as a superintendent of the maximum and medium security correctional institutions.

My department is responsible for the operation of the county jail and the Community Corrections Division. The populations that we encounter are adult men and women, 17 years of age and older, charged with crimes ranging from felonies and misdemeanors to county ordinance violations. The capacity of the jail at which I work is 1,232 inmates. In 2011 33,701 persons were booked at the jail, and the average daily population was 1,145 inmates. The population consists primarily of those inmates awaiting trial, but inmates are sentenced to the jail for periods up to 1 year. For sentences exceeding 1 year, inmates are normally sent to the state prison system operated by the Department of Corrections.

The management philosophy used in our general population housing area is considered direct supervision. Correctional officers are stationed inside the housing area pods enabling officers to take a proactive role in controlling inmate behavior and minimizing tension. We find that assaults against staff and other inmates are significantly reduced in our current direct supervision facility compared to our previous linear design facility. In the more traditional linear facility, officers only intermittently observe inmates when they conduct patrols in front of their cells. In direct supervision facilities, the officer is inside the

St. Louis County Department of Justice Services

St. Louis County Department of Justice Services
100 South Central Avenue
St. Louis, Missouri 63105
The St. Louis County Department of Justice Services is responsible for the operation of the St. Louis county jail and the Division of Community Corrections. The county jail provides 1,232 beds for the county's minimum, medium, and maximum security inmates. The Division of Community Corrections is located in a nearby building and is responsible for the operation of the Alternative Community Services Program, Mental Health Court and Probation Supervision Unit.

Photographs provided by Hellmuth, Obata, and Kassabaum, Inc.

living area and she or he can often stop problems early before they escalate.

Communication is the key skill for officers in working with inmates. Most inmates follow the rules because they want to live in a safe and secure environment. We set high expectations for inmate behavior, and this becomes a self-fulfilling prophecy. Inmates prefer to live in an environment in which the officer is the leader, not the toughest inmate. If an inmate consistently violates the rules, she or he is moved to an indirect housing unit with reduced privileges and restricted movement.

The most important part of the Corrections Department mission is to ensure inmate safety and security. As an administrator, I read daily reports and review incident reports. If there are numerous inmate assaults against other inmates or staff, we are not doing our job. Supervisors must make frequent inspections. Cells and inmate living areas must be routinely searched. If homemade weapons are being made, inmates cannot feel safe. Inmates are taught the rules and the possible sanctions for violating the rules. They also know that their right to a due process hearing to determine their guilt or innocence is affirmed.

The social worker in the corrections area works as a member of a multidisciplinary team. The social worker/case worker is responsible for conducting the initial assessment when the inmate is booked and processed into the jail setting. Often, this assessment involves crisis intervention, as the social worker must evaluate the inmate's current emotional state to identify issues such as suicidal ideation and mental illness. This assessment provides the basis for determining the part of the jail system in which the inmate will be housed. Second, social workers are responsible for coordinating and participating in the educational and treatment programs provided for the inmates. Casework also involves prioritizing the needs of the inmates through regular contact during their incarceration to assess how the inmate is functioning within the jail population and any issues that she or he is faced with from external sources (for example, family or financial). The social worker serves as a liaison with the legal system to monitor the inmate's case progress and with employers when inmates are participating in the work release program. Lastly, the social worker is often responsible for working with those inmates who need assistance upon release from jail to ensure that they are integrated effectively back into their communities.

One of the challenges of working in criminal justice is the high incidence of mental illness and substance abuse. In the early 1960s, there was an effort to deinstitutionalize vast numbers of persons with mental illness and provide the consequent community support and housing that would be needed. The community support for this effort fell woefully short. As a result, jails often became the place of last resort for those persons suffering from mental illness, not all of whom had committed crimes. We have certainly needed to hire psychiatrists, psychologists, and social workers to work with persons diagnosed with mental illness inside our jails. Many of those experiencing mental illness do not, however, belong in jail in the first place.

Because I was aware of the inappropriate placement of many persons suffering from mental illness, I was instrumental in forming a mental health court task force consisting of community mental health providers and criminal justice agencies. The goal of this task force was to establish a mental health court to divert persons with serious mental health disorders from the criminal justice system to appropriate mental health treatment and services in order to improve their mental health functioning and deter future criminal behavior. To ensure the provision of comprehensive services, we worked closely with the police department to implement their Crisis Intervention Team program. In this program, police officers are trained to intervene in situations involving persons with mental illness. Our other partners

included an advocacy group, the state mental health agency, a nonprofit mental health agency, and a university social work program along with judges, prosecutors, public defenders, probation officers, and our Corrections Department at the county jail.

Another challenge faced by social workers in criminal justice is the issue of substance abuse. Along with mental illness, the inmate population includes many persons who use and abuse alcohol and other drugs. My department has made a significant commitment to the treatment of substance abuse within the jail through the Choices Substance Abuse Recovery Program. Using a 12-step model, the program provides 90 days of treatment for male and female inmates with the goal of empowering participants to choose a lifestyle free of alcohol and other drug addictions and criminal behavior. During the past 12 years, the Choices program served 2,413 inmates. Judges have embraced the program, and there has been a waiting list since the program's inception.

Each year, faculty and students at a local university evaluate the program, and each year the program consistently shows positive results. For example, during years 2–11, 73% of those inmates who completed the program resided in the community without being arrested for a new crime, and 82% successfully remained on probation. By the ninth year of the program, 91% of the participants successfully completed the program.

I have learned that providing educational opportunities is also important for helping inmates to initiate changes in their life. Local school districts provide instructors to prepare inmates to take the high school equivalency exam. Inmates have the opportunity to be tested. In 2011, 138 inmates took the GED test, and 101 received their diploma.

Social workers are also often involved in the evaluation and supervision of inmates who are being placed on electronic home detention and pre-trial release programs.

The successful operation of our jail and the programs that I have described here also depends on volunteers. There are currently over 350 active volunteers at the jail. Programs conducted by volunteers include creative writing, individual counseling, religious services, literacy assistance, leadership classes, substance abuse education, and support groups for substance abusers. The volunteers have a positive influence on the well-being of the inmates both inside and outside confinement.

The field of social work in criminal justice has many challenges. Jails and prisons are being inundated with inmates with mental health and substance abuse problems. Jails and prisons have the highest rates of suicide in our society. In these times of scarce resources and reduced budgets, it is important to form partnerships with community leaders and organizations to provide services for inmate populations.

The future for social workers working in criminal justice is promising. There are a myriad of opportunities for correctional officers, social service staff, medical and mental health staff, and administrators in this field of practice. Innovations in inmate supervision and treatment, public health, technology, and community aftercare are examples of areas for growth and development. The vast majority of jail and prison inmates will be returning to their communities. The resources directed toward inmate populations during and after incarceration will pay significant dividends to the individuals, their families, and the community.

SOCIAL WORK PRACTICE IN HEALTH SETTINGS

The NASW reports that approximately 14% of social workers practice in health-related settings and this number is expected to increase by 34% in the coming years (Whitaker & Arrington, 2008; BLS, 2012b). All areas of health care practice will grow faster than the average job growth. The growing older adult population and baby boomer generation account for a significant portion of these expected growth rates. With the shortened length of stay in hospitals and the increase of the older adult population, social workers are employed in more outpatient health care settings than inpatient (BLS, 2012b).

Policy-Practice Considerations in Health Settings

Social workers who practice in any of the areas of health care social work, medical, mental health, substance abuse treatment, or public health have the opportunity to work in a variety of organizations with a wide array of client systems and with a range of other professions. While health care social workers provide services across the lifespan from neonatal intensive care to skilled nursing facilities, they share a common purpose: assist individuals and families to function in response to health issues; prevent social and emotional issues from impacting health; and address service inadequacies (NASW, 2006–2009b). Social workers work in interprofessional teams in inpatient hospitals, outpatient medical clinics, health-specific educational and advocacy organizations, residential care facilities, skilled nursing facilities, rehabilitation settings, public health agencies, hospice, home health care, and mental health and substance abuse treatment settings. Some of these organizations work with individuals across the lifespan, others are specific to adults of all ages, adolescents, or children. In other organizational settings, many are focused on a particular disease management such as HIV/AIDS, multiple sclerosis, Alzheimer's disease, or diabetes. A shift toward providing services in the primary care setting is providing new opportunities for social workers who can engage in screening, assessments, and treatment protocols in the outpatient setting (Rock, 2009). With $155 million allocated by President Obama in 2009 to fund 126 new community health centers, social workers have increased opportunities to serve the uninsured and underinsured in community settings.

Social work in the health field requires the social worker to have knowledge of the biological, psychological, spiritual, and social aspects of human functioning along with the skills to work with other professionals who provide health care services. Understanding the distinct and overlapping roles of all the professions that work with the health care consumer population is key to being an effective health care social worker. Health care social work involves an integration of direct practice with individuals and families as well as an awareness of the impact of policies and the willingness to serve as an advocate for patients' needs. In an effort to ensure quality practice, NASW established *Standards for Social Work Practice in Health Care Settings* (2005c), which provide guidelines in the areas of ethics, social justice, cultural competence, privacy and confidentiality, theory, interprofessional practice, and documentation. These standards apply to health social workers in all settings.

Whether they are working in an inpatient or outpatient medical setting, social workers perform a number of diverse functions. In the hospital or inpatient setting, the social worker is primarily responsible for helping the patient and her or his support network understand and cope with the presenting illness or health event (NASW CWS, 2011b, pp. 1–2). Exhibit 8.7 provides an overview.

- Screening and evaluating patients and families
- Conducting comprehensive psychosocial assessments, including mental health evaluation
- Helping patients and families understand the admission process, treatment options, and the consequences (i.e., role changes, responses to illness and treatment)
- Educating patients and families on the levels of health care, roles of the health care team and strategies for effective communication
- Facilitating health-related decision making
- Engaging in crisis intervention
- Educating professional staff on patient psychosocial issues and serving as a liaison between staff and patients and families
- Facilitating patient navigation of the health care system and discharge and continuity planning, including resource management
- Advocating for patient and family needs, including patient rights

EXHIBIT 8.7

Responsibilities for Practice in Health Care Settings

Source: NASW CWS, 2011b, pp. 1–2.

Similar to the roles of the social worker in inpatient settings, the social worker who works in the outpatient setting may engage in educating patients and families on health-related issues, conduct assessments of mental health issues, coordinate care management plans and resources, help patients and their support networks navigate the health care system, and engage in advocacy efforts on behalf of patients and families. While not exclusive to outpatient settings, social workers may also be involved in counseling patients and families in end-of-life issues; intervening in situations of intimate partner or child/abuse, and developing educational programming specific to health-related issues (Gibelman, 2004; Grobman, 2005; NASW CWS, 2011a).

Jane Sprankel, MSW, LCSW, Health Care Social Work Across Multiple Settings

In college, my first undergraduate major was education. I thought teaching would fulfill my desire to help people. I met other college students at a summer job and they were talking about their social work major. After I listened to what they were studying and their practicum experiences, a light bulb went on for me! I wanted to be a social worker. I changed my major and never looked back. My first practicum experience was in a community mental health center working with mental health consumers who had just been released from the state inpatient facility.

As I pursued my MSW, I studied both macro- and micro-level practice in health care. Upon completion of my MSW, as I was considering the best place for me to begin my MSW career, a friend encouraged me to consider social work in a hospital. She said she found it interesting, fast-paced, and challenging, and it required the use of all social work skills, from policy to clinical therapy. I took my friend's suggestion and entered the world of hospital-based social work. I discovered that her assessment of the work has been true throughout my career. While I have enjoyed all of the social work jobs I have had, it is health care where I have found my specialty.

As an MSW social worker in the health field, I felt it was important to obtain the credentials that certify my competence as a social work professional. I obtained my ACSW, a national credential that

certifies me as a member of the NASW Academy of Certified Social Workers (ACSW), and a license to practice clinical social work in my state.

As a new hospital social worker, I began my work at a community-based hospital assigned to the rehabilitation/skilled nursing unit. The population I served was primarily older adults who had experienced a health event and were in need of physical rehabilitation or skilled nursing care because they were no longer able to care for their own basic daily needs. I was a member of an interprofessional health care team comprised of practitioners in nursing; physical, occupational, and speech therapy; dietetics; and physicians. My responsibilities were to assist with discharge planning, skills for coping with illness and injury, patient and family education, and community resource referrals. During my time in this position, I developed a patient education program and support group for caregivers, became a part of an interprofessional team that provided diabetic education for patients and families, and facilitated a support group for patients with chronic pulmonary disease. When I first began to work with older adults, I realized I saw them through my eyes and my age; but with more experience, I now see them through their eyes and their years of wisdom and living.

Along with the direct practice opportunities, I saw the impact of state and federal policy on our patients' ability to access services. Through

Source: Comstock.

professional organizations, I participated in advocating for changing Medicare and Medicaid policies. Through these experiences, the issues affecting older adults and their families became an area of increased interest for me.

After 4 years in my first MSW social work position, I found myself wanting to specialize in the area of rehabilitation and obtained a position as rehabilitation social worker at an inpatient rehabilitation hospital. My work focused on young adults with spinal cord and brain injuries. Again I worked with patients and families in the areas of discharge planning, coping, patient/family education, and community resource referrals. As a member of the rehabilitation team, I participated in developing and maintaining program evaluation goals, team building, and staff education. I became active with the disability community, working on issues of access and services at the state and federal level.

In the 9 years I worked as a rehabilitation social worker, I saw a trend in the population we were serving. People were living longer and were more susceptible to acquiring a spinal cord or brain injury. Because I had previously worked with older adults, I understood the developmental issues of this population and their families. These older adults and their families often faced different types of caregiving situations, discharge planning, and coping issues than the younger adults on the unit.

I then had the opportunity to be involved in a new project in my community that was being developed to provide primary health care and social services to new refugees and immigrants. I was intrigued with the idea of applying my social work skills in another area of the health care delivery system, the physician's office. I was also intrigued with working with non-English-speaking refugees and immigrants.

My patients were primarily new refugees to the United States who may have arrived a few days or weeks prior to their visit to the community health care center. In most cases, the patients were coming from resettlement camps in countries willing to house them until they received approval to come to the United States. The health care they had received prior to coming here was often intermittent or minimal. These men, women, and children were entering a country they may have only known through the movies, a complex health care delivery system, and a culture different from their own.

My world as a social worker shifted dramatically with this new experience. I learned new skills, not the least of which was practice behaviors for interviewing and providing counseling services through an interpreter. Because I was dealing with individuals and families from multiple countries, cultural competence took on a whole new meaning for me. I became acutely aware that, although I was a competent health care social worker, I was going to have to reframe my practice to meet the needs of this new patient population better.

As we got to know our clients and their health and social service needs, the nurse practitioner, physician, and I began to realize that many of our clients were suffering from posttraumatic stress disorder (PTSD). Hearing the stories of their war-related experiences led us to understand that many of these people had suffered great physical harm, torture, and abuse at the hands of their captors. As the social worker on our team, I assisted these persons and their families in locating mental health professionals specially trained in war trauma and torture.

Issues of access to care, policy implementation, and policy formulation became central to my practice with this population. Working as a part of a coalition of agencies serving refugees and immigrants, I was able to advocate for interpreter services provided by Medicaid that increased access to quality medical care.

My later social work position at a university provided me the opportunity to work with BSW and MSW students as a mentor in health care social work. I assist as a field instructor for students in health care settings. I have taught courses in health policy and international social work in Mexico.

I often serve as a guest lecturer on topics ranging from immigrant and refugee health to social work with the older adult population and spirituality in social work practice. I volunteer to be part of a team that provides training to medical interpreters to serve the refugee and immigrant populations in my community better. I served on a community-based committee that worked toward policy change to provide our older refugees and immigrants better access to language skills, citizenship preparation, and social and health services. I served two terms on a board of directors that created an agency from the ground up to serve the mental health needs of refugees who experienced war torture and trauma. In addition, I also served three terms on a grants committee for a religious foundation that supports health and human service organizations.

Currently, I work with a religious organization where I engage in macro practice in nonprofit leadership, management, and governance of health and human service organizations. These organizations serve vulnerable children, adults, families, and communities. My practice as a health care social worker is a source of personal and professional satisfaction and has provided me with the expertise to serve as a mentor, teacher, and board member. My positions in health care settings have given me the opportunity to practice micro, **mezzo**, and macro skills across the lifespan, with diverse individuals, communities, and organizations.

Lisa Parnell, MSW, LCSW, St. Luke's Hospital

My first job was at a Baskin-Robbins ice cream parlor. I was 15 years old. Fortunately, I worked for a very kind couple who trained each of us thoroughly in the mechanics of the job and, more importantly, taught us to respect each customer. After high school, I continued to work for several years in the restaurant industry. It was not until I was 29 years old that I decided to find a career that made our world a better place, as well as a job that did not make my back and feet hurt so much at the end of the day.

My first field of study was business. I had a few elective classes left and my advisor recommended that I take a social work class. I knew within the first 15 minutes of the first class that this was the field for me and I have not been sorry since.

During my undergraduate studies, I met so many caring professors, who were extremely passionate about helping their communities, the underserved, and the world around them. I also found myself swept up in their teachings about giving people the tools they needed to have a decent life. At that same time, many of my good friends became ill with the AIDS virus and soon began to die. It was also during these years that I began to volunteer for an organization which provided food for persons living with AIDS. It was during this time that I began to understand the difference that a few compassionate individuals could make in the lives of so many who were suffering.

In my BSW program, I completed practicums with inner-city youth sports programs and neighborhood stabilization projects. I soon realized that politics was not my area of interest. Next, I worked with youth in the justice system. Even with the adolescents who had committed very serious crimes, I found myself drawn to support them. Unfortunately, once again, I found myself challenged by the bureaucracy of the legal system.

Finally, during my MSW program, I signed up for my final practicum with a local hospice organization. At last, I had a feeling of purpose and obtainable goals. Working in a hospice setting is not for the "faint of heart," but I felt very passionate about working with the terminally ill and their families. This experience helped me learn how to funnel my passion into giving these patients dignity and choices. All the while, I learned how to separate my own personal issues in order to mature into a true social work professional.

During my graduate program, I also had the opportunity to work on a former professor's new research project. They needed a graduate assistant for the study. Research was fascinating to me because I had never thought too much about the way in which programs were developed. I just assumed that someone came up with a good idea and then figured out how to get the money to start the new program. Spending those years assisting with two extremely important research projects was the best thing that could have happened to me. Now there is not a day that goes by where I do not think about the statistics involved in running a hospital and this helps me take into consideration the impact on patient care.

The first research project I worked on involved understanding the impact of caring for individuals suffering from Alzheimer's disease. My role as a research assistant was to call the family caregivers and ask them a series of questions related to their own well-being. Listening to these people share their struggles and heartaches taught me to pay attention not only to what they said, but how they said it and particularly to what they did not say. Often, they seemed to feel guilty for complaining about having to care for their loved ones. Often during my work now with patients' families, I can still hear that same frustration and I do my best to offer support and express compassion.

My next research position was as the coordinator for a mental health project that followed low-income pregnant women throughout their pregnancies. We collected information on both their mental health and substance abuse issues. We specifically studied women from both urban and rural health clinics, to evaluate potential differences in resources. Our goal was to identify deficiencies in current programs in order to provide improved services in the future. This position also offered many triumphs and sorrows, as I had never worked so closely with young women who had so many obstacles to overcome in their young lives. I am proud to say that the data I collected in this project has continued to be utilized in ongoing research, which will hopefully make life easier for future women in difficult situations.

About 11 years ago, after completing my part of the research project, I was offered a position as a medical social worker for a large suburban hospital. We are very fortunate as our hospital has a specific Social Work Department, led by a licensed clinical social worker, who understands our role and supports us in our goal to be advocates for the patients. While each social worker at our hospital is assigned to a particular division, we are all cross-trained and this has helped me stay current on social work policies and practices. We all have experience in working with every area of health care, including oncology, dialysis, stroke, alcohol and substance abuse, domestic violence, child abuse, psychiatric, infectious disease, respiratory, cardiology, women's health (including pregnancy and infant health issues), and any other health-related issue one could imagine.

My first position in the hospital was in the Rehabilitation unit. I held that position for 8 years. It was during this time that I learned the importance of a "team" approach to health care. The majority of our patients had suffered a stroke or other extremely serious health issue. Our Rehab team consisted of physiatrist (a physician who specializes in rehabilitative care), nurses, patient care technicians, physical therapist (who helps patients learn to transfer and ambulate after a serious health incident), occupational therapist (who helps patients learn how to perform activities of daily living, such as dressing, bathing, grooming, eating), speech therapist, recreational therapist, music therapist, registered dietician, case manager (who deals with insurance company approval for inpatient rehab days), and myself. My goal was to work with this team and create a safe discharge plan, which respected the patient's wishes and provided the necessary resources for resuming life outside the hospital.

I began working with each patient by completing a psychosocial assessment. It became obvious immediately that the more information I could gather about patients' prior life, the more opportunity we would have to help them reach their personal goals for their new life after this devastating illness. I would offer supportive counseling to patients and their families to help them adjust to recent changes that resulted from their new medical conditions. I would then work with the Rehab team in order to determine if a patient was going to be well enough to return home when medically stable for discharge or decide if she or he would require ongoing care in a skilled rehabilitation facility. Sometimes, the patient's condition declined and we had to help the patient make difficult decisions regarding end-of-life care, either at home or in a nursing facility.

If they did improve and were able to go directly home, I would help arrange home health care, durable medical equipment, and assistance with applying for prescription drug assistance or Medicaid insurance (which each state offers for chronically ill patients who meet certain financial guidelines), adult day care programs, or outpatient therapy. If it was determined that the patient would benefit from ongoing nursing care and therapy in a skilled setting, I would work with the patients and families to offer choices for this care and obtain insurance authorization. In addition to these duties, I also facilitated a support group for stroke survivors and their loved ones.

When my hospital decided to build a new rehabilitation hospital in a building down the street, I was offered the chance to move with them, but decided that I would miss the excitement of the acute hospital setting. An opportunity was available for a renal social worker. When I accepted this position, I took the skills I had used from Rehab to create a cohesive approach to working with patients suffering from kidney failure. It was apparent that I had much to learn about individuals suffering from chronic renal failure.

In addition to working with the renal patients, I also cover the Intensive Care Unit, which has offered me the chance to use my counseling skills and help families make life-and-death decisions under very stressful conditions. I am often called to handle situations in the Emergency Room, which requires me to think creatively and handle traumatic situations. What I have discovered about myself is that I function at my best in demanding settings. This job is always challenging. It gives me a sense of accomplishment and pride in my work and I know at the end of the day that my knowledge and empathy skills have helped people in crisis.

As the population of the United States continues to age, there will be multiple opportunities for social workers in the health care field. While I strongly encourage social work students to consider this area for their careers, I would suggest that they take practicum opportunities to explore several different settings. The future of medical social work is unlimited and there will not only be opportunities in hospitals, but in outpatient clinics, the mental health field, private practice, government agencies, and private industry, which is utilizing increasing numbers of social workers to provide care through their employee assistance programs. One of my favorite aspects of being a medical social worker is that every member on our team feels that we should always respect patients' goals and include them in all decision making regarding their care. This perspective may differ from the family members' thoughts and insurance company limitations; however, as a team we are able to stay focused and be effective advocates for our patients.

SOCIAL WORK PRACTICE IN MENTAL HEALTH SETTINGS

The social work profession is the largest provider of mental health services in the United States today, accounting for almost half of services. The remaining half of mental health services is provided by psychiatrists, psychologists, counselors, psychiatric nurses, and marriage and family therapists, as shown in Exhibit 8.8. Social work is recognized by the federal government as one of the four core mental health professions (Gibelman, 2004). As you might expect, mental health practice is also the largest area of practice for social workers, with over one-third of social workers reporting this category as their primary field of practice and 13% reporting they work in an outpatient mental health setting (Whitaker & Arrington, 2008). Moreover, social work practice in the area of mental health services is expected to grow by 31% in upcoming years (BLS, 2012b).

After 5 years of practice as a social worker, the number of social workers who identify mental health as the setting in which they work begins to increase, supporting the idea that, immediately following graduation, social workers gravitate to employment in the areas of aging, family and children services, and health settings and then shift their focus to the provision of more traditional clinical services after gaining experience. Mental health services are most often provided by social workers with an MSW or Ph.D. These social workers tend to be older, more experienced practitioners. Fewer social workers who are persons of color and of diverse ethnic groups identify themselves as mental health practitioners, indicating a need for greater diversity among mental health providers (CHWS/CWS, 2006).

Policy-Practice Considerations in Mental Health Settings

Mental health services are provided in a variety of settings and geographic locations with diverse client populations. Social workers provide mental health services to children, adolescents, adults of all ages, families, groups, persons with physical and/ or developmental disabilities; in correctional facilities, family service or mental health organizations, military and veteran programs, private practice, employee assistance programs, disaster relief programs, crisis intervention programs, victim assistance programs; and to persons from all races, ethnicities, and cultures. In sum, we are all potential consumers of mental health services provided by social workers.

Mental health services can be provided in the form of clinical therapy with individuals, families, and groups in both in- and outpatient mental health settings. Social workers facilitate support groups related to mental health issues, provide mental health education, and serve as advocates for those persons suffering from mental illness. More social workers providing mental health services are employed in outpatient mental health settings than in inpatient (hospital) settings (Whitaker & Arrington, 2008). The shift of service provision to the outpatient setting is due, in part, to a decreasing availability of "beds" in inpatient psychiatric facilities (Substance Abuse and Mental Health Services Administration (SAMHSA), 2010). The outpatient settings now providing the majority of mental health services include public and nonprofit mental health centers and group and solo private practices located in urban, suburban, and rural locations.

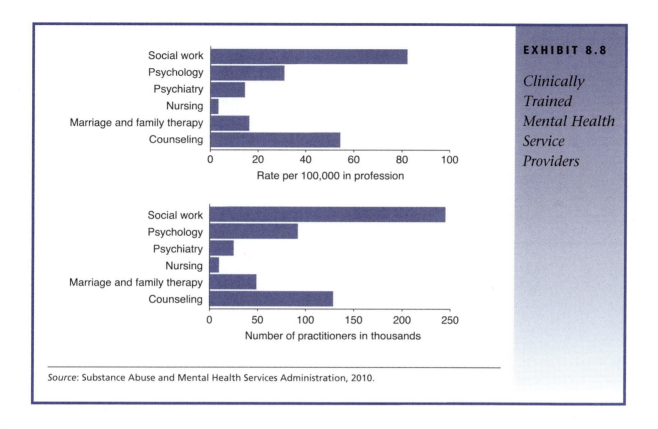

Source: Substance Abuse and Mental Health Services Administration, 2010.

A growing area of mental health practice for social workers is private practice. Seventeen percent of licensed social workers report they are engaged in private or group clinical practice, making this the third-ranked setting in which social workers practice (CHWS/CWS, 2006). Nearly every major health insurance provider recognizes the graduate social work degree as a provider of mental health services, thus making clinical practice (private or agency-based) a viable employment option for social workers with MSWs. Social workers in private clinical practice tend to garner the highest salaries within the social work practice community (CHWS/CWS, 2006).

While social workers providing mental health or behavioral health services work with a wide range of clients and client situations, most work primarily in either the community-based outpatient setting or an inpatient psychiatric setting. Exhibit 8.9 provides an overview of social work responsibilities in the community clinic and psychiatric setting.

Contemporary issues facing social workers working in the area of behavioral health services include increases in the numbers of persons experiencing mental health issues, particularly when mental illness co-occurs with another issue, and those individuals and families seeking services. With an estimated 46 million adults

EXHIBIT 8.9

Responsibilities for Practice in Mental Health Settings

- Determining service eligibility
- Conducting biopsychosocial (and spiritual) assessments, including identification of psychiatric disorders, physical and emotional functioning, financial stability, safety, substance abuse and addictions, and suicidal or homicidal ideation
- Developing and implementing therapeutic treatment and discharge plans in the form of individual, family, or group interventions
- Providing crisis intervention and case management services
- Engaging in nondirect services on behalf of clients, including advocacy, promotion of mental health services, grant writing, and evaluation

Source: National Association of Social Workers Center for Workforce Studies and Social Work Practice, 2011c, d, p. 1.

and 2 million adolescents experiencing a mental illness, the capacities of social workers and other providers of mental health services are being highly sought (SAMHSA, 2012). As a result of these high numbers of clients seeking treatment, several challenges have emerged, including increases in the number of co-occurring disorders (nearly 20% of persons with mental illness), nonspecialized providers that are delivering mental health services, number of psychotropic medications being prescribed (often in lieu of behavioral treatment), and lack of available emergency and residential treatment facilities (SAMHSA, 2010).

Barbara Flory, MSW, LCSW

As a licensed clinical social worker, I was employed in a program for families that have experienced domestic violence. My education includes an undergraduate degree in human services and a graduate degree in social work from a private university. My postgraduate training includes a certificate in family conflict management from a state university, and family therapy training from a program accredited by the American Association of Marriage and Family Therapy. My combined experience of family therapy and mediation has prepared me for the unusual position that I held in today's social services environment.

For more than 10 years, I was employed in a nonprofit mental health agency in a large metropolitan area. In my capacity as a program manager, I was responsible for all phases of program

development, implementation, supervision of staff, and evaluation of program outcomes. Implemented in 1997, the program is a supervised visitation and custody exchange center implemented to meet the needs of family court and a special needs population of separated, divorced, and never-married families. The families are court-mandated to participate in the programming out of three family court divisions: domestic relations (divorce and post-divorce child custody modifications), civil adult and child protection (time-limited protection orders sought by an adult), and juvenile dependency (child abuse and neglect cases resulting from a hotline call to child protection services). In rare cases, families were referred from the criminal child abuse and/or domestic violence dockets (e.g., domestic violence and/or child physical and/or sexual abuse cases that rose to a level that criminal prosecution was warranted).

As a public–private partnership between the local family court and the agency in which I worked, this formal collaboration required me to work at the interface between social services and the law, a unique position that requires knowledge beyond that which is traditionally a part of social work education.

Historically, supervised visitation between noncustodial parent and child is judicially ordered when the court determines that a child's safety is threatened by parental behavior. *Supervised visitation* is third-party guided contact between noncustodial parent and child for the purpose of maintaining or forming a relationship. Service delivery occurs on three levels to: (1) ensure the safety of children when abuse is alleged; (2) reintroduce parent and child after a prolonged separation; and (3) introduce parent and child when no prior relationship exists. *Custody exchange transfer* is defined as the transfer of children from custodial to noncustodial parent for the purpose of temporary custody. In the context of child abuse and neglect, supervised visitation services have a well-established history as a means to facilitate family reunification. Supervised visitation is a relatively new service within the domestic relations arena that is gaining credibility as an effective intervention when domestic violence is an issue. Over time, the judiciary has slowly embraced the practice of ordering supervised visitation on domestic violence cases to help ensure the protection of mothers and the children for whom they are responsible.

The population served was largely a violent group that engaged in psychological and/or physical aggression as a way of resolving interpersonal conflict. Approximately 70% of the client population had a history of abusive behavior, most often male-on-female intimate partner abuse (generally referred to as battering). In some instances, parental behavior excludes physical or sexual child abuse, and in other instances the children are abuse victims

as well. Whichever the case, a violent home environment almost ensures diminished overall child well-being. Therefore, the program is structured to meet the unique physical and emotional safety needs of this abusive population.

In order to meet the needs of families, the program operated during nontraditional business hours, meaning evenings, weekends, and holidays, including Christmas Day. Weekday and Sunday work hours started at 4:00 p.m. when parents began arriving to visit with their children under the supervision of a social worker. The social worker's responsibilities included ensuring children's safety during noncustodial parent/child visitation, teaching parenting skills and age-appropriate communication skills, and facilitating attachment and bonding as needed. Modeling and coaching are two important skills that social workers must possess to be successful in this practice area. Other noncustodial parents arrived at the center to pick up their children to spend time with them in an unprotected setting (for example, at home). The center was open on Saturday from 10:00 a.m. to 4:00 p.m., thus enabling parents to have flexible hours in which to spend time with their children.

Many parents who used the center had untreated, often undiagnosed, mental health disorders that contributed to their violent tendencies. Consequently, safety was paramount, and off-duty police officers had oversight responsibilities. A no-contact policy was necessary; that is, participating parents did not come face to face with each other while at the center, or communicate with each other outside the center.

It was encouraging to see that most parents could be good parents when offered the right circumstance. Unfortunately, sometimes circumstances dictated third-party intervention and court-restricted parental contact to mediate their violent behavior. The level of anger and distress exhibited by parents using the centers was often disproportionate to the event, resulting in violent outbursts with little provocation. I often found myself called upon to negotiate situations that were a crisis for overly stressed parents, whereas the situations were of little consequence for most parents. Consequently, staff members were hypervigilant about safety and took all necessary precautions to ensure their personal safety as well as client system safety.

The program that I managed is only one small piece on a continuum of care needed to sustain families in the modern-day world. The agency in which I worked offered a broad scope of intervention services to include individual and family counseling, addictions treatment, workforce development, employee assistance services, suicide prevention, youth mentoring services, teen pregnancy prevention, and in-home geriatrics support services. I am fortunate that my employer valued and supported innovative programming.

Supervised visitation is an emerging field of practice in social services that enjoys both praise and criticism from mental health and legal professionals. There is limited research about the effectiveness of services, with my team and myself being among a handful of social workers who have conducted research in this field. As practitioners, in conjunction with a local graduate social work school, we conducted an exploratory study that showed that the service can be very efficacious in promoting noncustodial parent/child safe contact, reducing interparental violence, and promoting child well-being (Dunn, Flory, Berg-Weger, & Milstead, 2004; Flory & Berg-Weger, 2003; Flory, Dunn, Berg-Weger, & Milstead, 2001).

Since few social workers conduct research in their settings, my research experience and professional publications have resulted in private consulting roles, such as judicial training for a national organization and participation in a federal task force charged with developing standards and guidelines for the profession. The national task force of which I was a member demonstrated a commitment to shape an emerging field to meet public policy expectations, thus legitimizing services and helping to ensure the future evolution of the field.

Supervised visitation and safe custody exchange services emerged out of grassroots organizing that will support future programming, albeit at a limited level. Future expansion of services is largely in the hands of family courts faced with budgetary cuts due to shrinking state and federal budgets. There are, however, promising legislative efforts at the federal level to support noncustodial parental access to children. One effort has resulted in the development of some statewide networks of programs focused on keeping noncustodial fathers and their children connected. This effort is attuned to the fact that too many fathers withdraw from their children's lives postdivorce, both emotionally and financially. Another federal effort is focused on developing centers designed to serve domestic violence victims and their children. This effort is attuned to the fact that battering does not stop after separation and/or divorce and the victims, ergo the children, remain vulnerable to abuse in the unprotected presence of the batterer. Both efforts recognize the benefits of keeping two parents safely involved in children's lives.

Like me, many social workers are employed in intense, highly conflictual, often violent, settings. Nothing in our training prepares us for the assaultive nature of the work, which often leads to vicarious traumatization of the professional.

It was not until I left this area of practice that I realized just how stressful and debilitating the daily exposure to the stories of violence and the aggressive behaviors of the individuals were on my own psyche. Therefore, I learned that education in self-care is essential to support professionals who have chosen to work in this field. Developing awareness of the need to care for oneself is one of the real issues facing the profession that requires attention by social workers of tomorrow.

After leaving this position, I became involved in the emerging field of collaborative family law. I chose this area of work—often referred to as a "peaceful" divorce process—because it is a stark contrast to the highly conflictual arena in which I worked, yet it allows me to continue to work with families in transition. The collaborative divorce process is a family-law procedure in which the two divorcing parties agree that they will not go to court. The parties engage in a series of meetings with a team of divorce attorneys, mental health professionals, and accountants who work collaboratively to help the parties make fully informed, carefully considered, settlement decisions that are consistent with the parties' priorities, goals, needs, and interests. My former position in supervised visitation prepared me to train and work as a divorce coach and/or child specialist. My specialized knowledge about divorce as an emotional process, postdivorce communication issues, child custody parenting plans/schedules, and the effects of divorce on children helped me become an integral part of the team process. This remaking of a career as a solo clinical practitioner is an example of how specialized knowledge and skills developed in one social work domain can be transferred into another more personally desired area of practice.

My expertise in family and organizational systems and collaborative processes has opened doors to yet another area of social work practice. Currently, I am engaged as a consultant on a state-wide strategic planning effort to re-examine and make alterations to improve the state's network of supervised visitation centers. I am also tasked with writing a policy and procedure manual that completes the state's standards for programming. The goal is to make service delivery more uniform, and thereby improve the quality of programming. I am also engaged in writing training curricula for this client: a documentation manual based on a hybrid model of case recording/note taking that I developed during my career that is specifically tailored to the supervised visitation profession.

In retirement, I am using my social work skills in community volunteerism. As a Court Appointed Special Advocate/Guardian ad Litem (CASA/GAL) volunteer, I advocate for abused and neglected children to help ensure permanency for children in a timely manner (the term "permanence" means that children are placed in a safe, permanent home within the established public policy guidelines). The GAL is essentially a legal and investigative role with duties such as meeting with the parents and foster parents, doing home visits to ensure the child's needs are being met, following medical and educational progress and other duties, as deemed appropriate based on the case facts. In addition to serving as a GAL, I have been privileged to provide content and skills training to other volunteers at conferences and/or in-service trainings. It is a very satisfying responsibility in that volunteers bring few skills to the volunteer arena, and, thus, are very eager to learn. Moreover, they are very appreciative of any training that will help them increase their effectiveness in serving children, especially social work skills training.

As described herein, my career includes clinical therapy, parent and divorce coaching, mediation and conflict management, program development and implementation, program administration, staff supervision, research and teaching, system reform, and consulting. The variety of work in which I am engaged is a good example of the depth and breadth of the social work education and the many opportunities an advanced degree in social work affords the social worker. My story demonstrates that the skills and knowledge that social workers possess are important tools that can be used in various ways to benefit the diverse client populations that we serve.

SOCIAL WORK PRACTICE IN THE PUBLIC HEALTH SETTING

Public health is a societal commitment to individual and population health (Tsay, 2010). It embraces concerns ranging from health education, prevention services, epidemiology, health care delivery, and immunization to environmental and occupational safety and bioterrorism.

The field of public health shares with the profession of social work a dedication to serving the disadvantaged and vulnerable populations. For this reason, social workers have a longstanding history of practicing in public health settings, including local departments of public health, clinics, and public health policy organizations. Over 150,000 U.S. social workers are employed in medical and public health settings (Baden, 2010).

The focus on public health concerns began in the early 19th century in England (Tsay, 2010). As the world became more urbanized, environmental and infectious diseases began to affect entire communities. The early public health activists focused their efforts on improving sanitation.

In contemporary times, public health workers address lifestyle issues that impact health (e.g., dietary and nutrition concerns, smoking, substance abuse, and obesity). In developing countries, the public health emphasis has included a focus on disease prevention and promotion of community health (Tsay, 2010).

The *Healthy People* initiative (www.Healthypeople.gov) occurs each decade to establish the nation's public health objectives. Those objectives shape program and funding priorities for public health organizations throughout the country. *Healthy People 2020*, issued in 2010, has identified the following goals:

- Attain high-quality, longer lives free of preventable disease, disability, injury, and premature death.

- Achieve health equity, eliminate disparities, and improve the health of all groups.

- Create social and physical environments that promote good health for all.

- Promote quality of life, healthy development, and healthy behaviors across all life stages.

Of special interest to the social work profession are the new topic areas that have been added to *Healthy People 2020*: health of older adults, lesbian, gay, bisexual, and transgender health, adolescent health, global health, preparedness, and dementias.

Ten essential services for public health in every community have been identified by the Centers for Disease Control and Prevention. First developed in 1994, these guidelines charge local public health agencies with a range of responsibilities. Depicted in Exhibit 8.10, these mandates share a number of similarities with the mission of the social work profession.

Policy-Practice Considerations for Social Work in the Public Health Setting

Many factors can significantly influence the health and well-being of an individual and family, including socioeconomic and employment status, ethnicity, health care access, education, social relationships, neighborhood/housing conditions, and

- Monitoring health status to identify and solve community health problems.
- Diagnosing and investigating health problems and health hazards in the community.
- Informing, educating, and empowering people about health issues.
- Mobilizing community partnerships and acting to identify and solve health problems.
- Developing policies and plans that support individual and community health efforts.
- Enforcing laws and regulations that protect health and ensure safety.
- Linking people to needed personal health services and assuring the provision of health care when otherwise unavailable.
- Assuring competent public and personal health care workforce.
- Evaluating effectiveness, accessibility, and quality of personal and population-based health services.
- Researching for new insights and innovative solutions to health problems.

Source: Centers for Disease Control and Prevention, 2010.

EXHIBIT 8.10

Responsibilities for Public Health Practice

personal behaviors (Collins, 2011, p. 2). A recent report focused on state funding for public health programs is adamant, however, that one's residential location should not negatively influence individual health (Trust for America's Health, 2012).

Social workers employed in public health organizations during these challenging economic times must be aware of the way in which the fluctuating economy affects their work. For a number of years, public health initiatives at the federal, state, and local levels have been underfunded, thus hampering the ability of public health departments to invest as fully as desired in disease prevention, a key factor in the campaign to improve the health of our citizens. The Trust for America's Health (2012) calls for increased funding, with more emphasis on evidence-based, prevention-focused programs prioritized by local health departments.

Social workers make effective partners at all levels of public health practice, from working with individuals and families to developing programs and policies that will provide guidance for communities and organizations. Social work and public health have much in common, including an embrace of both social action and scientific knowledge (Tsay, 2010, p. 1099). In addition, both types of professionals often examine the intersection between the physical and social environments (Tsay, 2010). Finally, with our profession's commitment to social justice and expertise in advocating for equitable access to needed resources, social workers can be on the forefront of advocacy efforts to increase public health funding.

Chae Li Yong, MSW, MPH

When I entered college, I wanted to help people discover and fix their problems. I thought medical school was the answer. Then I became ill and had to have two surgeries. I became disillusioned with the medical field when I realized the difficulty in accessing affordable medical care. To live in such a prosperous nation and still be forced to choose between food and medicine really troubled me.

When I stumbled into my first health education class, I knew I had found my niche. Health educators improve individual and community health by assisting in the adoption of healthy behaviors. Prevention through education saves money and lives. When I took my first epidemiology class, I knew I had found my career choice.

As an undergraduate student, I completed an internship at a local health department with a focus on communicable disease and confirmed that I wanted to be an epidemiologist. My mentor encouraged me to "job shadow" different professionals within the field of public health. Some of my diverse activities as an intern included collecting mosquitoes, setting pest traps, finding homes for animals, administering medications to a patient with tuberculosis, and inspecting restaurants and swimming pools. I respected the courage shown by the public health worker who closed the pool of an upscale hotel. I admired the compassion of the public health worker who interviewed a prisoner confirmed with a sexually transmitted disease. Being rather naïve, I was amazed at the places we searched for suspected cases of illness. Through those experiences, I came to admire all that public health professionals do to keep the public healthy and safe.

After I completed my undergraduate degree, I worked as a health educator at a local health department. I learned that many of the activities I observed during my internship were not performed in all local health departments. Funding was listed as the primary reason for the discrepancy in services offered at the local level. My position was supported through state funding.

As a health educator, I taught numerous target populations, depending on the focus of grant funding received by the agency. I taught children about unintentional and intentional injury prevention. I worked with parents regarding child passenger safety. I collaborated with various populations on smoking prevention and cessation. These are just a few of the target populations, community groups, and collaborative projects I had the opportunity to work with during my time as a health educator.

After several years working in public health, I returned to school to complete dual graduate degrees in Social Work (MSW) and Public Health (MPH). My premise for attaining the dual degrees was simple. Public health issues often cannot be addressed if the social work issues are too overwhelming. For example, a single mother struggling to find affordable child care may not be concerned with a car seat or a bike helmet. A father trying to feed his family may not be concerned about lead abatement or emergency response.

The public's perception regarding public health is often related to high-profile incidents such as the 2009 H1N1 and national foodborne outbreaks. There is less awareness of the day-to-day operations and accomplishments of those working in the field of public health. They include the following:

- Monitoring health status. If an unhealthy trend is associated with a specific subset in the population, public health workers might consult social workers to determine the best approach to use with the population. On one occasion, I consulted a social worker about an increase in infant deaths due to, in part, a unique cultural practice.

- Diagnosing and investigating health problems. If an outbreak of a particular disease is associated with a certain practice, public health workers can consult with social workers to determine the most effective approach to gain the cooperation of the persons impacted by the illness. For example, outbreaks of *Salmonella* have occurred in the MSM (men who have sex with men) population. Social workers can suggest strategies for providing education, prevention, and resource information to this population.

- Informing, educating, and empowering individuals about health issues. Breast cancer awareness is an excellent example of collaborative synergy. Many states have funded local health departments with programs for free mammograms. Treatment and case management would likely be handled by the medical and social services groups. As a health educator, I regularly sent out press releases educating the community on breast cancer and resources in the community, including social service agencies.

- Mobilizing community partnerships. Local health departments regularly assess community needs and create plans for the community based on those needs. The health departments then collaborate with community partners on different projects to improve the quality of life in that community. Several years ago, I was involved in a project that focused on improving the morbidity and mortality rates of children who were improperly restrained in a car. The National Highway Traffic Safety Administration offered week-long training that allowed me to become a certified child passenger seat technician. The health department funded and coordinated some of the first technician classes and car seat checks. After public health funding for the project ended, community partners— hospitals, police, fire departments, social service agencies, and private businesses—still checked car seats while educating families on proper installation.

- Developing policies and plans that support individual and community health efforts. The Master Settlement Agreement (MSA) of 1998 was a legal settlement between tobacco companies and the Attorneys General of 46 states to recover billions of dollars in

costs associated with treating smoking-related illnesses. The percentage of the MSA funding allocated for smoking cessation and prevention messages varied among the states. Public health and community partners, including social workers at various agencies, competed for state funding from the MSA in order to establish partnerships that would prevent the ravages of smoking.

- Enforcing laws and regulations that protect health and ensure safety. Local health departments inspect restaurants looking for potential vectors in the transmission of an organism, which may include individuals who are infected. In my experience, restaurants voluntarily close at public health's recommendation if their site is associated with a known outbreak. It is in their best interest to cooperate with public health to stop the transmission of illness. However, regulations restricting individuals in sensitive occupations from working can be difficult. If someone in a sensitive occupation is restricted from working for several months because she or he continues to shed an organism such as *Salmonella*, a public health worker might refer the employee to a social worker to help find a different occupation, obtain training, or address the emotional impact of the experience. If there are religious and cultural issues that make transmission of disease more likely, social workers have the cultural competency skills to work with public health officials to find realistic solutions.

- Linking people to needed personal health services and assuring the provision of health care when otherwise unavailable. As a coordinator for a local chapter of Safe Kids, I distributed safety devices such as bicycle helmets, gunlocks, and car seats. In that role, I often had the opportunity to refer clients to various sites for their public health (e.g., vaccines or physical examinations) and social work (e.g., parenting support or rehabilitation services) needs.

At this point in our history, funding is probably the greatest challenge facing public health departments. Strong leadership is needed at the federal, state, and local levels. Leaders at each of these levels need to be politically astute and knowledgeable about public health issues as they compete for funds.

Collaboration is an important skill for the social worker in a public health setting. We often partner with other community organizations. For example, I worked on a committee whose goal was to ensure appropriate emergency medical care and disaster preparedness for children. We established a partnership with Telephone Pioneers, a nonprofit charitable organization consisting primarily of employed and retired telecommunications employees. The Pioneers provided shoes and socks for area children who were in need, worked with area schools to identify children who would receive the shoes and socks, and worked with local businesses to obtain more donations. Members of our committee and the Pioneers accompanied the children as they selected their new shoes and socks.

Social workers in this field continually need to update their knowledge and competencies. For example, I am currently employed as an epidemiologist at a county health department. After the events of 9/11, some of the federal funding to prepare for a bioterrorism attack was disseminated to local health departments for the hiring of bioterrorism planners and epidemiologists. I became a Certified Emergency Response Coordinator and now spend my days working with surveillance systems that provide situational awareness during an emergency response.

Public health agencies have also been tasked with establishing clinics to respond in an emergency and thus conduct exercises to prepare for these clinics. (The majority of public health organizations had the opportunity to test those skills "for real" during the 2009 H1N1 outbreak.) While working in any emergency clinic, I am always the collector of the data, which allows adjustments to the clinic's flow. For example, on one occasion the data confirmed that one line in the clinic was taking a much higher patient load. Adjusting that load was necessary to prevent errors due to fatigue.

Collecting and analyzing data in order to make decisions based on the evidence is a key requirement for public health officials. For example, we may receive anecdotal reports about ill people in the community. By reviewing data from different sources, I can determine if there really is an increase of illness. In addition, because there is historical data regarding influenza and its characteristics, public health workers knew the 2009 influenza was an anomaly that needed to be addressed.

The future of the public health field is exciting and yet uncertain. Most people, including politicians, have difficulty distinguishing between public health (population-driven) and health care (individual-based). This means, in today's environment, the rhetoric surrounding health care reform will likely impact public health. The debate surrounding government authority at the federal, state, and local level will also influence public health's future. There has long been, and will continue to be, a role for social work in the public health arena.

Yet a shortage of competent public health workers seems likely. The current workforce has suffered considerable attrition. Facing budget cuts, public health agencies are not replacing workers who resign or retire and are, in fact, offering early retirement when funding falls short.

SOCIAL WORK PRACTICE IN SCHOOL SETTINGS

School social work has been around since social work has been a profession. The early settlement houses sent "visiting teachers" out to the homes of immigrant families to establish a link between home, school, and community, a mission that still characterizes the goals of school social work today. Unfortunately, the Depression of the 1930s and the rise of psychoanalysis in the helping professions limited the expansion of school social work until the 1960s.

In the 1960s the federal government became formally involved in providing funds to support educational achievement for special populations. First was the Title I program, which provided resources to schools to help improve the reading skills of children from poor neighborhoods. Title I remains part of the massive education funding bill known today as No Child Left Behind. In the mid-1970s the Individuals with Disabilities Education Act (IDEA) was passed, providing states with funds for special education programs.

These federal mandates required social services for students, which precipitated significant growth in the number of school social workers hired by school districts during the past 30 years. During this time, the field of school social work became one of the special practice sections in NASW. Social workers were specifically mandated to work in special education, but became increasingly present in regular educational settings. Depending on the way in which a school district manages special education services, a school social worker may work only in special education, only in regular education, or both.

School social workers assist children whose difficulties with behavior or learning interfere with their ability to succeed in school but who are not qualified for special education services. In this context, social workers primarily provide individual and group counseling, case management, crisis intervention, support and information for students' families, and assessments for special education eligibility, and collaborate with teachers on behavior plans and with community resources, particularly child welfare services.

Policy-Practice Considerations in School Social Work

Today, school social work responsibilities can differ across states and districts, even between schools in the same district. In order to provide consistency across the field and help clarify the role of the school social worker, the NASW (2012) has developed standards for school social work services. These standards address a wide spectrum of practice areas, including ethics and values, qualifications, assessment, decision making and practice evaluation, record keeping, workload management, professional development, cultural competence, interdisciplinary leadership and collaboration, and advocacy. Exhibit 8.11 provides a selection of the NASW's guidelines.

School social workers have an array of responsibilities within the various school-based and school-related settings (NASW CWS, 2010, p. 1):

- Conducting biopsychosocial assessments.

- Assessing students for substance use/abuse, support systems, physical and emotional functioning, barriers to academic performance, peer issues, suicidal/homicidal ideation, and mental health issues.

- Developing and implementing treatment and discharge plans that support student self-determination.

- Providing direct therapeutic services (e.g., individual, family, and group treatment).

- Providing crisis intervention services and safety assessments.

- Advocating for students' best interests and services.

- Providing case management services (e.g., referrals to community resources and collaboration with other professionals).

- Providing educational programs for teaching staff, students, and parents.

- Conducting home visits.

- Identifying and resolving ethical issues.

- Contributing to the multidisciplinary team.

EXHIBIT 8.11

Guidelines for School Social Work Services

Qualifications: School social workers shall meet the provisions for professional practice set by NASW and their respective state department of education and possess knowledge and understanding basic to the social work profession as well as the local education system.
Assessment: School social workers shall conduct assessments of individuals, families, and systems/organizations (namely, classroom, school, neighborhood, district, state) with the goal of improving student social, emotional, behavioral, and academic outcomes.
Intervention: School social workers shall understand and use evidence-informed practices in their interventions.
Workload Management: School social workers shall organize their workloads to fulfill their responsibilities and clarify their critical roles within the educational mission of the school or district in which they work.
Cultural Competence: School social workers shall ensure that students and their families are provided services within the context of multicultural understanding and competence.
Interdisciplinary Leadership and Collaboration: School social workers shall provide leadership in developing a positive school climate and work collaboratively with school administration, school personnel, family members, and community professionals as appropriate to increase accessibility and effectiveness of services.
Advocacy: School social workers shall engage in advocacy that seeks to ensure that all students have equal access to education and services to enhance their academic progress.

Source: Adapted from National Association of Social Workers (NASW), 2012.

All school social workers do not work for public school districts. An increasing number work in parochial or private schools. Some school social workers are employed by public or not-for-profit agencies and are placed in schools as *school-based social workers*. There are also special schools within districts that may operate as *community education centers, full-service schools* (schools that provide health, mental health, and social services on site), or *alternative schools* (may be private or part of a public school district). These schools seek a wider, more meaningful role for parent and community involvement than usually found in regular public school districts.

R. Jan Wilson, MSW, Ph.D., LCSW, School of Social Work

As a school social worker, I have always worked in alternative school settings. I served for a time as a social worker in an on-grounds school at a residential shelter; we provided education and therapeutic support for adolescents in residential care and for students expelled from local school districts for behavior problems. I provided support services to students at an independent GED program.

I was also a school-based social worker working for a not-for-profit agency. There I carried out a program for teen parents in five school districts and partnered with Parents As Teachers, a program focused on helping develop teens' parenting skills. As part of that program, I worked with the community to start a day care center for teen mothers. I worked for other not-for-profits in which my job responsibilities were associated with schools.

In yet another role, I provided support services for families who had children with disabilities. This position required that I work closely with the special education cooperative to help parents to learn the services system. These parents need to learn strategies for advocating for their children to receive appropriate services for which they are eligible.

School-based social workers tend to have responsibilities for students with mental health issues. Working with these complex and ongoing issues means that social workers stay involved with their clients throughout the entire year despite the fact that the school year is typically 9 months long. Providing services for students and families

experiencing mental illness also requires the social worker to have a community perspective on social work practice. While social workers working in alternative school settings have a collaborative, contracted relationship with the school district in which they are placed, they have some degree of freedom from district governance and are responsible primarily to the agency where they are employed. In the agency, social services are likely to be the primary mission of the organization—as opposed to school settings, in which education is the focus. For the last decade, school social workers have been working in *charter schools*, which, by definition, are independent of public school structures. For the parochial school, charter school, alternative school, or school-based school social worker, being able to practice independently is important because these types of education placements may only have one social worker.

However, any social work job that involves working with children and youth inevitably includes having to work with the school system. School social work provided me with a systemic view of the social service and education systems. I was constantly learning new information and resources because I was always challenged by the two systems.

Working as a generalist practitioner within the specialized area of school social work meant that I had to integrate practice across a wide range of specialties, from health to counseling to community

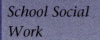

School Social Work

Source: Getty Images.

organization and program evaluation. I worked on all levels of social work practice: micro, mezzo, and macro. School social work presents a wide range of practice options and requires one to be a lifelong learner in order to maintain current expertise in the changing world of students and their families. I found that I enjoyed the fast pace of school social work.

SOCIAL WORK PRACTICE IN RURAL SETTINGS

Rural communities are defined by the U.S. Census Bureau in the 2010 Census as those areas that lie outside of more densely populated areas known as urbanized areas or urban clusters. Social work practice in rural communities is an important area of practice, but one that can go unnoticed. The availability of social workers is particularly low in states with more nonurban, or rural, areas. For example, the number of licensed social workers per 100,000 persons ranges from a high of 408 (Maryland, which abuts Washington DC) to a low of 23.7 (in largely rural New Hampshire) (CHWS/CWS, 2006).

Rural, nonmetropolitan areas have a chronic need for social workers with expertise in mental health treatment (Gibelman, 2004). Oftentimes, social workers are the only providers of mental health services in these areas (Clark, 2003).

Social workers with BSW degrees tend to be more commonplace in rural communities than MSWs and doctoral-level social workers. However, despite the small numbers of citizens and lack of services, rural communities are diverse populations. Social workers are thus required to function at multiple levels, for which they are prepared as generalists, and to be knowledgeable about a wider array of issues and resources than may be needed in an urban area. While practicing in a rural community has many advantages, including a sense of community, recruitment of and adequate number of social workers in rural communities may require organizations to consider offering benefits such as loan forgiveness, support for licensure and continuing education, and job security (Phillips, Quinn, & Heitkamp, 2010).

Early pioneers in rural social work focused on political and policy changes that were needed to increase the availability of social work services in rural communities (Brown, 1933; Ginsberg, 1998; Martinez-Brawley, 1983). The Rural Social Work Caucus notes that social work employment opportunities in rural communities are on the rise.

Policy-Practice Considerations in Rural Settings

As generalist social work practice is the method best suited to practice in rural areas, social work educators are being called upon to include rural social work practice within social work curricula to enable students to understand the sophisticated level of skill and knowledge that is required for competent rural practice (NASW, 2012–2014l). Such a focus can help rural social workers to conceptualize the possible differences between urban and rural practice and incorporate these differences into the training of other social workers. A set of 19 assumptions has been developed by the Southern Regional Education Board Manpower Education and Training Project's Rural Task Force that includes guidelines for social workers in rural settings (Southern Regional Education Board, 1998). For example, rural communities may be diverse, but the people who live in them, as well as their needs, are more similar to people who live in urban areas than they are different. Although rural communities may lack basic services, greater priority is placed on services to sustain life than on those to enhance the quality of life. Rural communities have unique characteristics that can include geographically scattered poverty; existence of generational poverty; resistance to formal services and professionals, particularly those who are not members of the community; and more informal service networks.

Practice in small communities can provide social workers with a uniquely rewarding and challenging opportunity. In addition to being trained in generalist practice, social workers who practice in rural communities are required to develop knowledge, skills, and values appropriate for that community. These may include an understanding of the unique aspects of that community and the ability to use the community's customs and traditions as a basis for interventions; the willingness to respect the culture and values of the community; the ability to work within the informal network of services and resources; and the skills to develop new resources as needed (Southern Regional Education Board, 1998).

The social worker often plays overlapping roles in a small community. Whereas an urban setting typically offers a social worker anonymity, in smaller communities, social workers often have not only a history with, but also multiple ties to, persons to whom they will provide services. Such complex roles are not impossible in a larger community, but the potential is greater in a rural area due to the smaller population. Multiple roles can serve as both a strength and a liability in the social work relationship. Knowing a person's background, support system, and resources can be an asset in engaging her or him, assessing the situation, and developing and implementing an intervention. On the other hand, having extensive prior knowledge can compromise the social worker's professional objectivity. To practice with competence, social workers must work within the culture and communications patterns of the community and anticipate potential ethical issues (e.g., dual relationships) (Daley, 2010). Understanding that interactions may entail a personal connection and information travels through community networks are key aspects to rural social work practice (Ginsberg, 2005).

Ellen Burkemper, Ph.D., MSW, LCSW, LMFT, RN, School of Social Work

For the last 25 years, I have provided a number of social work professional services in my small, rural community. I have found that social work practice in the small community is varied and requires that I be flexible and able to engage in services at the individual, family, group, and community levels. Through funding from the Department of Health, I participated in a program in which social workers obtain MSWs to provide mental health services through and in rural physicians' offices. Already a registered nurse, I was particularly well suited to this program, as I was familiar with the medical setting and terminology and lived in a rural community.

Upon completing my MSW, I had the opportunity to work in my community's mental health center as the center's coordinator and social work clinician. This practice opportunity brought forth all of my MSW generalist and clinical education and training. I was already knowledgeable about the services in my community and knew the local physicians and clergy who serve as the primary gatekeepers for referrals for mental health services. I felt this was a proactive way to bring the practice of social work to my community.

My responsibilities in the rural community mental health center included working with individuals, families, groups, organizations, and the community. Some of my practice activities included:

- Providing clinical services (therapy) for individuals and families.

- Working with other agencies to identify and develop community services.

- Representing the center at community meetings and events.

- Organizing fund-raising events.

- Collaborating with other programs involved in the provision of services to persons living with chronic and persistent mental illness.

- Making presentations to community groups on the services provided by the center.

- Serving as a member of the agency's advisory board.

- Writing newspaper articles regarding mental health concerns.

Due to a lack of funding and a need to consolidate services, the center closed after I had worked there for 10 years. Having the center close might have been a crisis, but I realized that I had gained considerable expertise in clinical and administrative practice. Because of the confidence that I had gained as a social worker, I decided to establish a private clinical practice as a solo practitioner. Concurrent with the opening of my private practice, I continued my education, ending with a doctoral degree in marriage and family therapy. I also began to work as a trainer and consultant for therapeutic foster parents for child protective services in my county.

The opportunities I have had to provide services in my small community have been rewarding. In small communities, there is a need for mental health services, and social workers are ideally suited to provide these services. As generalists, social workers are trained to engage in all levels of practice, and that versatility enables us to exercise our talents and education.

Working in a small community can present challenges. I had to be familiar with the NASW *Code of Ethics* (2008). In particular, rural social workers are knowledgeable about the special implications of the possible dual relationships that can occur in a small community. My family and I are active in my community, and living and working in a small community means that I am likely to run into clients while grocery shopping, attending weddings, church, professional gatherings, or school events. I learned to be careful to keep office work at the office. Of considerable importance is ensuring that client systems have knowingly provided informed consent for the social worker to discuss their cases with other professionals and that the social worker will not discuss them with friends, family members, or acquaintances. Clients must fully understand the social worker's role and functions, and the special implications of confidentiality in a small community. I talk with the client about the likelihood that we will encounter one another outside the professional social work setting. I inform clients that should that occur, I will not acknowledge them until they acknowledge me. By placing the decision to communicate in a public setting with clients, I am providing them with the right to self-determination.

Social workers are needed in small communities. Social workers who live and work in the small community have a view that is fuller than those who drive to the job and return home to other communities. Having been a member of a family in this farming community, my knowledge of the community helps me understand the culture in which the client system lives. This insight has provided me with a more efficient understanding of my clients' backgrounds, social environments, and rural ethic.

I see small-community social work as a viable field of practice. It offers the opportunity to engage in all levels of practice. In some cases, a benefit of rural practice is the ease of getting tasks accomplished due to the fewer numbers of individuals who need to be consulted. Social workers living and working in small communities are a minority, but rural areas can be an opportunity for employment, and for the expression of professional talents and education.

CONCLUSION

Although vastly different in terms of the settings in which they practice, populations with whom they work, and challenges they face, these "voices from the field" share a number of similarities and themes. Each social worker possesses a social work degree, not a degree in a field like gerontology, substance abuse treatment, or counseling. Upon completion of the requirements for the social work degree, the social worker is, thus, equipped with a set of knowledge, skills, and values that enable her or him to practice at multiple levels with diverse populations in different settings. Specific knowledge of a population and setting is required, but the engagement, assessment, intervention, and evaluation process is common regardless of the targeted client system or setting. Having knowledge of the social work role within a wide range of populations and settings is critical for all social workers.

Another similarity is that each of the social workers emphasizes a strengths-based perspective regardless of their fields of practice. Being able to identify the assets and resources that a client system or population possesses is essential to being an effective advocate, an ethical practitioner, and a partner with the client system in the change process.

The narratives also provide evidence of the importance of critical thinking as a social work skill. For example, in Jon's narrative on working in chemical dependency and addiction treatment, he describes a traditional treatment modality for substance abuse. Moreover, he voices skepticism regarding the effectiveness of that particular approach for all substance abusers and offers his insights into an alternative framework. Jon's social work training instilled in him the value of questioning and examining his social work practice so that all possibilities can be explored.

Advocacy and policy practice are two additional areas about which the social workers are united in their perceptions. Advocacy is a vital skill, especially when resources are a critical factor and policies are limiting. To provide better access to services, social workers must advocate with legislators on issues such as universal health insurance coverage, equity in mental health benefits, economic reform, and the needs of oppressed groups whose voices are not being heard (for example, older adults, children, persons with disabilities, refugees and immigrants, battered women, persons in the criminal justice system).

Several of the narratives provide insights into the opportunities to build on the practice skills used with individuals and families in order to move into administrative and management roles. Herb, Suzanne, and Barbara all write of their administrative functions, but each is grounded in her or his knowledge of the issues that social workers that work with individuals, families, and groups face in working in their respective fields of practice.

I want to point out that shortages do exist in several of the fields of practice described here. More social workers are needed to work with older adults, in substance abuse and addiction treatment, the child welfare arena, and rural communities. Specifically, employment opportunities in the area of mental health, substance abuse treatment, and marriage and family therapy are expected to grow 16–41% in these areas (BLS, 2012a & b). Initiatives have been launched to increase the number of degreed social workers working in areas such as gerontology and child welfare, but still more initiatives are necessary. To gain the experience to respond to these emerging needs, social work students can seek out coursework, field experiences, research opportunities, and service or volunteer experiences. Gaining knowledge and experience in a variety of areas not only can help you identify the areas that are the best professional fit for you, but can help to meet the needs of the profession. Using a strengths-based approach, you can assess your strengths and explore areas in which those strengths can be assets. To help you in your exploration, check out the information provided in Exhibit 8.12.

EXHIBIT 8.12

Activities for Learning About Fields of Practice

Social work organizations:

NASW, the policy-making and standard-setting body for the social work profession and specific fields of practice. www.naswdc.org.

NASW's Career Center. http://careers.socialworkers.org/.

Latino Social Workers Organization, a group for social workers to share experiences regarding education, employment, and the Latino community. www.lswo.org.

National Association of Black Social Workers, an organization committed to enhancing the quality of life and empowering people of African ancestry through advocacy, human service delivery, and research. www.nabsw.org.

North American Puerto Rican and Hispanic Social Workers, a group for social workers and other human service professionals to strengthen, develop, and improve the resources and services that meet the needs of the Puerto Rican and Hispanic communities. www.naprhsw.org.

Rural Social Work Caucus, an organization focused on issues related to rural social work practice. www.ruralsocialwork.org/.

School Social Work Association of America, an organization of social workers working in public and private schools. www.sswaa.org.

International Federation of Social Workers, a global organization striving for social justice, human rights, and social development. www.ifsw.org.

Socialworkhelper.com, an international social networking site to provide connections for students and professionals in the helping professionals. www.socialworkhelper. com/index.html.

Books for general reference and informational reading:

Barker, R.L. (2003). *The social work dictionary*. Washington, DC: NASW Press.

Grobman, L.M. (2012). *Days in the lives of social workers (4th edition)*. Harrisburg, PA: White Hat Communications.

Grobman, L.M. (2005). *More days in the lives of social workers*. Harrisburg, PA: White Hat Communications.

Grobman, L.M. (2007). *Days in the lives of gerontological social workers*. Harrisburg, PA: White Hat Communications.

Mizrahi, T. & Davis, L.E. (2008). *Encyclopedia of social work (20th edition)*. Washington, DC & New York, NY: NASW Press and Oxford Press.

National Association of Social Workers. (2009). *Author's guide to social work journals (5th edition)*. Washington, DC: NASW Press.

National Association of Social Workers. (2012–2014). *Social work speaks. NASW policy statements 2012–2014 (9th edition)*. Washington, DC: NASW Press.

Continued

EXHIBIT 8.12	Roberts, A.R. (2009). *Social workers' desk reference (2nd edition)*. Washington, DC: NASW Press.
continued	

Roberts, A.R. (2009). *Social workers' desk reference (2nd edition)*. Washington, DC: NASW Press.

Easily accessible and informative journals:

BPD Update Online. Published by The Association of Baccalaureate Social Work Program Directors. http://bpdonline.org.

Journal of Social Work Values and Ethics. Dedicated to examining ethical and values issues that impact social work practice, research, and theory development. www.socialworker.com/jswve.

The New Social Worker. Published by White Hat Publications, targeted for social work students and new professionals. www.socialworker.com.

Social Work. Official publication of the National Association of Social Workers.

Social Work Today. Biweekly magazine for social workers. Free subscriptions at www.socialworktoday.com.

Social work-related databases:

http://www.search.com/search. Constantly updated, free search engine; articles can be printed in their entirety at no cost.

http://ifp.nyu.edu/archive (Information for Practice). News and new scholarship from around the world that is relevant for social work practice.

www.pueblo.gsa.gov and www.access.gpo.gov. Government documents.

MAIN POINTS

- Social workers' range of knowledge and skills should include knowledge of human behavior and biology; the philosophy of other disciplines; awareness of cultures, faith traditions, laws, policies, and social systems; and the ability to work with a diverse population of clients and other professionals.

- With a generalist social work degree, you can practice in a variety of different fields within the same career, including mental health, chemical dependency, and criminal justice. Within the field, you can work with a variety of client systems at the micro, mezzo, and macro levels.

- In this chapter, 13 social workers present their experiences in 12 different fields, from working with older adults to working in a rural community, with the goal of sharing the diversity, challenges, and rewards of the social work profession.

- The diverse fields are held together by the commonality of social work practice. For example, working with older adults requires knowledge of medical and health issues. Working in mental health involves interactions with the legal and health systems.

EXERCISES

1. Use the Sanchez family interactive case (www.routledgesw.com/cases) to get a better sense of some of the practice issues mentioned in this chapter:
   a. Review the case file for Roberto Salazar. Then select Roberto and answer his Critical Thinking Questions.
   b. Review the case file for Carmen Sanchez. Then select Carmen and answer her Critical Thinking Questions.
   c. Review the case file for Gloria Sanchez Quintanilla. Then select Gloria and answer her Critical Thinking Questions.

2. Go to the Carla Washburn interactive case at www.routledgesw.com/cases and read her case file. Develop a list of questions you have about working with older adults. Utilizing the section in this chapter and other sources you can locate, identify the specific gerontological knowledge and skills needed for providing social work services to an older adult.

3. Go to the NASW website at www.naswdc.org/pressroom/features/issuefactsheets. asp. Click on Issue Fact Sheets and read about the various fields of practice that are included in this chapter. Choose three fields that interest you and reflect on your reasons for being interested in those fields. Develop a list of questions regarding areas in which you would like to have more information.

4. With assistance from your instructor, identify a social work student with whom you can conduct an interview regarding her/his primary field of practice interests. Your goal is to gain insight into the reasons that your fellow student has chosen social work for a career, the pros and cons of majoring in social work, and the life and academic experiences that she or he perceives to be helpful in pursuing a social work career.

5. With your instructor's assistance, identify a social worker with whom you can conduct an interview regarding her/his primary field of practice. Develop a set of questions to pose to the social work professional, and conduct an interview regarding her or his training, experiences, philosophy, and practice wisdom.

6. You have been given the opportunity to read about various fields of practice in social work. Imagine that you are working in one of these fields. Given your own experience, respond to the following questions:
   a. How might political, economic, and social issues impact your work?
   b. What are the potential "isms" that you might encounter in this field of practice?
   c. How might you adjust to the issues that you identified in the previous two questions?

CHAPTER 9

Social Work Practice With Individuals and Families

Emily's career has taken her down many paths, but the knowledge and skills she developed for working with individuals and families have proved invaluable in all her practice experiences. She has learned to develop rapport, establish trust, build relationships, conduct interviews, and employ skills of engagement, assessment, intervention, and evaluation, and these skills have formed the foundation of Emily's social work career. Emily has applied these skills when working with children, families, young adults, and older adult client systems.

In this chapter, we explore the area of **individual and family social work practice**. Providing services to individuals, couples, and families is the cornerstone of social work practice. Also known as **micro social work practice**, working one-on-one with individuals and families is the primary focus of most practicing social workers.

In fact, almost all (96%) of social work practitioners spend a portion of their time providing direct services to clients. Over two-thirds report direct services with individuals and families as their primary practice area, where they spend more than half of their overall work time (Center for Health Workforce Studies & Center for Workforce Studies, 2006; Whitaker & Arrington, 2008). Social work practice with individuals, couples, and families is an area that continues to have increasing opportunities. Not surprisingly, a larger proportion of younger and more recently graduated social workers are employed in direct practice areas, while many older, more experienced social workers often move into supervisory, administrative, management, teaching, and research positions.

Practitioners who work with individuals and families continue to work primarily in traditional settings such as health and mental health and family service settings, but they are also found in educational, faith-based, and correctional settings. This chapter focuses on the history and meaning of this level of practice. It also identifies practice skills that are essential for direct practice with individuals and families.

HISTORICAL PERSPECTIVE ON SOCIAL WORK PRACTICE WITH INDIVIDUALS AND FAMILIES

As you learned in Chapter 2, the history of social work is, in many ways, the history of social work practice with individuals and families. The friendly visitors, outdoor relief, and eventually, the Charity Organization Society movement of the 19th century all served as the forerunners of modern-day social work practice with individuals and families.

The work of these early practitioners evolved into a methodology referred to as **social casework**. Recall from Chapter 1 that this is a method of social work practice in which social workers, through direct contact with the client system, help individuals and families to resolve personal challenges.

In her 1922 book, *What Is Social Case Work?*, Mary Richmond provided the basis for the teaching and practice of social casework for many decades to come. Richmond proposed that practitioners help individuals adjust to their situations by identifying needs, goals, and resources (McNutt & Floersch, 2008). Early social workers were trained in the idea that the social casework approach could be used to help individuals and families resolve problems caused by "deviations from accepted standards of normal social life" (Brieland, 1995, p. 2251). For example, social workers who engaged in casework during this period may have worked with an immigrant family to obtain housing and jobs, helped a widow to obtain financial assistance, or facilitated the adoption of an orphaned child. Social casework continued to be the prevailing model for social work practice well into the 20th century.

This exclusive focus on the individual changed when the social upheaval of the 1960s brought the issues of race, ethnicity, poverty, and human rights to the forefront of societal attention (McNutt & Floersch, 2008). This attention prompted social workers to incorporate a broader, more holistic perspective when intervening with client systems. In the 1960s and 1970s, practice with individuals and families shifted to include the emergence of the ecological model, which encompassed the environmental perspective, the need for research to support and guide practice, and the birth of the generalist social work practice model. The generalist practice model emphasized an ecological, systemic, and strengths-based approach to working with individuals, groups, organizations, and communities.

THE PLANNED CHANGE PROCESS IN SOCIAL WORK PRACTICE WITH INDIVIDUALS AND FAMILIES

Change is the purpose of the social worker's involvement with client systems at all levels of practice. Change for the client system involves embracing new attitudes or behaviors. Establishing goals for change is a key component of the social work relationship.

Social workers become involved in a wide variety of change efforts in working with individuals and families, such as:

- Beginning or ending a phase of life, for example, marriage, divorce, parenting, career change, caring for a family member, retirement, or grief.

- Relationship difficulties, for example, friendship, family, marital, parent/child, or employment.

- Life crises, for example, physical or mental health challenges, violence, natural or economic disasters, or legal problems.

- Chemical dependency and addictions, for example, alcohol, drugs, food, gambling, sexual, or spending.

All interventions revolve around **planned change**, a process in which the social worker and client collaborate to plan and then execute a series of actions designed to enhance the client's functioning and well-being. Planned change for interventions with individuals, families, groups, organizations, and communities consists of four phases:

1. Engagement.

2. Assessment.

3. Intervention.

4. Evaluation.

See Exhibit 9.1 for a depiction of the planned change model.

Change is a fluid process that involves unexpected starts and stops. Even if the client system is able to establish goals for change, the process may be interrupted when real-life factors intervene. For example, the client may be seeking employment, but that goal is jeopardized or delayed when her or his car breaks down or child care arrangements fall through. The social worker's responsibility is to monitor and support the change process by helping the individual anticipate and respond to challenges and crises.

To facilitate planned change, the social worker must understand the situation from the client's perspective. Some clients want to change something in their lives and feel capable of doing so, whereas others who desire change feel incapable. Still other clients perceive no need for change. The saying *"starting where the client is"* guides social workers in gaining insight into the client's perception of the problem, its origins, and the desired goal. It is a mistake for the social worker to make assumptions regarding the client's thoughts, feelings, and values. The social worker must understand the client's motivation and capacity for change and not impose her or his desired goals on the client.

Recall from Chapter 7 that the strengths-based perspective is based on the belief that the client is the expert on her or his life, and the social worker's role is to support and empower the client to enhance her or his function and well-being.

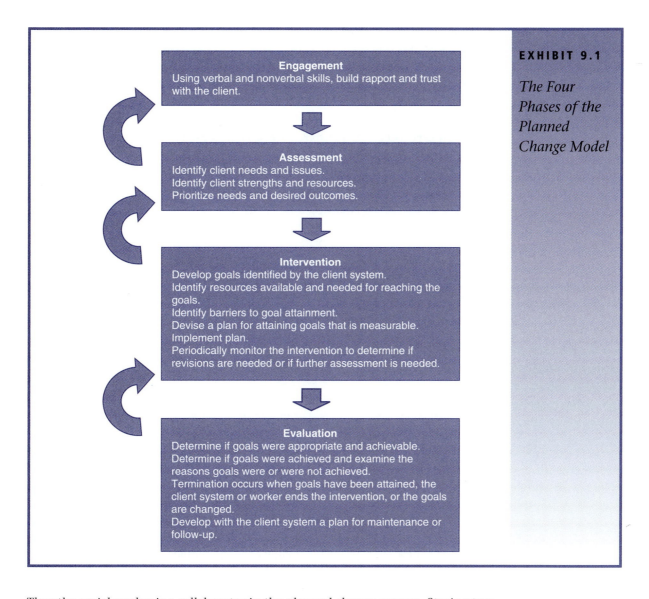

EXHIBIT 9.1

The Four Phases of the Planned Change Model

Thus the social worker is a collaborator in the planned change process. Staying true to this social work approach often requires social workers to take stock of their thoughts and feelings about the client's situation, choices, and goals. Social workers must consistently compare the client's goals with their own to ensure that the goals being worked toward are the client's and not those of the social worker. As we all know from our personal experiences, our motivation is likely to be much higher when the goal we are working toward is one in which we are invested and one that we think has the most possibility for success.

The difference in goals may be particularly dramatic when working with clients who do not voluntarily seek assistance. These clients may want nothing more than to end the professional relationship as soon as possible. Even then, the social worker's responsibility is to "start where the client is" and identify common ground on which to build a working relationship. In this case, the common ground may be the mutual desire to terminate the relationship.

SKILLS FOR SOCIAL WORK PRACTICE WITH INDIVIDUALS AND FAMILIES

To practice social work with empathy and efficacy, the social worker must possess a repertoire of specialized skills. In this section, we explore beginning social work skills for each of the four phases of the planned change intervention—engagement, assessment, intervention, and evaluation. These basic skills are essential for practice at all levels, and they serve as the foundation for the more advanced skills that social workers develop to address specific situations.

Engagement of Individuals and Families

While working at the sexual assault response program, Emily responded late one night to a call from a convenience store manager. A woman had come to the store and asked to use the telephone. Her swollen face and bleeding lip suggested that she had been physically assaulted. Recognizing the customer from previous visits to the store, the manager asked if the woman needed help. The woman, Victoria, burst into tears and told the manager she had been attacked as she was entering her apartment by a man she did not know. He dragged her into some bushes, beat and sexually assaulted her, and then left her in the bushes as he fled on foot. Victoria agreed to allow the manager to call Emily's agency, but not the police.

Emily first met Victoria in the manager's office. As Emily entered the room, she observed Victoria lying on a couch in a fetal position and crying. When Emily moved toward her and said her name, Victoria visibly flinched. Emily recognized that, as a result of the trauma that Victoria had experienced, building trust with Victoria was critical to being able to help her.

Emily's first step was to sit down near Victoria, but not too close to threaten her. She told Victoria who she was and that she was there to help in any way that she could. She asked Victoria if she could get her a tissue. As she spoke to Victoria, Emily spoke slowly in a warm and soft tone. She leaned forward toward Victoria but made no attempt to touch her.

Emily told Victoria that the manager had informed her that Victoria had been attacked. Emily then suggested that if Victoria was willing and when she was ready, they go to the hospital so that Victoria could be examined and could call the police to report the assault. Emily was careful not to use graphic, medical, or legal jargon at this point, focusing instead on helping Victoria to feel safe.

Emily sat with Victoria for an hour before Victoria said she was ready to go to the hospital. Emily assured Victoria that she would stay with her through the examination and the police interview. As Victoria rose from the couch, Emily asked for Victoria's permission to physically assist her in getting up and walking to the car. During the trip to the hospital, Emily explained to Victoria what she could expect when they reached the hospital. She continued to speak softly, calmly, and with empathy, assuring Victoria that she was now safe and in control of the procedure.

In order to conduct a complete and accurate assessment of the client situation, the social worker's first task is to establish a working relationship that encompasses rapport, trust, and respect—three distinct phenomena. Rapport is the "state of harmony, compatibilities, and empathy that permits mutual understanding and a working relationship between the client and the social worker" (Barker, 2003, p. 359). A component of building rapport is to display empathy for the person with whom you are working. Empathic responses convey to the client that you have compassion for her or his feelings and are responding to the emotions being experienced at that moment (Barker, 2003). When the social worker respects the client, she or he will treat the client with esteem and dignity. Engaging the client is the first step in building a successful relationship.

Engagement is the process of eliciting information in an open and sincere manner using both verbal and nonverbal communication. To engage the client and build rapport, the social worker should attend to the following aspects of verbal communication:

- Speak at a pace that the client can easily follow, particularly with clients whose first language is different from yours or clients who have a hearing impairment.

- Speak at a level that the client can easily hear, but not too loud.

- Speak with warmth and empathy.

- Use language appropriate to the client's culture, ethnicity, and social group, but do not attempt to use language that is unfamiliar to you.

- Use language appropriate to the client's educational level.

- Avoid professional jargon that may be unfamiliar to the client.

- Use respectful language to refer to individuals and groups, paying particular attention to avoiding language that promotes the "isms."

- Patiently listen while the client tells her or his story without interrupting, prompting, or interjecting words.

- Avoid "ums," "you knows," and other unnecessary language.

Attention to nonverbal communication is as important as verbal communication. Important nonverbal issues to consider include:

- Ensure that you and the client are both physically on the same level (for example, both sitting).

- Maintain direct eye contact, when culturally appropriate. When working with a family or small group, maintain equal eye contact with all members of the group. To look at one or some persons more than others can imply a preference or bias and can hamper your ability to establish trust with all members.

- Look at the client while speaking instead of looking out the window, at forms, or the client's chart, for example.

- Maintain physical and emotional focus on the client when the client speaks, as opposed to thinking ahead to the next question or comment.

- Avoid distractive behaviors (for example, playing with pencil/hair, swinging leg, tapping on the desk, checking your phone/computer).

- Directly face the client.

- Lean slightly forward to indicate attentiveness.

- Use nonverbal gestures that are typical and comfortable, but ensure that they are not excessive to the point of distraction.

- Demonstrate appropriate facial expressions such as interest, warmth, and varied responses that are appropriate to the client's remarks. Facial expressions should be consistent with the words.

Having insight into your style of communication is critical to the helping process. Exhibit 9.2 provides a checklist of questions that you can use to inventory your personal communication style. After answering the questions, identify those areas that may warrant attention in order to enhance your communication style as a social worker.

EXHIBIT 9.2

Inventory of Personal Communication Habits

- Are you more comfortable listening or talking?
- Do you view your role being to give advice or explore options?
- When listening to someone describe a difficulty or challenge, do you feel compelled to offer solutions immediately?
- Do you find it difficult to pay attention when others are talking?
- Do you find that while others are talking, you are thinking of what you are going to say next?

EXHIBIT 9.2

continued

- Do you find that you notice nonverbal communication as well as the verbal message?
- Do you become so consumed with the details of a "story" that you miss the essence of the story?
- Do you have a difficult time listening to a "story" without interjecting your own personal experiences or biases?
- How do you determine if you got the essence of the story?
- Do you find that you are easily distracted when conversing with another person (i.e., watching other activities, thinking of things you have to do later)?
- How do you react to people who have difficulty communicating in a straightforward manner (i.e., non-focused, tangential), are uncommunicative, or hostile?
- Does your speech include "ums," "ers," "you knows?"
- Do you feel that you communicate in a straightforward manner?
- What is your nonverbal communication style—use of hands and gestures, volume and tempo of your voice, posture?

Source: Updated from Corey & Corey, 1998, p. 69.

Assessment of Individuals and Families

Emily stayed with Victoria through the physical examination, the collection of evidence for the rape kit, and the police interview. Because these events took several hours, Emily had an opportunity to become more familiar with Victoria's situation. She learned that Victoria had moved to the city several years earlier to attend college. She was now a management trainee at a department store in the mall and lived alone in a ground-floor apartment. She was engaged, but her fiancé lived in another state and visited only once a month. Her family was in her hometown several hours away.

By asking questions in a gentle, unobtrusive manner, Emily was able to begin the assessment process. Emily was careful not to ask questions that were not relevant to gathering information for responding to Victoria's immediate need of safety. Emily learned that Victoria's attacker likely knew where she lived and possibly that she lived alone. She learned that Victoria had friends from school and work, but did not know anyone at her apartment complex, as she had just recently moved there. Victoria admitted that she was terrified to return to her apartment, but she did not want to leave town because she had work and school commitments.

Assessment is the professional activity conducted with the client that provides the basis for understanding the client's situation and planning the social work intervention. In conducting an assessment at any level, the social worker focuses on three main tasks:

1. Use theoretical frameworks to guide the gathering of relevant information and the evaluation of the information to determine its meaning for the client system.

2. Evaluate the level of functioning for the client—with a focus on strengths—as well as the resources available to the entire client system.

3. Work with the client to define and prioritize the issues to be addressed within the intervention.

The social worker then begins to develop the intervention, paying specific attention to the desired outcomes of the client system and the resources and strategies appropriate to achieve the mutually agreed-upon goals (Logan, Rasheed, & Rasheed, 2008).

In order to develop an accurate assessment and effective intervention plan, the assessment process, when possible, should be multifaceted so that it may capture the complexity of the client's life. Information should be gathered from multiple sources, including the client and collaterals (e.g., family members, friends, health and social service providers, and other professionals); archives (e.g., medical, legal, or educational records); direct observation of activities; and standardized measures (O'Hare, 2009).

Interview Practice Behaviors While an array of diverse methods and sources of information is needed to understand fully the client system, much of the information is gathered through an interview with the client; therefore, the next step in the assessment process is for the social worker to consider the types and quality of questions to ask the client. Questions should be focused on gathering only that information relevant to the situation at hand (and not just interesting). They should be grounded in the strengths-based perspective, and they should convey a sense of genuine support and empathy to the client. Following the interviewing guidelines below will help to elicit as much relevant information as possible and to optimize client comfort (Collins & Coleman, 2000):

- *A balance of open-ended questions and responses and closed-ended questions and responses:* **Open-ended questions** and responses (questions that ask what, how, and feelings questions) are helpful for gathering information and affirming the client's control of the situation. **Closed-ended questions** and responses (questions that can be answered by yes, no, or short answers) are more directive and allow the social worker to control the interview.

- *Avoidance of excessive questioning:* A good rule to follow is to ask no more than two questions in succession without pausing for reflection.

- *Periodic reflection:* Recapping or paraphrasing the client's response, known as **reflection**, enables the social worker to clarify her or his understanding of the client's words. Recapping not only makes the client feel validated and understood, but also enables her or him to clarify any misunderstandings by the social worker. At the same time, it enables the social worker to consider the information that has been shared and to plan for future comments and directions for the interview.

- *Silence:* Not speaking is an important social work skill. Pausing after asking a question enables the client to consider her or his response in a thoughtful manner.

In addition to these guidelines, there are numerous practice behaviors that social workers should either embrace or avoid in developing an assessment. Exhibit 9.3 gives additional examples of assessment that are effective and those that should be avoided.

ASSESSMENT "DON'TS"	EXAMPLE	ASSESSMENT "DO'S"
Excessive utterances, excessive head nodding	Frequent use of "That's good." "Really?"	Occasional use of these comments can serve as prompters or encouragers.
"Why" questions	"Why did you hit your son?"	"What were you feeling when you struck your son?"
Use of poor grammar (e.g., "that," "it," etc.)	"What did it feel like when it happened?"	"How did you feel when your daughter told you about the abuse?"
Closed questions	"Do you want to tell me what brought you here today?"	"What brought you here today?"
Talking more than clients talk	Social worker does the majority of the talking.	Client does the majority of the talking.
Machine gun questioning—series of "grilling" questions	"Where were you when that happened? How did it feel? What did she say?"	The client's response should guide the next question.
Leading questions	"I'm sure you told him that you would leave him if he didn't stop drinking, didn't you?"	"What did you say to your husband about his drinking?"
Placating	"Now, Mrs. Smith, there is nothing to worry about."	"Mrs. Smith, I will be here to support you through this experience."
Minimizing	"I'm sure you're keeping so busy that you don't really miss him that much."	"Missing a loved one who dies is a normal reaction."

EXHIBIT 9.3

Assessment "Don'ts" and "Do's"

continued

EXHIBIT 9.3

continued

ASSESSMENT "DON'TS"	EXAMPLE	ASSESSMENT "DO'S"
Rescuing	"I'll make sure that you don't get evicted."	"How can I help you with your housing situation?"
Fidgeting	Twirling hair, playing with a pen/pencil, or moving about in the chair.	Movement is a normal action, just not to the point of distraction.
Poor attending skills	Looking out the window, through papers, or responding to a phone.	Focusing on the client during the encounter is essential to the social work relationship.
Giggling at inappropriate times or during silences	Giggling, in general, conveys an unprofessional air and is offensive.	Laughing with the client at appropriate times is supportive.
Use of repetitive words (e.g., "you know," "like," "okay," "uh huh")	"I'm like, you know, happy to set another appointment with you, okay?"	"I will be happy to schedule another appointment with you."
Advice giving	"I definitely think you should have the procedure."	"Let's explore the pros and cons of having the procedure."
Multiple, double-barreled questions	"When did you separate?" "Have you filed for divorce?" (Client may not know which to answer or answer one and leave worker with the wrong impression.)	Ask a question, wait for a response, and continue.
Slouching	Slouching implies a posture that suggests this is a casual relationship and the worker may not be taking the situation seriously.	Sitting upright and leaning slightly forward suggests a professional, interested posture.
Letting the client ramble	Allowing the client to wander off the topic to the point that assessment cannot be completed.	Clients can often provide useful information while talking, but the social worker should monitor.
Mimicking cultural traits or language or client's behaviors	Using language or gestures that are not typical, but done only for the benefit of the client.	Use appropriate language, but do not "experiment" on the client.
Taking sides with the clients	"I know you meant well."	"My role is to be objective and neutral."

ASSESSMENT "DON'TS"	EXAMPLE	ASSESSMENT "DO'S"
Giving false reassurances or agreeing when that is inappropriate or unknown	"I'm sure the doctor will be able to give you good news on your tests."	"If you would like, I can be with you when you get your test results."
Ignoring cues about the client's subjective experiences and only focusing on the objective issues (i.e., getting the form completed)	"Now, what was your annual income last year?" (asked while client is sobbing)	"You seem very upset. Would you like to talk about it?"
Judgmental responses	"I am sure you want to take care of your mother at home instead of putting her in a nursing home."	"Have you thought about your mother's care? Let's discuss the options."
Inappropriate use of humor	"You know how they (fill in the group) can be."	If initiated by the client, the social worker should confront the inappropriate humor.
Premature problem solving	"I've heard enough. Let me tell you what I think."	"I need more information before we can discuss options."
Criticizing or belittling clients or condescending behaviors	"You're not being fair." "You shouldn't worry about that."	"You seemed concerned about that."
Over-reliance on "chit-chat"	Anything beyond the usual greeting and pleasantries is too much casual conversation.	Greeting the client, asking about her/his well-being and responding briefly to her/his inquiries is appropriate.
Overprotecting clients by avoiding clear cues to implicit information	"I think there may be some concern about your son's academic performance." (when, in fact, the son is failing)	"I am concerned that your son's grades are below the level needed for him to pass."
Inappropriate response to information shared by client	With wide eyes, "Wow, you have got to be kidding!"	Empathetically stated, "You must have been surprised."
Communicating displeasure when a client does not appear grateful	"I hope you know how difficult it was to get you an appointment today."	Commenting on a client's lack of gratitude is not appropriate.

Source: Adapted from Collins & Coleman, 2000.

EXHIBIT 9.3

continued

Family Assessments When conducting an assessment with a family, the social worker employs the same skill set that is appropriate for use with individuals, but with several additional considerations for the challenges inherent in assessing family issues. The family is a system, and working with a family essentially means working with a group and can be overwhelming at first. The family assessment provides the social worker and the family with insights regarding patterns of individual behaviors, family functioning, relationships, communication patterns, and dynamics among family members.

The first step in conducting a family assessment is to determine the composition of the family. This process requires the social worker to have a broad concept of family, given that people's living arrangements have changed considerably in recent years. As defined by the U.S. Census Bureau, Statistical Abstract (2012), the number of households increased 12% between 2000 and 2010, but "family" households (co-residents related by birth, marriage, or adoption) rose only 9%. During the same period, however, nonfamily households grew by 18% and one-person households grew by 17%, suggesting that social workers need to rethink traditional definitions of family.

Today the accepted social work definition of **family** is a group of persons, usually residing together, who acknowledge a sense of responsibility for one another and function as a unit. Social workers routinely intervene with gay, lesbian, bisexual, and transgender couples; people who share a residence but are not biologically or legally related; blended families that include the children of multiple marriages or relationships; single parents; grandparents rearing grandchildren; multigenerational family units; and foster and other kinship relationships.

When conducting a family assessment, the social worker must determine which family members are to be included in the change effort. Several factors may contribute to the composition, including the goals of the persons seeking services, the willingness and availability of family members to participate, and the relationships of the family members with one another. For example, in an adoption process, all members of the family should be involved, as the addition of a new member will affect everyone.

Engaging with each family member can be particularly difficult if one or more members do not voluntarily seek the services of a social worker or have different needs and agendas for the intervention. Involuntary participants may feel anger, resentment, or hostility.

The skills of engagement described in this section become critical as the social worker strives to establish rapport with each family member and the family unit as a whole, while observing the interactions among family members and between the family and their external environment.

Intervention With Individuals and Families

Using the information that she had gathered from Victoria during the assessment process, Emily developed both an immediate and a short-term plan for intervention, with the agreement that Victoria would allow Emily to follow up the next day. With

Emily's help, Victoria was able to state that her immediate need was a safe place to stay. In response, Emily arranged with one of Victoria's friends from work for Victoria to stay with her. Being sensitive to the trauma that Victoria had experienced, Emily did not want to overwhelm her with a request to establish long-range goals.

Over the next several weeks, Emily had regular contact with Victoria. Emily told Victoria that she was there to support her through this period, but their goal will include phasing Emily out of Victoria's life as Victoria recovers and regains emotional strength. Together, they established a list of objectives as prioritized by Victoria. Victoria wanted to return to living independently, feel safe, and be able to talk with her family and fiancé about her experience. Emily offered several strategies that could be helpful to Victoria.

Working together toward the goals identified by Victoria, Emily helped Victoria to relocate to a new third-floor apartment. Emily referred Victoria to several services that helped her to meet her goals: the community police program for an in-home safety assessment, a support group for survivors of sexual assault, and a clinical social worker to help her address her feelings of guilt and violation and to work with Victoria's family and fiancé.

Once the social worker has engaged with the client and gathered relevant information to assess the client's situation, the worker and the client can jointly begin the process of planning and carrying out the intervention. **Intervention** is the phase of the social work relationship in which the actual work is completed. During the assessment phase, the social worker and the client system engage in the process of identifying needs, issues, strengths, and resources. Using that information, the focus shifts to prioritizing the client's needs and mobilizing the client's strengths and resources to facilitate the desired change.

The social work intervention involves two steps:

1. *Planning*. The social worker and the client identify the areas of change on which the client wants to focus the intervention. Initially, the goals may be broad, be overwhelming, or seem unattainable. Through discussion, the social worker and the client will prioritize the goals and define each goal in specific behavioral and achievable terms. This is the point in the intervention in which the social worker and the client negotiate and document a contract that is mutually agreed upon, clear, measurable, and specific.

2. *Implementation*. Once the intervention is planned, the next step is implementation. Reviewing the contract on a regular basis enables the client and the social worker to monitor progress and determine whether

the goals and strategies are realistic or if they should be changed or eliminated.

Applying the strengths-based approach to planning and implementation, the social worker recognizes the client as the expert on her or his life and respects the client's right to self-determination in facilitating the change process. Exhibit 9.4 provides guidelines for facilitating the planned change social work intervention.

EXHIBIT 9.4

Steps in Social Work Intervention

ENGAGEMENT

Practice Behaviors
- Substantively and affectively prepare for action
- Use empathy and other interpersonal skills
- Develop a mutually agreed-on focus of work and desired outcomes

Possible Strategies
- Engage the client in a focused, goal-directed way
- Build rapport with warmth, interest, empathy, and genuineness
- Demonstrate culturally competent communication skills

ASSESSMENT

Practice Behaviors
- Collect, organize, and interpret client data
- Assess client strengths and limitation
- Develop mutually agreed-on intervention goals and objectives
- Select appropriate intervention strategies

Possible Strategies
- Allow the client to tell her or his story
- Use assessment tools (e.g., ecomap or culturagram) to gather and organize client information
- Evaluate information
- With the client, prioritize the needs and issues raised by the client and establish clear, achievable goals

INTERVENTION

Practice Behaviors
- Initiate actions to achieve organizational goals
- Implement prevention interventions that enhance client capacities
- Help clients resolve problems
- Negotiate, mediate, and advocate for clients
- Facilitate transitions and endings

Possible Strategies

- Mobility client strengths and resources
- Develop a mutually agreed-on plan (contract)
- Reflect on the plan
- Develop a timeframe for the intervention, identifying respective responsibilities
- Monitor implementation plan and make changes as needed

EVALUATION AND TERMINATION

Practice Behaviors

- Critically analyze, monitor, and evaluate interventions

Possible Strategies

- Review goals and objectives
- Develop plan for maintenance and continued contact
- Express feelings about termination
- Conduct process and/or outcome evaluation

Sources: Council on Social Work Education, 2008; Logan et al., 2008.

EXHIBIT 9.4

continued

Developing social work interventions with families builds on the skills used with individuals but is generally more complex. The focus may encompass the immediate or extended family along with formal and informal support networks. **Family group conference (FGC)** is a relatively new approach that can be used in situations involving children, adults, or intergenerational families. FGC brings together professionals, client systems, extended family, and others in the support networks to discuss and collaborate together to determine the optimal way to serve the client (Brodie & Gadling-Cole, 2008).

A written contract, mutually agreed upon by both the social worker and the client, is a valuable tool in the development and implementation of an intervention. Contracting with a client can help the social worker and client to clarify goals, tasks, and activities, the individual responsible for each task and activity, and a timeframe for the intervention. Exhibit 9.5 provides an example of a contract that can be used to develop goals and strategies for the planned change effort.

The intervention phase can be a time of gratification and fulfillment, but it can also be a time of challenges. Changing lifelong behaviors and patterns of interaction is sometimes difficult and even painful for clients. Social workers, too, can be challenged when clients are unable or unready to change their lifestyles. Nevertheless, when social workers and clients commit to mutually agreed-upon goals and agree to make adjustments as needed, the intervention can produce a positive outcome.

Client Name(s):

Victoria H.

Client System's Description of Issues to be Addressed:

Feel safe

Remain independent

Goals and Tasks:

Goal	Client Tasks/Date	Social Worker Tasks/Date
1. *Arrange for safe alternative housing.*	*Inquire about apartment above ground floor.*	*Provide referral to community police program.*
2. *Talk with my family and fiancé about the rape.*	*Attend survivor support group and meet with therapist.*	*Provide referral to survivor support group and therapist specializing in rape trauma.*
3. *Assume control of my life.*	*Journal daily and share journal with social worker.*	*Provide support as needed.*

Date Contract will be reviewed

3 months from date of contract

I agree with the above stated goals, to complete the contracted tasks, and participate in a review and evaluation of the contract on the specified date.

Victoria

Client

Emily

Social Worker

Date

Date

Evaluation and Termination of Intervention With Individuals and Families

After Emily worked with Victoria for 3 months, she reminded Victoria that their goal was to terminate the relationship when Victoria felt she no longer needed Emily's support. The two of them took this opportunity to evaluate their work together. Using the contract they had negotiated as a basis for their evaluation, they reviewed each of the objectives.

By that time, Victoria had settled into her new apartment. With the community police officer's help, she had taken a number of personal and environmental safety measures. She was regularly attending the sexual assault survivor support group and had seen the clinical social worker three times. She wanted to continue with the support group because she felt they understood her fears, setbacks, and uneasiness in talking about the event with others.

Because the goals that they established were specific and measurable, Emily and Victoria were able to determine that their work together was a success and Victoria was ready to terminate her relationship with Emily.

Although the intervention phase may seem to be the culmination of the client–social worker relationship, evaluation and termination of the intervention are equally important. **Evaluation** is the process by which the social worker and client assess the progress and success of the planned change effort and determine whether it is time to terminate the relationship.

In order for the social worker and the client to conduct a meaningful evaluation, the assessment and intervention phases must have been conducted in a comprehensive, well-conceived, and collaborative manner. In turn, these phases can be completed successfully only if the goals and objectives were developed with specificity and clear-cut strategies for measurement.

Evaluation   Evaluations can occur in two forms:

1. *Process evaluations* focus on the way in which the service was delivered to the client within the context of the organization, environment, and the persons facilitating the implementation (Chen, 2006, p. 183). In essence, a process evaluation enables the social worker and client to explore the nature of the client–social worker relationship (e.g., communication and rapport), the way in which the two worked together to plan and implement the intervention, and the tasks and activities completed (Grinnell, Unrau, & Gabor, 2008).

2. *Outcome evaluations* are typically completed at the termination of the client–social worker relationship and are empirical examinations of the

change that occurred (Grinnell et al., 2008). Standardized tools or protocols may be used to measure a behavior or belief at the onset of the intervention compared with its level at the ending of the working relationship.

The social worker may want to conduct periodic evaluations throughout the course of the intervention to monitor its progress. If progress is not being made, the social worker and client can refocus the intervention strategy in a direction that is more likely to promote a successful outcome. Developing the contract to identify mutual goals, strengths, and resources; strategies for achieving the goals; and barriers to goal achievement will give the social worker and client a working document for evaluating change throughout the intervention.

In addition to the contract, social workers typically document each encounter with and about the client, recording information such as facts related to the situation, your observations, and client activities. Such documentation cannot, under most circumstances, be shared or released without the client's informed consent (written permission granted by the client or the client's legal representative, usually a parent or guardian). Documentation can be used for a variety of purposes: accounting to supervisors, funders, or legal system; monitoring client progress; and improving the social worker's practice skills (Kagle, 2009). Therefore, documenting can become key to the evaluation process.

Although periodic evaluations are helpful, evaluating the intervention at the time agreed upon in the contract is critical. Some fundamental questions that the social worker and client can address are these: Can the relationship be terminated because the goals have been successfully achieved? Were the goals not achieved and should they be renegotiated? Should the relationship be terminated because there is no longer a need?

Determining whether the intervention facilitated the change that the client desired also serves as a way of evaluating the social worker's practice (for example, is the social worker offering appropriate and helpful input?). Using the contract as a basis for evaluation, the social worker and client can scrutinize each aspect of the intervention to determine whether the social worker upheld her or his commitment to the client and the change effort, adhered to professional ethical standards, and met the obligations to which she or he contracted. Client satisfaction measures should be interpreted with caution, however, as satisfaction, or lack thereof, does not necessarily determine success or effectiveness.

Agencies that fund social work programs and services have placed increasing importance on evaluating social workers' services as a way to determine funding levels. In other words, social workers can no longer just try to "help people." Rather, they now must verify that people were helped, and they must identify change that occurred as a result of the intervention. Within the profession itself, evaluating social work methods and practices enables social work educators to develop curricula that will train new social workers to be effective and efficient.

Termination

After completing their evaluation of their work together, Emily and Victoria planned for termination. They agreed they would meet one more time. At that meeting, they again reviewed the goals they had established and the progress that Victoria had made in meeting her goals. They discussed plans for handling situations in which Victoria felt her safety was being threatened, and they anticipated events such as the anniversary of the rape and her upcoming marriage. Emily offered Victoria the option to contact her in the future if she felt a need to talk or just to let Emily know how she was doing. Emily commended Victoria on her strength in handling this situation, and she told Victoria she appreciated Victoria's willingness to work with her. Victoria told Emily that she had been a "lifesaver" and she would forever be grateful to her. She admitted that she would miss Emily, and she was grateful to know that she could call Emily if she felt a need to talk with her.

Termination, defined as the official ending of the social worker–client relationship, is the goal from the first encounter. Failure to establish termination as the ultimate objective can lead to situations in which the client becomes dependent on the social worker. Individuals and families can come to feel comfortable in their relationships with the social worker and may be reluctant to lose the support and caring that the worker provides. Because the mission of social work is to empower clients to enhance their functioning and well-being, social workers are obligated to engage the client, assess the situation, plan and carry out an intervention, evaluate the intervention, and then terminate the planned change relationship.

The social worker who empowers the client to make changes in her or his life and devises a plan for maintaining that change provides a greater service than a worker who creates a relationship in which the client continues to look to the worker for help with each life crisis. Of course, if future events create a real need for assistance, services can be resumed.

Terminations occur for a variety of reasons and in a variety of ways. The social work relationship can be terminated in the following situations:

- The goals have successfully been achieved.

- The client withdraws from the relationship because she or he no longer agrees with the plan established within the contract.

- The client is no longer eligible to receive services.

- The social worker feels that the goals cannot be achieved or the client is unwilling to comply with the contract.

- The social worker or agency is no longer the most appropriate service provider for the client.

- The social worker leaves the agency.

Ideally, the concept of termination is introduced at the first social worker–client encounter. It is then built into the intervention, routinely discussed, and carried out in a planned manner. Planned terminations enable the client to enter into the contract and work through the intervention with a clear focus on the desired outcome, knowing that when the specified goals are reached, the planned change relationship will be terminated.

Determining the point at which termination can occur often influences the planning and implementation of the intervention. For example, when working with a person who identifies self-sufficiency as a priority, the social worker can design an intervention aimed toward independent living and economic stability. When the person has secured housing and a regular income, the planned change relationship can then be successfully terminated.

Successful termination of the social work relationship includes the following processes:

- Reviewing the goals and objectives included in the contract to determine whether these goals have been met, to identify barriers to meeting the goals, and consider future goals.

- Developing a plan for maintaining change after the relationship has been terminated. This plan must anticipate issues such as the client's response should the crisis occur again, as well as the skills, resources, and strengths developed and needed for the client's response.

- Discussing continued professional contact between the social worker and the client, anticipating questions such as when and under what conditions future contact would be acceptable and the appropriate parameters for that contact.

- Expressing feelings about ending the relationship. The nature of the social work relationship can be intense and personal, and both the client and social worker can feel anxious or sad about ending that part of their lives. Therefore, discussing feelings is an important ingredient in a successful termination.

A skillfully facilitated termination can be gratifying for both the client and the social worker. Clients can achieve a sense of closure and, if permitted by agency policy, can be reassured that they can contact the social worker in the future if the need arises. The social worker also benefits from feeling a sense of closure.

CONCLUSION

Social work practice with individuals and families can be approached systematically using the steps of engagement, assessment, intervention, evaluation, and termination. Although such an approach provides a structure for working with individuals and families, facilitating a planned change is not always straightforward, simple, or without complications.

Working with client systems whose lives can be steeped in crises, unexpected twists and turns, and external pressures requires social workers to be flexible and patient. Social workers must be willing to renegotiate or delay plans for interventions in order to respond to unplanned changes in the planned change effort. The change process is not typically a linear process, but a fluid one that requires returning to steps that may previously have been addressed or completed.

In the next two chapters, we explore the process of engagement, assessment, intervention, and evaluation/termination in the context of social work practice with groups, organizations, and communities. Although the client systems at the group and community levels are larger, the same basic premise provides the foundation for the social work intervention. Having the knowledge and skills to build rapport and trust, gather information, develop a planned change effort, and evaluate and terminate the intervention is the same regardless of the size or makeup of the client system. You will find that you use the skills and practice behaviors that you have learned for working with individuals and families when you are planning and implementing social work interventions with groups, organizations, and communities of all sizes and compositions.

This chapter has provided you with the framework from which you can expand your social work knowledge and skills. The agency in which you work will determine the specific assessment tools, intervention protocols, and evaluation methods that you will use, but having a well-grounded knowledge of the change process will enable you to transfer the knowledge and skills to the setting.

MAIN POINTS

- Direct social work practice with individuals and families is the process of working one-on-one with the client system to identify and assess a need and develop a plan for facilitating a planned change.

- The client's investment in the change process is key to the success of the social work intervention. The social worker is a collaborator with the client in the planned change process.

- Developing a social work intervention using the strengths perspective is essential for identifying the assets and resources possessed by the client system and for planning a successful intervention.

- Social workers practicing with individuals and families use a variety of skills and practice behaviors within the context of engagement, assessment, intervention, and evaluation/termination.

- Engagement is the building of rapport and trust with the client system.

- Assessment includes gathering information about the client system and the client's perception of her or his strengths, resources, and needs.

- With the client, the social worker plans an intervention that includes determining desired goals, priorities, barriers to change, and strategies for making change.

- Evaluation consists of assessing the progress and/or success of change and the change process, the effectiveness of the social work intervention, and readiness to terminate the client–social worker relationship.

- The knowledge and skills for intervening effectively with individuals and families are also relevant in social work practice at the mezzo and macro levels.

EXERCISES

1. It is now your turn to apply the knowledge of individual and family social work practices that you have acquired by reading this chapter. Using the Sanchez family, Carla Washburn, or Hudson City interactive case (www.routledgesw.com/cases), you will have the opportunity to experience a social work relationship from engagement through evaluation.
   a. Locate the Case Study Tools and select Biopsychosocial. Review each of the four perspectives for the Sanchez family, Carla Washburn, or Hudson City. Answer each of the questions that appear.
   b. Go to the Intervene tab. Following the prompts, respond to each of the questions that will enable you to define goals and needs, identify tasks for the intervention, complete the timeline, and identify coalitions.
   c. Next, go to the Case Study Tools and select the Interaction Matrix. Match a client with the members of the client system by clicking on Plot the Interaction. Identify the issues or barriers that exist between your client and system members.
   d. Go to the Evaluate tab. Review the Introduction. Continuing with your selected client, complete the Intervention Evaluation and Closing the Case sections.
   e. Provide a written analysis of your experience in developing a social work intervention.

2. This chapter highlighted the importance of "starting where the client is." Review the following scenario and prepare a response to the questions that follow:

Mr. J. is a 61-year-old male. He was diagnosed with probable dementia of the Alzheimer's type. Mr. J. is experiencing increasing memory problems; he has been unable to find his car in the mall parking lot on three occasions and has begun to lose his possessions (e.g., glasses, keys) on a regular basis. He works as a shipping and receiving foreman for a discount chain store.

Given that the typical course of Alzheimer's disease is 8–10 years from time of diagnosis to death, the physician has recommended that Mr. J. consider early retirement within the next year and that he be evaluated by the Department of Motor Vehicles to determine if he is safe to drive. The physician has asked you to follow up with Mr. J. and his family to implement these recommendations.

Mr. J. and his family—which includes his wife and adult son—are adamantly opposed to both recommendations, stating that his forgetfulness is just normal aging and that everyone misplaces small items and gets lost in large parking lots. Where do you begin?

a. Identify the person(s) you consider to be your client(s).
b. Describe the way in which you would start where the client(s) is(are).
c. Reflect on the possible strengths and challenges related to starting where the client(s) is(are) in the scenario you have just read.

3. Write a script, as though it were a play, for a social worker interviewing an individual or family client system. Include in the script the questions that the social worker would ask in an assessment of the individual or family. Insert directions regarding the facial and body language of the social worker and the client system. Include the client system's responses to the social worker. At the close of the script, draw an ecomap of the individual or family system and identify the individual and family strengths and areas for growth and change.

4. Personal reflection: Describe a change you have made in your life, how you were able to do so, why you made the change, and the long-term effects of the change on you and those in your environment. Discuss how this experience might impact your work and professional development.

CHAPTER 10

Social Work Practice With Groups

Over a period of time, Emily began to notice that the clients staying at the shelter for women who had experienced intimate partner violence shared a common concern regarding parenting. Emily heard many women voice apprehension about the effects of domestic violence on their children.

Emily was uncertain as to the most effective method for addressing this issue. After talking to co-workers and conducting research regarding options, Emily determined three possible strategies for responding to the need for parenting information:

1. *Emily could suggest that the Community-wide Domestic Violence Coalition develop a program to address the issue.*

2. *Emily could approach a local clinical social worker about forming a therapy group for women who had experienced intimate partner violence, and parenting could be incorporated as a therapeutic goal.*

3. *Emily's agency could form a support group for current and former residents of the shelter.*

In this chapter, we will learn more about each of the options Emily proposed and the one that best addressed the needs of Emily's clients.

Working with groups has long been a part of social work practice. Also referred to as mezzo (**meso**) practice, **group work** is a practice method in which the social worker works with multiple clients to develop a planned change effort that meets the needs of the group. The goals of group work focus on addressing individual issues, the need for information and education, the need for support, or social problems. The social worker's role in a group can be that of initiator, facilitator, therapist, resource person, consultant, or evaluator or a combination of these roles.

Group practice is built on the concept that change occurs as a result of the ongoing and changing group dynamics and group members' interactions with one another.

Thus, social work practice with groups emphasizes group interdependence, interaction, and support as the vehicle for change. It focuses on both the individual and the group as a whole, balancing both the needs and autonomy of each (Association for the Advancement of Social Work with Groups, Inc. (AASWG, Inc.), 2010). Essentially, the strength of group work is that a group can accomplish more as a group than a person can alone, whether the desired change is on the individual or community level.

Multiple helping relationships coexist with a group intervention (AASWG, Inc., 2010). Group members address both their own and other members' individual needs as well as the needs of the group:

> The very act of forming a group is a statement of our belief that every member of the group has something to offer the others, something to give to others, not just to get from them. (Kurland, 2007, p. 12)

Group work is increasingly a part of a social worker's career experiences. While only 18% of social workers identify group work as their primary area of practice (Whitaker & Arrington, 2008), most social workers engage in some form of group practice. The NASW *Code of Ethics* (2008) includes working with groups as one of the ethical principles and key competencies for social work practice. The *Code* charges social workers to strengthen relationships and the well-being of people at all levels of social work practice, including groups.

This chapter highlights the historical development of group work as a method of social work intervention and the role of group work within generalist social work practice. We will explore the types of group work methods along with an introduction to skills needed to deliver group services effectively.

HISTORICAL PERSPECTIVE ON SOCIAL WORK PRACTICE WITH GROUPS

As with practice approaches with individuals and families, the roots of group work are found in England. Emerging in the English post-Industrial Revolution era, group work first took the form of mutual aid groups (Alissi, 2009).

In the United States, group methods were initially used as a strategy for working with youth through organized activities (e.g., YMCA/YWCA and boys' and girls' clubs). In the settlement houses of the late 19th century, groups were formed to achieve educational and cultural goals. Workers in the settlement house movement also embraced group approaches as a means for furthering social action agendas.

Group work for the promotion of recreational and educational activities emerged after World War I. The decade of the 1920s saw group work flourish within agency settings to address "recreational, educational, character-building, and community organized group activities" (Alissi, 2009, p. 8). However, no formalized structures or training existed until the first university-level course on group work was offered at a social work program in 1923.

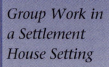

Group Work in a Settlement House Setting

Source: Corbis.

By the 1930s and 1940s, group work had become an intervention method for professional social workers working with hospitalized patients, persons with developmental disabilities and mental illness, and returning World War II veterans. During the Great Depression of the 1930s, social workers mobilized groups to lobby for workers' rights and simply survive the depression (Alissi, 2009; Toseland & Horton, 2008). Grace Coyle first wrote about group processes in the 1930s, emphasizing the effectiveness of group interventions for educating adults and promoting social action, social justice, and social change (Toseland & Horton, 2008, p. 2:299). Other professionals debated whether group work was a recreational activity, a social work method, or a separate profession.

Interest in incorporating group methods into social work practice continued to grow and expand into more settings over the next several decades. During the 1940s, scholars began to develop formalized knowledge regarding the practice of group work and group work began to be an accepted and integrated aspect of clinical practice (Alissi, 2009). By the 1960s, group work practice played a less central role in the social work profession as a philosophical shift was underway to consider social work in a more generic context without specialized methodologies (Alissi,

2009). By the 1970s, social workers were participating in a variety of experimental groups focused on self-improvement. Over the next 20 years, group work became an integrated part of social work practice for social workers addressing clients' challenges and issues at the individual and family, organizational, and community levels. Social workers adopted the roles of broker, teacher/educator, enabler, advocate, mobilizer, mediator, and case manager.

Group social work practice is now recognized as part of the profession's mission to empower and promote well-being. It can be applied in a range of settings, can be used with diverse populations, uses a variety of practice approaches, and is applicable for intervention at the individual, group, and community levels (Garvin & Galinsky, 2008).

The profession recognizes the value of educating all social workers in group knowledge and skills. As a result, all social work students are exposed to group work theory and practice through coursework and field experiences. Quick Guide #8 provides an overview of the standards for group work established by the AASWG, Inc., specifying the core knowledge and values needed for social work practice with groups as well as the key steps in the process.

QUICK GUIDE #8   Standards for Social Work Practice With Groups

Core Values

- Respect for persons and their autonomy.
- Creation of a socially just society.

Core Knowledge

- Knowledge of individuals.
- Knowledge of groups and small group behavior.
- Knowledge of the function of the group worker.

Phases of Group Work

1. *New Group Formation*

   - Identify the group's aspirations, needs, and goals.
   - Determine the group structure and process.
   - Recruit and orient members.
   - Develop the group's purpose and methods.

2. *Beginning Phase*

   - Establish a beginning contract.
   - Cultivate group cohesion.
   - Shape norms of participation.

3. *Middle Phase*

   - Assist progress on individual and group goals.
   - Attend to group dynamics and processes.
   - Assist members to identify and access resources from inside and outside the group.

4. *Ending Phase*
    - Prepare members for group ending.
    - Identify gains and changes.
    - Discuss impact of the group on systems outside the group and the movement the group has made over time.
    - Identify direct and indirect signs of members' and worker's reactions to ending.
    - Evaluate achievement.
    - Help members make connections and apply new knowledge and skills.

Source: Excerpted from AASWG, 2010.

MODELS OF CHANGE IN SOCIAL WORK PRACTICE WITH GROUPS

Building on the knowledge and skill base established for working with individuals and families, group work practice has evolved into four distinct models with similar theoretical underpinnings. The first three—respectively emphasizing social goals, remediation or therapy, and reciprocal aid—were developed during the 1960s by a variety of scholars (Alissi, 2009). All three models are grounded in systems theory and emphasize a goal-oriented outcome. More recently, a fourth goal-oriented model—based on group tasks—has been added (Toseland & Horton, 2008).

Each of the models described in this section has multiple uses and distinctive characteristics. Thus, as you will learn from Emily's situation, one issue can be addressed by more than one type of intervention. What all four have in common, however, is that change is a result of group effort and could not be reached as effectively with only individual efforts.

Social Goals Groups

Social goals groups, or **social action groups**, aim to facilitate social change on the organizational or community level. They are rooted in concepts of social responsibility, social action, democracy, and social justice and strive to change society by changing social structures (Toseland & Horton, 2008). This type of group originated from the early work of reformers, but has continued to be a primary approach used by social workers striving to achieve social change today. Social goals groups are a key component of social work practice with organizations and communities.

Social goals groups may be established for the purposes of accomplishing specific tasks, carrying out the goals of an organization, changing a law or policy, or developing a new program. The social worker may serve as initiator, participant, or consultant of a social change group. Professionals or nonprofessional persons may lead social action groups. Typically, the group's goals determine the leadership.

Groups whose aim is goal-specific can be short-term if there is no need for the group to continue once the goal is achieved or the time limit has expired for the goal to be achieved. For goal-specific groups that have an ongoing mission, longevity may be indefinite.

The following are examples of social action groups:

- *Neighborhood groups that promote a safe environment:* Such a group may hold regular meetings to strategize ways to improve and monitor neighborhood safety. The group may be composed of neighborhood residents, social service professionals who work in the neighborhood, and law enforcement personnel. Such a group is likely to be long-term, but the focus may shift from establishing a plan for safety to one of maintaining the plan. Due to their involvement in the community, social workers are often in a position to identify the need for a neighborhood group; so they may serve to mobilize the group, but not to lead the group. Neighborhood residents with an investment in their community are usually most effective as group leaders.

- *Members of the Alzheimer's Association advocating for legislation:* Such a group may be formed to lobby legislators to introduce and pass legislation requiring mandatory dementia education for long-term residential care workers caring for patients with Alzheimer's disease. This group may be composed of family members of persons suffering from dementia, representatives from the residential long-term care industry, and health and social service professionals. This group may exist over multiple legislative sessions, but the lifetime of the group will be determined by the success or failure of proposed legislation. Should the legislation be enacted, the group may refocus its efforts on implementing and monitoring the mandatory educational requirements, or they may redirect their efforts to other legislation to protect persons living with dementia. The social worker's employment position or personal interest in the issue will determine her or his role.

- *Child welfare workers from various public and private agencies that monitor the foster care system:* To ensure that children in the foster care system have timely and permanent plans for their futures, such a group might meet regularly to provide oversight of all foster care cases in a city, county, or region. Group members can represent multiple professions, such as social work, education, health, and law. This group essentially provides a quality assurance function and could continue to meet indefinitely. The social worker's role may be as a leader, facilitator, chair, participant, or a combination of these roles.

Faced with the dilemma regarding the best approach for strengthening the parenting needs of women receiving services from the domestic violence program, Emily asked to have the issue placed on the agenda for the monthly meeting of the Community-wide

Domestic Violence Coalition. This group of social, health care, and legal service profes-
sionals had organized for the purpose of enhancing communication among the commu-
nity's domestic violence services, influencing legislation, and training members of the
community to respond effectively to persons experiencing intimate partner violence.
Because they developed programs to address specific partner violence-related needs,
Emily thought the group might be appropriate for creating a program for parenting.

After hearing Emily's proposal that such a program be developed, Coalition
members determined that the provision of direct client services was outside the
purview of their mission. Coalition members felt that such a service should be provided
by individual agencies to simplify issues such as group leadership, funding,
practitioner competence, and comfort level of potential participants.

Remedial Groups

Remedial, or therapeutic, **groups** (also known as treatment groups, group therapy, group psychotherapy, and clinical group work) are professionally facilitated groups aimed at helping group members enhance their social functioning. The goal is typically to develop the individual's ability to solve problems, change behavior, or develop coping skills in order to eliminate or cope with a specific social, emotional, or behavioral issue (Barker, 2003; Toseland & Horton, 2008). Remedial groups are distinguished from other groups focused on individual growth and change by the presence of a professional group leader and the development of treatment goals specific to each individual. Group dynamics—interacting with other group members, hearing their experiences, and strategizing personal attitudinal and behavioral change—is influential in promoting change within the group members, but group goals are secondary to the goals of each group member.

Remedial groups were first introduced into clinical practice during the early 20th century. It was not until mid-century and later that clinically oriented group work became a widely accepted treatment intervention in hospitals, clinics, and rehabilitation settings with a variety of populations (Alissi, 2009, p. 10).

The role for the social worker in a remedial group is typically as a leader or facilitator. Social workers may also serve as co-leaders of certain types of therapy groups, particularly in cases of single-gendered groups, groups that are conflictual in nature, or groups that encompass emotionally sensitive issues. Having co-leaders/facilitators provides multiple benefits. In groups that are emotionally intense or conflictual, members' needs can be better met with multiple perspectives. The leaders are also able to respond and can support each other in and outside of the group experience.

Therapeutic groups often arise when a professional identifies several individuals within the agency's client population who share a common issue. Therapeutic groups may meet for a specified number of sessions or weeks or have an open-ended time limit or number of sessions. They may also be closed or open: Closed groups have a designated group membership that does not change during the lifetime of the group, whereas membership of an open group can move in and out of the group as needs arise.

The following are examples of groups that might be formed for the purpose of therapeutically focused group work:

- *Persons hospitalized for mental health issues:* Social workers working in mental health facilities often conduct group therapy on a daily or weekly basis with patients hospitalized for newly diagnosed or chronic or persistent mental illness. These social worker-led groups usually supplement individual therapy, but the interactions among group members serve to support and enhance individual treatment. The group itself is typically open and ongoing, the membership changing with admissions to and discharges from the facility. Group membership may be determined by diagnosis, time and duration of admission, or gender.

- *Survivors of childhood incest:* A group composed of persons who are survivors of incest is likely to be single-gendered due to the emotional intensity of the issue and the fact that incest raises considerable trust problems for the survivors. A survivor group may be formed within an agency by the administrative or clinical staff and can either be time-limited or ongoing and open or closed. In determining the type and timing of a survivor group, the social worker is sensitive to the nature of the trauma and the situations of the individual members of the group.

- *Male abusers:* A group of men identified by the social service or legal system as being violent toward their partners can be composed of involuntary or voluntary members. Involuntary groups, particularly ones with members that have a history of violence, can be challenging groups to facilitate due to members' hostility and resentment regarding their participation in the group. A group for abusers is typically a highly structured group with a focus on behavioral change. Such groups are often led by co-facilitators to enable a balanced response to disputes and angry outbursts. Behaviorally focused groups are typically time-limited and closed in order to enhance the therapist's ability to provide information and promote individual change and group cohesion.

In the case of the mothers at Emily's shelter, Emily determined that the agency was serving a number of clients who shared a common concern. She considered forming a therapy group to respond to their need for parenting information. With a BSW, Emily was not trained to conduct a therapy group, so she explored the possibility of co-leading a treatment group with a local clinical social worker in private practice.

Emily developed a concept that the therapist would offer a weekly therapy group for women who had been abused by their partners. The voluntary, open-ended group would be accessible to women in the community. Emily hoped that the therapist could address the issues involved in parenting children who have also experienced the domestic violence.

Emily and the clinical social worker jointly agreed that a therapy group was one effective approach for addressing the women's feelings regarding their life experience, and parenting issues would naturally become a part of the discussion. The two social workers agreed that they would not include a formal parenting education curriculum in this group.

Reciprocal Groups

Reciprocal groups—also referred to as mutual aid, self-help, and support groups—emphasize the concept of common goals, interests, and exchange as the basis for change. Group members come together out of a shared interest or experience. Personal growth and change occur as a result of group members sharing those commonalities, exchanging support with one another and receiving information about their shared issue. Receiving support from others who have similar experiences can be validating and empowering for the membership. Based on a member's needs and personality, support groups can augment individual treatment or can be a stand-alone resource.

Reciprocal aid groups differ from therapy groups in several areas: leaders can be professional or nonprofessional, individual members do not typically have specified treatment goals, and the intervention occurs as a result of the members' interpersonal relationships. Support groups are typically less formal than therapy groups and are open so that members can move in and out of the group as they feel a need.

The group and the reasons for its origins often determine the social worker's role. The social worker at an agency may identify a common need among her or his clients and be instrumental in creating a support group. The social worker may serve initially as the group's facilitator and then turn that role over to the group itself. The leader's role can be multifaceted. She or he can serve as a mediator between group members, encourage an environment to enable members to work as a group, and facilitate interactions between members to support individuals in meeting their goals (Toseland & Horton, 2008).

The following are examples of self-help, support-focused groups:

- *Addictions groups:* The 12-step model that originated with Alcoholics Anonymous is an example of a self-help group with members providing the leadership. Addictions self-help groups have expanded beyond alcohol to include other drugs, food, gambling, and sexual behavior. Social workers can play a leadership role in addictions groups, but in a traditional 12-step model, there is no formal or professional leadership. Most addictions-focused groups are open-ended, with members using the group to sustain their recovery process. Members may stop participating when they feel confident in their behavioral change.

- *Adoption or sibling groups:* Groups for families that are acquiring new members through adoption, remarriage, or birth may focus on providing education about issues such as the adoption or birth, but they also provide an opportunity for the members to identify and share their feelings about the change.

- *Disease/health condition groups:* Groups for persons experiencing a particular health condition are often facilitated by hospital social workers or social workers in organizations that advocate for and educate the public on specific health concerns. Groups are formed for persons with a variety of conditions, such as cancer, multiple sclerosis, stroke, and pregnancy.

- *Significant-other groups:* Support groups for the families and friends of persons experiencing a particular life event or transition or health condition have increased in recent years. For example, such groups provide considerable support for the family and friends of persons newly diagnosed with a serious or disabling illness or injury; gay, lesbian, bisexual, and transgender persons; and persons experiencing an addiction.

*Investigating the third option in her pursuit of a parenting program, Emily approached the administration of her own agency. Emily described the need that she and other social workers had identified among the mothers being served by the agency and the results of her research and consultation. She proposed that the agency offer a **psychoeducational** group (one that includes both education and emotional support) so that the clients could be exposed to parenting education, share their concerns, and strategize about ways to respond to their children's experience with domestic violence. Emily felt she could make a greater impact on this issue through a group, as she could provide information on parenting, a group experience could complement the individual work she and her co-workers were engaging in with each woman, and the women could support one another.*

The agency director agreed with Emily's assessment and gave approval for Emily to develop the group and advertise it to her co-workers and former and current residents. Although several potentially viable options for responding to a client need emerged from Emily's ideas and research, she was confident that the support group approach could provide the parenting support and information needed by the mothers.

Task Groups

A fourth model of group practice, the **task group** model, brings together features of the three previously described models. The focus of a task group is to work collaboratively toward creating solutions to specific problems or issues that affect a larger group, as agreed on by the task group members (Furman, Rowan, & Bender, 2009; Toseland & Horton, 2008). The group relies on reciprocal respect, information sharing, and a decision-making process to achieve its goals. A task group can encompass a focused goal (like the social goals model), the return of stability or function (like the remediation model), or mutual support (like the reciprocal model).

Building on a strengths-based foundation, the social worker strives to help members of a task group to identify their strengths and potential contributions. The social worker's role also includes facilitating group communication, consensus, and progress toward the agreed-upon goals. While typically structured with a designated leader, agenda, and work plan, task groups can also hold meetings that involve brainstorming, planning, and conflict resolution (Furman et al., 2009).

Examples of task groups include the following:

- *Individual education plan group:* Along with parents or guardians, school and community staff members meet regularly to discuss the educational progress and social and emotional needs of students who have been identified as having special needs. The social worker brings a systemic and strengths-based perspective to this interprofessional team.

- *Senior immigrant project task force:* A group of co-workers at a community-based agency serving older adults wants to provide culturally appropriate services to the growing population of older immigrants that live in the area. The social worker convenes a group to collaborate on a grant proposal to submit to a private foundation to develop a program for the older adults and their families.

- *Volunteer appreciation task force:* The volunteer coordinator at the food pantry calls a meeting of the staff to develop plans to show appreciation to the agency's volunteers for the countless hours spent helping the organization collect, sort, and distribute food donations. By consensus, the group developed a plan to host a dinner where they would prepare the food and serve the volunteers.

Facilitating a psychoeducational group was a new experience for Emily and she wanted to ensure that she considered the full range of issues related to content and process. In order to accomplish this goal, she formed a task group whose function was to advise her on the development and facilitation of a support group for residents and former residents of the shelter program. In addition to recruiting co-workers who had support group experience, she sought out community professionals with expertise in parenting and child development. The group met several times prior to the support group launch to support Emily in strategizing about recruitment, phases of group work, and content for the educational component related to parenting. She reconvened the group several more times to provide input regarding the group process, needed adjustments, and evaluation.

SKILLS FOR SOCIAL WORK PRACTICE WITH GROUPS

Social work practice with groups builds on many of the skills that are used in working with individuals and families. Both levels of practice have five things in common: (1) systems approach; (2) understanding of group dynamics; (3) intervention approach; (4) understanding of intervention processes; and (5) commitment to evidence of effectiveness (Garvin & Galinsky, 2008). The skill set required for group practice is not unique to group work; it is the purpose of those skills that are unique to group work (Ephross & Greif, 2009). The skills required for a social work planned change intervention with individuals and families are similar to those utilized at the group level, the difference being that the client system is the group as opposed to an individual.

Group work uses the skills of engagement, assessment, intervention, and evaluation that were introduced in Chapter 9 as the planned change process for working with individuals and families. However, at the group level, these phases can be fluid and dynamic, particularly in groups that are open-ended or in groups in which the goal or purpose may change after the group is formed. Monitoring individual and group progress toward goal achievement requires the social worker to move back and forth comfortably between phases of work.

Another characteristic of group work is that it requires sensitivity to group dynamics. Establishing a group for persons with a common cause, need, or agenda does not ensure that the group process will be mutually beneficial for all members (Shulman, 2009). Moreover, the social worker may attempt to be the sole "helper" in the group instead of activating the power of group members as contributors to the helping process (AASWG, Inc., 2010). Also, as the group intervention moves through the planned change effort, conflict may become a normal part of the group process; a skilled social worker makes that conflict part of the intervention itself.

As with all other areas of social work practice, social workers must keep ethical issues at the forefront of the group intervention process. Some of the ethical issues that arise in facilitating groups include dilemmas related to sharing information obtained during the group process (i.e., can or should the information be shared with or reported to others outside the group?), mediating values conflicts among group members, and resolving conflicts between the group process and the sponsoring agency's policy or mission. Social work's standards for ethical practice are the best guide in these situations (Pullen-Sansfaçon, 2011).

Social workers engaged in group practice are also ethically bound to be aware of potential issues of social justice. Social inequities, discrimination, power, privilege, oppression, and marginalization—whether among the members or between group members and those outside the group—can be present. The group leader's role is to increase knowledge and awareness regarding these experiences so group members learn to view such issues from a systemic perspective and thus feel empowered to engage in change (Singh & Salazar, 2011). Framing group members' issues and concerns within a context of social injustices often leads to "courageous conversations" about empowerment (Singh & Salazar, 2011, p. 214). Professionals committed to maintaining a social justice perspective can reflect on the potential impact of personal experiences, can challenge the appropriateness of practice interventions, and take action to remedy any identified social inequities (Constantine, Hage, Kindaichi, & Bryant, 2007).

Engagement of Groups

Before the planned change process can begin, the group must be formed and membership determined. When social workers have the opportunity to determine group membership, they may be able to ease potential group conflict and enhance group dynamics. Forming a group that is optimally configured in terms of goals, member characteristics, and logistical issues helps the group to progress more quickly to the tasks at hand. However, social workers may not always have free rein in determining group membership.

The following suggestions affect group dynamics and processes. Again, however, they may or may not be influenced by the social worker:

- Individual and group eligibility criteria and goals determine who may be eligible for or interested in joining the group.

- Logistical issues such as time, location, cost, duration, and accessibility (for example, open versus closed) should accommodate group members' needs.

- Optimal size for a therapy group is 6–8 members and for a support or educational group 15–20.

- Some groups thrive on a mixture of personality types, ages, and gender, while other groups need homogeneity of personality types for a successful experience. For example, young children can be in mixed-gender groups, but adolescents may find mixed-gender groups uncomfortable, particularly if issues of sexuality are to be discussed.

After the group is formed, the first step in engaging the group is to perceive the group as the client system. Although groups are made up of individual members and the social worker engages each of those individual members, she or he engages the entire group as well.

Regardless of the type of group work being practiced, the beginning stage includes group formation and first-meeting activities:

- *Making introductions:* Group members have the opportunity to introduce themselves by the name they wish to be called during group meetings and to share with the group any information they feel is relevant for the group experience. Social goals and task group members may share their affiliation, particular knowledge, or expertise that brought them to the group.

- *Explaining the purpose of the group:* The person who convened the group (this may be the group leader) is responsible for explaining the reason the group has been formed and sharing her or his role and expectations for participating in the group.

- *Establishing group rules, norms, and boundaries:* An important step in engaging group members is to provide the opportunity for each person to voice her or his feelings about individual and group goals and expectations for the group experience. Enabling all the members of a group to contribute to a set of group rules, norms, and boundaries enhances their connection to the leader and to one another, thus motivating them to continue with the group's work. For example, group members may choose to establish rules regarding attendance, timeliness, meeting time and location, conflict management, sharing information outside the group, and even responsibility for refreshments.

- *Attending to group members:* Just as attending skills are important for engaging individuals and families, a similar set of practice behaviors is required for developing effective group work skills. Using verbal and nonverbal skills to enhance communication, clarify exchanges, and create an environment in which the person feels safe is somewhat more complex at the group level, however, as the social worker attends to all members of the group at the same time. In addition, group work involves facilitating relationships with individual group members and the group itself, which is different from attending to an individual (Shulman, 2009). During this early phase of group development, social workers also want to be aware of and sensitive to members' feelings about participating in a group (AASWG, Inc., 2010).

The engagement, or beginning, phase in group practice is essential for the process of building group cohesion and trust. Regardless of the type or structure of the group, individual members need to take risks in sharing thoughts, feelings, and ideas. Members of groups that are effectively engaged by the group leader are likely to feel a higher level of connection to each other and the leader and trust the safety of the group process.

In the case of members who have not joined the group voluntarily, because they were mandated or forced to attend, the engagement phase is equally critical but more difficult. In spite of the anger or resistance portrayed by a less-than-willing member, the social worker must demonstrate acceptance of this member, particularly during the engagement phase (Levin, 2009).

Once Emily had permission to form a parenting support group for current and former residents of the shelter, she began by gathering information from her co-workers regarding their perceptions of client needs in the area of parenting. She also obtained input from clients at one of the weekly house meetings in which staff and current clients discuss house issues. Her idea was favorably received, and she went ahead with the planning. Because this group has a psychoeducational focus, Emily felt that diversity in age, race, and ethnicity would be an asset. The group was scheduled for a time and location that Emily felt best served the clients. She arranged for the group members' children to be supervised by a volunteer. Emily created flyers to post around the house and to mail to those former clients that she knew it was safe to contact. For their safety, women who return to live with their partners who had been violent cannot always be contacted by the social worker.

During the first session, Emily began by explaining the origins and purpose of the group. She asked each member to introduce herself and say as much or as little about herself as she wished and to state one goal she had for herself in joining this group.

Next, Emily and the group developed some general rules related to frequency of sessions, attendance, speaking out of turn, handling conflicts, and sharing information about group members outside the group meeting. Because Emily knew the group members from their stays at the shelter, the first session was comfortable, and the members began to bond with one another.

Assessment of Groups

Following engagement, the next phase of the group process is the assessment of individuals within the group as well as the group as a whole. Ongoing assessment is particularly important in group practice. Because the group experience involves a variety of individual personalities and life experiences, the goals, concerns, and dynamics change constantly.

Focusing on the following issues will help the group process benefit all members:

- *Group development:* To promote group cohesion, which is critical to the group process, the social worker can help the members connect to one another as well as to the social worker her-/himself. Helping members to identify shared experiences and similarities can aid the group in coalescing (AASWG, Inc., 2010). Throughout the group experience, the social worker can help group members become aware of their commonalities and their ability to support the goals of the individual members as well as the group. Even the process of establishing group norms, rules, and goals can provide the social worker with information for assessing individual members' communication and interpersonal styles as well as the group's ability to function collectively.

- *Group diversity:* As part of the assessment of group development, the social worker should remain aware of the influence of member diversity on the group building and work processes (AASWG, Inc., 2010). Group member characteristics that can impact group dynamics include race, ethnicity, gender, cultural background, age, values, and professional affiliation. The group process can be a useful strategy for increasing awareness of and educating individuals on stereotypes and diversity issues.

- *Group members' strengths and resources:* In conducting initial and ongoing assessment of the group and the individual members, the social worker helps both individuals and the group as a whole to identify strengths, resources, and areas for growth and change. Group assessment shifts the emphasis to members of the group, who ask questions, share experiences and insights, and identify resources previously unknown to other members or the social worker.

- *Balance of personal and group goals:* Each group member shares her or his motivation for participating in the group experience and identifies her or his expectations for that participation. The social worker helps link personal needs to group needs and goals (AASWG, Inc., 2010). Group members can be a resource for identifying the concerns and priorities of other members, thus involving all members of the group in the personal change process. Such a strategy fosters development of individual assessment as well as group cohesion. To achieve balance and involvement of all members, the worker uses a combination of open- and closed-ended questions and encourages other members to engage in questioning one another as well.

The social worker's role in practice with groups is to be aware of the interactions among group members and to monitor individual and group progress toward goals. Individual and group goals, as well as group structure and dynamics (for example, rules, norms, or membership), are always in flux. With vigilance and flexibility, group members and the social worker can develop plans and interventions to fit the changing needs of the group members as well as the group itself.

Despite the fact that Emily knew all of the group members before they joined the group, she needed to assess their current situations and, specifically, their concerns and strengths in the area of parenting children who have been exposed to intimate partner violence. Emily began her assessment of the group members as they introduced themselves, shared their stories, and stated their expectations for the group. This process enabled Emily to learn about the level of violence to which the children had been exposed, the way in which the mothers had handled that exposure, whether the children had been physically abused as well, and behaviors exhibited by the children that concerned the mother.

In addition to assessing each individual, Emily was able to assess the group members in terms of their strengths as parents and the areas in which they could build on those strengths to enhance their parenting skills. Other factors she thought were important to address included the members' investment in the group process, their ability to bond with and support one another, and the ways in which the members might handle emotional and conflicted situations that could occur within the group.

Intervention With Groups

As with social work interventions at the individual and family practice level, group interventions occur in two phases: planning and implementation. The social worker needs to keep the dual emphasis on individual and group goals in mind for both planning and implementing. Even if the group is able to develop a mutually agreed-upon set of goals, individual perceptions of the tasks and activities needed to achieve those goals may vary considerably. In addition, the group may reach consensus on group goals, but individual goals are bound to be distinct and unique, just as the group members are distinct and unique persons. Moreover, both individual and group goals may change over the lifetime of the group, requiring periodic review of goals. The social worker is responsible for monitoring and overseeing the changing balance of issues.

Planning interventions at the group level requires that the social worker help to establish goals and document the agenda for the group experience:

- *Establishing goals:* The social worker helps the group create goals for the group itself and for the individuals in the group, using specific and measurable tasks and outcomes. The social worker provides input into the development of the goals, weighs the advantages and disadvantages of proposed goals, identifies barriers and available and needed resources, and provides links between the individual and group proposals (AASWG, Inc., 2010).

- *Documenting the agenda for the group experience:* For groups with the general goals of remediation and reciprocity, developing individual and group working agreements helps each participant focus on her or his personal commitment as well as the commitment to the larger group. For social action and task groups, the agreement can be in the form of a working statement of the purpose, goals, and activities of the group and a delineation of the roles of the individual members. Exhibit 10.1 shows an example of a working agreement, similar to the individual contract in Chapter 9 that can be used in remedial, reciprocal, and social action goals groups.

EXHIBIT 10.1

Sample Working Agreement for Individual and Group Intervention Planning

Group Members:

Olivia M.	_Tammy R._
Shirley B.	_Megan S._
Cynthia W.	_Angela G._

Group Goals as Agreed on by All Group Members:

Identify our strengths as mothers

Improve parenting skills

Have a safe place to talk about our experiences

Group Rules and Expectations:

Group will meet weekly; members attend as needed

Members will respect one another's right to speak

All information shared will be confidential

Individual Group Member Goals and Tasks:

Group Member	Goal	Client Tasks/Date	Social Worker Tasks/Date
Olivia	1. _Be able to share my situation with others_	_I will share at least one personal item each meeting_	_Each meeting, I will support Olivia by asking if she would like to share_
	2. _Identify my strengths as a parent_	_I will report at least one positive thing I did during the week as a mother_	_I will provide information on "parenting without spanking"_
	3.		

Date Contract Will Be Reviewed:

8 weeks from today

I agree with the above-stated goals, to complete the contracted tasks, and participate in a review and evaluation of the contract on the specified date.

Olivia M.	_Emily_
Client	Social Worker
Date	Date

Implementation begins by putting into action the individual and group goals that have been established. As they proceed, the social worker and the group members engage in ongoing assessment of their individual and collective work to determine whether goals need to be revised.

The implementation stage of group practice may provide the greatest challenges for the social worker and group members, as this stage involves actually changing attitudes and behaviors and completing tasks. The social worker watches for and addresses individual and group issues that can impede the work of the group. These are some of the group dynamics that may impede the implementation process:

- *Conflict:* Differences may arise for several reasons, including the varying paces at which group members work toward their contracted goals, differences in individual and group values, and changing individual and group needs. The social worker may often be confronted with member-to-member conflict or member-to-social worker conflict. The social worker can model conflict resolution by responding directly to the conflict and involving group members in facilitating a positive outcome.

- *Violation of group rules and norms:* Even if rules are clearly outlined during the group's early development, members may find themselves unable to comply with them or to fulfill expectations. Responsibility for confronting violations falls to the group leader. Asking the group to review the previously established rules and to address the infraction empowers the group to act as a unit in determining an appropriate response.

- *Disruptive members:* The group process can suffer when a member creates obstacles to achieving the desired goals. Behaviors that impede the group's progress include talking too much or too little, not fulfilling obligations (for example, attendance or tasks), and being overly critical. A group leader minimizes the disruption by monitoring for such behaviors and addressing the disruptive behaviors either within the group session itself or outside the group meeting. Offering alternative strategies for interacting with the group and modeling appropriate behaviors while in the group are two ways to provide members with options for appropriate interaction.

The established purpose and goals of the group can influence the development and implementation of the intervention. For example, an intervention for an anger management group focused on helping the members learn appropriate skills for handling their anger may be highly structured and formalized, whereas a group for persons recently widowed may be less structured to foster the sharing of feelings and supporting one another. Regardless of the type of intervention, the social worker is responsible for building on individual and group strengths, meeting individual and group needs, and focusing on specific and measurable outcomes.

> *Using the individual and group goals identified by the group members, Emily proposed that each session have two components: education and support. Each meeting would begin with a "checking-in" period in which the members could share successes or ask for help with their parenting. The second half of the session would include a presentation by Emily or another professional on a topic specific to parenting children who have experienced trauma. Together, Emily and the group developed a list of possible topics to cover, while acknowledging that they needed to be flexible in case additional topics arose.*
>
> *Throughout each session, Emily monitored the interactions of the group members with her and with one another and noted individual growth and change. Emily routinely provided feedback to the group on her observations and asked the members to do the same with her and one another.*

Evaluation and Termination of Groups

The final phase of group work includes evaluation and possible group termination. This segment of group work provides the opportunity for the social worker and the group members to reflect on the gains, changes, and learning that have occurred for the individual group members; consider the impact of the group experience on members as well as persons outside the group; and react to the ending of the group experience (AASWG, Inc., 2010). Final group meetings are also a time to discuss application of the new learning and review follow-up plans (including referrals or ongoing treatment, in the case of client-focused groups).

Evaluation at the group level can be more complicated than when working with individuals and families. Individual and group goals are evaluated along with the group process.

In general, strategies for evaluating a group experience evolve from the structure of the group, the goals of the group and its members, and intervention tasks and activities. For example, structured groups benefit from more formalized evaluations, while less structured groups (for example, ongoing support groups) may be able to informally evaluate process and progress on a regular basis.

Evaluation is part of the group process from the time the group is formed, but building evaluation into the ending phase can be empowering. The social worker and group members identify personal and group changes that have occurred, assess the impact of the group experience on the members' lives, and determine whether future intervention is needed (AASWG, Inc., 2010). In the event that individual or group goals have not been achieved, the social worker can use the termination and evaluation phase to help individual members and the group to identify those areas that were positive, reflect on possible reasons that the goals were not reached, and develop strategies for continuing to work on the original or new goals (Garvin & Galinsky, 2008).

To capture the complexities of the group experience, a multifaceted plan for conducting a group evaluation might be needed. It could include the following:

- Audio- or videotaping, with group members' informed consent, to enable the social worker to observe group dynamics and her or his intervention skills.

- Obtaining information from group members through needs assessments, measures of attitudes or behaviors, or physical measures before and after the group experience.

- Obtaining group member feedback regarding satisfaction with the group experience and the leadership.

- Reviewing individual and group goals.

- Reviewing processes used to accomplish goals.

Groups that are time-limited or based on a specific goal or activity may terminate as a group at this stage. In these situations, the termination process encompasses the entire group. In open-ended groups, however, termination occurs for individuals as they leave the group. Evaluation in these situations may occur for the individual and still involve members who are not leaving the group.

The social worker facilitates termination using a common set of skills:

- The social worker and group members share feelings about ending the group experience and leaving the group.

- The social worker and group members develop plans for maintaining change.

- Group members discuss their feelings about having contact after termination from the group (for example, returning to the group, having contact outside the group, or having group reunions).

During the beginning phase of the group's work, Emily and the members had agreed that the group would meet weekly for 8 weeks, and then evaluate the future of the group. To help to evaluate their progress, the members completed a standardized parenting questionnaire at the first and eighth sessions to determine changes in parenting style and knowledge. At the eighth session, the group asked that Emily continue the group but open it to other current and former shelter residents to join.

Through these two evaluation strategies, Emily and the group members were able to assess both individual and group goals and make decisions for the future.

CONCLUSION

Group work can be a powerful experience for both the social worker and the members of the group. Groups often achieve far more than a person could alone, but a group intervention is not for every person or every issue. The effective social worker uses her or his engagement and assessment skills to determine whether a group intervention is the optimal approach to use in a given situation.

In group work, the social worker uses the skills of engagement, assessment, intervention, and evaluation that were introduced in Chapter 9 for work with individuals. In group practice, however, the social worker must simultaneously build rapport with the individual group members and facilitate group cohesiveness, being careful not to focus too much attention on one group member or issue. With leadership from a social worker, group members can provide input into the individual and group intervention plans and participate in a group-wide evaluation of the experience. Working with a group of people at one time may seem like a daunting task, but the social worker's skill in viewing strengths from a systemic perspective can be an asset.

MAIN POINTS

- Group work is a method of practice in which the social worker works with a group of persons to address individual issues; to address a need for information and education; to provide mutual support; or to address social conditions. Following the first course on group methods offered in 1923, group work soon became an established part of the social work educational curriculum.

- The main group work models are in the areas of social action, individual growth (or remediation), self-help and support (or reciprocity), and tasks. The goal of a social action group is to initiate or change a policy, law, or program; individual growth groups emphasize clinically oriented treatment for a personal issue or concern; support groups are mutual aid groups based on a common life experience; and task groups complete a predetermined goal that is typically focused outside the group members themselves.

- In the practice of social work with groups, the social worker forms the group, facilitates group meetings, provides resources for the group, and works with the group to develop strategies to meet the desired goals.

- The outcomes for the group are based on the individual members' ability and willingness to be interdependent and interact with one another for the purpose of achieving the goals. Although change occurs for the individual members of the group, the focus of the intervention is the group as a whole.

- As with social work practice with individuals and families, skills for group work focus on the areas of engagement, assessment, intervention, and termination and evaluation.

EXERCISES

1. Below are descriptions of four groups in which Sanchez family members (www.routledgesw.com/cases) may be participants. Read the descriptions and, using the group practice models highlighted in this chapter, complete the exercises that follow the descriptions.

- *Group 1—Grandparents Raising Grandchildren*. Hector and Celia are members of this group. The group meets for a monthly potluck meal, and members share strategies and resources related to rearing grandchildren. The group was organized by a social worker who has custody of her granddaughter. Occasionally, the group meeting includes a presentation by a professional on a topic of interest to the group (e.g., legal and financial issues and childrearing strategies).

- *Group 2—Women's Group*. Celia Sanchez is a member of a group for persons experiencing depression. The group meets weekly for 90 minutes at the mental health center. The group addresses issues such as identifying causes and symptoms of depression, treatment strategies, and strategies for coping with depression. Facilitated by two clinical social workers, the group is composed of eight women who were referred by other mental health professionals. Each group member was then interviewed by the group leaders to determine her appropriateness for the group. Celia was referred by the social worker working with Hector and her to facilitate Joey's adoption. The adoption social worker noted that Celia had experienced episodic depression throughout her life and was currently reporting depressive symptoms.

- *Group 3—Grandparents for Justice*. Through their involvement with the grandparents group, Celia and Hector became members of a group in their state that is working for improving the state laws that determine the rights of grandparents. The group was formed by several grandparents who struggled with the state's child welfare system to gain custody of their grandchildren. The group's goal is to see legislation passed that will protect the rights of grandparents.

- *Group 4—Grandparents and Grandchildren Together*. During one of the meetings of Grandparents Raising Grandchildren, one grandmother suggested that the group form a special committee to plan social and recreational activities that the grandparents could attend with their grandchildren. While the group unanimously supported the initiative, they were concerned about the cost of activities being prohibitive for some of the families. Several members of the group, including Celia, volunteered to form a committee to organize and raise funds for the activities.

   a. Identify the type of group that each of these four groups is and at least three reasons for your decision about the type of group:

Group 1—Grandparents Raising Grandchildren.

Group 2—Women's Group.

Group 3—Grandparents for Justice.

Group 4—Grandparents and Grandchildren Together.

   b. After completing exercise 1a, select one of the group scenarios. Using that scenario, identify at least three skills appropriate for each phase of the group process:

- Engagement.

- Assessment.

- Intervention.

- Evaluation and termination.

2. As you read in exercise 1, Hector and Celia have become involved in a group working to improve the state laws that dictate the rights of grandparents, Grandparents for Justice. Using the knowledge that you have gained regarding the phases of the group process, develop a list of strategies that the group might use to develop a plan and focus local and state attention on their issue.

3. Go to the Riverton interactive case at www.routledgesw.com/cases. As a new resident and social worker in the Alvadora neighborhood of Riverton, you have become aware of the neighbors' concerns about public drinking. Using a social goals approach, your task is to convene a group of neighborhood residents who will develop a plan to advocate with city officials to address the problems.

   After familiarizing yourself with the residents of Alvadora, determine the potential strengths and contributions of each one. From a social goals perspective, develop a plan for organizing a group and provide strategies for recruiting members and creating a goal.

4. Go to the Carla Washburn interactive case at www.routledgesw.com/cases. Following the death of her husband, Carla Washburn joined a widows' group at her church. Not only was she able to benefit from participation in this group, she

was able to help other widows with their adjustments as well. With the loss of her grandson, Mrs. Washburn has once again found herself grieving the loss of a loved one. Respond to the following:

   a. How could a group experience benefit the client system in her current grief?

   b. Describe the group model that you would recommend for Mrs. Washburn.

   c. Develop a draft of a contract that you would negotiate with Mrs. Washburn if she were to join a group.

5. Using the information you have available regarding the Hudson City case located at www.routledgesw.com/cases, develop detailed descriptions of social work group interventions that are appropriate for each of the four group approaches presented in this chapter. Include the goals, purposes, membership, and basic rules for each type of group.

CHAPTER 11

Social Work Practice With Organizations, Communities, and Policy Practice

In working with a senior homemaker/chore program, Emily helped Marietta, a 78-year-old widow with several physical challenges, to arrange home-based services so that she could continue independent living. One of those services was home health care. However, as a result of state policy changes in the reimbursement of home health agencies, Marietta and a number of the older adults with whom Emily worked had their home health services decreased or terminated altogether. Emily began to see negative consequences among these older adults. Some were no longer able to live independently and had to move in with family members or into a residential care facility.

Viewing her role as an advocate as well as a case manager, Emily compiled case examples detailing the negative effects of the policy changes. With her agency's support, Emily shared her data with a community coalition of agencies and organizations that engage in legislative advocacy on issues related to older adults. The advocacy group used Emily's data in their campaign to gain a legislative sponsor and to write and introduce state-level legislation that would increase the reimbursement rates for home health service providers.

Emily then worked with the advocacy group to prepare testimony for a legislative committee. She arranged for family members of the home health care recipients to travel to the state capitol and testify before the committee on the negative impact of the cutbacks.

After a 2-year sustained, collaborative effort, legislation was passed to increase reimbursement for home health services for older adults.

In this chapter, we explore social work practice that targets change efforts at the organizational, community, and societal levels. **Community-level social work practice**, also referred to as **macro practice**, promotes changes in practices, policies, and legislation that impact groups of people in an organization, community, state, country, or even the world. **Policy practice** is an important aspect of macro-level social work practice that encompasses the formulation and implementation of social policies within the context of social and economic development (Iatridis, 2008).

Social workers have worked for change at the organizational, community, national, and societal levels throughout the history of the profession. Macro-level interventions are often initiated in response to government incentives (e.g., the economic stimulus programs of 2009); significant funding decreases (e.g., Medicaid cuts); or a large-scale social movement to address oppression (e.g., Occupy Movement) (Gibelman, 2004). When policies are punitive or bureaucracies are large and impersonal, the social worker can serve as an advocate for clients in facilitating change in the system that is intended to serve them. Community-level practice serves a range of purposes, including improving the quality of life; advocacy; human social and economic development; service and program planning; service integration; political and social action; and social justice (Weil & Gamble, 2009, p. 883).

While 14% of practicing social workers describe their primary practice focus as macro practice, organizational and community practice is also often combined with direct practice. In fact, over half (51%) of social workers surveyed report spending their time in direct services to clients, but the remaining time spent is in activities such as administration, management, supervision, consultation, training, planning, teaching, research, project management, policy/legislative development, fund-raising/grant-writing, and community organizing (Whitaker & Arrington, 2008, p. 8). Exhibit 11.1 shows the percentage of time that social workers engage in macro practice activities.

Social workers often begin their careers by working with individuals and families and then move into areas that include administration, management, teaching, or research. This career path means that administrators, supervisors, and teachers have insight into the issues and challenges of social work practice with individuals and families.

In addition, although organizational and community-level practice may not be their primary focus, all social workers are ethically and professionally obligated to advocate for social justice. In the National Association of Social Workers (NASW) *Code of Ethics* (2008), four of the six ethical principles emphasize this responsibility. For social work practice at the community level, the *Code* charges social workers with the responsibility to: (1) promote social change "with and on behalf of vulnerable and oppressed individuals and groups" in the areas of poverty, unemployment, discrimination, and other areas of social injustice; (2) serve both client systems and the larger society and address the needs of organizations and communities as well as individuals, families, and groups; and (3) practice with integrity within organizations (NASW, 2008). Moreover, Standard 6 of the *Code of Ethics* (NASW, 2008) focuses on social work practice within the broader society in the areas of:

- Social welfare.

- Public participation through influencing policies, and institutions.

- Public emergencies.

- Social and political action through working toward equity in access to resources, opportunities, and policies.

Addressing social injustice is considered to be a social work responsibility because social injustice "harms people and limits their opportunities to live as fully human persons with inherent worth and dignity" (Horejsi, 2002, p. 12).

In this chapter, we explore the third level of generalist social work practice, beginning with a brief overview of policy practice and then a review of the historical

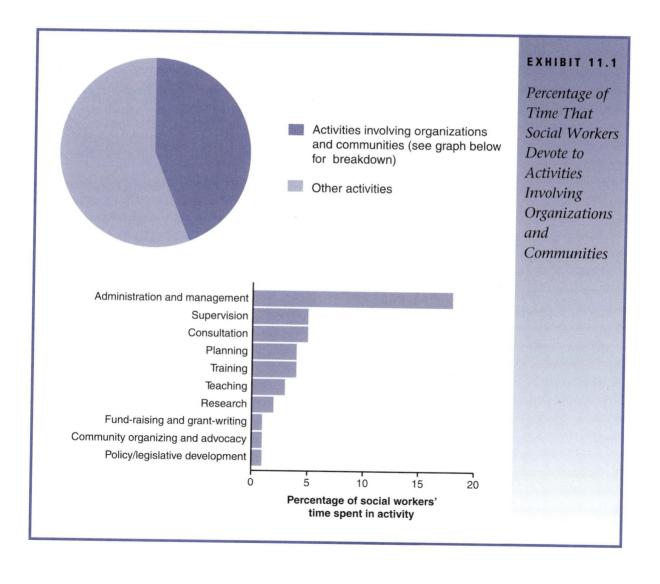

EXHIBIT 11.1

Percentage of Time That Social Workers Devote to Activities Involving Organizations and Communities

development of social work practice with organizations and communities. To understand the underpinnings of the many and varied facets of working with organizations and communities, we will examine the models of change used in this level of practice and the skills that are essential for being an effective practitioner.

A WORD ON POLICY PRACTICE

Although many of the terms and concepts that describe social work practice with organizations and communities are used interchangeably, they are, in fact, distinct practice approaches and are not synonymous. Policy practice, which specifically addresses the formulation and implementation of social policies, is a critical area of competence for all social workers regardless of whether they practice at the individual and family, group, or organization and community level.

As an example, one policy practice strategy is advocacy. The advocacy effort made by Emily on behalf of her individual client, Marietta, resulted in a policy change, but only because Emily understood the intricacies of the policy, analyzed the impact of the policy, and worked with her clients and within the system to effect a change that enhanced her client's well-being. This systematic process highlights one of the many roles that a social worker can play while practicing at the organizational and community level.

All social workers are obligated to develop a working knowledge of social policies and to understand the impact of policies on the populations they serve (Iatridis, 2008). In fact, as one social worker noted, the 2012 closure of Jane Addams's Hull House signaled the need for the social work profession to reinvest in the practice of macro-level policy work (Gale, 2012, p. 19).

HISTORICAL PERSPECTIVE ON SOCIAL WORK PRACTICE WITH ORGANIZATIONS AND COMMUNITIES

The origins of social work practice with organizations and communities can be found in the early efforts of the Charity Organization Society (COS) and settlement house movements. While the focus of the COS movement was primarily individuals and families, COS workers found they also needed to advocate on behalf of their clients. Early settlement house activists organized and advocated at the local and state levels for social, economic, and political change in areas such as housing, child welfare, workers' rights, and the environment (Fisher, DeFilippis, & Shragge, 2012; Pyles, 2009).

Jane Addams and her colleagues at Hull House were the first to engage in large-scale advocacy efforts. They were concerned about sanitation problems in Chicago. The result was Addams's appointment as sanitation inspector (L. Quam, 2008).

The role of community practice continued to grow throughout the first half of the 20th century. The Great Depression of the 1930s, in particular, focused the country on the need for community-level interventions to address the issues of widespread poverty, unemployment, and hunger. Through the New Deal programs, the federal government assumed responsibility for the development and implementation of community-level interventions for the first time in U.S. history.

The social upheaval of the 1960s galvanized social workers into taking a greater role in community organization and advocacy. Social workers of this era were involved in advocacy efforts in the areas of civil rights, employment, the Vietnam War, and welfare rights.

Interest in organizational and community change waxed and waned through the 1970s and 1980s; the emphasis was social work practice with individuals and families. By the 1990s, the efforts of several social work organizations had created a resurgence of interest in arenas such as political campaigns and advocacy.

Eventually, the profession acknowledged the need to have competence at multiple levels of intervention, which has contributed to the development of the generalist social work practice model. In the 21st century social workers strive to address social problems with individuals, families, groups, and organizations and communities. Practice at the organizational and community level is thus an integral part of the profession and essential knowledge for all social workers.

Social workers practicing at the organizational and community level often face funding challenges; however, the profession's commitment to community organization, advocacy, and other organizational and community-level service activities remains strong. The Council on Social Work Education has shown its commitment to ensuring that all social workers have knowledge and skills for organizational and community practice in the current curriculum guidelines, which state that social workers should be prepared to work with organizations and communities as well as individuals and families and to be competent in policy practice to promote effective service delivery (2008).

MODELS OF CHANGE IN SOCIAL WORK PRACTICE WITH ORGANIZATIONS AND COMMUNITIES

In an effort to address social injustices at the organizational or community level, social workers must be ready to work toward change within political, social, and economic systems. Achieving change within a system is a challenging endeavor due to the many and varied persons, policies, and needs involved. In order to facilitate system-wide change, social workers need to determine whether the system is ready for a change or alternatives can be explored. If a change is viable, the social worker's role may focus on identifying the key persons and resources that are needed to facilitate the change process.

The first step is to define the community to be targeted, which may include the physical or geographic environment or a social group or organization. Upon defining the community to be targeted, the goal of the change effort is defined.

Then the social worker selects the most appropriate approach to achieve the desired outcome.

The models of community organization that have been developed to enable social workers to match the community, the goals, and the strategies for intervention include the following (Streeter, Gamble, & Weil, 2008):

- Geographic-community organizing.

- Functional-community organizing.

- Community development.

- Program development.

- Social planning.

- Coalition building.

- Political and social action.

- Movement for progressive change.

Exhibit 11.2 summarizes these models of change and provides examples of possible interventions to address problems of neighborhood and community safety.

EXHIBIT 11.2 Models of Community Action	SOCIAL WORK APPROACH	DEFINITION	EXAMPLE: INTERVENTION FOR IMPROVING NEIGHBORHOOD AND COMMUNITY SAFETY
	Geographic-community organizing	Within a specified geographic area that shares a common concern related to a social problem, facilitating the creation or maintenance of a "collective body" to work toward resolution of the shared concern	Organizing a monitoring committee to document instances of vandalism within the neighborhood
	Functional-community organizing	Facilitating a change in attitudes or behaviors within a community of shared interests by raising awareness	Providing public information and education about the potential effects on a community if vandalism becomes widespread

SOCIAL WORK APPROACH	DEFINITION	EXAMPLE: INTERVENTION FOR IMPROVING NEIGHBORHOOD AND COMMUNITY SAFETY	EXHIBIT 11.2 *continued*
Community development	Systematically developing or improving the standard of living or the economic, physical, or social infrastructure within a geographic or interest-based community	Increasing commerce in a community through development of neighborhood watch programs to enhance customer safety	
Program development	Providing leadership at the agency level to identify and attain goals, seek and allocate resources, supervise personnel, and oversee service delivery	Helping a group of neighborhood residents to address personal, home, and business safety by facilitating links to the police and fire departments	
Social planning	Using a systematic, data-driven, evidence-based process in concert with other experts and professionals to identify a need for social change and conduct an assessment, develop a plan for service delivery, and implement an evaluation	In response to community complaints, working with police and community leaders to study crime statistics and trends in the community, conducting a community needs assessment, and developing a new safety program	
Coalition building	Bringing together groups and organizations that are committed to a common cause or concern in order to have a greater impact on decision makers	Coordinating a collaborative effort by organizations that serve older adults to develop a program that educates their clients on safety issues and provides safe escort and transportation services	
Political and social action	Building political pressure to resolve a social problem or address a social need at the institutional or policy level, by working to elect candidates who support issues important to a group, organization, or community or advocating for legislation promoting those interests	Supporting candidates who are committed to increasing community policing and safety and providing them with sample legislation or data to support legislation	

Continued

EXHIBIT 11.2 *continued*	SOCIAL WORK APPROACH	DEFINITION	EXAMPLE: INTERVENTION FOR IMPROVING NEIGHBORHOOD AND COMMUNITY SAFETY
	Movement for progressive change	Undertaking large-scale community, national, and international efforts in order to address social injustices targeting specific populations	Helping advocacy groups across the country to unite in order to address the issue of hate crimes perpetrated on the gay, lesbian, bisexual, and transgender community

Sources: Barker, 2003; Butterfield & Chisanga, 2008; Sager, 2008; Streeter, Gamble, & Weil, 2008; Weil & Gamble, 2009.

Geographic-Community Organizing

Overall, geographic-community organizing aims to improve the economic and social quality of life in a specific neighborhood or other geographic locale, whether in the domestic or international arena. Building connections among community members to achieve a desired change is a primary focus of this model of practice. The goal is to bring together individuals and groups who share the common goal of gaining or regaining power that they perceive to be held by another group (Pyles, 2009).

Common to most efforts to build community is the concept that a community is complex and dynamic. Growth begins with recognizing the community's existing infrastructure, its many potential collaborations, and the capacity for change (Milligan, 2008).

The process of community organizing has four key elements (Pyles, 2009, p. 81):

1. *Empowerment:* Emboldening people to act for change.

2. *Accountability:* Involving individuals and groups in the organizing effort so they will feel more committed to the cause.

3. *Relationship:* Using the skills of listening and "starting where the client is" to develop a rapport with community members that can evolve over time into a trusting relationship.

4. *Social change:* Facilitating an alternative approach or a solution to a social injustice.

Examples of community organizing initiatives by social workers include the following:

- *Organizing for better housing:* Residents of an apartment complex request help from a community-based social services agency in getting needed repairs made to their apartment buildings. The landlord has refused to replace inefficient, potentially dangerous heating and cooling equipment, maintain the exterior of the buildings, and replace hallway and outdoor lighting. With the assistance of the residents, the agency's social worker conducts an on-site assessment of their concerns and contacts a local attorney in the housing division of a legal services agency. Together, the legal services attorney and the social worker compile a report and form a team made up of the attorney, the social worker, and representatives from the residents' group. The team presents the report to the landlord, and the landlord promises to make repairs. Repairs are not made within the 6-month period promised. With the social worker's help, the residents organize a picket outside the landlord's office. The changes are then made promptly.

- *Organizing for improved transportation:* A neighborhood group unites around the issue of having the public transportation system extend to their neighborhood so that access to and from the neighborhood is enhanced. The social worker begins by convening a gathering of stakeholders who have an interest in this issue. The stakeholders make a commitment to advocate for this issue and develop a plan for advocating for expanded transportation services. With the social worker's help, the group conducts a needs assessment, formulates a plan to approach the city government, and implements the campaign. While the plan required several modifications and compromises, the city government agreed to conduct a feasibility study—the first step in reaching their goal.

Functional-Community Organizing

In addition to being based on a geographic area, a community can also be interest-based. These functional communities share commonalities such as ethnicity, values, faith traditions, or socioeconomic levels (Butterfield & Chisanga, 2008). As when organizing a neighborhood, the focus of the change effort in functional community organizing is to identify and raise awareness regarding the need for an action, provide education, change attitudes or behaviors, and organize and lead an advocacy effort for change (Weil & Gamble, 2009).

Examples of functional community organizing include the following:

- *Students organizing for students:* A group of social work students who have been completing a service learning project in a faith-based after-school program discover that the children are having difficulty getting to the program from their elementary schools. The social work students organize a campaign to help the children's parents advocate for the school district to include the program on its bus route.

- *Faith community organizing for immigrants and refugees:* A group of immigrants and refugees living in the neighborhood approach the ministerial alliance in a community to request assistance in locating a site for religious services. The alliance comes together to offer their individual facilities to be used on a rotating basis until the community of immigrants and refugees is able to raise funds to obtain a permanent home for their services.

Whether organizing a neighborhood, community, or a group of individuals united by some other characteristic, the social work organizer strategically and proactively considers the "client's" goals, available and needed resources, the power held by the various stakeholders (e.g., politicians, consumers, and legal system), and strives to implement the best strategy to meet the group's goals and needs (Pyles, 2009). Having a diverse repertoire of organizing skills is essential for effective community organizing, including the skills of legislative and legal advocacy, asset-based community development, mobilization for direct action, and negotiation (Pyles, 2009).

Community Development

The goal of the community development model is to help communities to enhance and strengthen their cohesion, capability, and competence, also known as capacity development (Rothman, 2008). As with community organizing, change efforts in the community development approach can be focused on geographic or interest-based groups (Butterfield & Chisanga, 2008). Although developing communities may seem similar to organizing communities, community development is more focused on creating opportunities for members of the community to engage in civic activities and tends to be less politically focused than community organizing (Traynor, 2012).

Whether working in the local, national, or international arena, social workers engaged in community development focus on mobilizing the community's members to confront unmet needs that traditional social and economic systems are not adequately addressing. The change effort can be directed toward areas such as economic development or community empowerment (Butterfield & Chisanga, 2008).

The community development model assumes that members of the community are invested in changing the environment in which they live. Change is based on the community members engaging in a cooperative, self-help process with one another and with outside individuals and groups. The effectiveness of the change intervention increases as member participation increases. In essence, the client system and the change agent system are the same population.

The best approach for community development is generally a democratic, "bottom-up" approach. Members of the community are called on to define the targets for change, assess their needs and resources, and envision and carry out an intervention strategy (Walker, 2010).

The most efficient way to effect change is to use existing networks to build stronger, more effective services and resources and to help individuals, families, and groups in the community to gain more control over their lives, communities, and futures (Walker, 2010, p. 195). For example, community development efforts often aim to eliminate poverty (Midgley, 2010). One way to optimize a low-income/low-wealth community's efforts is to seek partnerships with public and for-profit entities to help build the community's assets and economic capacities (Sherraden, 2008, p. 1:382).

The social worker's role in community development varies. As a professional working in the community and interacting with a range of people and groups, the social worker may be in a unique position to identify a community need that residents or members of the community do not view as a community-wide problem. In this capacity, the social worker may initiate a social change effort by mobilizing key persons within the community, following the social goals model of group practice described in Chapter 10. The social worker may train a community member to assume leadership and then relinquish the leadership role to that individual. In situations in which community members identify the condition needing change, the social worker helps to facilitate the change. The social worker may also be a participant in the change effort based on her or his residence in the community or position within an organization. Or the social worker may be an outside consultant to the change effort due to a particular expertise or by virtue of membership in the community.

Community development interventions focus on such diverse target areas as employment, community enterprise, alleviation of poverty, social exclusion, improvements to physical/environment spaces, improvements to educational and social resources, and development of social capital (Walker, 2010). For instance, NASW has called for social workers to actively engage in advocacy for protecting and improving the environment, in general, and those areas of the environment that detrimentally impact disadvantaged communities (NASW, 2012–2014d). Let us now look at some examples of community development change efforts:

- *Neighborhood residents concerned about health care access:* A social worker in a community center becomes aware of the decreasing access to health care of residents in a neighborhood largely composed of older adults living on limited incomes. With the help of the agency's neighborhood advisory committee, the social worker conducts a needs assessment to determine the extent of access problems and learns that many older adults have not seen a physician regularly since the nearby clinic closed several years earlier. The advisory committee approaches the local medical school to propose opening a small free clinic in the agency to serve outpatient needs. The medical school faculty seizes the opportunity to provide a training site for medical students, and a partnership is born.

- *Refugee-owned businesses:* Clients and former clients of a refugee resettlement agency approach social work staff about refugee-owned business owners being harassed. In recent months, a number of the refugee-owned businesses have been vandalized. With the support of the local business owners, the social worker convenes a task force comprising representatives from the refugee-owned businesses, Chamber of Commerce members, law enforcement personnel, and the community development agency. The task force conducts an assessment of the neighborhood and finds the problem to be widespread. They agree to address the issues of vandalism, security, and community relations. The social worker assists initially by chairing the task force but later works to identify a leader from the refugee business community to assume that role.

- *Micro-financing of small businesses:* A faith-based organization located in an economically developing Central American country provides low-interest loans to community members to start or grow their small businesses. The businesses are primarily retail enterprises, are owned by women, and target local residents' need for goods and supplies. The social worker's role is to locate potential borrowers, determine eligibility for the loans, provide education regarding the loan and repayment processes and small business development, and provide services and support during the loan period.

In community development activities, the experts are the members of the community. The social worker's role is to support and assist the community in developing and implementing a change to enhance the lives of those in the community.

Program Development

Development at the program level can originate in several areas. Social workers working in direct services may identify a need that is not being filled by their organization or another. Current or former recipients of services may also bring attention to the need for a new or expanded service. In essence, the social worker involved in program development serves as a liaison to the community.

The role for the social worker can be multifaceted. The social worker may be the person who draws attention to the need for a service to be implemented. She or he may then be the one who develops and implements the service. Conversely, the social worker may be approached to aid in the development of a service, thus serving as a liaison for her or his organization. Social workers can also engage in the development of a program or funding proposal, advocacy for the program, and facilitation of the program (Streeter et al., 2008).

Examples in which social workers may engage in program development include the following:

- *Service expansion:* Former recipients of services provided by an urban domestic violence program contact the agency requesting that a satellite office be opened in their rural area. The domestic violence program conducts its own needs assessment to determine that the rural community indeed lacks services for women who are survivors of intimate partner violence, approaches key persons in the community for support, and establishes the program. A social worker working for the shelter may be called on to conduct the needs assessment, develop the program, or manage the satellite program. If the social worker is already a key person in the rural community, her or his support and involvement can help the program to gain acceptance.

- *Programming for preschoolers:* A county provides child care and other programs for children up to age 3 and for children 5 and older, but parents of children ages 3–5 must make their own arrangements. A BSW student works with an interagency team to develop a needs assessment and a program proposal that includes a proposal for funding (Bollig, 2009).

Social Planning

Social planning is an intervention model in which change efforts are aimed at community or policy-level issues. Social planning involves working at the institutional and bureaucratic levels to facilitate the desired change at the community and policy levels.

Social planning is based on the belief that experts, who have access to empirical data and technical expertise, best orchestrate change. Change may be instigated by members of the community who seek outside professional expertise. Planning may also be initiated by professionals, outside consultants, and influential decision makers and may not involve members of the community themselves. Those who are impacted by the planning effort should, however, be involved in the planning itself (Rothman, 2008).

The social worker's role may be as a member of a professional team involved in identifying issues, collecting data, analyzing policy, and planning a program to address needs. With the profession's values and knowledge of planned change efforts and training in identification, assessment, resource development and management, and human needs, social workers' participation in social planning is an asset (Sager, 2008).

The following are examples of social planning change efforts:

- *Neighborhood redevelopment:* Municipal officials, concerned about the deterioration of one of the city's historic neighborhoods, conduct a community assessment to determine the extent of decline. Upon determining that the number of businesses, owner-occupied households, and the tax base have drastically decreased, the city's Office of Community and Economic Development applies for federal funding to restore the neighborhood. The funding enables the city to offer tax breaks for new homeowners, low-interest loans for new business owners, funds for rehabilitation and beautification of buildings, and grants for development of social service programs. The social worker may be in a position to gather and analyze data, facilitate the interactions of local officials, publicize the redevelopment effort, review applications, assist with locating and securing funding, and oversee program development.

- *International social work education:* Dramatic social, political, and economic changes in some countries (e.g., former Soviet Union and Haiti) have created a need to restructure social service delivery systems. Recognizing that the expertise to build a social service system did not exist within the professional community of these countries, social workers from the United States are called in to assist in the rebuilding effort. The social worker's role in this change effort is to serve as a trainer, facilitator, educator, and consultant, working with professionals to develop organizational practices, fund-raising mechanisms, and evaluation processes that are consistent with the new social structure.

- *Rural domestic violence services:* Consider the earlier example of the domestic violence agency establishing a satellite program in a rural community from a different perspective: While the idea can originate with the former recipients of services, another possibility for a social planning effort may occur when staff of a local hospital identify a need and begin the process. Noticing an increase in the number of women presenting to the emergency room who report being abused by their partners, the hospital staff determine that local services are needed. The nearest domestic violence program is 30 miles away in the county seat. The hospital administrator contacts that program and asks for their help in establishing a satellite program at the hospital. The administrator and shelter director apply for a grant to provide start-up funding for a hospital-based social worker to provide services for women who are seen at the hospital for abuse-related injuries. Once that program is in place, an advisory group is formed and plans are made to seek long-term funding to keep the program running on a permanent basis.

Coalition Building

The concept of "strength in numbers" is the basis for coalition development. **Coalitions** are collaborative initiatives that unite groups such as agency professionals, client systems, governmental organizations, educational institutions, and legislative groups around a common interest or goal. Building a coalition is typically aimed at impacting a large-scale change over a long period of time. It involves influencing the decision-making process and focuses on accessing resources (Streeter et al., 2008).

The social worker may initiate the building of a coalition or participate as a member of a coalition. With skills in micro-, mezzo-, and macro-level practice, social workers are well positioned to serve in coalition leadership, mediation, and organizing roles (Streeter et al., 2008).

Coalition-building examples may include:

- *Coalition for community development:* This type of intervention is similar to the previous example of neighborhood redevelopment. In this case, however, a social worker working in an agency in a neighborhood may invite resident associations, social service organizations, and representatives from the faith community to come together as a coalition. They would then advocate for the funding organization to approve the request for neighborhood redevelopment.

- *Coalition for human rights:* A social work student has completed a practicum in a country in which women's rights are being oppressed. She calls on her network of students interested in social justice issues to build a coalition for increasing awareness of this issue. She invites student organizations from across her campus to co-sponsor an educational and awareness-raising event outside the student center. At the event they provide information on the oppression women are experiencing in this country, sign petitions to be sent to legislators, and educate the public about the needs of the women in that region of the world.

Political and Social Action

Aimed at addressing a social injustice, **political and social action** change efforts increase political pressure on decision-making processes so that oppressed groups receive equitable services, resources, and power. Social action often involves advocating for rights on behalf of or with a group that does not have a strong voice within the decision-making process. Advocacy for policy change and development can occur at the organizational, community, governmental, and legislative levels and may involve a range of activities, from public education campaigns to confrontational meetings and public protests. Working from a systems framework enables the social worker to grasp the meaning and inadequacies of the client–system interaction and to facilitate change that will enhance the functioning of both parts of the system (Shulman, 2009). Social workers also help candidates to get elected to political office.

Social action is typically accomplished through lobbying or mobilizing (Mondros, 2009). When engaged in lobbying activities, social activists direct their resources toward the passage of legislation or election of political candidates who support political agendas that would enhance the quality of life for clients. Mobilizers focus on long-term change efforts, such as fairer treatment of students who were born in the United States to parents who are not legally residents of the country through the provision of education, public awareness, health care strategies, and improving access to health care.

When advocating to policy and decision makers, particularly legislators, an organized, evidence-based strategy is key to success. Policy makers need well-researched data presented to them by experts or persons with direct experience in that area; the data needs to be derived from credible sources, be easily accessible for them, and be timely and up to date (Borgenschneider & Corbett, 2010). Personal stories are a particularly effective strategy for gaining the attention of decision makers. See Quick Guide #9 for strategies that social workers and others can utilize when advocating with legislators.

The following are examples of political and social action change efforts:

- *Welfare reform:* In the wake of budget cuts that reduced the state's public cash assistance programs, the director of a statewide welfare rights organization puts together a coalition of welfare recipients, social service professionals, and the ministerial alliance to engage in a high-profile advocacy effort. Pooling their resources, the coalition mounts an advocacy campaign that uses social media and e-mail along with the more traditional letters, local visits, and telephone calls to legislators; educational sessions to teach effective lobbying techniques to faith groups; trips to the state capitol to lobby key legislators; and web-, radio-, and television-based public service announcements. The social worker may be involved in any of these activities directly or indirectly as a facilitator.

- *Political action:* The political action committee for NASW members (PACE— Political Action for Candidate Election) has chapters in every state. On behalf of NASW members, state chapter PACE committees endorse candidates at the local and state level, and the national PACE committee endorses candidates

---

QUICK GUIDE #9   Guidelines for Approaching Policy Makers

1. Aim to inform, not influence.
2. Separate facts from opinions.
3. Provide standards for judging the information.
4. Be fair and nonpartisan.
5. Provide private and safe locations for sharing information.

Source: Adapted from Borgenschneider & Corbett, 2010, p. 251.

at the national level. Candidates are endorsed based on their platform on issues related to the social work profession. NASW members participate in campaigns, assist with voter registration, and contribute to campaigns.

Movements for Progressive Change

The social work profession has a long and rich history of participation in and support of social movements aimed at promoting social justice, eliminating oppression and discrimination, and fostering opportunities for groups and communities that have previously been unable to access services or rights. Such movements are large-scale and impact change on the national and international level. The movement to gain the vote for women and the civil rights movement are historical examples of major initiatives within our society that have addressed the need for progressive change. Social workers may be involved in organizing and supporting social movements in their professional capacity. They may also be involved personally with social movements.

The following are examples of current social movements that are directly related to the populations served by social workers or in which social workers are involved:

- *Gay rights movements:* Beginning in the 1960s and 1970s, many in our society have been engaged in seeking rights for persons who are gay, lesbian, bisexual, and transgender so that they can live without discrimination, adopt children, and marry.

- *Immigration rights movements:* Many people across the United States have been advocating for the comprehensive reform of immigration laws and rights. Undocumented workers and low-income immigrants have limited resources and are frequently the target of discrimination and unfair labor and financial practices.

- *Occupy Movement:* The Occupy Movement began in 2011 and quickly spread across the country. Members of this movement have focused our attention on the need for reforms in the U.S. environmental, financial, and electoral practices in our country so that they benefit "the 99%" of the population who are not wealthy and powerful.

Social workers have a unique vantage point on movements, and on other models for intervention with organizational, community, and public policy issues, because of the profession's commitment to social justice, client and community well-being, and empowerment. Having a working knowledge of the multiple models of change described here enables the generalist social worker to use the most effective aspects of each for any given intervention. Exhibit 11.3 provides descriptions and examples of community-level interventions that social work students, faculty, and professionals can be involved in to make a difference.

EXHIBIT 11.3

What Students and Faculty Can Do to Influence State Policy

- Get out of your comfort zone.
- Ask your professors for advocacy and policy assignments.
- Identify an issue or problem that you want to change.
- Form a group at work or school to help you advocate.
- Contact your legislators and ask them to help you introduce a bill.
- Develop fact sheets and policy briefs.
- Identify and track a bill in the state legislature that affects your field agency.
- Enter the national contest, State Policy Plus, for a cash prize and commitment.
- Plan a social work "rally day" at the state legislature annually.
- Serve as an intern in the office of a state legislator.
- Visit state senators and representatives personally or as a class and inform them of your concerns on a particular bill.
- Organize a group to prepare testimony at a public hearing or subcommittee.
- Write letters to your state legislators.
- Track state legislation using the internet. Visit www.statepolicy.org.
- Work with your state chapter of NASW in lobbying for its legislative agenda.
- Design a research project analyzing the current impact of state welfare reform.
- Join a coalition or advocacy group and assist them in setting their agenda.
- Organize a forum or luncheon for state legislators, lobbyists, service providers, and clients on a proposed bill or policy.
- Prepare and deliver testimony before a legislative committee.
- Analyze and compare a particular policy or bill among all 50 states or internally.
- Write position papers for candidates who are campaigning for legislative office.
- Volunteer to work in a political campaign to support a candidate.
- Conduct a survey of candidates or legislators on their views about proposed bills or significant issues.
- Persevere and be very determined.

Source: Robert Schneider, Virginia Commonwealth University.

SKILLS FOR SOCIAL WORK PRACTICE WITH ORGANIZATIONS AND COMMUNITIES

Organizations and communities are made up of persons and groups; the client in organizational and community practice is a group of individuals. For example, the client system may be residents in a neighborhood or community; social service agencies seeking adequate funding; or persons that share a common diagnosis, life event or style, or need. Therefore, effective practice with organizations and communities is built on the skills learned in working with individuals, families, and groups. Just as with individual, family, and group work, social work at the organizational and community level can be practiced using the concepts of engagement, assessment, intervention, and evaluation as a method for structuring social work practice processes and activities.

As in social work practice with individuals, families, and groups, practice with organizations and communities encompasses multifaceted and varied roles. The role of the social worker is the same as it is at other levels of practice but focuses on a larger client system. At the macro level of social work practice, the social worker may function in one or more of the following ways:

- *Broker:* The social worker forms connections by building collaborations, coalitions, networks, and partnerships.

- *Enabler:* Community-level practitioners empower clients and others to participate in change by organizing and coordinating the efforts of individuals and groups committed to a common issue or concern. As many of the tasks and activities of organizational and community practice involve group meetings, social workers can use their skills to plan meetings, develop agendas, lead meetings, and facilitate good group dynamics. Also included in the enabler role is evaluation. Because funding sources increasingly require verification that funding is supporting programs that are making a positive impact, social workers are required to develop and carry out evaluations, analyze findings, and compile evaluation reports to staff, boards of directors, and funders.

- *Advocate:* Advocacy involves articulating the needs of a group to those in decision-making positions in the form that is most effective with the targeted decision makers (for example, social media, press releases, letters, lobbying, public education campaigns, demonstrations, political lobbying, and petitions). Advocates must be willing to take risks and have realistic expectations regarding success. Legislative advocacy requires an array of strategies: providing research and technical information, understanding legislators' biases, having insights into all perspectives on the issues, and presenting issues in ways that can be embraced by the legislators (Reisch, 2009).

- *Mobilizer:* Social workers may take an active role in writing grant applications and organizing fund-raising campaigns (for example, events, mailings, and telethons). This role also encompasses program development and planning. Organizational and community practice often involves establishing new programs or expanding existing ones, which means identifying the need for a program, conceptualizing and designing the program, securing funding or administrative support, overseeing program operations, and evaluating program outcomes.

- *Mediator or negotiator:* Through reflective listening, the social worker can aid opposing groups in establishing a common ground and a mutually agreed-upon resolution of the issues. In the role of mediator, the social worker serves as an unbiased party, while the role of negotiator typically involves the social worker having a preference for one side over the other.

- *Administrator:* Social work administration activities include overseeing program development and operations, budgets, fund-raising, and personnel.

These roles may come into play within each phase of the social work intervention—engagement, assessment, intervention, and termination and evaluation—at the organizational or community level.

As a BSW student, Emily completed a practicum at a multiservice community center that provides social services to the residents of an urban neighborhood. Emily had the opportunity to gain generalist social work experiences working with children in the after-school program, taking applications for the utility assistance program, and co-facilitating a job skills group with mothers in the welfare-to-work program. To provide Emily with organizational and community experiences, the field instructor invited her to participate in the Neighborhood Advisory Council. This group provided input to the staff on the needs of the community.

During Emily's first meeting with the Neighborhood Advisory Council, one of the neighborhood resident council members suggested that neighborhood children and youth needed access to an after-school tutoring program. The council voted to create an ad hoc committee to explore the development of a tutoring program. Together with Caroline, Emily's field instructor, Emily served as co-chair of the ad hoc committee. The committee began to investigate the possibility of adding tutoring to the services provided by the center.

Engagement of Organizations and Communities

The first task of Emily and Caroline, the ad hoc committee chairs, was to identify persons and organizations that would have an interest in this issue of tutoring and could provide support for launching the program. The first meeting was scheduled at the center (in the room that could house the tutoring program) with representatives from the center's Children and Youth Department, the school district's Office of Administration, the neighborhood council, and neighborhood parents.

At the beginning of the meeting, participants introduced themselves and described their personal or professional role. Caroline explained the reason for forming the ad hoc committee and the purpose of the gathering and asked each member to share her or his thoughts (or the feelings of the constituency being represented by the member) regarding the need for a tutoring program.

Although the group was generally in agreement on the concept of a tutoring program, questions were raised regarding neighborhood residents' support for a tutoring program, resources needed to mount a program, and staff or volunteers to operate the program. Emily volunteered to conduct a needs assessment and research best practices in tutoring programs and report back to the committee at the next month's meeting.

Organizational and community-level concerns or needs are often addressed in a fragmented manner. All relevant parties may not be regularly communicating with one another, and key participants may not be involved in the change process. In order to work effectively in this situation, social workers must use a systems approach and involve all those persons who can influence the change or be affected by the change.

As with group work, the first step in engaging the client system is to identify the persons and groups that can contribute to the change effort. Contributions may come in the form of knowledge, resources, influence, funding, credibility, or access to other groups or resources. Several different groups may be involved, depending on the type and goal of the organizational or community change effort. For example, a welfare rights coalition (group one) may be representing welfare recipients (group two), and front-line workers in the welfare agency may have insight into the needs of the target group (group three). A collaborative group may come together naturally, as in the case of the earlier example of refugee business owners, or may have to be formed, as in the case of the neighborhood redevelopment example.

During the engagement phase of an organizational and community change effort, all participants have the opportunity to articulate the needs, resources, contributions, and barriers to participation for themselves or the groups they represent. In addition, each participant contributes to the development of the purpose, goals, decision-making process, and allocation of resources and responsibilities.

A key to sustaining participants' investment in the change process is to ensure that each participant has a clear understanding of the tasks and activities for which she or he is responsible and ensure that the individuals are invested in the goals of the group. Each participant's contribution is affirmed and valued in the process.

The social work skills of reflective listening, interpretation of both verbal and nonverbal communications, and negotiation can contribute to the group's ability to bond around a common concern. As with social work practice at the individual, family, and group levels, the social worker practicing at the community and organizational level will use empathy and rapport-building skills to engage with individuals and groups.

Assessment of Organizations and Communities

In formulating a strengths-based assessment approach, Emily and her field instructor developed the following needs assessment plan for the ad hoc committee they had convened:

- *Clarification of purpose: The council wanted to know if there was an interest in and need for a tutoring program as well as the viability of launching and sustaining such a program.*
- *Data collection strategy: In an effort to determine neighborhood interest in and need for a tutoring program, Emily and Caroline developed a multimodal approach to collecting data. To ascertain community attitudes regarding a tutoring program, Emily and a representative from the residents' committee conducted a door-to-door survey of 50 neighborhood households using a survey developed by Emily and approved by the committee. Next, Emily contacted the local Board of Education to gather information on existing tutoring resources in the area and the process for creating a tutoring program that would build on current resources. Emily then contacted other tutoring programs and gathered information regarding development, staffing, funding, and evaluation. Additionally, she consulted the scholarly literature on tutoring programs to determine if there is a body of research-based literature to support the use of tutoring.*
- *Compilation of data: Emily compiled information from the various sources, contacted possible volunteer sources, and at the next meeting of the ad hoc tutoring committee, presented a written and verbal report highlighting the interest, assets, and potential outcomes for a neighborhood-based tutoring program.*

An essential component of developing a plan of intervention for effecting change within an organization or community is the assessment process. The first assessment activity is to identify the organization or community targeted for change. Once the targets for change have been identified, the organization is assessed to determine whether change is needed, desired, feasible, and sustainable.

Assessment of organization and community needs encompasses an array of activities, including determination of goals in order to identify the information to be gathered and the way in which the information will be used. The goal-setting phase may actually be an important aspect of the overall intervention, particularly when the members of the community are invited to contribute to identifying the issues and concerns and participating in the gathering of information (Tropman, 2008). Gaining familiarity with the target group and identifying and organizing a core group of supporters can, in fact, contribute to the change process. With any change effort, however, macro practitioners should assume the possibility of

GUIDING PRINCIPLES

1. Value participation from diverse constituencies.
2. Use multiple methods (quantitative and qualitative data).
3. Encourage civic participation and technical elements.
4. Keep the assessment realistic.
5. Value asset building.

TYPES OF INFORMATION TO COLLECT

- *Strengths and available resources:* Identify the resources and assets possessed by and available to the target group or community.
- *Organizational and community attitudes:* Collect input from the key players and others involved in the change process.
- *Barriers to change:* Determine the existence of any obstacles to change, such as attitudes, perceptions, funding, political support, space, and participation.
- *Viability of sustaining a change:* Determine the organization's or community's ability to maintain a change.
- *Assessment of similar change efforts:* Identify organizations and communities that have developed similar programs, policies, or changes. Evaluate the success or failure of those efforts and factors that led to their ending.

Source: Mulroy, 2008, pp. 385–386.

EXHIBIT 11.4

Guidelines for Conducting Organizational and Community Assessments

---

resistance, passive as well as active, and incorporate that into the assessment process (Mizrahi, 2009).

The next step is to develop and conduct an assessment. Exhibit 11.4 summarizes the principles for conducting a community-level assessment as well as some of the categories of information to seek.

Having a plan for gathering information or data is critical for organizing, analyzing, and interpreting the data. Data may be gathered by various methods: in-person, telephone, or mail surveys; focus groups; official government data; agency records on services provided; and indepth interviews with key stakeholders.

Intervention With Organizations and Communities

Using the data from Emily's needs assessment, the ad hoc committee developed the following plan:

- *Goal: Develop a plan to establish a tutoring program, building on the assets and capacities of the neighborhood residents, and implement it by the start of the next school year.*

- *Objectives: Using information gathered from the Board of Education and other tutoring programs, develop a schedule, curricular plan, budget, and staffing coverage.*
- *Present plan to the ad hoc committee and council for approval.*
- *Publicize the program to neighborhood parents and youth and school personnel.*

After receiving approval of the plan from both the ad hoc committee and the council, Emily and Caroline implemented the intervention by developing a curricular plan for tutoring and a training program for the tutors; obtained funding from the agency for supplies and refreshments; recruited volunteers to serve as tutors; advertised the program to parents, youth, and teachers; and prepared the room designated for the program. Once the program was under way, Emily served as on-site supervisor, and she and Caroline met weekly with the volunteer tutors. With permission from students' parents, Emily contacted teachers on a monthly basis to monitor student performance.

Planning and implementation for organizational and community interventions must balance multiple sets of needs, agendas, and resources. The social worker's role may be to negotiate a plan and intervention between groups whose goals and perceived obligations conflict. Having a realistic understanding of the organizations, policies, and limitations involved in accomplishing the goals can help the social worker create viable alternatives for addressing the need(s) identified during the needs assessment.

Then, helping the opposing parties to establish a common goal and to compromise on an intervention plan falls within the purview of the social worker's responsibilities to the group and draws on the skills that a generalist social worker possesses. Goal development means prioritizing the needs identified during the needs assessment process, articulating overall goals, and attending to the individual needs of constituent groups. Just as with micro- and mezzo-level interventions, a priority in establishing goals is achievability. The strategies for action contain specific objectives toward achieving the desired change. The goals, action strategies, and evaluation methods are mutually agreed upon, documented, and shared with all relevant constituencies. As members of the change effort carry out the tasks and activities designed to meet the goals, regular communication and ongoing evaluation are used to monitor progress.

Practitioners ensure that responsibility for meeting the objectives is equitably shared by all groups. Although participants may contribute different skills, resources, and influence, all participants have a clear role that contributes to the achievement of the established goal. Moreover, each objective that relates to the overall goal should be specific and measurable so that the change effort can be evaluated.

To summarize, the strategies for action contain specific objectives toward achieving the desired change. The goals, action strategies, and evaluation methods are mutually agreed upon, documented, and shared with all relevant constituencies. As members of the change effort carry out the tasks and activities designed to meet the goals, regular communication and ongoing evaluation are used to monitor progress.

Evaluation and Termination of Organization and Community Interventions

Evaluation of Emily's tutoring program began with the development of the program plans. The needs assessment yielded information to suggest that a program was needed; therefore, creating the program fulfilled that need. However, simply creating a service to meet a need does not equate to success. Maintaining regular contact with the volunteers, students' parents, and teachers provided ongoing input into issues such as student participation, parent and student satisfaction with the program, and student performance at school. Documenting the input from the involved groups enabled Emily and Caroline to report to the council that the tutoring program was meeting a neighborhood need, to recommend continuation, and to make needed adjustments to the program.

Evaluation of organizational and community interventions is an ongoing and complex process. Because many interventions are long-term change efforts that are implemented over months or years with a large and varied number of persons and groups, evaluation may need to be compartmentalized and conducted on an ongoing basis.

Evaluation strategies that are applicable for organizational and community interventions include the following:

- Review of the needs assessment and goals to determine whether identified needs and goals have been met.

- Pre- and postintervention measures to determine whether change occurred and the extent of change.

Program outcomes and continuous quality assurance can be evaluated by assessing change-related efforts such as quantity and quality of services provided, revenue generated, decreased spending, or behavior change.

Termination of organizational and community-level change may indicate either success or failure of the change effort. In the case of program development, the intervention can be terminated when the program is operational, but then a stabilization effort may be incorporated to enable the program to be sustained. In an advocacy effort, termination may occur when a policy is or is not changed, when a law is or is not passed, or when needs change. In these situations, the intervention may shift in response to the change. In other situations, termination is moot because the purpose of the intervention is to facilitate an ongoing change.

CONCLUSION

Social workers have skills that can influence large-scale changes in organizations, communities, and the society as a whole. To facilitate change at these levels, social workers use the knowledge and skills learned for working with individuals, families, and groups but apply them on a larger scale. Working at the organizational and community level, social workers have to advocate on behalf of a client, develop a new program, obtain funding, interpret data for program evaluation, or analyze the impact of a new policy on their clients.

Therefore, social workers must keep abreast of the policy issues that could affect the lives of the persons they serve. Working at the organizational and community level also often requires the social worker to have vision and patience—vision to see the possibility of large-scale change and patience to traverse the multiple and complex steps to achieve the change.

For additional information on social work practice with organizations and communities, check out the following groups and websites:

- Influencing State Policy (www.statepolicy.org) is an organization for social work students, faculty, and professionals that provides information on advocacy and current legislation. On the website, you will also find a comprehensive listing of policy-related resources.

- NASW (www.naswdc.org) provides the latest information on the association's advocacy efforts, issues, updates, and political action. See information on the NASW publication *Social Work Speaks: NASW Policy Statements, 2012–2014*, a comprehensive guide to social and political issues that affect the social work profession.

- Association for Community Organization and Social Administration (http://acosa.org) is an organization for community organizers, planning activists, administrators, policy practice specialists, students, and faculty.

- International Federation of Social Workers (http://www.ifsw.org) is a global organization striving for social justice, human rights, and social development.

- Alliance for Justice (http://www.afj.org/) is an association of organizations focused on civil rights in the areas of mental health, women, children, consumers, and the environment. This group sponsors the First Monday Campaign, an effort to raise awareness about public policy and advocacy.

- National Budget Simulation is a website that will allow you to see the impact of budget decision making on the federal budget. To learn more about the budget simulation, go to: http://www.nathannewman.org/nbs/.

MAIN POINTS

- Social work practice with organizations, communities, and public policy is defined as working toward large-scale change in a practice, policy, program, or law that affects people's lives.

- The roots of the social work profession are well grounded in practice at the macro level, as evidenced by the work of the settlement house workers, whose goal was to improve the living conditions for persons in the neighborhoods in which they worked.

- Models for facilitating change within organizations and communities include neighborhood and community organizing; functional-community organizing; community development and program development; social planning; coalition building; political and social action; and movements for progressive change. Development activities bring about change in a specific geographic or functional area; planning focuses on organizing a group of people to facilitate change that may span different groups but affect people experiencing similar life situations; the goal of a social action intervention is to organize people around a particular issue in an effort to influence decision making related to that issue.

- As at the other two levels of social work practice, skills for working with organizations and communities use the approaches of engagement, assessment, intervention, and evaluation.

- Specific social work skills needed for organizational and community practice include negotiation, fund-raising, collaboration, organization, advocacy, analysis, administration, program planning, evaluation, and supervision.

EXERCISES

1. In the Sanchez family interactive case (www.routledgesw.com), go to the Engage tab and select "Explore the Town Map."
   a. After familiarizing yourself with the community in which the Sanchez family lives, select one of the family members and identify those community resources that could be accessed by her or him to address the need(s) that you have identified for that individual. What are the assets of the community for meeting the needs that you have identified for the family?

      b. Staying with the client you selected, return to the Engage tab and complete the Critical Thinking Questions for that family member.

2. You have learned from the Sanchez family case that Hector and Celia have two children with disabilities. They have become involved in a community group that advocates for additional funding for children with disabilities. Based on the knowledge you have gained from the current chapter, strategize about ways in which this group can be successful in launching a fund-raising campaign.

3. In the Riverton interactive case (www.routledgesw.com), go to the Engage tab and select the Riverton Town Map.

      a. Using the Town Map, complete the Critical Thinking Questions.

      b. You are now familiar with the many aspects of the community system, including potential partners for developing an intervention to address the issue of the Alvadora neighborhood being used for public drinking and inappropriate disposal of refuse. Because of your professional knowledge and your personal investment, you have been asked by your agency to establish a task force to "clean up Alvadora."

          i. Identify key stakeholders to invite to join the task force who will be effective in establishing common goals for the area.

          ii. Develop a preliminary and prioritized strategy for the group.

4. Following a disaster, social workers often serve as members of a team that works to rebuild communities. Utilizing the information presented in the Hudson City interactive case (www.routledgesw.com/cases) and this chapter, select five areas of social work practice with communities and organizations and describe the roles and activities that the social worker would perform at this level of practice.

5. Being able to conduct research and evaluation is key to macro-level social work competency. Go to www.routledgesw.com and select the RAINN interactive case. Familiarize yourself with the aspects of this case and then respond to the Phase III Critical Thinking Questions.

6. Because laws impact the lives of everyone in our society, but particularly those persons served by social workers, having an awareness of legislative activity in your state is essential for effective social work practice. Select a state and explore the current legislative activities for that state by going to the internet site for Influencing State Policy at www.statepolicy.org. Click on Resources, then State Links.

    You might want to investigate current and pending legislation that can impact the client systems with whom social workers work. From within the State Link you have chosen at the website, choose All State-Local Government Servers. Select one legislative issue and prepare a 2-minute presentation on an example of that state's policy and deliver it orally in class. Provide your classmates with a one-page written version of the 2-minute presentation with enough copies for your fellow students and the instructor. (Source: R. Schneider, Virginia Commonwealth University, 2002.)

7. Advocacy is an important social work skill. In this exercise, you will have the opportunity to advocate for an issue that has been written about in a newspaper, periodical, or online publication by writing a commentary. The opinion or comments section is one of the most popular.

Identify an article from a printed or digital newspaper, periodical, or journal that describes an issue, event, or pending legislation about which you have an opposing view. Post a comment or write a letter to the editor of that publication articulating your point of view.

Editors tell us the first reason they reject commentaries or "op-eds" is because they are too balanced or only offer facts and figures. A good opinion piece is not a survey of both sides of an issue, but a strong, concise argument.

The second reason op-eds often are turned down is that writers have failed to grab the reader's attention in the first sentence. Instead they alienate the reader by delaying the point of the piece until the end.

The guidelines in Exhibit 11.5 may help you in advocating capably for your point of view and in being published.

Share your opinion, make a point, keep it clear!

- *Respond in a timely manner.* An opinion piece is usually only as hot as the news of the day.
- *Take a position.* Facts and figures are OK to back your case, but don't rely on them. Don't be afraid to offer your opinion.
- *Write a compelling first sentence.* Summarize your viewpoint and tell the readers why they should care.
- *Offer solutions.* Don't just address the problem, but discuss ways it can be fixed.
- *Write with clarity.* Keep your sentences short, simple, and to the point. Use language the average person can understand. Avoid jargon suited only to your expertise.
- *Keep it short.* Most pieces should not be more than 500–600 words.
- *Do not forget the last sentence.* Give your ending as much thought as your start. A concise summary is vital.

Source: Adapted from Saint Louis University Marketing and Communications.

EXHIBIT 11.5

Guidelines for Writing Strong Commentaries

CHAPTER 12

The Social Work Profession

Emily has been fortunate to provide a range of services to a diverse group of people in a variety of agency settings. Her social work degrees have enabled her to secure employment easily with each of her transitions. She values being part of a profession that not only embraces people with empathy and compassion but also provides her with the knowledge, skills, and values to empower others to enhance their lives. As Emily's story ends, yours begins.

As you have learned in this introductory course, social work as a profession has a long and rich history. But you might also want to know where the profession of social work is going in the future. Where will the jobs be? What will these jobs pay? What type of preparation will social workers need to be effective in the coming decades? In this final chapter, we will complete our exploration of the social work profession by considering the future trends and opportunities for the social work profession, examining the route to becoming a social worker, and, most importantly, moving toward answering the question: Is social work a career for you?

PROFESSIONAL OUTLOOK FOR SOCIAL WORKERS

> *Social work does not exist in a vacuum. As much as any profession, social work activity is woven into the very fabric of society. Social work acts and reacts to that which transpires in society.*
> (Allen-Meares & DeRoos, 1997, p. 384)

As we consider social work practice into the mid-21st century, the future looks bright for the profession. Employment opportunities continue to expand, compensation for social workers is increasing, and society recognizes the valuable contributions that social workers can and do make to the well-being of people they serve. As the social work profession is well into its second century, the profession will continue to be viewed as a major service profession and, as noted in the opening quotation, remain an integral part of society.

Social work will continue to be a profession that emphasizes diversity and will be involved in public controversy, because social workers are often involved in sensitive and highly publicized social issues.

Employment Trends and Opportunities

The future appears extremely promising for social workers. Increases in diversity of all kinds—ethnic, cultural, age, and family structure—will continue to provide expanded opportunities. Projections suggest that social work will have a distinctive focus on the concerns of women, children, older adults, immigrant populations, and military veterans and their families as these continue to be the persons in our society who are most vulnerable and are most at risk of negative outcomes (U.S. Department of Labor, Bureau of Labor Statistics (BLS), 2012b).

Increases in social work opportunities are expected in all the practice areas in which social workers may be employed: social and community service managers (up 27%), mental health counselors and marriage and family therapists (up 37%), and probation officers and correctional treatment specialists (up 18%) (BLS, 2012c). The BLS projections of the fastest-growing occupations for 2010–2020 includes marriage and family therapists (BLS, 2012c). For social workers interested in working in the area of advocacy, grant writing, and civic organizations, a 14% increase in employment is expected by 2016 (BLS, 2008). Employment prospects are expected to be most competitive in urban areas, but social work positions in rural communities will continue to provide significant opportunities for social workers, in general, and BSWs, in particular (BLS, 2012c).

Social workers in the United States already number approximately 650,000. This number is expected to reach 811,700 by 2020, an overall growth rate of 25%, or approximately 16–34% depending on area of practice (BLS, 2012). That is nearly twice the average growth rate (14%) for all careers. Areas of growth for social workers include aging, health care, substance abuse treatment, school social work, and mental health services (BLS, 2012c).

The popular press has proclaimed social work along with other social and public service-related opportunities to be one of the careers on the rise. Here is a sampling of these reports:

- U.S. News and World Report ranks social work as one of the 25 best jobs of 2012 (Graves, 2012).

- The *Wall Street Journal*'s on-line Career Journal lists social work as #51 on the list of "Top 200 Jobs of 2012," based on positive employment growth, positive work environments, and lower levels of stress and physical demands when compared with other occupations (*Wall Street Journal*, 2012).

- Social workers will be needed as members of teams to serve the baby boomer generation as they age, in long-term care facilities, hospices, and substance abuse treatment programs (Worldwidelearn.com, 2009).

- Mental health and substance abuse social workers are included on the list of Hottest Careers for College Graduates through 2018, with 61,000 jobs expected to be available (Collegeboard.com, 2012).

In addition to increasing opportunities for social work services involving older adults, substance abuse, and mental health, other settings expected to experience growth and employ larger numbers of social workers in the second decade of the 21st century include agencies that provide services in child protection, foster care, adoption, disabilities, human trafficking, veterans services, and homeless services. Social work employment opportunities in the criminal justice system, particularly with adolescents, will continue to grow, as will social work positions within elementary and secondary school systems. Private practice (in which self-employed clinical social workers provide individual, family, and group treatment) will be another growth area for social workers with MSWs.

The funding crises that have plagued the social work profession for much of its history will continue to dictate the growth that is realized in these settings. The need for social workers will remain constant, however. Our legislators and funding sources will determine whether the resources required to meet the need will be present as well, making advocacy efforts critical as an area of social work focus.

Areas of Practice The provision of services to families, children, and youth is expected to remain the primary area of practice for social workers, as evidenced by the fact that students enrolled in social work programs identify these populations as the largest area of concentration followed by mental health (Council on Social Work Education (CSWE), 2011). Approximately 30% of MSW students and over one-third of social work practitioners report their primary area of practice as mental health (Whitaker & Arrington, 2008).

As a result of increasing pressure on physicians to prevent or maintain shorter hospitalizations, patients are being returned to their homes with greater needs for in-home health services. Social workers serve as key members of the inter-professional team of health professionals that work with older adults and their families to provide home- and community-based care. Funding has been made available to social work educators in recent years to provide students with knowledge, skills, and values so they may work effectively with older adults and their families regardless of the area in which they specialize.

With the privatization of many social service systems, a number of social workers are expected to leave the public and nonprofit sectors to work in for-profit organizations. Privatizing social services shifts administrative responsibility for delivery to a privately owned company that contracts with governmental agencies and private insurance companies. These contract agencies then provide the services at a lower cost, as there are typically fewer bureaucratic requirements.

Salaries   Almost all students want to know the salaries they can expect when they choose social work as a career. Although it is common knowledge that social work salaries, like many other human service-related careers, have historically lagged behind other professions, the salaries for social workers are improving. In recent years, the profession as a whole has united to campaign for higher salaries and better overall compensation and has realized some success in this area. The statistics presented here are broad-based, nationwide salary ranges that differ considerably by region, field of service, educational level, and experience, but they serve as a useful reference point.

The U.S. Department of Labor reports that median annual salaries for all social workers in 2010 ranged from the mid-$30,000s to mid-$50,000s. Specifically, the median annual salary for social workers employed in child, family, and school settings was $40,210; in medical and public health setting, $47,230; and in mental health and substance abuse treatment services, $38,600. Exhibit 12.1 lists salaries for several categories, as well as the distribution of salaries in 2009 for social workers employed in full-time positions.

In examining the differences between the salaries of social workers, several factors impact earning potential, including gender, workload, employment sector, years of experience, licensure status, and geographic location. Those social workers who typically earn higher salaries are male, do not carry a client caseload in an agency setting, are private practitioners providing mental health services, and are more experienced social workers (National Association of Social Workers (NASW), 2007). For those social workers in the United States who possess a professional credential (e.g., license or certification), the annual incomes are typically higher by $5,000–8,000/year than those of social workers who do not obtain licensure or certification. Geographic location influences the annual salaries of social workers as well. Social workers working in the Pacific region earn the highest salaries, while those in the South Atlantic area earn the lowest salaries (NASW/CWS, 2010). Educational attainment is a factor as well: a 2009 study of social work compensation and benefits reported the median annual earnings for social workers at the BSW level is $40,000, MSW level is $55,000, and doctoral level is $72,000 (NASW/CWS, 2010). Of note, social workers with undergraduate and graduate degrees are among those graduates with the lowest levels of unemployment. The unemployment rate for recent BSW graduates is 6.6%, while MSW graduates experience only 2.9% unemployment (Carnevale, Cheah, & Strohl, 2011).

Overall, social work salaries are comparable to those of other helping professions (e.g., elementary and secondary teachers, school counselors, clergy, counselors, and nurses). BSW salaries are on par with nonsocial work counselors in substance abuse and mental health, while MSWs earn salaries comparable to teachers, librarians, nurses, and school counselors (CHWS/CWS, 2006).

EXHIBIT 12.1

Social Work Salaries

Salaries by specialization:

- Child, Family, and School Services
  - $35,120/year (individual and family services)
  - $39,750/year (state government)
  - $47,130/year (local government)
  - $54,260/year (elementary and secondary schools)

- Medical and Public Health Care Services
  - $39,310/year (individual and family services)
  - $41,860/year (nursing and personal care facilities)
  - $44,810/year (local government)
  - $48,530/year (home health care services)
  - $53,400/year (hospitals)

- Mental Health and Substance Abuse Treatment Services
  - $36,740/year (individual and family services)
  - $36,780/year (outpatient mental health and substance abuse centers)
  - $45,210/year (local government)
  - $47,710/year (psychiatric and substance abuse hospitals)
  - $48,010/year (hospitals)

Source: U.S. Department of Labor, Bureau of Labor Statistics, 2012b.

Salaries for Social Workers Employed in Full-Time Positions:

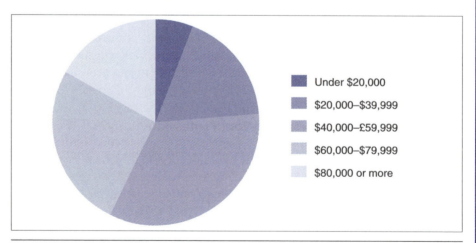

Legend:
- Under $20,000
- $20,000–$39,999
- $40,000–£59,999
- $60,000–$79,999
- $80,000 or more

Source: National Association of Social Workers Center for Workforce Studies.

Two possible explanations have been offered for these lower salaries:

- *Gender*: Social work will continue to be somewhat unique among major professions, as its members are predominantly women (85% of the total), and women increasingly hold many of the leadership positions. Professions that are made up largely of women (for example, nursing and education) routinely receive lower levels of compensation.

- *Economic sector*: Social workers are typically employed in organizations that may struggle for financial stability, thus paying lower salaries. As many social workers feel drawn to the profession out of a commitment to working in services for and with the disenfranchised, social workers are undervalued by dominant society in the area of compensation.

Although these explanations may be a valid commentary on salaries in the social work profession, they can also serve as a call to social workers to engage in more aggressive advocacy for the profession.

Social workers provide valuable, much-needed services to a large segment of our population and therefore deserve recognition and compensation for the work they do. Social workers routinely focus professional advocacy efforts on behalf of client systems, but to maintain high-quality education and training opportunities social workers also need to advocate for salaries that recognize the valuable services provided. To learn more about median salaries across the country, check out the NASW Center for Workforce Studies Salary Calculator at http://workforce.social workers.org/calc.asp.

Despite these challenges, 90% of social workers surveyed report feeling they are helping their clients to improve their quality of life; more than two-thirds view their salaries as "adequate" to "very adequate"; and the same number perceive they are respected and supported in their work setting (CHWS/CWS, 2006).

Societal Perceptions of the Social Work Profession

Social work is a profession that is visible and valued within our society. Social workers are employed in an increasingly wide-ranging number and type of settings and are being sought to fill needs in the social service delivery system.

In addition to the traditional settings that have been described throughout this book, social workers are entering the political arena. Over 170 social workers have been elected in recent years to political office at the local, state, and national levels. For a listing of social workers in elected office and information on getting involved, visit the NASW Political Action for Candidate Election (PACE) website at http://socialworkers.org/pace. Social workers are also being called on to use their knowledge and skills to develop state and national policy. State government officials also recognize the need to increase the number of social workers.

Social workers must continue to advocate for the profession by educating the public regarding the role that they play in society. They do this by taking every opportunity to represent the profession favorably in the public eye. For instance, they write letters, make telephone calls, send e-mail messages, blog, and twitter when social workers are negatively portrayed in the news, on television, and in the movies. They can ensure that when the media highlight social workers, they are identified as degreed social workers. Conversely, when a person who does not possess a social work degree is identified in the media as a social worker, professional social workers challenge that label and provide clarification that only those persons who have been awarded social work degrees from CSWE-accredited programs are social workers.

PROFESSIONAL SOCIALIZATION

Developing the competencies, knowledge, skills, and values needed for social work practice is only one aspect of becoming a social work professional. Along with learning the theories and methods of practice, becoming a social work professional involves being socialized into the profession.

Professional socialization involves becoming acquainted with the values, norms, and culture of the profession, establishing a professional identity, identifying with the social work profession, feeling comfortable with that self-identity, and understanding the role of social work within the community and society. Being a social worker becomes part of who you are.

You have begun your socialization process by gaining an overview of the profession; experiencing social work through class discussions and exercises; possibly volunteering or working in a social service agency; and hopefully, interacting with other social work students and social work practitioners. In the following sections, we explore the next steps in the professional socialization process.

Social Work Education: Pursuing a Degree

Do you see yourself as a social worker? Twenty-two percent of social workers knew before they started college that they wanted to join the profession. For others, the feeling of connection comes later in other courses or their field experience: 45% identified their goals during college and 33% after college (Whitaker, 2008).

Professional identification begins with introspection and soul searching. Essentially, you are asking yourself, "Is social work the right career for me?" "Do I see myself working in those settings that I have been learning about and doing the work I have been reading about and seeing?" The decision to become a social worker lies solely in your hands.

As you learned in the first chapter of this book, to become a social worker requires a bachelor's or master's degree in social work awarded by a college or university accredited by the CSWE. In 2012, there were 697 social work programs accredited by the CSWE—218 MSW and 479 BSW programs. An additional 15 MSW and 24 BSW programs were awaiting word on their accreditation (CSWE, 2012). In 2010, 19,673 MSW degrees were awarded and 13,836 BSWs degrees were granted (CSWE, 2011). In both degree areas, the overwhelming majority of graduates are female (87–89%) and approximately one-third of new social workers are members of an underrepresented ethnic or racial group (CSWE, 2011).

A competency-based social work education at the baccalaureate level is grounded in liberal arts studies and prepares graduates for generalist practice. At the master's level, practitioners are trained for advanced practice in a specific area of concentration.

Due to anticipated retirements of social workers and the growing need for services for a number of populations—older adults and children, in particular—the number of practicing social workers is not expected to meet the needs of our society. Societal changes that heighten the need for competently trained social workers include but are not limited to the impact that the Affordable Care Act is intended to have (pending the Supreme Court ruling), the emphasis on reducing the number of children living in out-of-home care arrangements, the need for bridging the health and mental health care service areas, demand for increased interprofessional service delivery teams, and the need for more social workers able to work in the military/ veteran and business sectors (Social Work Policy Institute, 2011).

Bachelor of Social Work   Social work courses at the BSW level focus on preparing generalist social work practitioners. A brief description of the social work curriculum appears in Exhibit 12.2. As was briefly noted in Chapter 1, the CSWE *Educational Policy and Accreditation Standards* (2008) provide competency-based guidelines for BSW and MSW social work curricula, which are summarized in the exhibit, but individual social work programs determine the best model for delivering course-work in their own environment.

Although programs vary considerably, courses typically taken by social work majors at the bachelor's level include English, communications, human biology, history, mathematics and/or statistics, political science and/or economics, fine arts, sociology and/or anthropology, foreign language, psychology, and philosophy. Each of these areas of study is key to becoming an articulate, effective social worker who has a broad base of knowledge about people, culture, and society. The competent social worker understands the way in which the human body and mind function, the role of culture in our society, the impact of the economy and the political system on the lives of the people that social workers serve, and the use of statistical analysis for the purposes of funding and evaluation. The arts and humanities courses that social work students take provide an understanding of the motivations of human beings.

In addition to the general liberal arts courses and required social work courses, social work students complete elective coursework in individual areas of interest. Most BSW programs offer electives, but students can also choose to take their elective coursework in other departments to round out their knowledge base. Using our

EXHIBIT 12.2

Council on Social Work Education (CSWE) Guidelines for a Competency-Based Social Work Curriculum

Core Competencies

Competency-based education is focused on student learning outcomes that are measurable and relevant to the social work foundations of knowledge, values, and skills in the practice areas of individuals, families, groups, organizations, communities, and public policy.

- *Identify as a professional social worker and conduct oneself accordingly*—social workers are committed to: (1) advocating for client access to the services of social work; (2) practicing personal reflection and self-correction to assure continual professional development; (3) attending to professional roles and boundaries; (4) demonstrating professional demeanor in behavior, appearance, and communication; (5) engaging in career-long learning; and (6) using supervision and consultation.
- *Apply social work ethical principles to guide professional practice*—social workers have knowledge about the profession's value base, ethical standards, and relevant laws.
- *Apply critical thinking to inform and communicate professional judgments*—social workers have knowledge of principles of logic, scientific inquiry, and reasoned discernment and use critical thinking along with creativity and curiosity.
- *Engage diversity and difference in practice*—social workers understand diversity and its impact on the human experience. Diversity encompasses age, class, color, culture, disability, ethnicity, gender, gender identity and expression, immigration status, political ideology, race, religion, sex, and sexual orientation.
- *Advance human rights and social and economic justice*—social workers are committed to the belief that all persons have basic human rights including freedom, safety, privacy, adequate standard of living, health care, and education.
- *Engage in research-informed practice and practice-informed research*—social workers use practice experiences to inform research and research to inform practice, policy, and delivery of services.
- *Apply knowledge of human behavior and the social environment*—understanding human behavior across the lifespan and the systems in which people live is essential for social work practice.
- *Engage in policy practice to advance social and economic well-being and to deliver effective social work services*—social workers are prepared to understand the history and structure of policies that impact client systems and engage in policy practice.
- *Respond to contexts that shape practice*—in order to respond to the evolving and dynamic nature of society and social work practice, social workers must be informed about current issues, events, and service delivery methods.
- *Engage, assess, intervene, and evaluate with individuals, families, groups, organizations, and communities*—social workers have the knowledge and skills to practice at multiple levels and with a range of populations. Practice in any context includes engagement, assessment, intervention, and evaluation.

Field Education

Field education, the signature pedagogy, is the integration of theory and practice that occurs when the student is able to apply the knowledge and skills learned in the classroom in an agency-based social service setting. Under the supervision of social work practitioners, students gain experience in engaging, assessing, intervening in, and evaluating client systems that include individuals, families, groups, organizations, and communities.

Source: Adapted from CSWE, 2008.

past to look into the future, you can seek out elective coursework, readings, projects, and experiences to enable you to approach your social work career armed with a broad-based repertoire of skills. There are a variety of areas you may want to cultivate during your social work training, some of which are listed in Exhibit 12.3.

An increasing number of BSW students are finding it helpful to complete a second major or minors, certificates, and/or specializations to prepare them better for the challenging world of social work practice.

For social workers to maintain knowledge and skills that are relevant for contemporary society, they require regular, ongoing education. Areas for

EXHIBIT 12.3

Useful Electives for BSW Students

- *Critical thinking.* This skill, which is essential for effective social work practice, comes from a broad understanding of the liberal arts. Reading and writing on complex issues help to hone critical thinking skills.
- *Social sciences.* Coursework in areas such as economics and domestic and global political environments can enhance your ability to understand the various societal systems and advocate for your clients' and profession's needs.
- *Legal studies.* Having an understanding of the legal system can be invaluable to a practicing social worker. Most fields of social work practice intersect at some point with the legal system. Client systems may encounter the legal system as a victim of crime or as the accused, when they need guardianship, have end-of-life decisions that require legal intervention, or need legal help with immigration concerns.
- *Gerontology.* Knowledge of aging and effective practice methods for working with older adults and their families will be essential for social work practice in the coming decades as the baby boomers become older adults (CSWE/SAGE-SW, 2001).
- *Community systems and dynamics.* Knowledge of communities is needed, particularly for assessment and intervention at the community level.
- *Leadership.* Social workers need leadership skills to be at the forefront of policy development instead of reacting to established policies.
- *Communication skills.* Public speaking, working with the media, and providing testimony are essential skills for those who want to be effective advocates for the social worker's constituencies.
- *Applied research skills.* Social workers who intend to conduct agency- or community-based research need the ability to conduct needs assessments and to develop and evaluate programs with measurable outcomes.
- *Evidence-based practice.* In order to choose the most effective intervention approaches, a social worker needs a thorough knowledge of how effective those approaches have proved to be, based on well-designed research.
- *International studies.* Whether a social work student gains proficiency in a second or third language, experiences a study-abroad semester or course, or completes a practicum focused on an international population, becoming skilled in working with diverse populations and cultures is essential.

intervention and employment opportunities are extremely varied and constantly in a state of change.

Master of Social Work   At the graduate level, coursework is delineated into two levels: foundation and concentration. The foundation coursework, comparable to the generalist courses completed as part of the BSW, consists of social work practice with individuals, families, groups, organizations, communities, and public policy; human behavior and the social environment; social policy; research methods; and the field experience. Also typically infused and integrated throughout the foundation coursework are understanding and respect for social work values and ethics, diversity, populations at risk, and social and economic justice.

Following the successful completion of the foundation coursework, students select an area of concentration. Each social work program establishes its own areas of specialized study, but the curriculum typically includes advanced coursework in the areas introduced at the foundation level: practice, human behavior, policy, research, and field experiences. Although concentration areas in MSW programs are wide-ranging, areas of specialization you are likely to find include children, youth, and family practice; mental and physical health practice; gerontology; administration; community and policy practice; and social and economic development. Emerging areas of practice that may be offered include services to the military and veteran communities, international services, and services to immigrants and refugees.

Many schools offer **advanced standing** into MSW programs to students who have graduated from a CSWE-accredited BSW program. Their coursework may be applied to part or all of the foundation coursework, thus decreasing the total number of credits required for completion of the MSW degree. With advanced standing, students may complete their master's degree in a shorter period of time or take more elective coursework in areas of interest.

Additional options for completing both the BSW and MSW degrees are the 5-year and "bridge" programs offered at some institutions. The 5-year program typically requires the student to complete a joint BSW and MSW degree within a structured 5-year plan. A bridge program typically enables the student to complete 3 years in another major or institution and begin MSW coursework during the senior year of the undergraduate experience.

Current Issues Influencing Social Work Training for the Future

Because social work is a profession that responds to the personal and societal needs and concerns of the times, social work knowledge and education must also reflect current societal changes and needs. For example, in recent years, a struggling economy has created personal financial challenges for a broader array of people, including many who previously were financially stable. As one social worker notes: "Times like this push people to re-examine their core values, those core values of caring for each other. Those values fit very well with the core values of social work"

(Smith, 2009). As we progress through the 21st century, some new opportunities are emerging for social workers.

Some of those opportunities were identified during the historic 2005 Social Work Congress, which was convened to establish the profession's agenda for the next decade (Clark et al., 2006). Building on that congress, over 400 social workers gathered for the 2010 Social Work Congress. They examined the "internal challenges facing the social work profession with a special focus on transferring leadership from established leaders to emerging leaders" (NASW, 2010, p. 1). Of those attending, 30 participants were emerging leaders under the age of 30 years. From that gathering, 10 imperatives for the next decade were established (NASW, 2010), as shown in Exhibit 12.4.

EXHIBIT 12.4

Social Work Imperatives for the Next Decade

Business of Social Work

1. Infuse models of sustainable business and management practice in social work education and practice.

Common Objectives

2. Strengthen collaboration across social work organizations, their leaders, and their members for shared advocacy goals.

Education

3. Clarify and articulate the unique skills, scope of practice, and value added of social work to prospective social work students.

Influence

4. Build a data-driven business case that demonstrates the distinctive expertise and the impact and value of social work to industry, policy makers, and the general public.

5. Strengthen the ability of national social work organizations to identify and clearly articulate, with a unified voice, issues of importance to the profession.

Leadership Development

6. Integrate leadership training in social work curricula at all levels.

Recruitment

7. Empirically demonstrate to prospective recruits the value of the social work profession in both social and economic terms.

Retention

8. Ensure the stability of the profession through a strong mentoring program, career ladder, and succession program.

9. Increase the number of grants, scholarships, and debt forgiveness mechanisms for social work students and graduates.

Technology

10. Integrate technologies that serve social work practice and education in an ethical, practical, and responsible manner.

Adopted at 2010 Social Work Congress, April 23, 2010.

Source: NASW, 2010.

Throughout this book, a number of the issues addressed in the imperatives have been highlighted. Following is a discussion of the issues and opportunities related to a selected sample of the needs and issues that will impact the social work profession.

Health Care Social Work Practice   Social work is becoming more integrated within the health and mental health care delivery system. Therefore, social workers need to understand the biopsychosocial and spiritual dynamics that impact people's lives. Among the ways that the social work profession is being affected by health care issues are these:

- As our population grows more diverse, social workers are needed to help individuals and families who may have limited exposure to the health care system to gain access to health care services and resources (Whitaker, Weismiller, Clark, & Wilson, 2006).

- Care coordination among providers was a centerpiece of the 2010 health care reform legislation. New opportunities for social workers include patient-centered medical homes (multipurpose medical facilities), accountable care organizations (evidence-based health care collaborations), and guided care (patient-centered care for those with chronic conditions) (Fink-Samnick, 2011).

- As the population ages and social workers become more involved in older adult and end-of-life issues, they will need greater understanding of developments in prolonging life, psychopharmacology, and genetic counseling. Knowledge of biochemistry, neuroscience, and genetics will be a marketable asset.

- Social workers already play a significant role in the provision of interprofessional physical and mental health and social services to persons across the spectrum of the service delivery system. To prepare for practice in an interprofessional setting, social workers need skills in teamwork, contracting, group process, leadership, and conflict resolution (Abramson, 2009).

Gerontological Social Work Practice   The baby boomer generation (those persons born between 1946 and 1964), as the largest generational cohort in our history, has already changed our society in significant ways. Not surprisingly, their entrance into older adulthood is changing the face of aging considerably. Compared with previous generations, as they age they will be healthier, more technologically sophisticated, and better-informed consumers; will work longer; and will require more focused, specialized services and care.

To meet the needs of this population, more social workers with specialized expertise in aging are needed. Opportunities have begun to emerge and will continue to increase in a variety of practice areas, including these:

- While social workers are already on the forefront of gerontological services, they will be needed to take on larger roles as part of interprofessional teams in all geographic areas, but especially in nonurban communities (Whitaker, Weismiller, & Clark, 2006b).

- Social workers will be needed particularly in the areas of mental and physical health services.

- To serve the older adults who require alternative living arrangements in retirement, social workers will be needed in residential care facilities, to include assisted living, skilled care, and hospice.

- With improvements in medical care and access, older adults of all racial, ethnic, and cultural groups are living longer. Social workers are needed to work with healthy, productive older adults in direct practice, administrative, and policy areas.

- Baccalaureate social workers will be in high demand for their skills to work effectively in direct practice and advocacy roles with older adults who are caregivers and older adults who require the assistance of a caregiver (Williams & Joyner, 2008).

Child Welfare Services   The professionalization of child welfare services is at a critical point in the United States. Historically, due to large caseloads and inadequate salaries, child welfare agencies in nearly every state have faced challenges in attracting competent and appropriately trained professionals to work in the area of child welfare (Whitaker, Weismiller, & Clark, 2006a). In addition, the national turnover rate is as high as 90% annually in some regions (U.S. Department of Health and Human Services, n.d.). High turnover results in less effective and inconsistent services for children and families. Although turnover rates are considerably less for degreed social workers who work in child welfare, there are not enough licensed social workers to provide the range of services for children and families. Thus many states do not require a social work degree for these positions.

It is quite apparent that more social workers, at both the BSW and MSW level, are needed to work in child welfare services. Employment opportunities for social workers who want to work with children are expected to grow by 58,200 (20%) jobs by 2020 (BLS, 2012b).

Opportunities in this field of practice include the following:

- Qualified and competent social workers are needed to provide services for children who are born into poverty (one in every five), are abused or neglected (one every 47 seconds), or are being reared by grandparents (2.6 million) (Children's Defense Fund, 2012).

- Career possibilities for generalist, baccalaureate social workers in the area of child welfare include micro, mezzo, and macro opportunities. For instance, social workers' skills at all levels can be utilized in public or private agencies in child protective services, family preservation, and foster care. An emerging area of focus for social work practice includes transitional and independent living for older adolescents, particularly those "aging out" of the foster care system.

- Student loan forgiveness programs have been offered to encourage the development of skilled workers in certain professions. Your state may have loan forgiveness for social work practitioners in areas such as children and family, health and mental health care, or school social work. To inquire about these opportunities, check with your NASW state chapter or your state's department of professional licensing. Information on loan forgiveness programs may also be available at the federal level and your college or university's student financial services office. For a sampling of some additional resources, see Exhibit 12.5.

Technology and Social Work Social workers must have increasing levels of sophistication in the use of information technologies—for providing services, keeping records, analyzing data for funding and program evaluation, communicating, and participating in distance education. Information technology has enabled social workers to conduct online therapy and support groups, facilitate discussion/chat rooms for clients interested in similar issues, provide long-distance social work education and training, maintain up-to-date knowledge of legislation and policies, and reach numerous policy makers in a matter of seconds around the world. In short, technology has enhanced social workers' abilities to reach more people more often in less time.

However, we must use technology in an ethical and responsible manner. Social workers are ethically obligated to ensure integrity at all times when using technology.

EXHIBIT 12.5

Some Sources of Information About Student Loan Forgiveness Programs

- NASW: www.socialworkers.org/loanforgiveness/default.asp
- National Health Service Corp: nhsc.hrsa.gov/loanrepayment/
- U.S. Department of Education's Income Contingent Repayment (ICR) Program: www.ed.gov
- U.S. Department of Education: studentaid.ed.gov/PORTALSWebApp/students/english/PSF.jsp
- Smart Student Guide to Financial Aid: www.finaid.org/
- Income Contingent Repayment: www.finaid.org/loans/icr.phtml
- Volunteer organizations: www.finaid.org/scholarships/service.phtml
- Military: www.finaid.org/military/
- Income-Based Repayment and Public Service Loan Forgiveness: www.ibrinfo.org/

For example, confidentiality is essential when communicating with or about client systems via a cell phone, e-mail, and text messaging. Websites should be checked to ensure they are credible and secure sources of information. Social networking sites (Facebook, LinkedIn, and micro-blogging) present the profession with both opportunity and risk. While these forms of communication enable increased access for both clients and providers, the ethical obligation for privacy may be virtually impossible to maintain, making informed consent critical (Sfiligoj, 2009).

In an effort to ensure that social workers and client systems have access to and use technology appropriately and ethically, the NASW and the Association of Social Work Boards developed Standards for Technology and Social Work Practice (2005). The standards encompass technology-related issues such as competent, appropriate, legal, and ethical use of technology; accurate representation of self when using electronic communication technologies; strict adherence to privacy of communication; advocacy for community access to helpful technology; and understanding of the dynamics of electronic communications.

Examples of knowledge, skills, and opportunities related to technology include the following:

- Technological enhancements enable social workers to conduct groups and meetings in a virtual environment through telephone/video/web conferencing and internet groups (e.g., chat rooms, bulletin boards, e-mail, and listservs). Social workers must be aware of group dynamics in the absence, in some cases, of verbal and nonverbal communications (Toseland & Horton, 2008).

- Just as traditional records are subject to scrutiny, electronic records (including e-mails, text messages, and online postings) may be used in legal proceedings and insurance determinations. Therefore, social workers must be sensitive to the information included in these forms of communication.

- Opportunities for technological social work interventions exist in the areas of online support, advocacy, fund-raising, education, policy development, innovative services, and one-on-one support available for crises (Smith, 2009).

- When facilitating an online support group (OSG), for example, the social worker must develop a unique skill set in order to foster group interaction without the face-to-face contact (Perron & Powell, 2009).

Disaster Response and Crisis Intervention   Disaster is defined as an extraordinary natural or human-made event that can bring harm to property and human life. Social workers are increasingly on the scene in times of disaster and crisis to provide support and mental health services. For example, approximately 50% of the volunteers trained by the American Red Cross to provide mental health services in emergency and disaster situations are professional social workers (Dale, 2011).

Social workers' knowledge and skills in crisis intervention make them valuable assets for working with persons traumatized by a disaster or crisis. More social workers are learning to intervene in cases of "disaster syndrome," which is a term coined to describe the phases experienced by a disaster or crisis survivor (preimpact, impact, postimpact, and disillusionment or long-term impact) (Barker, 2003). A specialized skill set is needed as well: knowledge of stress and coping responses; ability to individualize an intervention to the situation and the phase of recovery with sensitivity and in the context of the circumstances; and ability to support other disaster responders (NASW, 2012–2014c).

Here are some examples of disaster and crisis situations in which social workers become involved:

- Social workers have been prominently represented in the aftermath of such natural disasters as the swarm of deadly tornadoes during the 2011 season and Hurricane Katrina. They have contributed to the profession's knowledge and skill base regarding disaster and crisis response. Critical skills needed in working with survivors include listening, anticipating and normalizing reactions and recovery, recognizing resilience, and building on strengths (McPartlin, 2006).

- Social workers are needed to work with members of the military involved in deployments and combat and with their families. Social workers have accompanied troops in virtually every deployment in recent times and are working with the families on the home front before, during, and after the deployment.

- Social workers working in crisis and disaster response must be vigilant about attending to their own self-care. Crisis and disaster work can be intense and emotionally challenging for the responders. As helping professionals, social workers recognize the obligation to care for self to avoid burnout, also known as compassion fatigue. Strategies include maintaining healthy lifestyle habits (e.g., exercise, nutrition, and sleep), finding time for relaxation, seeking supportive supervision, continuing education regarding disaster responses, and practicing spirituality or meditation (Arrington, 2008; Wharton, 2008).

International Social Work and Multilingualism   With increased focus on international and global issues, social workers will continue to play a larger role both domestically and internationally. Social work employment opportunities will continue to grow within the United States in virtually every area of the social service delivery system, particularly in community-based social service agencies, health care facilities, and schools that serve immigrant and refugee populations. Internationally, social workers have established a presence within the nongovernmental organizational (NGO) community, with 95% of program director and co-ordinator positions in 20 NGOs held by degreed social workers (Claiborne, 2004).

As the U.S. population becomes increasingly diverse, having written and oral proficiency in more than one language enables a social worker to communicate more effectively with and advocate for clients. When we think about being bilingual in the United States today, Spanish is typically the first language that comes to mind. However, there is a need for social workers who are fluent in other languages as well, including but not limited to Russian, Bosnian, Chinese, Korean, and American Sign Language.

These are some of the opportunities emerging in the area of international and multicultural social work:

- If you are considering a career in the international arena, having certain experiences are key. Therefore, it is helpful to develop internationally focused knowledge and skills through coursework, volunteer/service or paid internships abroad or in immigrant communities, and personal cultural experiences (McLaughlin, 2007).

- Multilanguage fluency and community organization, fund-raising, and clinical skills are useful in this arena (McLaughlin, 2007).

- Opportunities continue to grow for social workers to assume leadership and administrative roles in international organizations located both in the United States and abroad.

- Maintaining awareness of global issues is critical regardless of the setting in which you practice social work. You are obligated to be aware of international and global issues, because today they impact every facet of our society and our practice.

Your Career in Social Work

With these insights into some of the societal and social work practice challenges and opportunities that are on the horizon for social workers, let us end the journey by turning our attention to your socialization as a social work professional within this context. Exhibit 12.6 provides an array of possible activities that will help you identify further with the social work profession.

Although formalized education is an essential part of your professional socialization as a social worker, many informal aspects of your educational experience are equally important for your professional development. Key to your success in determining whether the social work profession is for you is gaining experience. Volunteer and service-related activities are valuable opportunities for developing insights into the world of social work. Working as a volunteer in a social service setting can also provide you with access to social workers who can share with you the rewards and realities of being a social worker.

Network

- Through social work organizations, get acquainted with other social workers who have interests similar to your own.
- Join a social work listserv or chat room for the opportunity to converse with other social work students and faculty.
- See if your school has a student social work association or student/faculty special-interest groups (for example, social workers interested in working with older adults or a group for students that are gay, lesbian, bisexual, or transgender).
- If you join a group, get involved! There is no better way to get connected than to serve in a leadership position.

Join NASW

- Join as a student member at a discounted rate. You will get a transitional membership rate following graduation.
- Take advantage of member benefits: a monthly newspaper, *NASW News*; the journal, *Social Work*; and your local-chapter newsletter.
- Join one of the Specialty Practice Sections (a member benefit), including aging; alcohol, tobacco, and other drugs; child welfare; health; mental health; poverty and social justice; private practice; and school social work.
- Take advantage of membership in one of the Specialty Practice Sections: online forums for section members and two newsletters per year, with information on the trends, specific activities, and practice updates of interest to members of that section.
- Run for a position as student representative for your NASW chapter or the national organization.
- Check the NASW website (www.naswdc.org) for a wealth of information on the profession. For example, check out 50 Ways to Use your Social Work Degree at http://50ways.socialworkblog.org/ to read the stories of 50 practitioners, view a video on the profession, learn surprising facts about social work, and even calculate your future salary.

Get More Experience

- Continue volunteering at the site where you received community service experience for this introductory course.
- Gain a different experience by volunteering at another organization.
- Seek paid employment at an agency. Many social service organizations have part- or full-time positions for students seeking to gain social service experience.

One group of graduating BSW students shared their wisdom for optimizing your professionalization during your time as a social work student (Clewes, 2001):

- Be prepared to grow and change by being open-minded and having your values and beliefs challenged, but do not plan to change anyone but yourself.

- Maximize your learning opportunities by challenging yourself and recognizing that every person that comes into your life can teach you something. Venture into areas of learning that are new for you.

- Ask for help when you need it, and see mistakes as opportunities for learning.

- Be prepared for your social work program to change you and provide you with the tools to go out and continue this change.

Your social work training will be a lifelong process; therefore, the list of educational and professional socialization opportunities provided here is just the beginning. Our society is in a constant state of flux, and the knowledge and skills needed by social workers must be regularly updated and refined over the course of their career. Before the dawn of the 21st century, the social work profession acknowledged that the social worker of the 21st century needs a broad array of knowledge and skills to enable her or him to work with equal effectiveness on private issues (individual, family, and group work) and public issues (organizational, community, and public policy practice) (Reeser, 1996).

CONCLUSION

Is a career in social work for you? Social work is a unique helping profession that is dually committed to providing social services to vulnerable groups in our society, such as disaster victims and abused and neglected children, while advocating for positive change to alleviate social problems, such as lobbying for affordable housing policies. Social work is a profession striving to make a difference. It is a fulfilling profession shaped by the totality of the social worker's life experiences and professional knowledge, skills, and values. You can begin the process of identifying with the social work profession as early as this first social work course and revisit that process many times throughout your career.

You are almost at the end of your first social work course. You have been exposed to a wide range of information about the profession and have, hopefully, gained a sense of what a career in social work would entail. Your task now is to determine how your journey will continue. I would like to end our time together by asking you to consider the inspirational theme for Social Work Month 2012 (NASW, 2012, para 5, lines 1–3):

Social Work Matters. Social Workers fundamentally believe that a nation's strength depends on the ability of the majority of its citizens to lead productive and healthy lives. What drives these professionals? They help people, who are often navigating major life challenges, find hope and new options for achieving their full potential.

MAIN POINTS

- The outlook for the social work profession is promising. Employment trends suggest that social work jobs will be expanding in areas such as aging, health care, substance abuse treatment, school social work, and mental health services, although provision of mental health services will continue to be the primary area of practice for social work professionals.

- The current median annual salary for social workers is in the mid-$30,000 to mid-$50,000 range.

- Societal perceptions of the social work profession are improving, but social workers must stay focused on self-advocacy efforts to ensure that such perceptions continue to improve.

- The BSW prepares social workers to function as generalist practitioners. Both the BSW and MSW foundation curricula encompass a broad spectrum of content that includes human behavior, social policy, research, and social work practice and is integrated through the field experience.

- Socialization as a social work professional encompasses the formal educational process along with the informal strategies for developing a professional identity. Be prepared for a lifelong process of growth and change if you decide to pursue a career in social work.

EXERCISES

1. You are now ready to bid farewell to the Sanchez family. Begin your evaluation and termination by going to the Evaluate tab for this interactive case at www.routledgesw.com/cases.
   a. Review the Evaluation Introduction and complete Task 1 for the entire Sanchez family case (notebook review).
   b. To conduct an overall review of the Sanchez family case, complete Task 2, which includes intervention evaluation, case closed, and final thoughts. In the final thoughts section, reflect on the work you have done with the Sanchez family throughout this course. How would you know that you were effective in your work? For example, would you ask the family to complete a satisfaction survey?

Would you review the goals the family set for themselves and measure progress against those goals? If you failed to reach certain goals, how would you respond?

2. You are now familiar with social work interventions at the micro, mezzo, and macro levels. Referring to the community's concerns in the Riverton neighborhood of Alvadora (www.routledgesw.com/cases), identify an issue or challenge and develop an intervention that can be approached from all three levels of social work practice.

3. Social workers practicing in disaster response situations can experience secondary trauma. Review the information presented in this chapter and the Hudson City interactive case (www.routledgesw.com/cases) regarding the impact of crisis intervention on the practitioner, then complete your own self-care plan.

4. Along with completing an introductory social work course and learning about the social work profession, talking with practicing social workers is an excellent strategy for determining if social work is the right career for you.

   a. With the help of your instructor for this course or other faculty in the social work program, identify a social work practitioner that you can interview in person at her/his agency. Consider an area of social work that is of interest to you and select a practicing social worker that works in that area—for example:

Health/medical	Child welfare	Gerontology
Policy practice	Community organizing	Administration
Advocacy	Mental health	School social work
Law/justice system	Children and families	Adoption
Substance abuse treatment	Domestic violence	Youth

   b. After you have identified a social worker to interview, contact the person by telephone or e-mail to request the interview. Be certain to discuss a convenient time and duration for the interview. Confirm the interview time and location. Before the interview, you may want to e-mail or mail your questions to the interviewee (see Exhibit 12.7 for some suggestions). Remember to send a thank you note after the interview.

   c. Upon completion of the interview, reflect on the information you learned from the social worker and submit your reflection to your instructor. Summarize the information you gained, but also reflect on your thoughts and reactions to what you learned. (Exhibit 12.8 offers some suggestions.) You may want to consider audiotaping the interview to help with your reflection paper.

5. Personal reflection: Discuss your current perception of social work. Issues to consider: Has your attitude toward or perception of the profession changed since the beginning of the semester? If so, how? What is your perception of the future of social work?

EXHIBIT 12.7

Sample Questions for Interviewing a Practicing Social Worker

Do not feel limited to these suggestions. Be creative and inquisitive! Ask about the things that matter to you.

- Tell me about your journey into social work. What about social work appealed to you? How did you decide to become a social worker?
- What is your educational background for being a social worker?
- What social work experiences have you had, including practical and paid employment?
- How did you determine the area(s) in which you wanted to work?
- Tell me about your current social work position. What are your responsibilities? How long have you been employed in this position?
- What do you like/dislike about your job?
- What are the positive aspects of being a social worker?
- What are the negative aspects of being a social worker?
- What suggestions would you offer to someone who is considering a social work career?
- Based on what you now know, what suggestions do you have for courses or field experiences that a social work student might seek out during training?

EXHIBIT 12.8

Sample Questions for Reflecting on an Interview With a Social Worker

- Before the interview, how would you have described or defined social work?
- Did the social worker you interviewed confirm or change your perception of the social work profession?
- What was it about the social worker's job that appealed or did not appeal to you? Can you see yourself working in the area or job of the social worker you interviewed? Why or why not?
- What new information did you learn about social work that you did not previously know?
- Did the social worker discuss how she or he applies the values of the social work profession?
- Did the social worker discuss any ethical conflicts that she/he has encountered? How would you handle similar situations?

6. The following exercise provides an opportunity to engage in a planned change intervention:

Lydia Dennyson: A Social Work Planned Change Intervention

This exercise brings together the social work knowledge that you have gained throughout this course. In order to determine an appropriate intervention plan for the client, you will first need to learn about the aging-related changes that are occurring in her life and the impact of those changes on her ability to maintain a functional quality of life. You will also need to learn about resources in your community at the individual, family, and organizational level that can be developed or mobilized for the benefit of the client system and about policies that impact older adults and their families.

Background Information   Mrs. Dennyson is an 82-year-old woman who lives alone in the home she shared for four decades with her husband, who has been deceased for the past 11 years. She has remained in the home since the death of her husband and has, until recently, been highly functional, active, and productive. She retired at age 66 from her career as a human resources specialist for a large corporation. With the retirement income from both her husband and herself, she has been financially comfortable—able to travel to visit family, update her home and car, and pursue her cultural and social interests. She has three children, all of whom live several hundred miles away. She sees them several times a year, but typically only around holidays and on periodic visits to their homes.

Over the past several years, Mrs. Dennyson has begun to experience increased difficulty with her vision. Attributing this to "normal" aging, she did not seek specialized medical care. She has been compensating for her visual impairment in many areas of her life. She developed a strict routine from which she seldom strayed, and generally hid from family, friends, and her physician that she was becoming less functional. In the area of driving, she limited her driving to daylight, nonpeak hours, stayed close to her home, and used only those routes familiar to her. It was not until she caused a motor vehicle incident that the severity of her impairment was discovered.

During a follow-up with her physician, she was informed by the physician that her visual condition was degenerative and it would no longer be safe for her to drive. She informed the physician that she had no one who could help her and she had no choice but to continue driving. The physician again cautioned her against driving.

Over the ensuing months, Mrs. Dennyson discontinued virtually all of her social, volunteer, and religious activities, her travel, and her medical appointments. When her daughter, Janice, came to visit, she was appalled to see the condition of her mother, the house, and the car. Her usually well-kempt mother was disheveled, somewhat confused, and significantly thinner. The previously immaculate house was in disarray and the car was covered with scratches, dents, and evidence of multiple fender-benders. Upon further inspection, Janice found multiple unpaid bills, late-payment notices, and large sums of cash hidden throughout the house.

Despite the fact that her mother denies any problems and insists that she will continue living in the home alone, Janice is distraught. She contacts the Senior Services Center and asks for an immediate appointment for her mother. You are the case manager assigned to see Mrs. Dennyson.

The Intervention   Your task is to develop a strengths-based intervention plan for Mrs. Dennyson that encompasses the phases of engagement, assessment, intervention, and termination/evaluation. You must identify the practice implications for each phase and, ultimately, consider the lessons learned from this experience.

Phase I—Engagement of the client system

    a. Who is your client?

    b. How do you engage the client system?

    c. How do you interact with the nonclient "actors" in this system?

Practice implications for the engagement phase

- What additional information is needed?
- What are the sources of the information?
- What are your initial impressions?
- What knowledge is needed?
- What skills are needed?

Phase II—Assessment

    a. What are the strengths of the client system?

    b. What are the goals and needs of the client system?

    c. What community and family resources are available to meet those goals and needs?

    d. What are the barriers to reaching those goals and needs?

    e. What is your assessment of the client system's goals and needs?

Practice implications for the assessment phase

- What knowledge is needed?
- What skills are needed?
- Are you aware of the client system's values?
- What is your ethical obligation in this situation?
- What is your legal obligation in this situation?
- Who are potential partners in gathering information?
- How might you manage conflicting goals within the client system?
- What policies might impact the case?

Phase III—Intervention

    a. What is an intervention plan that is realistic and potentially helpful to this situation—for the client, the daughter, and the service delivery system?

    b. How does the intervention plan build on the strengths of the client system?

    c. Are there adequate and viable resources available to fulfill the plan—at the individual, family, organizational, or community levels?

    d. What new or different resources are needed to implement the intervention plan?

    e. What are the barriers to obtaining those resources?

f. What is an appropriate timeframe for the implementation of this intervention plan?

g. Are the barriers at the individual, family, or community level?

h. What policies impact the situation?

Practice implications for the intervention phase
- What knowledge is needed?
- What skills are needed?
- Who are potential partners in developing and implementing an appropriate intervention plan?
- Is the intervention plan achievable? Measurable? Ethical?
- How might you manage conflicting views of the intervention plan?

Phase IV—Termination and Evaluation

a. What constitutes a successful intervention? How will you know when you have completed the intervention?

b. What evaluation process would help you to gauge the success of the intervention?

Practice implications for the termination and evaluation phase
- What knowledge is needed?
- What skills are needed?
- How will the intervention be evaluated?

Lessons Learned

Upon completing the planned change process, consider the following:

a. What information did you realize that you possessed?

b. What information did you realize you needed?

c. What knowledge did you realize you possessed?

d. What knowledge did you realize you needed?

e. What skills did you realize you possessed?

f. What skills did you realize you needed?

g. What are the value and ethical issues related to this scenario?

h. What are the legal implications of this scenario?

i. What is your knowledge of community resources?

j. What is your awareness of strategies to develop or mobilize needed community resources?

k. What policy information about older adults did you realize that you possess?

l. What policy information about older adults did you realize that you need?

REFERENCES

Abramson, J. (2009). Interdisciplinary team practice. In A.R. Roberts (Ed.), *Social workers' desk reference* (2nd ed.) (pp. 44–50). New York: Oxford Press.

Adams, M., & Joshi, K.Y. (2010). Religious oppression. In M. Adams, W.J. Blumenfeld, C. Castañeda, H.W. Hackman, M.L. Peters, & X. Zúñiga (Eds.), *Readings for diversity and social justice* (pp. 226–234). New York: Routledge.

Akin, J. (1998). *100 skills of the professional social worker.* Tallahassee, FL: NASW Florida chapter.

Albelda, R. (2012). Different anti-poverty programs, same single-mother poverty. *Dollars & Sense, 298,* 11–17.

Albelda, R., Folbre, N., & the Center for Popular Economics. (1996). *The war on the poor. A defense manual.* New York: The New Press.

Alissi, A.S. (2009). United States. In A. Gitterman & R. Salmon (Eds.), *Encyclopedia of social work with groups* (pp. 6–13). New York: Routledge.

Allen, K. (2012). What is an ethical dilemma? *The New Social Worker, 19*(2), 4–5.

Allen-Meares, P. (2000). Our professional values and the changing environment. *Journal of Social Work Education, 36*(2), 179–182.

Allen-Meares, P., & DeRoos, Y. (1997). The future of the social work profession. In M. Reisch & E. Gambrill (Eds.), *Social work in the 21st century* (pp. 376–386). Thousand Oaks, CA: Pine Forge Press.

Angelis, T. (2012). Social workers help military families. Available at: http://www.naswdc.org/pressroom/events/peace/helpFamilies.asp.

Annie E. Casey Foundation. (2011). *The changing child population of the United States: Analysis of data from the 2010 Census.* Baltimore, MD: Annie E. Casey Foundation.

Arrington, P. (2008). *Stress at work: How do social workers cope? NASW membership workforce study.* Washington, DC: NASW.

Association for the Advancement of Social Work with Groups, Inc. (2010). Standards for social work practice with groups (2nd ed.). Available at: http://www.aaswg.org/files/AASWG_Standards_for_Social_Work_Practice_with_Groups.pdf.

Association of Baccalaureate Social Work Program Directors. (2007). Definition of social work practice 2007. Available at: http://bpdonline.org/.

Austin, D.M. (1997). The profession of social work in the second century. In M. Reisch & E. Gambrill (Eds.), *Social work in the 21st century* (pp. 396–407). Thousand Oaks, CA: Pine Forge Press.

Baden, B. (2010). Best careers in 2011: Medical and public health social worker. Available at: http://money.usnews.com/money/careers/articles/2010/12/06/best-careers.

Baldino, R.G. (2000). Wearing multiple hats as a social worker. *The New Social Worker, 7*(2), 25.

Barker, R.L. (1999). *The social work dictionary* (4th ed.). Washington, DC: NASW Press.

Barker, R.L. (2003). *The social work dictionary* (5th ed.). Washington, DC: NASW Press.

Bell, L.A. (2010). Theoretical foundations. In M. Adams, W.J. Blumenfeld, C. Castañeda, H.W. Hackman, M.L. Peters, & X. Zúñiga (Eds.), *Readings for diversity and social justice* (pp. 21–26). New York: Routledge.

Bishaw, A. (2011a). *Poverty: 2009 and 2010.* Washington, DC: U.S. Census Bureau.

Bishaw, A. (2011b). *Areas with concentrated poverty: 2006–2010.* Washington, DC: U.S. Census Bureau.

Blank, B.T. (1998). Settlement houses: Old idea in new form builds communities. *The New Social Worker*, 5(3), 4–7.

Blank, B.T. (2006). Racism—the challenge for social workers. *The New Social Worker*, 13(4), 10–13.

Bliss, D.L., & Meehan, J. (2008). Blueprint for creating a social work-centered disaster relief initiative. *Journal of Social Service Research*, 34(3), 73–85.

Blundo, R. (2008). Strengths-based framework. In T. Mizrahi & L.E. Davis (Eds.), *Encyclopedia of social work* (20th ed.) (pp. 4:173–177). Washington, DC: NASW Press and Oxford University Press.

Boes, M., & van Wormer, K. (2009). Social work with lesbian, gay, bisexual, and transgendered clients. In A.R. Roberts (Ed.), *Social workers' desk reference* (2nd ed.) (pp. 934–938). New York: Oxford Press.

Bollig, K. (2009). Personal communication. April 2, 2009.

Borgenschneider, K., & Corbett, T.J. (2010). *Evidence-based policymaking*. New York: Routledge.

Borzutzky, S. (2010). Developing countries. In T. Fitzpatrick, H. Kwon, N. Manning, J. Midgley, & G. Pascall (Eds.), *International encyclopedia of social policy* (pp. 297–300). London: Routledge.

Brieland, D. (1995). Social work practice: History and evolution. In R.L. Edwards (Ed.), *Encyclopedia of social work* (19th ed.) (pp. 2247–2257). Washington, DC: NASW Press.

Briggs, D. (2012). Diversity rising: Census shows Mormons, nondenominational churches, Muslims spreading out across U.S. Available at: http://blogs.thearda.com/trend/featured/diversity-rising-census-shows-mormons-nondenominational-churches-muslims-spreading-out-across-u-s/.

Brodie, K., & Gadling-Cole, C. (2008). Family group conferencing with African-American families. In C. Waites (Ed.), *Social work practice with African-American families: An intergenerational perspective* (pp. 123–143). New York: Routledge.

Brown, J. (1933). *The rural community and social casework*. New York: Family Welfare Association of America.

Buila, S. (2010). The NASW *Code of Ethics* under attack: A manifestation of the culture war within the profession of social work. *Journal of Social Work Values and Ethics*, 7(2), 1–8.

Buss, J.A. (2010). Have the poor gotten poorer? The American experience from 1987–2007. *Journal of Poverty*, 14, 183–196.

Butterfield, A.K.J., & Chisanga, B. (2008). Community development. In T. Mizrahi & L.E. Davis (Eds.), *Encyclopedia of social work* (20th ed.) (pp. 1:375–381). Washington, DC: NASW Press and Oxford University Press.

Carnevale, A.P., Cheah, B., & Strohl, J. (2011). *Hard times: Not all college degrees are created equal*. Georgetown: Georgetown University, Center on Education and the Workforce.

Casio, T. (2012). Approaching spirituality as a client strength. In Transcendent worldviews: Understanding spirituality in practice, *Families in Society Practice & Policy Focus* (1).

Center on Budget and Policy Priorities. (2009). American Recovery and Reinvestment Act of 2009: State-by-State Estimates of Key provisions Affecting Low- and Moderate-Income Individuals. Washington, DC: Center on Budget and Policy Priorities.

Center for Health Workforce Studies & Center for Workforce Studies. (2006). *Licensed social workers in the US, 2004*. Rensselaer, NY: University of Albany School of Public Health Center for Health Workforce Studies and NASW Center for Workforce Studies.

Centers for Disease Control and Prevention. (2010). 10 Essential Public Health Services. Available at: http://www.cdc.gov/nphpsp/essentialServices.html.

Centers for Disease Control and Prevention. (2012). Prevalence of autism spectrum disorders—autism and developmental disabilities montioring network, United States 2008. *Morbidity and Mortal Weekly Report (MMWR) 61*(3).

Chace, W.M. (1989). The language of action. *Wesleyan LXII*(2), 36.

Chawla, N., & Solinas-Saunders, M. (2011). Supporting military parent and child adjustment to deployments and separations with filial therapy. *American Journal of Family Therapy*, 39, 179–192.

Chen, H.T. (2006). *Practice program evaluation: Assessing and improving planning, implementation, and effectiveness*. Thousand Oaks, CA: Sage.

Children's Defense Fund. (2012). Children in the United States. Available at: http://www.childrensdefense.org/child-research-data-publications/data/state-data-repository/cits/2012/2012-united-states-children-in-the-states.pdf.

Claiborne, N. (2004). Presence of social workers in nongovernment organizations. *Social Work*, 49(2), 207–218.

Clark, E.J. (2003). The future of social work. In R.A. English (Ed.), *Encyclopedia of social work* (19th ed., 2003 supplement) (pp. 61–70). Washington, DC: NASW Press.

Clark, E.J., Weismiller, T., Whitaker, T., Waller, G.W., Zlotnik, J.L., & Corbett, B. (2006). *2005 social work congress—final report*. Washington, DC: NASW.

Clark, S. (2007). Social work students' perceptions of poverty. *Journal of Human Behavior in the Social Environment*, 16(1/2), 149–166.

Clewes, R. (2001). Experto credite: New social work graduates share their wisdom. *The New Social Worker*, 8(4), 14–16.

Coleman-Jensen, A., Nord, M., Andrews, M. & Carlson, S. (2011). Household food security in the United States in 2010. Available at: http://www.ers.usda.gov/Publications/ERR125/ERR125.pdf.

Collegeboard.com. (2012). Hottest careers for college graduates. Available at: https://bigfuture.collegeboard.org/explore-careers/careers/hottest-careers-for-college-graduates#bachelors.

Collins, D., & Coleman, H. (2000). Eliminating bad habits in the social work interview. *The New Social Worker*, 7(4), 12–15.

Collins, P.H. (2010). Toward a new vision. Race, class, gender. In M. Adams, W.J. Blumenfeld, C. Castañeda, H.W. Hackman, M.L. Peters, & X. Zúñiga (Eds), *Readings for diversity and social justice* (pp. 604–609). New York: Routledge.

Collins, S. (2011). Healthy People 2020: Social work values in a public health roadmap. *Practice Perspectives*, *03*, 1–4.

Colon, E., Appleby, G.A., & Hamilton, J. (2007). Affirmative practice with people who are culturally diverse and oppressed. In G.A. Appleby, E. Colon, & J. Hamilton (Eds.), *Diversity, oppression, and social functioning: Person-in-environment assessment and intervention* (2nd ed.) (pp. 294–311). Boston, MA: Allyn & Bacon.

Comartin, E.B., & Gonzáles-Prendes, A.A. (2011). Dissonance between personal and professional values: Resolution of an ethical dilemma. *Journal of Social Work Values and Ethics*, 8(2), 5-1–5-14.

Congress, E.P. (2009). The culturagram. In A.R. Roberts & J. Watkins (Eds.), *Social workers' desk reference* (2nd ed.) (pp. 969–975). New York: Oxford University Press.

Constantine, M.G., Hage, S.M., Kindaichi, M.M., & Bryant, R.M. (2007). Social justice and multicultural issues: Implications for the practice and training of counselors and counseling psychologists. *Journal of Counseling and Development*, 85(1), 24–29.

Corbett, B.S. (2008). Distinctive dates in social welfare history. In T. Mizrahi & L.E. Davis (Eds.) *Encyclopedia of social work* (20th ed.) (pp. 4:403–424). Washington, DC: NASW Press and Oxford University Press.

Corcoran, J. (2008). Direct practice. In T. Mizrahi & L.E. Davis (Eds.), *Encyclopedia of social work* (20th ed.) (pp. 2:31–36). Washington, DC: NASW Press and Oxford University Press.

Corey, M.S., & Corey, G. (1998). *Becoming a helper* (3rd ed.). Pacific Grove, CA: Brooks/Cole Thomson Learning.

Council on Social Work Education. (2006). *Statistics on social work education in the United States: A summary*. Alexandria, VA: CSWE.

Council on Social Work Education. (2008). *Educational policy and accreditation standards*. Washington, DC: Council on Social Work Education.

Council on Social Work Education. (2009). *Guide to the economic stimulus bill*. Available at: http://www.cswe.org/NR.

Council on Social Work Education. (2010). *Advanced social work practice in military social work*. Alexandria, VA: Council on Social Work Education. Available at: http://www.cswe.org/File.aspx?id=42466.

Council on Social Work Education. (2011). *2010 statistics on social work education in the United States: A summary*. Available at: http://www.cswe.org/File.aspx?id=52269.

Council on Social Work Education. (2012). *Accreditation*. Available at: http://www.cswe.org/Accreditation.aspx.

Council on Social Work Education/SAGE-SW. (2001). *Strengthening the impact of social work to improve the quality of life for older adults and their families: Blueprint for the new millennium*. Washington, DC: Council on Social Work Education/SAGE-SW.

Cummings, S.M., & Adler, G. (2007). Predictors of social workers employment in gerontological work. *Educational Gerontology*, *33*, 925–938.

Cummings, S.M., Adler, G., & DeCoster, V.A. (2005). Factors influencing graduate-social-work students' interests in working with elders. *Educational Gerontology*, *31*, 643–544.

D'Aprix, A.S., Boynton, L.A., Carver, B., & Urso, C. (2001). When the ideal meets the real: Resolving ethical dilemmas in the real world. *The New Social Worker, 8*(2), 20–23.

Dale, M. (2011). Building resilience after disaster. *NASW News, 56*(8).

Dale, M.L. (2001). Your summer vacation—or is it? The value of experiential learning as part of the new social worker's career campaign. *The New Social Worker, 8*(1), 4–6.

Daley, M.R. (2010). A conceptual model for rural social work. *Contemporary Rural Social Work, 2,* 1–7.

Daniel, C.L. (2008). From liberal pluralism to critical multiculturalism: The need for a paradigm shift in multicultural education for social work practice in the United States. *Journal of Progressive Human Services, 19*(1), 19–38.

Danziger, S.K. (2010). The decline of cash welfare and implications for social policy and poverty. *Annual Review of Sociology, 36,* 523–545.

DeJong, P. (2009). Solution-focused therapy. In A.R. Roberts & J. Watkins (Eds.), *Social workers' desk reference* (2nd ed.) (pp. 253–258). New York: Oxford University Press.

DeJong, P., & Cronkright, A. (2011). Learning solution-focused interviewing skills: BSW student voices. *Journal of Teaching in Social Work, 31,* 21–37.

DeNavas-Walt, C., Proctor, B.D., & Smith, J.C. (2008). *Income, poverty, and health insurance coverage in the United States: 2007. U.S. Census Bureau, current population reports,* pp. 60–235. Washington, DC: U.S. Government Printing Office.

DeNavas-Walt, C., Proctor, B.D., & Smith, J.C. (2011). *Income, poverty, and health insurance coverage in the United States: 2010. U.S. Census Bureau, current population reports,* pp. 60–239. Washington, DC: U.S. Government Printing Office.

de Shazer, S. (1982). *Patterns of brief family therapy: An ecosystemic approach.* New York: The Guilford Press.

de Shazer, S. (2005). *More than miracles: The state of the art of solution-focused therapy.* Binghamton, NY: Haworth Press.

Diller, J.V. (2007). *Cultural diversity: A primer for the human services.* Belmont, CA: Brooks/Cole-Thomson Learning.

Dolgoff, R., Loewenberg, F.M., & Harrington, D. (2009). *Ethical decisions for social work practice* (8th ed.). Belmont, CA: Thomson Brooks/Cole.

Dolgoff, R., Loewenberg, F.M., & Harrington, D. (2012). *Ethical decisions for social work practice* (9th ed.). Belmont, CA: Thomson Brooks/Cole.

Dunlap, K.M., & Strom-Gottfried, K. (1998). Everyday ethics and values for social workers (part 1 in a series on ethics). *The New Social Worker, 5*(1), 16–18.

Dunn, C. (2002). The importance of cultural competence for social workers. *The New Social Worker, 9*(2), 4–5.

Dunn, J.H., Flory, B.E., Berg-Weger, M., & Milstead, M. (2004). An exploratory study of supervised access and custody exchange services: The children's experience. *Family Court Review, 42*(1), 60–73.

Ephross, P.H., & Greif, G.L. (2009). Group process and group work techniques. In A.R. Roberts & J. Watkins (Eds.), *Social workers' desk reference* (2nd ed.) (pp. 679–685). New York: Oxford University Press.

Fass, S., Dinan, K.A., & Aratani, Y. (2009). *Child poverty and intergenerational mobility.* New York: Columbia University: National Center for Children in Poverty.

Feeding America. (2011). *Map the meal gap. Child food insecurity 2011.* Chicago, IL: Feeding America.

Fink-Samnick, E. (2011). Understanding care coordination: Emerging opportunities for social workers. *The New Social Worker, 18*(3), 18–21.

Fisher, R., DeFilippis, J., & Shragge, E. (2012). History matters: Canons, anti-canons, and critical lessons from the past. In J. DeFilippis & S. Saegert (Eds.), *The community development reader* (2nd ed.) (pp. 191–200). New York: Routledge.

Flory, B.E., & Berg-Weger, M. (2003). Children of high conflict custody disputes: Striving for social justice in adult focused litigation. *Social Thought, 22*(2/3). (Also published in Stretch, J.J., Burkemper, E.M., Hutchison, W.J., & Wilson, J. (2003). *Practicing justice* (pp. 205–219). New York: Haworth Press.)

Flory, B.E., Dunn, J., Berg-Weger, M., & Milstead, M. (2001). An exploratory study of supervised access and custody exchange services: The parental experience. *Family and Conciliation Court Review, 39*(4), 469–482.

Frumkin, M., & Lloyd, G.A. (1995). Social work education. In R.L. Edwards (Ed.), *Encyclopedia of social work* (19th ed.) (pp. 2238–2246). Washington, DC: NASW Press.

Furman, J., & Parrott, S. (2007). *A $7.25 minimum wage would be a useful step in helping working families escape poverty*. Washington, DC: Center on Budget and Policy Priorities.

Furman, R., Rowan, D., & Bender, K. (2009). *An experiential approach to group work*. Chicago, IL: Lyceum Books.

Gale, L. (2012). Lessons from Hull House. *The New Social Worker*, *19*(2), 18–19.

Garvin, C.D., & Galinsky, M.J. (2008). Groups. In T. Mizrahi & L.E. Davis (Eds.), *Encyclopedia of social work* (20th ed.) (pp. 2:287–298). Washington, DC: NASW Press and Oxford University Press.

Gates, T. (2006). Challenging heterosexism: Six suggestions for social work practice. *The New Social Worker*, *13*(3), 4–5.

Germain, C.B., & Gitterman, A. (1980). *The life model of social work practice*. New York: Columbia University Press.

Germain, C.B., & Gitterman, A. (1995). Ecological perspective. In R.L. Edwards (Ed.), *Encyclopedia of social work* (19th ed.) (pp. 816–824). Washington, DC: NASW Press.

Gibelman, M. (2004). *What social workers do* (2nd ed.). Washington, DC: NASW Press.

Gibelman, M. (2005). *What social workers do* (2nd ed.). Washington, DC: NASW Press.

Ginsberg, L. (1998). Introduction: An overview of rural social work. In L. Ginsberg (Ed.), *Social work in rural communities* (3rd ed.) (pp. 3–22). Alexandria, VA: Council on Social Work Education.

Ginsberg, L.H. (2001). *Careers in social work* (2nd ed.). Boston, MA: Allyn & Bacon.

Ginsberg, L.H. (2005). Introduction: The overall context of rural practice. In L.H. Ginsberg (Ed.), *Social work in rural communities* (4th ed.) (pp. 1–14). Alexandria, VA: CSWE Press.

Gitterman, A., & Germain, A. (2008). Ecological framework. In T. Mizrahi & L.E. Davis (Eds.), *Encyclopedia of social work* (20th ed.) (pp. 2: 97–102). Washington, DC: NASW Press and Oxford University Press.

Glasmeier, A.K. (2012). Living wage calculator. Available at: http://www.livingwage.geog.psu.edu/.

Glaze, L.E. (2011). Correctional population in the United States, 2010 (NCJ236319). Available at: http://bjs.ojp.usdoj.gov/content/pub/pdf/cpus10.pdf.

Golden, G.K. (2008). White privilege and the mental health profession. *The New Social Worker*, *15*(2), 4–5.

Goode, T.D., & Jones, W. (2006). *A definition of linguistic competence*. Washington, DC: Georgetown University National Center for Cultural Competence.

Granich, S. (2012). Duty to warn, duty to protect. *The New Social Worker*, *19*(1), 4–7.

Graves, J.A. (2012). Best jobs 2012. Available at: http://money.usnews.com/careers/best-jobs/rankings/the-25-best-jobs.

Green, G.P., & Haines, A. (2002). *Asset building in community development*. Thousand Oaks, CA: Sage Publications.

Grinnell, R.M., Unrau, Y.A., & Gabor, P. (2008). Program evaluation. In T. Mizrahi & L.E. Davis (Eds.), *Encyclopedia of social work* (20th ed.) (pp. 3: 429–434). Washington, DC: NASW Press and Oxford University Press.

Grobman, L.M. (2005). *Days in the lives of social workers: 54 professionals tell real-life stories from social work practice*. Harrisburg, PA: White Hat Communications.

Gumpert, J., & Black, P.N. (2005). Walking the tightrope between cultural competence and ethical practice: The dilemma of the rural practitioner. In L.H. Ginsburg (Ed.), *Social work in rural communities* (4th ed.) (pp. 157–174). Alexandria, VA: CSWE Press.

Hagen, J.L., & Lawrence, C.K. (2008). Temporary assistance to needy families. In T. Mizrahi & L.E. Davis (Eds.), *Encyclopedia of social work* (20th ed.) (pp. 4:225–229). Washington, DC: NASW Press and Oxford University Press.

Hartman, A. (1978). Diagrammatic assessment of family relationships. *Social Casework*, *59*, 465–476.

Haynes, K.S. (1996). The future of political social work. In P.R. Raffoul & C.A. McNeece (Eds.), *Future issues for social work practice* (pp. 266–276). Boston, MA: Allyn & Bacon.

He, W., Sengupta, M., Velkoff, V.A., & DeBarros, K.A. (2005). *65+ in the United States: 2005*. *Current population reports*, pp. 23–209. Washington, DC: U.S. Census Bureau, U.S. Government Printing Office.

Hegewisch, A. & Williams, C. (2011). *The gender wage gap: 2010*. Research Report IWPR #C350.

Washington, DC: Institute on Women's Policy Research.

Hernandez, V.R. (2008). Generalist and advanced generalist practice. In T. Mizrahi & L.E. Davis (Eds.), *Encyclopedia of social work* (20th ed.) (pp. 2:260–268). Washington, DC: NASW Press and Oxford University Press.

HIPAASpace. (2011). "Social worker" professionals availability ratio by state. Available at: http://www.hipaaspace.com/Medical.Statistics/Healthcare.Professionals.Availability/Social%20Worker/201112.

Hoffman, K.S., Lubben, J.E., Ouellette, P.M., Westhuis, D., Shaffer, G.L., Hutchison, E.D., Alvarez, A.R., Biegel, D.E., & Colby, I.C. (2008). Social work education: Overview. In T. Mizrahi & L.E. Davis (Eds.), *Encyclopedia of social work* (20th ed.) (pp. 4:107–137). Washington, DC: NASW Press and Oxford University Press.

Hollister, M. (2011). Employment stability in the U.S. labor market: Rhetoric versus reality. *Annual Review of Sociology*, 37, 305–324.

Hopps, J.G., & Collins, P.M. (1995). Social work profession overview. In R.L. Edwards (Ed.), *Encyclopedia of social work* (19th ed.) (pp. 2266–2282). Washington, DC: NASW Press.

Hopps, J.G., Lowe, T.B., Stuart, P.H., Weismiller, T., & Whitaker, T. (2008). Social work profession. In T. Mizrahi & L.E. Davis (Eds.) *Encyclopedia of social work* (20th ed.) (pp. 4:138–168). Washington, DC: NASW Press and Oxford University Press.

Horejsi, C.R. (2002). Social and economic justice: The basics. *The New Social Worker*, 9(4), 10–12.

Howden, L.M., & Meyer, J.A. (2011). *Age and sex composition: 2010*. Washington, DC: U.S. Census Bureau.

Humes, K.R., Jones, N.A., & Ramirez, R.R. (2011). Overview of race and Hispanic origin: 2010 Census brief no. 2. Available at: http://www.census.gov/prod/cen2010/briefs/c2010br-02.pdf.

Iatridis, D.S. (2008). Policy practice. In T. Mizrahi & L.E. Davis (Eds.), *Encyclopedia of social work* (20th ed.) (pp. 3:362–368). Washington, DC: NASW Press and Oxford University Press.

Internal Revenue Service. (2012). Earned income tax credit (EITC) – Use the EITC assistant to find out if you should claim it. Available at: http://www.irs.gov/individuals/article/0,,id=130102,00.html.

Jackson, K.F., & Samuels, G.M. (2011). Multiracial competence in social work: Recommendations for culturally attuned work with multiracial people. *Social Work*, 56(3), 235–245.

Jenson, J.M., & Howard, M.O. (2008). Evidence-based practice. In T. Mizrahi & L.E. Davis (Eds.), *Encyclopedia of social work* (20th ed.) (pp. 2:158–165). Washington, DC: NASW Press and Oxford University Press.

Johnson, A.G. (2010). What can we do? In M. Adams, W.J. Blumenfeld, C. Castañeda, H.W. Hackman, M.L. Peters, & X. Zúñiga (Eds.), *Readings for diversity and social justice* (pp. 610–616). New York: Routledge.

Kagle, J.D. (2009). Record-keeping. In A.R. Roberts & J. Watkins (Eds.), *Social workers' desk reference* (2nd ed.) (pp. 28–32). New York: Oxford University Press.

Kaiser Family Foundation. (2012a). Adult poverty rate by gender, 2010. Available at: http://www.statehealthfacts.org/comparebar.jsp?ind=12&cat=1.

Kaiser Family Foundation. (2012b). Poverty rates by race/ethnicity, 2010. Available at: http://www.statehealthfacts.org/comparebar.jsp?ind=14&cat=1.

Kane, M.N. (2008). When I'm 75 years old: Perceptions of social work students. *Social Work in Health Care*, 47(2), 185–213.

Kendall, K.A. (2000). *Social work education: Its origins in Europe*. Alexandria, VA: Council on Social Work Education.

Kindle, P.A. (2006). The inherent value of social work. *The New Social Worker*, 13(4), 17.

King, M.L. Jr. (1963, June 23). Speech at the Great March on Detroit.

Kohli, H.K., Huber, R., & Faul, A.C. (2010). Historical and theoretical development of culturally competent social work practice. *Journal of Teaching in Social Work*, 30, 252–271.

Kondrat, M.E. (2008). Person-in-environment. In T. Mizrahi & L.E. Davis (Eds.), *Encyclopedia of social work* (20th ed.) (pp. 3:348–354). Washington, DC: NASW Press and Oxford University Press.

Kosmin, B.A., & Mayer, E. (2001). *American religious identification survey, 2001*. New York: The Graduate Center of the City University of New York.

Kurland, R. (2007). Debunking the "blood theory" of social work with groups: Group workers *are* made and not born. *Social Work with Groups*, 30(1), 11–24.

Landon, P.S. (1995). Generalist and advanced generalist practice. In R.L. Edwards (Ed.), *Encyclopedia of social work* (19th ed.) (pp. 1101–1107). Washington, DC: NASW Press.

Leachman, M., & Mai, C. (2011). *New CBO report finds up to 2.4 million people owe their jobs to the Recovery Act.* Washington, DC: Center for Budget and Policy Priorities.

Leachman, M., Williams, E., & Johnson, N. (2011). *Governors are proposing further deep cuts in services, likely harming their economies. Less-harmful alternatives include revenue increases and rainy day funds.* Washington, DC: Center for Budget and Policy Priorities.

Leighninger, L. (2000). *Creating a new profession: The beginnings of social work education in the United States.* Alexandria, VA: Council on Social Work Education.

Levin, K.G. (2009). Involuntary clients (engagement processes). In A. Gitterman & R. Salmon (Eds.), *Encyclopedia of social work with groups* (pp. 287–290). New York: Routledge.

Lofquist, D. (2011). Same sex households. American Community Survey Briefs. Available at: http://www.census.gov/prod/2011pubs/acsbr10-03.pdf.

Logan, S.M.L. (2003). Issues of multiculturalism: Multicultural practice, cultural diversity, and competency. In R.A. English (Ed.), *Encyclopedia of social work* (19th ed., 2003 supplement) (pp. 95–105). Washington, DC: NASW Press.

Logan, S.L., Rasheed, M.N., & Rasheed, J.M. (2008). Family. In T. Mizrahi & L.E. Davis (Eds.), *Encyclopedia of social work* (20th ed.) (pp. 2: 175–182). Washington, DC: NASW Press and Oxford University Press.

Longres, J.E. (2008). Hopkins, Harry Lloyd (1890–1946). In T. Mizrahi & L.E. Davis (Eds.), *Encyclopedia of social work* (20th ed.) (p. 4:339). Washington, DC: NASW Press and Oxford University Press.

Longres, J.F. (2008). Richmond, Mary Ellen (1861–1928). In T. Mizrahi & L.E. Davis (Eds.), *Encyclopedia of social work* (20th ed.) (p. 4:368). Washington, DC: NASW Press and Oxford University Press.

Lynch, D. & Vernon, R. (2001). You will need a social worker . . . For free distribution information visit: http://hsmedia.biz.

Mackelprang, R.W., & Salsgiver, R.O. (2009). *Disability: A diversity model approach in human service practice* (2nd ed.). Chicago, IL: Lyceum Books.

Mackelprang, R.W., Patchner, L.S., DeWeaver, K.L., Clute, M.A., & Sullivan, W.P. (2008). Disability. In T. Mizrahi & L.E. Davis (Eds.), *Encyclopedia of social work* (20th ed.) (pp. 2:36–60). Washington, DC: NASW Press and Oxford University Press.

Mackun, P., & Wilson, S. (2011). *Population distribution and change: 2000 to 2010.* Washington, DC: U.S. Census Bureau.

Marson, S.M., & MacLeod, E.H. (1996). The first social worker. *The New Social Worker, 3*(2), 11.

Martin, D.C. (2010). *Refugees and asylees: 2009. Annual flow report.* Washington, DC: Office of Immigration Statistics.

Martinez-Brawley, E. (1983). *Seven decades of rural social work.* New York: Praeger.

Maschi, T., & Killian, M.L. (2011). The evolution of forensic social work in the United States: Implication for 21st century practice. *Journal of Forensic Social Work, 1,* 8–36.

Mason, S.E. (2012). The Occupy Movement and social justice economics. *Families in Society: The Journal of Contemporary Social Services, 93*(1), 3–4.

McCartney, S. (2011). *Child poverty in the United States 2009 and 2010: Selected race groups and Hispanic origin.* Washington, DC: U.S. Census Bureau.

McLaughlin, A. (2007). How to snag a job in international social work. *The New Social Worker, 14*(2), 26–27.

McNutt, J., & Floersch, J. (2008). Social work practice. In T. Mizrahi & L.E. Davis (Eds.), *Encyclopedia of social work* (20th ed.) (pp. 4:138–144). Washington, DC: NASW Press and Oxford University Press.

McPartlin, T.K. (2006). Notes from the Gulf: A social worker reflects on hurricane relief. *The New Social Worker, 13*(1), 18, 23.

Midgley, J. (2010). Social development. In T. Fitzpatrick, H. Kwon, N. Manning, J. Midgley, & G. Pascall (Eds.), *International encyclopedia of social policy* (pp. 1236–1241). London: Routledge.

Miller, W.R., & Rollnick, S. (2002). *Motivational interviewing: Preparing people for change* (2nd ed.). New York: The Guilford Press.

Milligan, S.E. (2008). Community building. In T. Mizrahi & L.E. Davis (Eds.), *Encyclopedia of social work* (20th ed.) (pp. 1:371–375). Washington, DC: NASW Press and Oxford University Press.

Minahan, A. (1981). Purpose and objectives of social work revisited. *Social Work, 26*(1), 5–6.

Mindell, C.L. (2007). Religious bigotry and religious minorities. In G.A. Appleby, E. Colon, & J. Hamilton (Eds.), *Diversity, oppression, and social functioning: Person-in-environment assessment and intervention* (2nd ed.) (pp. 226–246). Boston, MA: Allyn & Bacon.

Mizrahi, T. (2009). Community organizing principles and practice guidelines. In A.R. Roberts & J. Watkins (Eds.), *Social workers' desk reference* (2nd ed.) (pp. 872–881). New York: Oxford University Press.

Mizrahi, T., & Davis, L.E. (2008). *Encyclopedia of social work* (20th ed.). Washington, DC: NASW Press and Oxford University Press.

Mondros, J.B. (2009). Principles and practice guidelines for social action. In A.R. Roberts & J. Watkins (Eds.), *Social workers' desk reference* (2nd ed.) (pp. 901–906). New York: Oxford University Press.

Mulroy, E.A. (2008). Community needs assessment. In T. Mizrahi & L.E. Davis (Eds.), *Encyclopedia of social work* (20th ed.) (pp. 1:385–387). Washington, DC: NASW Press and Oxford University Press.

National Association of Black Social Workers. (n.d.). *Code of ethics.* Available at: http://www.nabsw.org/mserver/CodeofEthics.aspx.

National Association of Social Workers. (1973). *Standards for social service manpower.* Washington, DC: NASW.

National Association of Social Workers. (1998). *Milestones in the development of social work and social welfare.* Washington, DC: National Association of Social Workers.

National Association of Social Workers. (n.d.). *Social work profession and issue fact sheets.* Available at: http://www.naswdc.org.

National Association of Social Workers. (2005a). *NASW standards for social work practice in child welfare.* Washington, DC: NASW Press.

National Association of Social Workers. (2005b). *NASW standards for social work practice with clients with substance use disorders.* Washington, DC: NASW Press.

National Association of Social Workers. (2005c). *NASW standards for social work practice in health care settings.* Washington, DC: NASW Press.

National Association of Social Workers. (2006–2009a). *Cultural and linguistic competence in the social work profession. Social work speaks: National Association of Social Workers policy statements 2006–2009.* Washington, DC: NASW Press.

National Association of Social Workers. (2006–2009b). *Health care. Social work speaks: National Association of Social Workers policy statements 2006–2009.* Washington, DC: NASW Press.

National Association of Social Workers. (2007). *Indicators for the achievement of the NASW standards for cultural competence in social work practice.* Washington, DC: NASW.

National Association of Social Workers. (2008). *Code of ethics.* Washington, DC: NASW. Available at: http://www.naswdc.org

National Association of Social Workers. (2009). *Social work profession.* Available at: http://www.socialworkers.org/profession/overview.asp.

National Association of Social Workers. (2009–2012a). *Economic policy. Social work speaks: National Association of Social Workers policy statements 2009–2012.* Washington, DC: NASW Press.

National Association of Social Workers. (2010). *2010 Social Work Congress final report.* Available at: http://www.socialworkers.org/2010congress/documents/FinalCongress-StudentReport.pdf.

National Association of Social Workers. (2011a). *Social workers and "Duty to Warn" state laws.* Available at: http://www.naswdc.org/ldf/legal_issue/2008/200802.asp?back=yes.

National Association of Social Workers. (2011b). *Social workers in Congress.* Available at: http://www.naswdc.org/assets/public/documents/pace/swInCongress.pdf.

National Association of Social Workers. (2012–2014a). *Confidentiality and information utilization. Social work speaks: National Association of Social Workers policy statements 2012–2014* (9th ed.). Washington, DC: NASW Press.

National Association of Social Workers. (2012–2014b). *Deprofessionalization and reclassification. Social work speaks: National Association of Social Workers policy statements 2012–2014* (9th ed.). Washington, DC: NASW Press.

National Association of Social Workers. (2012–2014c). *Disasters. Social work speaks: National Association of Social Workers policy statements 2012–2014* (9th ed.). Washington, DC: NASW Press.

National Association of Social Workers. (2012–2014d). *Environment policy. Social work speaks: National*

Association of Social Workers policy statements 2012–2014 (9th ed.). Washington, DC: NASW Press.

National Association of Social Workers. (2012–2014e). *Immigrant and refugees. Social work speaks: National Association of Social Workers policy statements 2012–2014* (9th ed.). Washington, DC: NASW Press.

National Association of Social Workers. (2012–2014f). *Language and cultural diversity in the United States. Social work speaks: National Association of Social Workers policy statements 2012–2014* (9th ed.). Washington, DC: NASW Press.

National Association of Social Workers. (2012–2014g). *Lesbian, gay, and bisexual issues. Social work speaks: National Association of Social Workers policy statements 2012–2014* (9th ed.). Washington, DC: NASW Press.

National Association of Social Workers. (2012–2014h). *People with disabilities. Social work speaks: National Association of Social Workers policy statements 2012–2014* (9th ed.). Washington, DC: NASW Press.

National Association of Social Workers. (2012–2014i). *Poverty and economic justice. Social work speaks: National Association of Social Workers policy statements 2012–2014* (9th ed.). Washington, DC: NASW Press.

National Association of Social Workers. (2012–2014j). *Public child welfare. Social work speaks: National Association of Social Workers policy statements 2012–2014* (9th ed.). Washington, DC: NASW Press.

National Association of Social Workers. (2012–2014k). *Racism. Social work speaks: National Association of Social Workers policy statements 2012–2014* (9th ed.). Washington, DC: NASW Press.

National Association of Social Workers. (2012–2014l). *Rural social work. Social work speaks: National Association of Social Workers policy statements 2012–2014* (9th ed.). Washington, DC: NASW Press.

National Association of Social Workers. (2012–2014m). *Social work in the criminal justice system. Social work speaks: National Association of Social Workers policy statements 2012–2014* (9th ed.). Washington, DC: NASW Press.

National Association of Social Workers. (2012–2014n). *Transgender and gender identity issues. Social work speaks: National Association of Social Workers policy statements 2012–2014* (9th ed.). Washington, DC: NASW Press.

National Association of Social Workers. (2012–2014o). *Welfare reform. Social work speaks: National*

Association of Social Workers policy statements 2012–2014 (9th ed.). Washington, DC: NASW Press.

National Association of Social Workers. (2012–2014p). *Women's issues. Social work speaks: National Association of Social Workers policy statements 2012–2014* (9th ed.). Washington, DC: NASW Press.

National Association of Social Workers. (2012). *NASW Standards for School Social Work Services.* Washington, DC: NASW Press.

National Association of Social Workers. (2012). *Social work month 2012.* Available at: http://www.socialworkers.org/pressroom/swMonth/2012/keymessages.asp.

National Association of Social Workers. (n.d.). *Issue fact sheets. Diversity and cultural competence.* Available at: http://www.naswdc.org.

National Association of Social Workers and Association of Social Work Boards. (2005). *NASW and ASWB standards for technology and social work practice.* Washington, DC: NASW Press.

National Association of Social Workers Center for Workforce Studies. (2004). *"If you're right for the job, it's the best job in the world." NASW Child Welfare Specialty Section members describe their experiences in child welfare.* Available at: http://www.socialworkers.org/practice/children/NASWChildWelfareRpt062004.pdf.

National Association of Social Workers Center for Workforce Studies. (2005). *Assuring the sufficiency of a frontline workforce: A national study of licensed social workers.* Washington, DC: NASW.

National Association of Social Workers Center for Workforce Studies. (2007). *More money—less money: Factors associated with the highest and lowest social work salaries.* Washington, DC: National Association of Social Workers.

National Association of Social Workers Center for Workforce Studies. (2010). *Summary of key compensation findings.* Washington, DC: National Association of Social Workers.

National Association of Social Workers Center for Workforce Studies. (n.d.). Workforce planning. Available at: http://workforce.socialworkers.org/planning.asp.

National Association of Social Workers Center for Workforce Studies and Social Work Practice. (2010). *Social workers in schools (kindergarten through 12th grade). Occupational profile.* Washington, DC: National Association of Social Workers.

National Association of Social Workers Center for Workforce Studies and Social Work Practice. (2011a). *Social workers in health clinics and outpatient health care settings. Occupational profile*. Washington, DC: National Association of Social Workers.

National Association of Social Workers Center for Workforce Studies and Social Work Practice. (2011b). *Social workers in hospital and medical centers. Occupational profile*. Washington, DC: National Association of Social Workers.

National Association of Social Workers Center for Workforce Studies and Social Work Practice. (2011c). *Social workers in mental health clinics and outpatient facilities. Occupational profile*. Washington, DC: National Association of Social Workers.

National Association of Social Workers Center for Workforce Studies and Social Work Practice. (2011d). *Social workers in psychiatric hospitals. Occupational profile*. Washington, DC: National Association of Social Workers.

National Association of Social Workers National Committee on Racial and Ethnic Diversity. (2001). *NASW standards for cultural competence in social work practice*. Washington, DC: National Association of Social Workers.

National Committee on Pay Equity. (2011). The wage gap over time: In real dollars, women see a continuing gap. Available at: http://www.pay-equity.org/info-time.html.

National Conference for Community and Justice—St. Louis Region. (2002). Action continuum: From discrimination to respect. Developed by Roni Branding, St. Louis, MO.

National Law Project. (2012). Federal minimum wage. Available at: http://www.nelp.org/content/content_issues/category/federal_minimum_wage/.

National Public Radio/Henry J. Kaiser Family Foundation/Harvard University Kennedy School of Government. (2001). Poverty in America. Available at: http://www.kff.org.

O'Hare, T. (2009). *Essential skills of social work practice. Assessment, intervention, and evaluation*. Chicago, IL: Lyceum Books.

Okun, B.F., Fried, J., & Okun, M.L. (1999). *Understanding diversity: A learning-as-practice primer*. Pacific Grove, CA: Brooks/Cole.

Open Society Foundations. (2010). *Defining the addiction treatment gap: Data summary*. New York: Open Society Foundations.

Paraquad. (n.d.). Words with dignity. Available at: http://www.paraquad.org.

Parrott, S. (2008). *Recession could cause large increases in poverty and push millions into deep poverty*. Washington, DC: Center on Budget and Policy Priorities.

Peck, S. (1999). Who are we? *The New Social Worker*, 6(1), 4–6.

Peebles-Wilkins, W. (2008). Wells-Barnett, Ida Bell. In T. Mizrahi & L.E. Davis (Eds.), *Encyclopedia of social work* (20th ed.) (pp. 4:385). Washington, DC: NASW Press and Oxford University Press.

Perron, B.E., & Powell, T. J. (2009). Online groups. In A. Gitterman & R. Salmon (Eds.), *Encyclopedia of social work with groups* (pp. 311–314). New York: Routledge.

Pew Research Center. (2012). The rise of intermarriage. Rates, characteristics vary by race and gender. Available at: http://pewresearch.org/pubs/2197/intermarriage-race-ethnicity-asians-whites-hispanics-blacks.

Phillips, A., Quinn, A., & Heitkamp, T. (2010). Who wants to do rural social work? Student perceptions of rural social work practice. *Contemporary Rural Social Work*, 2, 51–65.

Pollard, W.L. (2008). Civil rights. In T. Mizrahi & L.E. Davis (Eds.), *Encyclopedia of social work* (20th ed.) (pp. 1:301–309). Washington, DC: NASW Press and Oxford University Press.

Polowy, C.I., Morgan, S., Bailey, W.D., & Gorenberg, C. (2008). Confidentiality and privileged communication. In T. Mizrahi & L.E. Davis (Eds.), *Encyclopedia of social work* (20th ed.) (pp. 1:408–415). Washington, DC: NASW Press and Oxford University Press.

Pullen-Sansfaçon, A. (2011). Ethics and conduct in self-directed groupwork: Some lessons for the development of a more ethical social work practice. *Ethics and Social Welfare*, 5(4), 361–379.

Pyles, L. (2009). *Progressive community organizing: A critical approach for a globalizing world*. New York: Routledge.

Quam, J.K. (2008a). Brace, Charles Loring. In T. Mizrahi & L.E. Davis (Eds.), *Encyclopedia of social work* (20th ed.) (pp. 4:325–326). Washington, DC: NASW Press and Oxford University Press.

Quam, J.K. (2008b). Dix, Dorthea Lynde. In T. Mizrahi & L.E. Davis (Eds.), *Encyclopedia of social work* (20th ed.) (p. 4:334). Washington, DC: NASW Press and Oxford University Press.

Quam, J.K. (2008c). Perkins, Frances. In T. Mizrahi & L.E. Davis (Eds.), *Encyclopedia of social work* (20th ed.) (pp. 4:364–365). Washington, DC: NASW Press and Oxford University Press.

Quam, L. (2008). Addams, Jane (1860–1935). In T. Mizrahi & L.E. Davis (Eds.), *Encyclopedia of social work* (20th ed.) (pp. 4:318–319). Washington, DC: NASW Press and Oxford University Press.

Rank, M.R. (2004). *One nation, underprivileged: Why American poverty affects us all*. New York: Oxford University Press.

Rank, M.R. (2006). Toward a new understanding of American poverty. *Journal of Law and Policy*, *20*(17), 17–51.

Rank, M.R. (2008). Poverty. In T. Mizrahi & L.E. Davis (Eds.), *Encyclopedia of social work* (20th ed.) (pp. 3:387–395). Washington, DC: NASW Press and Oxford University Press.

Rank, M.R. (2009). Measuring the economic racial divide across the course of American lives. *Race and Social Problems*, *1*, 57–66.

Rank, M.R., & Hirschl, T.A. (2001a). The occurrence of poverty across the life cycle: Evidence from the PSID. *Journal of Policy Analysis and Management*, *20*(4), 737–755.

Rank, M.R., & Hirschl, T.A. (2001b). Rags or riches? Estimating the probabilities of poverty and affluence across the adult American life span. *Social Science Quarterly*, *82*(4), 651–669.

Rank, M.R., & Hirschl, T.A. (2002). Welfare use as a life course event: Toward a new understanding of the U.S. safety net. *Social Work*, *47*(3), 237–248.

Reamer, F.G. (2001). *Ethics education in social work*. Alexandria, VA: Council on Social Work Education.

Reamer, F.G. (2006). *Ethical standards in social work*. Washington, DC: NASW Press.

Reamer. F.G. (2008a). Ethics and values. In T. Mizrahi & L.E. Davis (Eds.), *Encyclopedia of social work* (20th ed.) (pp. 2:143–151). Washington, DC: NASW Press and Oxford University Press.

Reamer, F.G. (2008b) Ethical standards in social work: The NASW Code of Ethics. In T. Mizrahi & L.E. Davis (Eds.), *Encyclopedia of social work* (20th ed.) (pp. 4:391–397). Washington, DC: NASW Press and Oxford University Press.

Reamer, F.G. (2009a). Ethical issues in social work. In A.R. Roberts (Ed.), *Social workers' desk reference* (2nd ed.) (pp. 115–120). New York: Oxford University Press.

Reamer, F.G. (2009b). *The social work ethics casebook: Cases and commentary*. Washington, DC: NASW Press.

Recovery Act. (2012). Available at: http://www.recovery.gov/About/Pages/The_Act.aspx.

Reeser, L. (1996). The future of professionalism and activism in social work. In P.R. Raffoul & C.A. McNeece (Eds.), *Future issues for social work practice* (pp. 240–253). Boston: Allyn & Bacon.

Reid, P.N. (1995). Social welfare history. In R.L. Edwards (Ed.), *Encyclopedia of social work* (19th ed.) (pp. 2206–2225). Washington, DC: NASW Press.

Reisch, M. (1997). The political context of social work. In M. Reisch & E. Gambrill (Eds.), *Social work in the 21st century* (pp. 80–92). Thousand Oaks, CA: Pine Forge Press.

Reisch, M. (2000). Social work and politics in the new century. *Social Work*, *45*(4), 293–297.

Reisch, M. (2009). Legislative advocacy to empower oppressed and vulnerable groups. In A.R. Roberts & J. Watkins (Eds.), *Social workers' desk reference* (2nd ed.) (pp. 893–900). New York: Oxford University Press.

Reisch, M., & Jarman-Rohde, L. (2000). The future of social work in the United States: Implications for field education. *Journal of Social Work Education*, *36*(2), 201–214.

Responsible Reform for the Middle Class. (2010). Patient Protection and Affordable Care Act. Available at: http://dpc.senate.gov/healthreformbill/health bill04.pdf.

Rock, B.D. (2009). Social work in health care for the 21st century. In A.R. Roberts (Ed.), *Social workers' desk reference* (2nd ed.) (pp. 10–15). New York: Oxford University Press.

Rome, S.H. (2008). Forensic social work. In T. Mizrahi & L.E. Davis (Eds.), *Encyclopedia of social work* (20th ed.) (pp. 2:221–223). Washington, DC: NASW Press and Oxford University Press.

Rothman, J. (2008). Multi mode of community intervention. In J. Rothman, J. Erlich, & J. Tropman (Eds.), *Strategies of community intervention* (7th ed.) (pp. 141–170). Peosta, IA: Eddie Bowers.

Ruffing, K.A., & Horney, J.R. (2011). *Economic downturn and Bush policies continue to drive large projected deficits. Economic recovery measures, financial rescues have only temporary impact*. Washington, DC: Center for Budget and Policy Priorities.

Sager, J.S. (2008). Social planning. In T. Mizrahi & L.E. Davis (Eds.), *Encyclopedia of social work* (20th ed.) (pp. 4:56–61). Washington, DC: NASW Press and Oxford University Press.

Saint Louis University Marketing and Communications. (n.d.). *Guidelines for writing a strong commentary*. St. Louis, MO: Saint Louis University Marketing and Communications.

Saleebey, D. (1996). The strengths perspective in social work practice: Extensions and cautions. *Social Work*, *41*(3), 296–305.

Saleebey, D. (2006). *The strengths perspective in social work practice* (4th ed.). Boston, MA: Allyn & Bacon.

Sandoval, D.A., Rank, M.R., & Hirschl, T.A. (2009). The increasing risk of poverty across the American life course. *Demography*, *46*(4), 717–737.

Sargent Shriver National Poverty Law Center. (n.d.). Available at: http://www.povertylaw.org/.

Sawhill, I.V. (2012). Mapping the Obama administration's priorities. Available at: http://www.brookings.edu/opinions/2012/0213_obama_priorities_sawhill.aspx.

Schlesinger, E.G., & Devore, W. (1995). Ethnic-sensitive practice. In R.L. Edwards (Ed.), *Encyclopedia of social work* (19th ed.) (pp. 902–908). Washington, DC: NASW Press.

Schneider, R. (2002). Influencing "state" policy: Social work arena for the 21st century. *The Social Policy Journal*, *1*(1), 113–116.

Schott, L. (2008). *Summary of final TANF rules. Some improvement around the margins*. Washington, DC: Center on Budget and Policy Priorities.

Schott, L., & Pavetti, L. (2011). *Many states cutting TANF benefits harshly despite high unemployment and unprecedented need*. Washington, DC: Center on Budget and Policy Priorities.

Seccombe, K. (1999). *"So you think I drive a Cadillac?" Welfare recipients' perspectives on the system and its reform*. Boston, MA: Allyn & Bacon.

Segal, E.A. (2007). *Social welfare policy and social programs: A values perspective*. Belmont, CA: Thomson Brooks/Cole.

Senkowsky, S. (1996). Social work's religious roots. *The New Social Worker*, *3*(2), 10.

Sfiligoj, H. (2009). New technology transforming profession, *NASW News*, *54*(4), 4.

Shaw, H., & Stone, C. (2010). *Tax data show richest 1 percent took a hit in 2008, but income remained highly concentrated at the top. Recent gains of bottom 90 percent wiped out*. Washington, DC: Center for Budget and Policy Priorities.

Sheridan, M.J. (2002). Spiritual and religious issues in practice. In A.R. Roberts & J. Watkins (Eds.), *Social workers' desk reference* (pp. 567–571). New York: Oxford University Press.

Sherman, A., Greenstein, R., & Parrott, S. (2008). *Poverty and share of Americans without health insurance were higher in 2007—and median income for working-age households was lower than at bottom of last recession*. Washington, DC: Center for Budget and Policy Priorities.

Sherraden, M. (1990). *Assets and the poor: A new American welfare policy*. Armonk, NY: M.E. Sharp.

Sherraden, M.S. (2008). Community economic development. In T. Mizrahi & L.E. Davis (Eds.), *Encyclopedia of social work* (20th ed.) (pp. 1:381–385). Washington, DC: NASW Press and Oxford University Press.

Shulman, L. (2009). *The skills of helping individuals, families, groups, and communities* (6th ed.). Belmont, CA: Brooks/Cole, Cengage Learning.

Simmons, C.S., Diaz, L., Jackson, V., & Takahashi, R. (2008). NASW cultural competency indicators: A new tool for the social work profession. *Journal of Ethnic and Cultural Diversity in Social Work*, *17*(1), 4–20.

Singh, A.A., & Salazar, C.F. (2011). Conclusion: Six considerations for social justice group work. In A.A. Singh & C.F. Salazr (Eds.), *Social justice in group work: Practical interventions for change* (pp. 213–222). London: Routledge.

Smith, C.J. (2009). Hard times steer some toward social work. Available at: http://blog/syracus.com/progress_impact/2009/02.

Social Work Policy Institute. (2011). *Investing in the social work workforce*. Washington, DC: National Association of Social Workers.

Social Work Reinvestment Initiative. Available at: http://www.socialworkreinvestment.org.

Society for Research in Child Development. (2007). Head Start's benefits likely outweigh program costs. *Social Policy Report Brief, 21*(3), 1–2.

Society for Research in Child Development. (2008). Children in immigrant families key to America's future. *Social Policy Report Brief, 22*(3), 1–2.

Society for Research in Child Development. (2011a). Reducing prejudice and promoting equity in childhood. *Social Policy Report Brief, 25*(4), 1–2.

Society for Research in Child Development. (2011b). Food insecurity harmful to children's development. *Social Policy Report Brief, 25*(3), 1–2.

Southern Regional Education Board Manpower Education and Training Project's Rural Task Force. (1998). Educational assumptions for rural social work. In L. Ginsberg (Ed.), *Social work in rural communities* (3rd ed.) (pp. 23–26). Alexandria, VA: Council on Social Work Education.

Stone, C., Shaw, H., Trisi, D., & Sherman, A. (2011). *A guide to statistics on historical trends in income inequality*. Washington, DC: Center for Budget and Policy Priorities.

Streeter, C.L., Gamble, D.N., & Weil, M. (2008). Community. In T. Mizrahi & L.E. Davis (Eds.) *Encyclopedia of social work* (20th ed.) (pp. 1:355–368). Washington, DC: NASW Press and Oxford University Press.

Strom-Gottfried, K., & Dunlap, K.M. (1998). How to keep boundary issues from compromising your practice (Part 2 in a series on ethics). *The New Social Worker, 5*(2), 10–13.

Strom-Gottfried, K., & Dunlap, K.M. (1999). Unraveling ethical dilemmas. *The New Social Worker, 6*(2), 8–12.

Substance Abuse and Mental Health Services Administration. (2010). *Mental health, United States, 2008.* HHS publication no. (SMA) 10-4590. Rockville, MD: Center for Mental Health Services, Substance Abuse and Mental Health Services Administration.

Substance Abuse and Mental Health Services Administration. (2012). *Results from the 2010 national survey on drug use and health: Mental health findings.* NSDUH series H-42, HHS publication no. (SMA) 11-4667. Rockville, MD: Substance Abuse and Mental Health Services Administration.

Syers, M. (2008). Flexner, Abraham (1866–1959). In T. Mizrahi & L.E. Davis (Eds.), *Encyclopedia of social work* (20th ed.) (p. 4:338). Washington, DC: NASW Press and Oxford University Press.

Tapp, K., & Payne, D. (2011). Guidelines for practitioners: A social work perspective on discharging the duty to protect. *Journal of Social Work Values and Ethics, 8*(2), 2-1–2-13.

Terrell, P. (2010). Poverty, War on. In T. Fitzpatrick, H. Kwon, N. Manning, J. Midgley, & G. Pascall (Eds.), *International encyclopedia of social policy* (pp. 1061–1063). London: Routledge.

Tiehen, L., Jolliffe, D., & Gundersen, C. (2012). *Alleviating poverty in the United States. The critical role of SNAP benefits.* Washington, DC: U.S. Department of Economic Research Service. Available at: www.ers.usda.gov.

Toseland, R.W., & Horton, H. (2008). Group work. In T. Mizrahi & L.E. Davis (Eds.), *Encyclopedia of social work* (20th ed.) (pp. 2:298–308). Washington, DC: NASW Press and Oxford University Press.

Traynor, B. (2012). Community building: Limitations and promises. In J. DeFilippis & S. Saegert (Eds.), *The community development reader* (2nd ed.) (pp. 209–219). New York: Routledge.

Trisi, D., Sherman, A., & Broaddus, M. (2011). *Poverty rate second-highest in 45 years; record numbers lacked health insurance, lived in deep poverty.* Washington, DC: Center for Budget and Policy Priorities.

Tropman, J. (2008). Phases of helping. In J. Rothman, J. Erlich, & J. Tropman (Eds.), *Strategies of community intervention* (7th ed.) (pp. 127–133). Peosta, IA: Eddie Bowers.

Trust for America's Health. (2012). Investing in America's health. A state-by-state look at public health funding and key health facts. Available at: www.healthyamericans.org/assets/files/investing.pdf.

Tsay, J. (2010). Public health. In T. Fitzpatrick, H. Kwon, N. Manning, J. Midgley, & G. Pascall (Eds.), *International encyclopedia of social policy* (pp. 1098–1101). London: Routledge.

Urban Experience in Chicago. (n.d.). Available at: http://uic.edu/jaddams/hull/urbanexp/contents.htm.

U.S. Census Bureau. (2008a). An older and more diverse national by midcentury. Washington, DC: U.S. Census Bureau.

U.S. Census Bureau. (2008b). Income, poverty, and health insurance coverage in the United States: 2007. Available at: http://www.census.gov/prod/2008pubs/.

U.S. Census Bureau. (2009a). Census Bureau data show characteristics of the US foreign-born population. Available at: http://www.census.gov/Press-Release/www.releases.

U.S. Census Bureau. (2009b). 2009 Statistical abstract. Available at: http://www.census.gov/compendia/statab.

U.S. Census Bureau. (2011). People and families in poverty by selected characteristics: 2009 and 2010. Available at: http://www.census.gov/hhes/www/poverty/data/incpovhlth/2010/table4.pdf.

U.S. Census Bureau News. (2010). Census Bureau reports nearly half of U.S. residents live in households receiving government benefits. Participation in means-tested programs on upswing in 2008. Available at: http://www.census.gov/newsroom/releases/archives/employment_occupations/cb10-53.html.

U.S. Census Bureau, International Data Base. (2011). *World population growth rates: 1950–2050.* Washington, DC: U.S. Census Bureau.

U.S. Census Bureau News. (2011). Anniversary of Americans with Disabilities Act: July 26. Available at: http://www.census.gov/newsroom/releases archives/facts_features_special_editions/cb11.ff14.html.

U.S. Census Bureau, Statistical Abstract. (2012). Available at: http://www.census.gov/compendia/statab.

U.S. Department of Agriculture Food and Nutrition Service. (2012). Supplemental Nutrition Assistance Program (SNAP) pre-screening eligibility tool Available at: http://www.foodstamps-step1.usda.gov/fns/.

U.S. Department of Commerce, Bureau of the Census. (2012). *Preliminary estimate of weighted average poverty thresholds for 2011.* Washington, DC: U.S. Census Bureau.

U.S. Department of Health and Human Services. (2004). Protecting the privacy of patients' health information. Available at: http://www.hhs.gov/news/facts/privacy.html.

U.S. Department of Health and Human Services. (2006a). TANF 7th annual report to Congress. Available at: http://www.hhhs.gov/programs/ofa/data-reports/annualreport7/.

U.S. Department of Health and Human Services. (2006b). The supply and demand of professional social workers providing long-term care services: Report to Congress. Available at: http://aspe.hhs.gov/daltcp/reports/2006/Swsupply.htm#ref7.

U.S. Department of Health and Human Services. (2010). Child welfare outcomes 2006–2009. Report to Congress. Available at: http://www.acf.hhs.gov/programs/cb/pubs/cwo06-09/cwo06-09.pdf.

U.S. Department of Health and Human Services Administration on Aging. (2011). A profile of older Americans: 2011. Available at: www.aoa.gov/AoARoot/Aging_Statistics/Profile/2011/docs/2011profile.pdf.

U.S. Department of Health and Human Services Substance Abuse and Mental Health Services Administration. (2012). Results from the 2010 national survey on drug use and health: Mental health findings. Available at: http://store.samhsa.gov/home.

U.S. Department of Health and Human Services, Administration for Children and Families, Administration on Children, Youth, and Families, Children Bureau. (2011). Child maltreatment 2010. Available at: http://www.acf.hhs.gov/programs/cb/stats_research/index.htm#can.

U.S. Department of Health and Human Services, Administration for Children and Families (n.d.). Worker turnover. Available at: http://www.childwelfare.gov/management/workforce/retention/turnover.cfm.

U.S. Department of Health and Human Services Health Resources and Services Administration, Maternal and Child Health Bureau. (2008). *Women's health USA 2008.* Rockville, MD: U.S. Department of Health and Human Services.

U.S. Department of Labor. (2008). Career guide to industries, 2008–2009 edition. Advocacy, grantmaking, and civic organizations. Available at: http://www.bls.gov/oco/cg/cgso54.htm.

U.S. Department of Labor. (2009a). Employment situation summary. Available at: http://www.bls.gov/news.release/empsit.nr0.htm.

U.S. Department of Labor. (2009b). Minimum wage laws in the states—January 1, 2009. Employment Standards Administration Wage and Hour Division. Available at: http://www.dol.gov.

U.S. Department of Labor, Bureau of Labor Statistics. (2008–2009). Occupational outlook handbook, 2008–09 edition. Social workers. Available at: http://www.bls.gov/oco/ocos060.htm.

U.S. Department of Labor, Bureau of Labor Statistics. (2010). Career guide to industries, 2010–11 edition, state and local government, except education and health. Available at: http://www.bls.gov/oco/cg/cgs042.htm.

U.S. Department of Labor, Bureau of Labor Statistics. (2011). A profile of the working poor, 2009. Washington, DC: U.S. Department of Labor.

U.S. Department of Labor, Bureau of Labor Statistics. (2012a). Employment situation summary. Available at: http://www.bls.gov/news.release/empsit.nr0.htm.

U.S. Department of Labor, Bureau of Labor Statistics. (2012b). Occupational outlook handbook, 2012–13 edition, social workers. Available at http://www.bls.gov/ooh/community-and-social-service/social-workers.htm.

U.S. Department of Labor, Bureau of Labor Statistics. (2012c). Occupational outlook handbooks (mental health counselors and marriage and family therapists, probation officers and correctional treatment specialists, social and community service managers, and social workers). Available at: http://www.bls.gov/ooh/.

U.S. Department of State, Bureau of Population, Refugees, and Migration (PRM). (2011). Worldwide Refugee Admissions Processing System (WRAPS), fiscal years 1980 to 2010. Available at: www.dhs.gov/xlibrary/assets/statistics/yearbook/1020/table13.xls-2011-05-03.

Valutis, S., Rubin, D., & Bell, M. (2011). Professional socialization and social work values: Who are we teaching? *Social Work Education, iFirst Article*, 1–12.

Van Soest, D. (2008). Oppression. In T. Mizrahi & L.E. Davis (Eds.), *Encyclopedia of social work* (20th ed.) (pp. 3:322–324). Washington, DC: NASW Press and Oxford University Press.

Vaughn, M., Fu, Q., DeLisi, M., Beaver, K., Perron, B., & Howard, M. (2009). Are personality disorders associated with social welfare burden in the United States? Results from the National Epidemiologic Survey on Alcohol and Related Conditions. *The American Journal of Psychiatry, 24*, 709–721.

Walker, A. (2010). Community-based development. In T. Fitzpatrick, H. Kwon, N. Manning, J. Midgley, & G. Pascall (Eds.), *International encyclopedia of social policy* (pp. 195–196). London: Routledge.

Wall Street Journal. (2012). The top 200 jobs of 2012. Available at: http://www.careercast.com/content/top-200-jobs-2012-41-60.

Walsh, J. (2010). *Theories for direct social work practice* (2nd ed.). Belmont, CA: Wadsworth Cengage Learning.

Walters, N.P., & Trevelyan, E.N. (2011). *The newly arrived foreign-born population of the United States: 2010*. Washington, DC: U.S. Census Bureau

Walton, S. (1996). Getting real: Mastering the art of helping others. In *America's best graduate schools* (p. 63). Washington, DC: *U.S. News and World Report*.

Weil, M.O., & Gamble, D.N. (2009). Community practice model for the twenty-first century. In A.R. Roberts (Ed.), *Social workers' desk reference* (2nd ed.) (pp. 882–892). New York: Oxford University Press.

Werner, C. (2011). The older population: 2010. Available at: http://www.census.gov/prod/cen2010/briefs/c2010br-09.pdf.

Wharton, T.C. (2008). Compassion fatigue: Being an ethical social worker. *The New Social Worker, 15*(1), 4–7.

Whitaker, T. (2008). *Who wants to be a social worker? Career influences and timing. NASW membership workforce study*. Washington, DC: National Association of Social Workers.

Whitaker, T., & Arrington, P. (2008). *Social workers at work. NASW membership workforce study*. Washington, DC: National Association of Social workers.

Whitaker, T., Weismiller, T., & Clark, E. (2006a). *Assuring the sufficiency of a frontline workforce: A national study of licensed social workers. Special report: Social work services for children and families*. Washington, DC: National Association of Social Workers.

Whitaker, T., Weismiller, T., & Clark, E. (2006b). *Assuring the sufficiency of a frontline workforce: A national study of licensed social workers. Special report: Social work services for older adults*. Washington, DC: National Association of Social Workers.

Whitaker, T., Weismiller, T., Clark, E., & Wilson, M. (2006). *Assuring the sufficiency of a frontline workforce: A national study of licensed social workers. Special report: Social work services in health care settings*. Washington, DC: National Association of Social Workers.

Williams, L.D., & Joyner, M. (2008). Baccalaureate social workers. In T. Mizrahi & L.E. Davis (Eds.), *Encyclopedia of social work* (20th ed.) (pp. 3:322–324). Washington, DC: NASW Press and Oxford University Press.

Williams, M., & Smolak, A. (2007). Integrating faith matters in social work education. *Journal of Religion & Spirituality in Social Work*, *26*(3), 25–44.

Williamson, J. (2010). Demographic trends. In T. Fitzpatrick, H. Kwon, N. Manning, J. Midgley, & G. Pascall (Eds.), *International encyclopedia of social policy* (pp. 297–300). London: Routledge.

Wilson, M. (2010). *Criminal justice social work in the United States: Adapting to new challenges*. Washington, DC: NASW Center for Workforce Studies.

Worden, B. (2007). Women and sexist oppression. In G.A. Appleby, E. Colon, & J. Hamilton (Eds.), *Diversity, oppression, and social functioning.*

Person-in-environment assessment and intervention (2nd ed.) (pp. 93–114). Boston, MA: Allyn & Bacon.

Worldbank Group. (2003). Understanding poverty. Available at: http://www.worldbank.org/poverty/mission/up1.htm.

World Hunger (2012). Hunger in America: 2012 United States hunger and poverty facts. Available at: http://www.worldhunger.org/articles/Learn/us_hunger_facts.htm

Worldwidelearn.com. (2009). Five biggest trends impacting the job market. Available at: http://www.worldwidelearn.com/online-education-guide.

CREDITS

Exhibit 1.2: Lynch, Darlen and Robert Vernon, "You'll Need a Social Worker" © 2011. Reprinted with permission.

Chapter 3: Barkely, Donald C. "If . . . A Big Word With the Poor." 1976. Reprinted with permission of Faith and Life Press.

Chapter 5: Chace, W.M. (1989). "The Language of Action." Wesleyan LXII(2). Reprinted with permission.

Exhibit 6.2: D'Aprix, A.S., L.A. Boynton, B. Carver, and C. Urso. (2001). "When the ideal meets the real: Resolving ethical dilemmas in the real world." *The New Social Worker*. Reprinted with permission of White Hat Communications.

Exhibit 7.1: Akin, Jim. "100 Skills for Social Workers." (1995) NASW-Florida Chapter Reprinted with permission of the National Association of Social Workers, Inc.

Exhibit 7.2: Germain, C.B. and A. Gitterman. (2008). "Ecological perspective." In Edwards, R.L., *Encyclopedia of social work*, 20th edition. Reprinted with permission of NASW Press and Oxford University Press.

Exhibit 7.3: Hartman, A. (1978). Diagrammatic assessment of family relationships in *Social Casework*. Reprinted with permission of *Families in Society*.

Exhibit 7.4: Saleebey, D. (1996). "The strengths perspective in social work practice: Extensions and cautions." In *Social Work 41*(3). Reprinted with permission of Oxford University Press.

Exhibit 9.3: Collins, D. and H. Coleman. "Eliminating bad habits in the social work interview." *The New Social Worker*. Reprinted with permission of White Hat Communications.

Exhibit 11.3: Schneider, Robert. "Influencing state policy." Reprinted with permission.

Chapter 11: Berry, Clayton. "Guidelines for Publishing." Reprinted with permission of the author.

Photos

Wasserman Family Photo: Reprinted by permission of Mary Wasserman.

Photo of St. Louis County Jail: taken by Hellmuth, Obata, and Kassabaum for St. Louis County. Provided by Herb Bernsen. Reprinted with permission.

Alzheimer's Disease Advocates at State Lobby day. Reprinted with permission Alzheimer's Association.

GLOSSARY/INDEX

Note: Page numbers ending in *e* refer to exhibits. Page numbers ending in *t* refer to tables.

AASSW *see* American Association of Schools of Social Work

AASWG, Inc. *see* Association for the Advancement of Social Work with Groups, Inc.

ableism 130–132

abuse 160–161

  see also **child abuse and neglect**

Academy of Certified Social Workers (ACSW) 49

accommodation: Efforts of one group to make changes to enable another group to live within society. 126

acculturation: Socialization of one culture into the ways (i.e., values, beliefs, and behaviors) of another culture. 126

ADA *see* Americans with Disabilities Act

Addams, Jane 29, 30, 31, 34, 147, 153, 190, 318

addiction *see* substance abuse and addiction

administration and management: A field of practice in which the social worker supervises programs and people. 7

administrator 334

adoption groups 299

advanced standing: Many schools offer advanced standing into MSW programs to students who have graduated from a CSWE-accredited BSW program. 354

advocate: A social work role in which the social worker articulates client system needs on behalf of the client system. 3, 27–28, 179–180, 262, 333

  community-based programs 202

  economic environment 105, 106

  NASW policy 78–79

  NASW standards 117

  policy practice 148, 165, 318

  political environment 101, 102

  social environment 109–110

  social justice 316

Affordable Care Act 43

age 86, 87–89

ageism 127–128

Aid to Families with Dependent Children (AFDC): Former government program of social welfare that provides cash assistance to poor women and children; phased out with enactment of the 1996 Personal Responsibility and Work Opportunity Reconciliation Act (PRWORA). 71

Albelda, R. et al. 66

Alissi, A.S. 291

Allen, James 221–223

Allen, K. 160

Allen-Meares, P. 344

Alzheimer's disease 209–212, 242, 295

American Association of Schools of Social Work (AASSW) 47, 49

American Charities 44

American Recovery and Reinvestment Act (ARRA; 2009) 74, 99

Americans with Disabilities Act (ADA) 42, 72, 131, 212

Annie E. Casey Foundation 104

anthropology 196

Anti-Crime Bill 72

assessment: A component of the planned change effort in which the social worker collaborates with the client system to obtain information that provides the foundation for developing a plan of intervention. 273–274

  at community-level 336–337

  "Don'ts" and "Do's" 275–277

  ecomaps 186, 187

  family assessments 278

  of groups 304–306

  of individuals and families 273–278

  interview practice behaviors 274–277

assimilation: Adoption of one group's cultural practices (e.g., values, norms, and behaviors) by another group which adopts the culture of the majority group (e.g., refugees become "westernized" when they immigrate to the United States). 126

Association for the Advancement of Social Work with Groups, Inc. (AASWG, Inc.) 291, 293–294

Association of Baccalaureate Social Work Program Directors 176, 178

Austin, D.M. 99

Bachelor of Social Work (BSW): The degree awarded to a student who has fulfilled the requirements for a bachelor of arts or science that prepares the graduate for generalist social work practice. 14–16, 50, 176, 351–354

Bakely, Don 54–55, 79–81

Baldino, R.G. 151

Barker, R.L. 105, 147, 178, 271

Bell, L.A. 121

Bernsen, Herbert 233–236

bias: Also referred to as prejudice, bias is a positive or negative perception of an individual or group that is often based on stereotypes. 126

biology 197

Boes, M. 133

boundaries: Delineations between the professional and the client system that serve to separate the personal from the professional relationship. 163–164, 303

Brady (gun control) Bill 72

Bratcher, Angela 205–207

Brieland, D. 267

broker: A social work role in which the social worker aids the client in obtaining needed resources. 178, 179, 333

BSW *see* **Bachelor of Social Work**

Buila, S. 158

Burkemper, Ellen 260–261

Bush, George H.W. 41, 42–43, 71–72

Bush, George W. 42, 43, 73, 105, 106

Carter, Jimmy 71

case management: A method of social work practice in which the social worker conducts needs assessments, provides information and referral and enables client systems to access resources. *see* **social casework**

case manager: Role for social worker in which the focus is to mobilize the client system to achieve mutually-determined goals. 180

CCC *see* Civilian Conservation Corps

CETA (Comprehensive Employment and Training Act 1974) 41

Chace, William M. 142

Charity Organization Society (COS): The movement was based on the belief that the person was responsible for his or her own difficulties but could be rehabilitated through individual sessions with a "friendly visitor" as opposed to a financial handout. 29, 31, 33, 45, 46, 176, 318

chemical dependency *see* substance abuse and addiction

Chicago School of Civics and Philanthropy 45–46

child abuse and neglect: Perpetration of physical, emotional, or sexual harm to a child or the inadequate provision of physical, medical, emotional, or educational care to a child. 160–161, 204–205, 247, 249, 297

Child Abuse Prevention and Treatment Act (1974) 41

Child Tax Credit 61, 74

child welfare: Public or private social service and residential programs aimed at the protection and welfare of children who are being abused, neglected, or exploited. 202, 203–207

  action groups 295

  foster care 26, 204, 206–207

  future of 357–358

  history of 47–48

  impact of policies on 77

  NASW standards 205

  play therapy 207

  in practice 205–207

  practice considerations 203–204

  salaries 348

  settings 204

Child Welfare League of America 35

children and families 203–207

  practice considerations 203–205

  and risk of poverty 59, 60, 104

  salaries 348

  social work in practice 246–249

Children's Bureau 30, 34–35

civil rights 39, 40, 125

Civil Rights Act (1964) 39, 40

Civil Rights Restoration Act 72

Civilian Conservation Corps (CCC) 37, 70

classism 129–130

client/client system: The consumer(s) of services provided by the social worker. 185

client information, protection of 161

  see also **confidentiality**

client strength 191

clinical social work: A field of practice in which the social worker counsels individuals, families, and groups in settings such as hospitals, schools, mental health facilities, and private practices. 7

Clinton, Bill 41–42, 72–73

closed-ended questions: Eliciting information from a client system through asking questions that can be answered by "yes", "no", or short answers. 274

  see also **open-ended questions**

coalitions: Collaborations between professional organizations and client systems who share a mutual goal. 321, 329

code of ethics: A professional group's articulation of its values, ethical standards, and expected behaviors of its members.

Code of Ethics (NASW) 49, 154–158

  application of the Code 158

  definition of social work 4

ethical principles 156, 291, 316
mission and core values 95, 115–116, 122, 155, 175–176
organization of the Code 155–158
purposes 155–156
standards 156–158, 160, 162, 163, 316–317
cognitive disabilities 214–217
Coit, Stanley 29
Collins, P.M. 67
color 126
communication
nonverbal 272
personal habits 272–273
skills 15, 98, 114–115, 139, 141, 353
verbal 271
community development: A method of social work practice with organizations and communities, in which the planned change efforts are focused on enhancing a specific geographic area. 177, 202, 321, 324–326
community-level social work practice: A method of social work practice in which the social worker works with a client system comprised of organizations and communities to develop a planned change effort that meets the needs of the organization or community. 177–178, 315–341
assessment 336–337
coalition building 321, 329
community development 177, 202, 321, 324–326
engagement 334–335
evaluation 339
functional-community organizing 320, 323–324
geographic-community organizing 320, 322–323
historical perspective 318–319
intervention 337–339
models of change 319–332
movements for progressive change 322, 331–332
policy practice 315–316, 318
political and social action 321, 329–331
program development 321, 326–327
skills 332–340
social planning 321, 327–328
termination 339–340
Community Mental Health Center Act (1963) 39
community organization: A method of social work that involves working with groups and communities to identify conditions and develop strategies to address community-level conditions. 7, 48, 202
community service 16–17
Comprehensive Employment and Training Act (CETA; 1974) 41
confidentiality: Maintaining client-related information and disclosing only with the permission of the client or the client's guardian. 160–162, 167–170
Congressional Social Work Caucus 101–102
Contract with America 72
co-occurring disorders: Co-occurrence of two disease processes. 229–230
core values: Specified by the NASW *Code of Ethics*, beliefs and practices of the profession that include service, social justice, dignity and worth of person, importance of human relationships, integrity, and competence. 155, 175–176
COS *see* Charity Organization Society
Council on Social Work Education (CSWE): The organization that accredits baccalaureate and master of social work education programs. 49
accreditation 14
core competencies 15, 352
curriculum guidelines 319
Educational Policy and Accreditation Standards 7–8, 47, 50, 134, 176, 351
field education 352
military social work guidelines 218–221
Coyle, Grace 292
criminal justice 202, 232–236
practice considerations 232–233
social work in practice 233–236
crisis intervention 202, 359–360
critical multiculturalism 125
critical thinking 262, 353
cross-cultural knowledge/leadership/skills 117
CSWE *see* Council on Social Work Education
culturagram: Tool for assessing a family within the context of their culture. 137–138
cultural awareness 109, 110, 118, 119, 125, 137–139
cultural competence: Interactions with persons with respect and value of the individual's culture, race, ethnicity, religion, sexual orientation, age, and other factors that make them unique. 98, 125, 135–141
action continuum 139, 140
cultural awareness 109, 110, 118, 119, 125, 137–139
definition 114
language and communication skills 15, 98, 114–115, 139, 141, 361
multiracial awareness 138–139
NASW standards 114, 116–117, 125, 183
cultural identity 118, 119
culture: The characteristics that define a group, including beliefs, values, behaviors, ideas, and mores. 126
custody exchange transfer 247, 248

Dawes, Anna 47
Deficit Reduction Act (2005) 43, 73
deficits perspective 123, 189

demographic profiles: Profile of a population.
  85, 86
  age 86, 87–89
  children 86
  income inequality 90–93
  life expectancy 88
  race and ethnicity 85, 86, 87
  religious affiliation 93–94
  sex ratios 89–90
  of social work profession 109
Department of Health, Education and Welfare
  37–38, 70
DeRoos, Y. 344
developmental disabilities 214–217
direct practice: Social work with individuals, couples,
  families, and small groups. 6
  see also **group work; individual and family social
  work practice**
direct service provider: Social work professional who
  engages in direct practice with individuals and
  families. 180
disabilities, people with 212–217
  ableism 130–132
  autism spectrum disorder 213
  legislation 42, 212
  in practice 214–217
  practice considerations 213–214
  terminology 131–132
disaster response 359–360
discrimination: Bias perpetrated by one individual
  or group over another individual or group due
  to race, ethnicity, gender, religion, age, sexual
  orientation, mental and physical conditions,
  class, and lifestyle. 95, 123–124
  ableism 130–132
  ageism 127–128
  classism 129–130
  heterosexism 132–133
  racism 124–127
  religious discrimination 134–135
  self-awareness 118
  sexism 128–129, 132–133
disease/health condition groups 299
diversity 142
  ecological perspective 121–122
  in social work practice 114–142
  of social workforce 117
  strengths-based perspective 122–123
  in U.S. population 85
Dix, Dorothea 27
Doctorate of Philosophy in Social Work (Ph.D. or
  DSW) 14
Dolgoff, R. et al. 146, 158, 166
domestic and family violence 202, 246–247
  confidentiality 161

group work with male abusers 297
  rural services 328
Dorothy I. Height and Whitney M. Young Jr. Social
  Work Reinvestment Act 101
dual diagnosis: Co-occurrence of two disease
  processes or conditions 229–230

Earned Income Tax Credit (EITC): A program
  established for low-income working persons
  to receive a refundable tax credit based on the
  number of children and the total household
  income. 61, 74, 76, 106
eclecticism: The application of knowledge and skills
  that may be derived from multiple theoretical
  concepts because they are most appropriate to
  the client system. 196
ecological perspective: A theoretical framework
  in which the individual is viewed within the
  context of the environment in which she/he
  lives. 121–122, 183, 184
ecomap: A tool for assessing individuals, families,
  groups, and communities that provides a
  framework for understanding the interrelationships
  between members of the system. 186, 187
economic environment 103
  challenges 103–105
  opportunities 105–106
economic justice: All persons are able to have the
  resources needed to survive. 105
Economic Opportunity Act (1964) 39, 70
economic stimulus package *see* American Recovery
  and Reinvestment Act
economics 196
ecosystem: A component of systems theory, an
  ecosystem encompasses the relationship among
  individuals, families, and organizations within
  the environment in which they exist. 185
Education for All Handicapped Children Act (1975)
  41, 42
educator: Social work role of providing information
  on coping strategies and resources. 180
Eisenhower, Dwight D. 37–38
EITC *see* **Earned Income Tax Credit**
Elementary and Secondary Education Act (1965) 40
Elizabethan Poor Laws (1601) 23–24
employment trends and opportunities 345–349
  areas of practice 346–347
  salaries 347–349
empowerment: The process of working with a client
  system to optimize the system's capacity to
  function and change. 117, 190–193, 302
enabler: A social work role in which the social
  worker aids the client system in developing and
  implementing a mutually agreed-upon plan for
  change. 333

engagement: A component of the planned change effort in which the social worker establishes rapport with the client system based on trust and respect. 271–273
 at community-level 334–335
 of groups 302–304
 of individuals and families 270–273
Enhanced Ethical Decision-Making Matrix 165, 169
ethical dilemma: A situation in which a person's ethical position, based on personal values, contradicts that of other persons or the choice being faced. 146–147, 154, 158–170
 allocation of resources 164–165
 boundaries 163–164
 client self-determination 162–163
 confidentiality 160–162, 167–170
 criteria 160
 ethical decision-making 165–167, 169
 self-disclosure 164
Ethical Principles Screen 167
Ethical Rules Screen 166
ethics: The behaviors of an individual or group based on the value system to which the individual or group is committed. 153–171
 definitions 147–148
 NASW *Code of Ethics* 4, 95, 115–116, 154–158, 291, 316
 in practice 165–170
ethnicity: Perception of one's group membership based on race, cultural background, religion, or national origin. 126
 income and poverty 59, 60, 62, 90–91, 92
 and social welfare 71
 terminology 126–127
 U.S. diversity 85, 86–87
ethnocentrism: Belief that one's cultural beliefs and values should be considered the norm by others. 126
evaluation: A component of the planned change effort in which the social worker and the client system assess the progress and success of the planned change effort. 283
 at community-level. 339
 of groups 309–310
 with individuals and families 283–284
 outcome evaluations 283–284
 process evaluations 283
evidence-based practice: Social work practice that is derived from a theoretical approach that has been empirically tested using rigorous research methodology. 181, 353

family: A group of persons, usually residing together, who acknowledge a sense of responsibility for one another and function as a unit.

 assessments 278
Family and Medical Leave Act (1993) 72
family group conference (FGC): Convening client, professionals, and extended family to develop intervention plan. 281
Family Support Act (1988) 41, 72
Federal Bureau of Public Assistance 35
Federal Emergency Relief Administration (FERA) 37, 38
field education 16–17, 352
fields of practice 47, 201–264, 346–347
Flexner, Abraham 46, 50
Floersch, J. 84
Flory, Barbara 246–249
food insecurity: Nutritional deficiency due to inadequate types and quantities of food. 77
food stamps: Administered by the Department of Agriculture, this social program (renamed Supplemental Nutrition Assistance Program in 2008) provides a means for eligible persons to supplement their income through the purchasing of food items. 40, 57, 61, 71, 74, 76
Ford, Gerald 40, 71
forensic social work: Social work practice within the legal system, including the criminal and civil legal systems. *see* criminal justice
foster care 26, 204, 206–207
functional-community organizing 320, 323–324

Gates, Ellen 30
gay and lesbian rights 42, 43, 132–133, 331
gender
 demographic shift 89–90
 inequity 128–129, 132–135
General Assistance (GA): Also referred to as General Relief, this program provides cash assistance for low-income adults who do not qualify for any other cash assistance programs. 76
generalist social work practice: A method of social work practice that encompasses a broad-based set of knowledge, skills, and values that are applied to assessment and intervention with client systems at the individual, family, group, organizational, and community levels. 175–197
 definition 176–177
 ecological perspective 183, 184
 evidence-based practice 181
 history of 176–177
 levels of 177–178
 people:environment (P:E) perspective 182–183
 skills and roles 178–181
 solution-focused model 193–196
 strengths–empowerment perspective 188, 192–193
 systems theory 182, 186–188
 theory 181–197

geographic-community organizing 320, 322–323
Germain, Carel 183
gerontological social work: Social work practice
    focused on older adults that can include work at
    the individual, family, group, organizational, and
    community level. 202, 208–212
    competencies 209
    future of 43, 353, 356–357
    in medical social work 238–239
    policy practice 209–212
    in practice 209–212
    practice considerations 208–209
Gingrich, Newt 72
global awareness 100–101, 103, 110
Grace Hill Settlement House 31, 32
Great Depression 35, 67–68, 69, 292, 318–319
Great Society 39–40, 72
group work (mezzo-level practice): A method of
    social work practice in which the social worker
    works with a client system comprised of multiple
    persons to develop a planned change effort that
    meets the needs of the group. 177, 290–312
    AASWG standards 293–294
    assessment 304–306
    engagement 302–304
    evaluation 309–310
    group dynamics 301, 302, 305, 308
    historical perspective 48, 291–293
    intervention 306–309
    models of change 294–301
    reciprocal groups 298–299, 359
    remedial groups 296–298
    skills 301–310
    social goals groups 294–296
    task groups 299–301
    termination 309–310
    working agreement 306, 307

Hartman, Ann 186
hate crimes 108–109, 132
Head Start: A War on Poverty program, Head Start
    is a child development program for low-income
    children that includes early childhood education,
    health, and nutrition services. 39, 70–71, 76
health care 99, 105, 106, 107, 161–162, 325–326
health care social work *see* **medical social work**
health insurance 60
Health Insurance Portability and Accountability Act
    (HIPAA; 1996) 161–162
health professions 2
Healthy People 2020 250
heterosexism 132–133
high school dropouts 59, 60
Hill, Octavia 44, 45
HIV/AIDs 100, 161, 241

Hoey, Jane M. 35
homosexuality 42, 43, 132–133, 331
Hopkins, Harry 37, 38
Hopps, J.G. et al. 44, 67
Horejsi, C.R. 317
housing 70, 107–108, 323
Hudson, Jon 230–232
Hull House 29, 30, 318
human capital 63

IDA *see* **Individual Development Account**
IEP *see* Individualized Education Program
immigrants 87, 223–227
    culturogram 138
    origins of 224
    policy 225
    practice considerations 223–225
    and racism 124
    rights movements 331
    risk of poverty 44
    social work in practice 225–227, 240, 324
    task groups 300
income
    inequality 90–93
    living wage 93, 105–106
    and poverty 57, 60, 61, 73, 90, 109
individual and family social work practice
    (micro-level practice): A method of social
    practice in which the social worker works with
    a client system comprised of an individual or
    family to develop a planned change effort that
    meets the needs of the individual or family. 177,
    266–288
    assessment 273–278
    engagement 270–273
    evaluation 283–284
    historical perspective 48, 267
    intervention 278–282
    planned change process 267–270
    rapport 271
    skills 270–286
    termination 285–286
Individual Development Account (IDA): Savings
    are matched for use in home purchase, business
    startup, or education expenses. 76
individual racism 124
Individualized Education Program (IEP) 215–216, 300
Individuals with Disabilities Education Act 42, 255
"indoor relief" 23, 29
informed consent: Release of client-related
    information based on the client having full
    understanding of and agreement with the
    disclosure of the information. 161
institutional racism: Discrimination against persons
    in accessing resources. 124

institutional social policy: Policy that addresses a social need that is universal to a population. 67

integration: Bringing together of all diverse groups with the goal of unity. 126

inter-agency cooperation 111

international social work 202, 328, 353, 360–361

interpersonal perspective 1

intersectionality 124, 135

intervention: A component of the planned change effort in which the social worker and the client system develop and implement a plan of action to achieve the mutually agreed-upon goals. 279

  at community-level 337–339

  contract 282, 284

  with groups 306–309

  implementation 279–280

  with individuals and families 278–282

  planning 279

  steps in intervention 280–281

interview practice behaviors 274–277

"ism": A suffix that, when added to a word that describes an individual or group, signifies discrimination or prejudice (e.g., racism, sexism, or ageism). 123–135

  ableism 130–132

  ageism 127–128

  classism 129–130

  heterosexism 132–133

  intersectionality 124, 135

  racism 124–127

  religionism 134–135

  sexism 128–129, 132–133

Job Corps 39, 70

Johnson, Lyndon B. 39, 70, 72

Keeley, Mark A. 214–217

Kendall, K.A. 29, 50

Kennedy, John F. 39

Kindle, P.A. 106

King, Martin Luther, Jr. 95

Kurland, R. 291

language for cultural competence *see* **linguistic competence; person-first language**

language diversity 85, 87, 117, 125

Lathrop, Julia 35

Law of Settlement (1662) 24–25

LeLaurin, Suzanne 225–227

life expectancy 88

Lilly Ledbetter Fair Pay Act (2009) 105

linguistic competence: Demonstrations of communication skills that are applicable to a range of diverse populations. 15, 98, 114–115, 139, 141, 361

living wage: Minimum amount needed to maintain a standard of living that exceeds the poverty line 93, 105–106

locality development *see* **community development**

MA *see* **Medicaid**

Mackelprang, R.W. et al. 214

McNutt, J. 84

macro social work practice: Working with organizations and communities to facilitate planned change. *see* **community-level social work practice**

marginalization: Efforts by one group to disenfranchise or disempower another group typically based on self-perceptions of superiority. 126

marriage and family counseling 3

Massachusetts General Hospital 35, 47

Master of Social Work (MSW): The degree awarded to a student who has fulfilled the requirements for a master of social work that prepares the graduate for social work practice in an area of concentration. 14, 16, 49, 176, 354

MC *see* **Medicare**

mediator: A social work role in which the social worker aids in the negotiation of a mutual outcome for individuals or groups that are in disagreement. 333–334

Medicaid (MA): Health care coverage available to some recipients of the eligibility-based programs (TANF, SSI, and SSD). 40, 76, 106

medical social work: Serving as a case manager and counseling around specific health-related issues. 47, 202, 236–243

  across multiple settings 238–241

  future of 356

  in hospital 238, 241–243

  NASW standards 237

  practice considerations 236–238

  salaries 348

Medicare (MC): Health care coverage for persons who receive Social Security benefits. Any person who receives any type of Social Security payments is automatically eligible for Medicare. 40, 73, 74, 75, 106

Mental Health Parity Act (1996) 42

mental health services 202, 243–249

  Alzheimer's disease 209–212, 242, 295

  impact of policies on 77

  potential violence 161, 246–247

  practice considerations 244–246

  remedial groups 297

  salaries 348

  service providers 245

  social work in practice 242, 246–249

  substance abuse 108

Meyer, Don 216

mezzo (meso) social work practice: Working with a group of individuals toward the goal of planned change. *see* **group work**

micro social work practice: Working with individuals, couples, and families in direct social work practice toward the goal of planned change. *see* **individual and family social work practice**

military social work 202, 217–223
    in practice 221–223
    practice considerations 218–221
    services 217, 221
    settings 108, 217, 360

mobilizer: A social work role in which the social worker facilitates the organization of individuals or groups to gain access to needed resources or attain a goal. 333

Mothers' Pensions 35

motivational interviewing: Client-focused intervention strategy that utilizes listening. 192–193

movements for progressive change 322, 331–332

MSW *see* **Master of Social Work**

multicultural competence *see* **multiculturalism**

multiculturalism: The practice of embracing and honoring the values, beliefs, and culture of others. 125, 126

multilingualism 361

multiracial awareness 138–139

National Association for the Advancement of Colored People (NAACP) 28, 29

National Association of Black Social Workers (NABSW) 154

National Association of Schools of Social Administration 47

National Association of Social Workers (NASW): The professional organization for the social work profession that serves to provide information and education to the profession and advocate on behalf of its members. 49, 340
    on confidentiality 160
    establishment of 47
    on gender equity 129, 133
    language policy 114–115, 125
    membership 362
    on multiculturalism 125
    on people with disabilities 213
    political agenda 78–79, 101, 102
    on poverty 73, 78
    on social work 1, 4
    Standards for cultural competence in social work 114, 116–117, 125, 183
    Standards for school social work services 255, 256
    Standards for social work practice in child welfare 205
    Standards for social work practice in health care settings 237
    Standards for social work practice with clients with substance abuse disorders 228–229
    Standards for technology and social work practice 359
    see also Code of Ethics (NASW); Political Action for Candidate Election (PACE)

National Council on Social Welfare 30

National Urban League 34

National Youth Administration (NYA) 37

negotiator 333–334

neighborhood groups 295, 323, 324

neighborhood programs
    community development 325
    history of 31, 70
    social planning 328

Neighborhood Youth Corps 39

neurocognitive disabilities 213

New Deal 35, 37, 69, 70, 319

New York School of Philanthropy 47

Nixon, Richard M. 40

No Child Left Behind 255

NYA (National Youth Administration) 37

Obama, Barack 43, 74, 99, 100, 104, 105, 237

Occupy Movement 102–103, 331

older adults 43, 59, 238–239
    see also **gerontological social work**

Older Americans Act (1965) 40, 71

Omnibus Budget Reconciliation Act (OBRA; 1981) 41, 72

online support groups (OSG) 359

open-ended questions: Eliciting information from a client system through asking questions that address feelings. 274

oppression: The restriction by one group over an individual or another group in the areas of activities, access to resources or ability to exercise their rights. 95
    cycle of oppression 96
    hate crimes 108–109, 132
    and social work 97, 121, 122
    see also **racism**

organizer: Social work role utilized when mobilizing resources to meet needs of client system. 180

OSG (online support groups) 359

"outdoor relief" 29

PACE *see* Political Action for Candidate Election

Parnell, Lisa 241–243

Patient Protection and Affordable Act (2010) 60

Patten, Simon 44, 47

Peace Corps 39

people:environment (P:E): Perspective that emphasizes the interrelationship between individuals and the environment in which they live. 182–183

Perkins, Frances 35, 36

person-first language: Language in which the person is noted first followed by the situation or condition (e.g., "person with a disability" instead of "disabled person"). 132

person-in-environment perspective: A theoretical framework in which the client system is perceived as an integral component of a larger and dynamic physical and social environment' 182–183

Personal Responsibility and Work Opportunity Reconciliation Act (PRWORA) Act (1996) 42, 72–73

physical disabilities 213

planned change: A process in which the social worker and client system work together to develop and implement mutually agreed-upon goals for enhancing the functioning and well-being of the client system. 203, 267–270

planning: Intervention aimed at policy- or community-level change. *see* **social planning**

planning and program and policy development: Facilitation of policies and services to meet the needs of program goals more effectively. 202, 321, 326–327

play therapy 207

pluralism: Individual and group differences are held in esteem by all members of a society without discrimination or prejudice. 126

policy development and analysis 202

policy practice: Working to influence the development, implementation, improvement, and evaluation of policies at the organizational, community, state, and national levels that are aimed at creating social justice for those impacted by the policies. 148, 165, 262, 315–316, 318
  gerontological 209–212
  immigration and refugees 225–227
  mental health 246–249

political action: Achieving social change through political campaign, policy, or advocacy support. 321, 329–331

Political Action for Candidate Election (PACE) 101, 330–331, 349

political environmet 98–99
  challenges 99–101
  opportunities 101–103

political science 196

Poor Laws: Also known as the Elizabethan Poor Laws of 1601, these laws employed the concept of mandatory taxation to fund social and financial assistance. Public assistance was provided to persons deemed eligible in three distinct categories: (1) monetary help for poor people who were deemed unemployable (i.e., older persons and persons with disabilities); (2) work for poor people who were not elderly or disabled; and (3) apprenticeships for orphaned/dependent children. 23–24

population growth 84–85

posttraumatic stress disorder (PTSD) 108, 240

poverty: Having inadequate money or means of subsistence. 54–82
  absolute poverty 57
  approaches to 65–66, 75, 76–79
  at-risk groups 58, 59–60, 62, 90–92, 104
  causes of 62–64
  cycles of 64–65
  definition 56–57
  "feminization" of 93
  impact of policies on 70–75, 77, 105
  and income levels 57, 60, 61, 73, 90, 109
  individual differences 62–63
  legislation 60, 73–74
  lifetime chances of living in poverty 43, 61–62
  NASW policy on 73, 78
  "new face of poverty" 57
  poems 54–55, 79–81
  relative deprivation 57
  social structure 63–64
  War on Poverty 39, 70, 71
  the working poor 60–61

poverty line: The amount calculated at the federal government level that establishes the minimal income needed for a person or family or individual to maintain basic needs. 57, 59, 60, 74

practice theory: A subset of theory that has been empirically tested for use in the practice setting. 181

prejudice: Positive or negative opinion or attitude that is not evidence-based. 126

privacy 160–162, 168

private practice 12, 24, 25, 39

program development 321, 326–327

Progressive Reform movement 29, 34

Protestant work ethic: A belief system and "way-of-life" philosophy that emphasizes self-discipline and frugality and has had a significant influence on societal attitudes toward the poor. 24

PRWORA *see* Personal Responsibility and Work Opportunity Reconciliation Act (PRWORA) Act (1996)

psychiatric disabilities 213

psychiatric social workers 35, 47

psychoeducational group: Group work model that emphasizes education and emotional support. 299, 300

psychology 2, 196

PTSD *see* posttraumatic stress disorder
public assistance *see* **social welfare**
Public Health Service 25
public health services 249–254
    practice considerations 250–251
    salaries 348
    social work in practice 251–254
public welfare: A system of programs, benefits, and
    services that support those in need of financial,
    social, and health care support. Also referred to
    as social welfare or public assistance. *see* **social
    welfare**
Pyles, L. 322

questions
    open/closed-ended 274
    for solution-focussed approach 195

race: Human characteristics identified by physical
    traits (e.g., skin color or hair texture), geography
    (e.g., place or origin), or culture. 126
    Census categories 127
    income and poverty 59, 60, 62, 90–91, 92
    and social welfare 71
    terminology 126–127
    U.S. diversity 85, 86–87
racism: Discrimination or oppression based on an
    individual or group's race. 124–127
Rank, M.R. 63–64, 66, 75
rapport 122, 139, 164, 271
Reagan, Ronald 41, 71–72
"Reaganomics" 72
Reamer, F.G. 160
reciprocal groups: Group intervention model
    that emphasizes common goals, interests, and
    exchanges. 298–299, 359
reflection: Recapping or paraphrasing the
    client's response for the purpose of clarifying
    the statements made by the client system.
    274–275
refugee: Person who seeks refuge from danger or
    persecution in her or his home country. 87,
    223–227
    culturogram 138
    origins of 224
    policy 225
    practice considerations 223–225
    risk of poverty 44
    social work in practice 225–227, 240, 324, 326
Rehabilitation Act (1973) 131
rehabilitation social work 240, 242–243
Reisch, M. 100
religion
    discrimination based on 134–135
    and origins of social work 22–23, 24

    trends in affiliation 93–94
    and value conflicts 151–152
remedial groups: Professionally led group
    intervention focused on a therapeutic goal of
    enhanced social functioning. 296–298
residual social policy: Policy that addresses a
    population-specific social need. 67
resources for clients
    allocation of 76, 164–165
    value conflicts over 152
resources for social workers 263–264, 340–341, 358
respect for the client 158, 168
Richmond, Mary 44, 46–47, 267
Rodriquez, Carroll 209–212
Roosevelt, Franklin D. 34, 35, 38, 39, 69
rural social work 202, 258–261
    in practice 260–261
    practice considerations 259–260
Ruskin, John 45

Salazar, C.F. 302
Saleebey, D. 190–192
Sanchez, Hector 128
school social work: A field of social work practice in
    which social workers provide services to students
    and their families on emotional, social, and
    economic concerns to enable them to focus on
    the student's education. 202, 204, 255–258
    NASW standards 255, 256
    in practice 257–258
    practice considerations 255–257
    salaries 348
Scots' Charitable Society 25
secularism 134
segregation: The formal or informatl separation of
    groups for reasons such as race, ethnicity, culture,
    or religion. 127
self-awareness 116, 118–120, 153, 248
self-determination: The belief that the individual or
    group has the right to make decisions that affect
    her/himself or the group. 158, 162–163, 168
self-disclosure: The sharing of personal information
    with a client system. 164
self-help groups *see* **reciprocal groups**
service delivery 117
settlement house: A facility based in a geographically
    bound neighborhood whose purpose is to
    provide a center for the "neighbors" to come
    together for educational, social, and cultural
    activities. Settlement houses also provided
    social services and financial assistance. The
    settlement house movement is based on the
    concept that: (1) social change can occur; (2)
    social class distinctions can be narrowed through
    information and education; and (3) change

can come only when social workers immerse themselves into their clients' community 29, 31, 32, 33, 44, 291, 292, 318
sex ratios 89–90
sexism 128–129, 132–133
sibling groups 299
Sibshops 216
significant-other groups 299
Singh, A.A. 302
Smith, C.J. 354–355
SNAP *see* **Supplemental Nutrition Assistance Program**
social action: A method of social work practice with organizations and communities in which the planned change effort is focused on addressing issues of social injustice. 321, 329–330
    see also **social goals groups**
social casework: Conducting needs assessments, providing information and referrals, and accessing resources. 6–7, 44, 45, 46, 47, 267
social class: Classifications of groups of people within a society that are based on financial, social, educational, and family status. 127, 129–130
Social Diagnosis 44, 46, 47
social environment 107
    challenges 107–109
    opportunities 109–111
social goals groups: Group intervention approach focused on social action and societal change. 294–296
social justice 107, 118, 121, 158, 301–302, 316, 317
social planning: A method of social work practice with organizations and communities in which the planned change efforts are focused on policy or community-wide change. 321, 327–328
social policy: Legislatively and administratively defined regulations that guide procedures for social welfare programs. Social policies can be: (1) residual–targeted toward a specific population or (2) institutional–available to the entire population. 66–67
social policy research: A method of social work practice that involves analyzing conditions, programs, and policies and conducting and studying research in an effort to improve the social service system. 7
Social Security: Authorized by the Social Security Act of 1935, a retirement income for all workers who paid the system during employment based on the amount contributed by the employee. Benefits are also available to surviving spouses and children of deceased workers and workers who become disabled. 67, 69, 74, 75, 76
Social Security Acts 34, 35, 37, 69, 70

Social Security Disability (SSD): Administered by the Social Security Administration, SSD is case assistance for persons deemed to be unable to work for a period of at least 1 year due to a physical or mental disability. 75
social structure and causes of poverty 63–64
social welfare: System that helps people meet their basic needs in order to maintain stability and social and economic justice within society.
    17–19th centuries 25–26, 67
    20th century 67–73
    21st century 73–76
    definitions 21, 66–67
    programs 37, 43, 69–71, 72–73, 74, 75–76
    vs. social work 21
social welfare policy: A type of social policy that addresses the allocation of governmental resources designated for the provision of health and social services. 67
social work: The professional activity of helping individuals, groups, or communities to enhance or restore their capacity for social functioning and creating societal conditions favorable to this goal. 1–19
    1601 Elizabethan Poor Laws 23–24
    17th–18th centuries 24–25
    19th century 25–33
    20th century 33–42
    21st century and beyond 42–44
    choosing a career in 1, 4, 16–17, 18
    credentials 14, 347
    definition 3–4, 48, 50
    diversity in 114–142
    fields of practice 47–48, 201–264, 346–347
    goals 4
    origins 21, 22–23
    professionalization of 49–50
    scope 6–10
    settings 4–5, 7, 10–13
    skills 6–8, 179
    vs. social welfare 21
    terminology 44
    uniqueness of 1–3
    see also social work education; social work profession
Social Work (journal) 48
Social Work Congresses 355
social work education 14–16, 350–361
    Bachelor of Social Work 14–16, 50, 176, 351–354
    current issues and the future 354–361
    Doctorate of Philosophy in Social Work 14
    and earnings 347–349
    field experiences 16–17, 352
    focus 50–51, 117
    historical perspective 44–47, 50

Master of Social Work 14, 16, 49, 176, 354
ongoing professional development 109
skills 353
social work organizations 263
social work profession 49–50, 344–364
diversity of workforce 109, 117
employment trends and opportunities 345–349
interpersonal perspective 1
paths into the profession 13–14
professional associations 263
professional identification 361–363
professional outlook 344–350
professional socialization 350–363
purpose, principles, objectives 48–49
salaries 347–349
societal perception of 349–350
sociology 2, 196
solution-focused model: A theoretical framework
for social work practice that enables the social
worker and the client system to reconstruct the
perception of the current life situation.
concepts 194
in generalist practice 193–196
questions 195
Speenhamland system 57
Sprankel, Jane 238–241
SSD *see* **Social Security Disability**
SSI *see* **Supplemental Security Income**
state laws 161
stereotype: Individuals and groups are assumed to
be the same as one another by virtue of their
membership in that group. 127
strengths-based perspective: A social work practice
approach that recognizes the person and her/
his cultural experiences and beliefs as an asset on
which to develop a plan for change. 188–193
vs. deficits perspective 123, 189
diversity 122–123
in generalist practice 188, 192–193
principles 190–192
student loan forgiveness programs 358
substance abuse and addiction 108, 202, 227–232
addictions groups 298–299
NASW standards 228–229
practice considerations 228–230
salaries 348
social work in practice 230–232
supervised visitation 247, 248
**Supplemental Nutrition Assistance Program
(SNAP)**: Formerly known as Food Stamps, this
social program provides support for meeting
nutritional needs of eligible individuals and
families. 40, 57, 61, 71, 74, 76
Supplemental Security Income (SSI): Administered
by the Social Security Administration, SSI is

cash assistance provided to low-income adults,
older adults, and persons with disabilities or
visual challenges who meet income and health
standards. 40, 71, 76
support groups *see* **reciprocal groups**
system: A group of individual components that
interact with one another to create a dynamic
entirety. 185
systems-based perspectives 182–188
systems theory: A theoretical framework used to
guide social work practice that conceptualizes
client systems within the context of the
environment in which they exist and explains
the interactions of the components within the
system. 183, 185–186
concepts 185–186
ecomap 186, 187
in generalist practice 182, 186–188

TANF *see* **Temporary Assistance to Needy Families**
task groups: Group intervention approach that
emphasizes specific solutions for a designated
group, 299–301
Tax Equity and Fiscal Responsibility Act (1982) 41
tax policies 61, 72, 74, 106
technology and social work 358, 359
Temporary Assistance to Needy Families (TANF):
Government program of social welfare that
provides cash assistance to poor women and
children; established by the 1996 Personal
Responsibility and Work Opportunity
Reconciliation Act (PROWRA). TANF provides
monthly cash assistance to eligible low-income
families with children under age. 37, 42, 72, 73,
74, 75
termination: A component of the planned change
effort in which the social worker ends the
planned change relationship. 285
at community-level 339–340
of groups 309–310
with individuals and families 285–286
Terrell, P. 39
theory: Conceptualization that has been proved by
empirically based research that is used to explain
behavior and develop a plan for intervention.
181–197
eclecticism 196
influences from other disciplines 196–197
integration of 196–197
practice theory 181
solution-focused model 193–196
strengths and empowerment perspectives 188–193
systems-based perspectives 182–188
therapeutic groups *see* **remedial groups**
Thrifty Food Plan 57

Title XX amendment to the Social Security Act (1975) 41, 71
Towns, Edolphus "Ed" 101, 102
Toynbee Hall 29
transportation 71, 323
trust *see* **confidentiality**
Trust for America's Health 251

unemployment 74, 104

value conflict: One's values are incongruent with the value system of another. 149–152, 165
values: An individual or group's customs, beliefs, and behaviors. 147–153
    definition 147–148
    historical perspective 148–149
    importance in social work 148–149
    of social workers 152–153
    standards 116
values clarification: Self-exploration and assessment of one's belief system with the goal of developing a respect for others' values. 152–153
Valutis, S. et al. 153
Van Wormer, K. 133
Vincent de Paul, St. 24
violence
    and confidentiality 161
    domestic and family 202, 246–247
    group work with male abusers 297
    in rural services 328
volunteer task groups 300
Volunteers in Service to America (VISTA) 39, 70

War on Poverty 39, 70, 71
wealth: definition 91
wealth gap 91, 92, 102
welfare: Having stability in the areas of physical, emotional, and financial well-being. 66
    see also **social welfare**
welfare reform 328
welfare-to-work programs 42, 43
Wells-Barnett, Ida B. 27–29
Wilson, R. Jan 257–258
women
    and aging 88, 89–90
    and risk of poverty 58, 59, 60, 91, 92–93
    sexism 128–129
    single mothers 60, 71, 93, 109
Women, Infants, and Children (WIC): A federally funded program established to provide low-income women vouchers with which they can purchase certain foods for themselves and their children. 76
Work Incentive Program 71
workers' compensation legislation 35
workers' rights 106
working poor: A person who is employed, but whose income from employment falls below the poverty line because the employment is part-time or low-paying. 60–61
Works Progress Administration 37, 38
World War II 37, 69
Worldbank Group 57

Yong, Chae Li 251–254

NEW DIRECTIONS IN SOCIAL WORK

SERIES EDITOR: ALICE LIEBERMAN, UNIVERSITY OF KANSAS

....

New Directions in Social Work is an innovative, integrated series offering a uniquely distinctive teaching strategy for generalist courses in the social work curriculum, at both undergraduate and graduate levels. The series integrates five texts with custom websites housing interactive cases, companion readings, and a wealth of resources to enrich the teaching and learning experience.

Research for Effective Social Work Practice, Third Edition

Judy L. Krysik, Arizona State University and Jerry Finn,
University of Washington, Tacoma

HB: 978-0-415-52100-0
PB: 978-0-415-51986-1
eBook: 978-0-203-07789-4

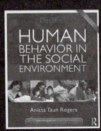

Human Behavior in the Social Environment, Third Edition

Anissa Taun Rogers, University of Portland

HB: 978-0-415-52081-2
PB: 978-0-415-50482-9
eBook: 978-0-203-07786-3

The Practice of Generalist Social Work, Second Edition

Julie Birkenmaier, Marla Berg-Weger, both at St. Louis University,
and Martha P. Dewees, University of Vermont

HB: 978-0-415-87457-1
PB: 978-0-415-87336-9
eBook: 978-0-203-82946-2

Social Policy for Effective Practice: A Strengths Approach, Second Edition

Rosemary Chapin, University of Kansas

HB: 978-0-415-87335-2
PB: 978-0-415-87339-0
eBook: 978-0-203-83484-8